Strategic Survey 2010
The Annual Review of World Affairs

Strategic Survey 2010: The Annual Review of World Affairs
is dedicated to the memory of Sidney Bearman (1925–2010),
Editor of *Strategic Survey* for 24 years until 2001.

Strategic Survey 2010
The Annual Review of World Affairs

published by

Routledge
Taylor & Francis Group

for

The International Institute for Strategic Studies

The International Institute for Strategic Studies
Arundel House | 13–15 Arundel Street | Temple Place | London | WC2R 3DX | UK

Strategic Survey 2010
The Annual Review of World Affairs

First published September 2010 by **Routledge**
4 Park Square, Milton Park, Abingdon, Oxon, OX14 4RN

for **The International Institute for Strategic Studies**
Arundel House, 13–15 Arundel Street, Temple Place, London, WC2R 3DX, UK

Simultaneously published in the USA and Canada by **Routledge**
270 Madison Ave., New York, NY 10016

Routledge is an imprint of Taylor & Francis, an Informa business

DIRECTOR-GENERAL AND CHIEF EXECUTIVE Dr John Chipman
EDITOR Alexander Nicoll

ASSISTANT EDITOR Dr Jeffrey Mazo
CONTRIBUTING EDITOR Jonathan Stevenson
MAP EDITORS Jessica Delaney, Sarah Johnstone
EDITORIAL Dr Ayse Abdullah, Janis Lee, Carolyn West
EDITORIAL INTERNS Aoife Breen, Sean Mulkerne, Harry White
DESIGN/PRODUCTION John Buck
ADDITIONAL MAP RESEARCH Henry Boyd
CARTOGRAPHY Steven Bernard

COVER IMAGES Getty Images
PRINTED BY Bell & Bain Ltd, Glasgow, UK

This publication has been prepared by the Director-General of the Institute and his Staff, who accept full responsibility for its contents, which describe and analyse events up to 30 June 2010. These do not, and indeed cannot, represent a consensus of views among the worldwide membership of the Institute as a whole.

British Library Cataloguing in Publication Data
A catalogue record for this book is available from the British Library

Library of Congress Cataloguing in Publication Data

ISBN 978-1-85743-563-4
ISSN 0459-7230

Contents

Strategic Geography (after p. 200)

Index of Regional Maps

Events at a Glance

July 2009–June 2010

July 2009

5 **China:** Rioting breaks out in Ürümqi, capital of Xinjiang Uighur Autonomous Region in northwest China, leaving more than 180 dead. Uighurs were protesting after a brawl in a factory in Shaoguan, Guangdong province, involving Uighurs and Han Chinese. Unrest continues for several months.

13 **Turkey:** An agreement is signed between Turkey, Austria, Hungary, Romania and Bulgaria to construct the Nabucco gas pipeline through southeastern Europe, intending to reduce European energy dependence on Russia. Iraq agrees to supply half of the pipeline's capacity by 2015.

14 **Mexico:** Bodies of 12 federal police officers are found tortured in Michoacan state, killed by members of La Familia in drug-related violence. Government sends 5,500 troops and police to the state.

15 **Russia:** Human-rights activist Natalya Estemirova, who had been gathering evidence of abuse by authorities in Chechnya since 1999, is kidnapped and killed.

17 **Indonesia:** Nine people are killed in attacks on the Ritz Carlton Jakarta and the J.W. Marriott hotels in Jakarta for which Jemaah Islamiah is blamed.

18 **Mauritania:** Mohamed Ould Abdel Aziz is elected civilian president a year after seizing power in a military coup.

20 **Bosnia:** Milan and Sredoje Lukic, two Bosnian Serb commanders, are found guilty of committing war crimes by the International Criminal Tribunal for the Former Yugoslavia. Milan is sentenced to life imprisonment, while Sredoje is sentenced to 30 years' imprisonment.

27 **Nigeria:** Hundreds are killed in clashes between the Islamist militant Boko Haram group and government forces in several northern Nigerian states.

29 **Moldova:** Europe's last Communist government is defeated in elections by the Alliance for European Integration, a coalition.

29 **Ireland:** Ireland accepts two Uzbek detainees from Guantanamo Bay.

August 2009

2 **Sudan:** At least 185 members of the Lou Nuer community, mostly women and children, are killed in a camp near Akobo during an attack by Murle fighters. Hundreds more were killed in intertribal violence earlier in the year.

4 **North Korea:** Former US President Bill Clinton, meeting President Kim Jong-il in Pyongyang, secures the release of American journalists Euna Lee and Laura Lin, who were sentenced in June to 12 years of hard labour for illegally entering North Korea.

8 **Taiwan:** Typhoon Morakot kills more than 600 people. On 10 September, Prime Minister Liu Chao-shiuan resigns over the government's handling of the disaster.

11 **Myanmar:** Opposition leader Aung San Suu Kyi is sentenced to a further 18 months of house arrest after an American man trespassed in her compound.

12 **Philippines:** At least 31 suspected terrorists and 23 soldiers are killed when government forces raid training camps of the Islamist militant organisation Abu Sayyaf.

17 **North/South Korea:** North Korea agrees to reopen border to allow family reunions and group tourist visits from South Korea.

19 **Iraq:** A series of bombings in Baghdad and Mosul kill at least 101 people, the deadliest attack in two years.

20 **United Kingdom:** Abdelbaset Ali Mohmed Al Megrahi, a Libyan convicted of participating in the 1988 bombing of Pan Am Flight 103 over Lockerbie, Scotland, and sentenced to life imprisonment, is released by the Scottish government on compassionate grounds as he was claimed to be suffering from prostate cancer and given a life expectancy of three months – a prognosis which proves not to be accurate.

20 **Afghanistan:** Presidential election brings allegations of electoral fraud, and President Hamid Karzai's apparent victory is contested.

25 **Pakistan:** Tehrik-i-Taliban Pakistan says its leader Baitullah Mehsud was killed in an American missile strike in South Waziristan. Hakimullah Mehsud succeeds him.

27 **Saudi Arabia:** Prince Muhammed bin Nayef, deputy interior minister and head of Saudi anti-terrorism efforts, survives an al-Qaeda suicide bomb attack, receiving minor injuries.

30 **Japan:** Democratic Party of Japan defeats the ruling Liberal Democratic Party-led coalition in a general election, and Yukio Hatoyama becomes prime minister.

September 2009

4 **Afghanistan/Germany:** NATO forces destroy two fuel tankers hijacked by Taliban militants, killing up to 150 militants and civilians. The air-strike, called in by a German officer, leads to intense public debate in Germany, a reassessment of policy in Afghanistan, and the resignation of Labour and Social Affairs Minister Franz Josef Jung, who was defence minister at the time, as well as armed forces chief General Wolfgang Schneiderhan.

14 **Somalia:** Saleh Ali Saleh Nabhan, an al-Qaeda leader in Africa, is killed in a helicopter raid in southern Somalia by American special forces.

15 **Israel/Palestine:** A UN fact-finding mission on the Gaza conflict of 2008–09 concludes that both Israeli forces and Palestinian militants committed war crimes and breaches of humanitarian law. The UN Human Rights Council votes to send the report to the Security Council for possible referral to the International Criminal Court. The US votes against the resolution.

17 **Somalia:** Al-Shabaab insurgents, driving stolen UN vehicles, detonate explosives at an African Union base in Mogadishu, killing 17 peacekeepers.

17 **United States:** President Obama scraps the Bush administration's plan to site missile defence facilities in Poland and the Czech Republic, planning instead to deploy a reconfigured system aimed at intercepting shorter-range missiles.

24 **Myanmar:** US government announces it will shift its policy towards Myanmar after concluding that sanctions have failed to sway the ruling junta. While keeping sanctions in place, it will seek engagement with Burmese leaders.

25 **United States:** G20 summit in Pittsburgh agrees that it will become the primary forum to discuss international economic developments, instead of the G8. It agrees on a 'peer review' process on economic policies, and to push forward new regulation of financial markets.

25 **Iran:** Iran reveals to the International Atomic Energy Agency that it has a second uranium-enrichment plant under construction, located inside a mountain near Qom.

27 **Germany:** CDU/CSU partnership led by Chancellor Angela Merkel wins largest number of seats in federal election and forms a centre-right coalition with Free Democratic Party, ending a grand coalition between CDU/CSU and the Social Democratic Party.

28 **Guinea:** Government forces open fire on protesters outside a stadium in Conakry, the capital, killing at least 57 people. Some 50,000 were protesting against the military leadership that came to power in a December 2008 coup.

October

4 **Greece:** Panhellenic Socialist Movement, led by George Papandreou, wins elections, defeating the government of the New Democratic Party. The new government revises the estimated 2009 budget deficit from 6% to 12.7%. This

triggers a crisis of investor confidence in Greek debt, and in the debt of other high-borrowing European countries. Government moves to reduce the deficit prompt violent protests.

4 **Nigeria:** Three rebel leaders in the Niger Delta region and hundreds of militants surrender their arms under a government amnesty.

9 **Norway :** US President Barack Obama is awarded the Nobel Peace Prize, 263 days after taking office.

10 **Turkey/Armenia:** Armenia and Turkey sign an accord to establish diplomatic relations, open borders and establish a commission to examine the 'historical dimension' of their relations.

12 **Italy:** A Libyan man attempts to detonate a bomb while entering an army barracks in Milan, injuring himself and one soldier. Two additional suspects are arrested and bomb-making chemicals are found in subsequent searches.

17 **Pakistan:** Pakistan's military begins a major military offensive in South Waziristan against the Pakistani Taliban and other militant groups.

18 **Iran:** At least 42 people, including six senior Revolutionary Guard commanders, are killed by a suicide bomber in the southeastern province of Sistan and Balochistan. Iran says Jundullah, an ethnic Baluch Sunni resistance group, claims responsibility.

20 **Afghanistan:** President Hamid Karzai bows to international pressure and agrees to a run-off election vote. Following allegations of vote-rigging in the first round held in August, the election commission stripped him of many votes, triggering the run-off. However, the opposition candidate, Abdullah Abdullah, withdraws, allowing Karzai to be sworn in for a second term on 19 November.

25 **Iraq:** Two car bombs at government ministry buildings in central Baghdad leave at least 155 people dead.

28 **Pakistan:** Car bomb in a crowded marketplace in Peshawar kills at least 91 people.

31 **Palau:** Six Uighurs, detained in 2001 by the United States at Guantanamo Bay, arrive in Palau for resettlement.

November 2009

5 **United States:** US Army Major Nidal Malik Hasan kills 13 people in a rampage at Fort Hood base in Texas.

5 **Italy:** A judge in Milan convicts in their absence 22 CIA agents, a US Air Force colonel and two Italian secret agents of the kidnapping of Egyptian cleric Usama Mostafa Hassan Nasr, otherwise known as Abu Omar, in 2003. He was taken to Egypt, where he was allegedly tortured.

9 **Lebanon:** Saad Hariri, head of the March 14 Alliance, becomes prime minister at the head of a unity government after five months of negotiations following 7 June elections.

11 **North/South Korea:** North and South Korean naval vessels exchange gunfire in disputed waters off the western coast of the peninsula. Each side blames the other for initiating the exchange, the first in seven years.

19 **Europe:** Leaders of the 27 countries of the European Union choose Belgian Prime Minister Herman van Rompuy as the Union's first president, and Catherine Ashton of the UK as its high representative for foreign affairs and security policy. The expanded positions were established by the Lisbon Treaty.

23 **Philippines:** President Gloria Macapagal-Arroyo declares a state of emergency in two southern provinces after 57 people, including 18 journalists, are killed in an attack on an election campaign convoy.

26 **United Arab Emirates:** State-owned investment company Dubai World asks creditors for a six-month moratorium on debt repayments, triggering months of negotiations on a $23bn debt restructuring.

28 **Russia:** Bomb blast causes a Moscow–St Petersburg express train to crash, killing 27 people.

29 **Switzerland:** Swiss voters, defying the government and clerics, back a referendum proposal to ban building minarets, with 57% of votes.

30 **Honduras:** Porfirio Lobo of the National Party wins presidential election with 56% of the vote, following the ousting of Manuel Zelaya in a military coup in June.

December

1 **United States:** President Obama announces 30,000 more US troops will be sent to Afghanistan, bringing the total to 100,000, and that a drawdown of troop numbers will begin from July 2011. On 4 December, other NATO members and partners commit an additional 7,000 troops.

7 **Iran:** Hundreds of people are arrested in a period of anti-government protests and clashes with police. Tensions are particularly high around the 21 December funeral of Grand Ayatollah Hossein Ali Montazeri, a critic of government policies.

8 **Iraq:** At least 112 people are killed by car bombs in Baghdad that coincide with the announcement of the date for parliamentary elections.

12 **North Korea:** A Georgian registered Il-76 cargo plane from Pyongyang, North Korea's capital, is detained during a refuelling stop in Thailand and 35 tonnes of weapons are seized. The plane's final destination is unknown.

18 **Denmark:** UN Climate Change Conference ends with a deal under which countries agree on the need to limit the global temperature rise above pre-industrial levels to 2°C, but are left to announce their own voluntary targets for carbon emissions to meet this goal. The Copenhagen Accord, which resulted from an agreement between the US, China, India, Brazil and South Africa, is 'recognised' by the 192 nations attending the conference. But it falls far short of a binding treaty to address the effects of climate change and replace the Kyoto Protocol.

23 **Eritrea:** UN Security Council votes to impose sanctions on Eritrea for providing support to insurgents in Somalia. Sanctions include an arms embargo and travel restrictions and asset freezes on some individuals.

25 **United States:** Umar Farouk Abdulmutallab, a Nigerian trained in Yemen, unsuccessfully attempts to set off an explosive device aboard a Northwest Airlines flight as it approaches Detroit from Amsterdam.

27 **United Arab Emirates:** A South Korean consortium wins a $20bn contract to build four nuclear power plants in the United Arab Emirates.

30 **Afghanistan:** Seven American CIA agents are killed by a suicide bomb at a CIA base in Khost Province, Afghanistan. The bomber was Humam al-Balawi, a Jordanian doctor of Palestinian origin, whom the CIA and Jordanian intelligence services had recruited to provide information on al-Qaeda. Balawi had entered the base for a meeting with the CIA personnel.

January 2010

1 **Pakistan:** Suicide bomb amidst a crowd at a volleyball tournament in the Lakki Marwat district of North West Pakistan kills at least 90 people.

11 **China:** China successfully intercepts a missile in mid-flight in a test of its ground-based mid-course missile-interception programme, becoming the second country after the United States to do so.

12 **Haiti:** An earthquake devastates the capital, Port-au-Prince, and kills an estimated 230,000 people. The headquarters of the UN stablilisation mission is destroyed and many officials, including its head, are killed. A massive international aid effort is launched to help the injured and displaced, and restore order, involving US and other militaries and aid agencies.

17 **Nigeria:** Violence erupts between Christians and Muslims in and around the central city of Jos, where up to 500 people are killed.

19 **Israel:** Hamas official Mahmoud al-Mabhouh is assassinated in a hotel in Dubai. The murderers appear to be Israelis using false passports from Britain, France, Germany, Ireland and Australia, causing a diplomatic furore.

25 **Iraq:** Ali Hassan al-Majid, a cousin of Saddam Hussein known as 'Chemical Ali', is hanged for offences including gas attacks on Kurds in the village of Halabja in 1988 in which 5,600 people died.

27 **Sri Lanka:** President Mahinda Rajapaksa is re-elected with 58% of votes, defeating former army chief Sarath Fonseka, who is later arrested for 'military offences'.

29 **Taiwan:** US approves $6bn arms sale to Taiwan. China condemns the deal, saying it harms Chinese security and Sino-US relations, and breaks off military-to-military exchanges.

February 2010

7 **Ukraine:** Presidential election is won by Viktor Yanukovich, defeating Prime Minister Yulia Tymoshenko. Mykola Azarov, former finance minister, becomes prime minister.

8 **Pakistan:** Afghan Taliban's second in command, Mullah Abdul Ghani Baradar, is arrested by American and Pakistani security forces in Karachi.

11 **Yemen:** Government and Houthi rebels agree a ceasefire in their six-year conflict.

13 **Afghanistan:** NATO-led forces launch *Operation Moshtarak*, intended to capture the Taliban stronghold of Marjah in Helmand province.

18 **Niger:** President Mamadou Tandja is deposed in a military coup.

20 **Netherlands:** Coalition government collapses in a dispute between two largest member parties over whether Dutch troops should stay in Afghanistan.

27 **Chile:** An earthquake measuring 8.8 on the Richter scale strikes off the coast of central Chile, killing about 500 people and displacing more than 1.5 million.

March 2010

7 **Nigeria:** Violence between Christians and Muslims erupts in three villages near the city of Jos. Up to 500 people, predominantly Christian, are killed.

7 **Iraq:** Parliamentary elections produce a close result that triggers months of discussions on the formation of a new government.

9 **Israel/United States:** A sharp downturn in US–Israeli relations occurs as the Israeli Interior Ministry announces it has approved the building of 1,600 new homes in East Jerusalem during a visit by US Vice President Joe Biden.

22 **China:** Google closes its Internet search service in China, and redirects Chinese users to an uncensored version of its search engine based in Hong Kong. The move follows cyber attacks on Google which it says originated in China.

23 **United States:** President Obama signs into law a landmark bill to reform health care, extending insurance to 32m additional people, after House of Representatives backs it by 219 votes to 212.

24 **Saudi Arabia:** Security forces arrest more than 100 people, mostly Yemenis and Saudis, suspected of involvement with al-Qaeda.

26 **South Korea:** The *Cheonan*, a South Korean naval corvette, sinks with the loss of 46 of its 104-strong crew. An investigating team including foreign experts concludes that it was hit by a North Korean torpedo. South Korea refers the incident to the United Nations.

29 **Russia:** Two female suicide bombers kill 40 people in Moscow subway stations. Chechen separatists claim responsibility for the attack.

April 2010

6 **India:** Maoist rebels, known as Naxalites, kill 76 paramilitary police in an ambush in the Dantewada region of Chhattisgarh state.

7 **Kyrgyzstan:** President Kurmanbek Bakiyev is ousted in a revolt as protesters storm government buildings. Roza Otunbayeva, former foreign minister, becomes president.

8 **United States/Russia:** Presidents Obama and Medvedev sign an arms control treaty to replace the 1991 Strategic Arms Reduction Treaty (START), agreeing to new limits on nuclear warheads.

10 **Poland:** President Lech Kaczynski and many senior officials are killed in a plane crash in Russia.

10 **Thailand:** Protests by 'red-shirt' anti-government campaigners in Bangkok turn violent. Clashes continue until Thai soldiers move in and break up red-shirt encampments on 19 May, and protest leaders surrender. By the end of the unrest about 85 people have died.

11 **Sudan:** Sudan holds first multiparty elections for 24 years. On 26 April President Omar al-Bashir is declared the winner with 68% of the vote.

13 **United States:** President Obama hosts a Nuclear Security Summit, with representatives from 47 countries, focused on stopping non-state groups gaining access to nuclear materials.

15 **Iceland:** An ash cloud from the erupting volcano Eyjafjallajokull disrupts European air travel.

20 **United States:** An explosion aboard the *Deepwater Horizon* oil rig in the Gulf of Mexico kills 11 workers and causes a large oil spill. The rig was owned by Transocean and was being operated under lease to BP. A series of attempts to plug the leak fail, and oil reaches the coasts of all US Gulf states. On 16 June BP, at a meeting with President Obama, agrees to pay $20bn into a fund to meet claims arising from the spill.

21 **Ukraine/Russia:** Russia and Ukraine sign a deal cutting the price for gas supplies to Ukraine by 30% in exchange for an extension of Russia's lease on the naval port of Sevastopol, where Russia's Black Sea fleet is based.

May 2010

1 **United States:** A car-bomb in New York's Times Square fails to explode. Faisal Shahzad, a US citizen of Pakistani origin, is arrested two days later at JFK airport as he attempts to fly to Dubai. He pleads guilty to terrorism charges.

2 **Greece:** Eurozone countries agree a €110bn bailout for Greece, including €80bn from eurozone countries and €30bn from the International Monetary Fund. Greece promises austerity measures.

5 **Nigeria:** President Umaru Yar'Adua dies after an illness. Acting President Goodluck Jonathan succeeds him.

6 **United Kingdom:** General election gives no party a clear majority. After five days of negotiations, a coalition between Conservatives and Liberal Democrats is formed and David Cameron, the Conservative Party leader, becomes prime minister, replacing Gordon Brown who quits leadership of Labour Party.

9 **Europe:** European Union finance ministers agree to set up a €750bn three-year stabilisation mechanism to support eurozone countries that run into financial difficulties. Eurozone members contribute €440bn in loan guarantees, the European Commission €60bn in emergency funding and the International Monetary Fund €250bn.

10 **Iraq:** At least 102 people are killed in a series of suicide bombings throughout Iraq.

13 **Nigeria/China:** Nigeria and China agree to build three oil refineries in Nigeria at a cost of $23bn.

17 **Iran:** Iran reaches agreement with Turkey and Brazil to send 1,200kg of low-enriched uranium to Turkey in return for 120kg of further-enriched uranium for use in a medical reactor.

17 **India:** Maoist rebels blow up a bus in Dantewada district of Chhattisgarh state, killing at least 30 people including many police officers.

28 **India:** More than 100 people are killed when Calcutta to Mumbai train is derailed in West Bengal. Police accuse Maoist Naxalite rebels of sabotaging track.

28 **Pakistan:** At least 90 members of the Ahmadi Muslim sect are killed when six men apparently affiliated with the Pakistani Taliban attack two mosques in Lahore.

31 **Israel:** Nine Turks are killed when Israeli commandos, enforcing blockade, board an aid ship bound for Gaza. Turkey demands apology, compensation, a UN inquiry and lifting of the blockade.

June 2010

2 **Japan:** Japanese Prime Minister Yukio Hatoyama resigns after being unable to keep an election promise to move an American military base at Futenma on the island of Okinawa. He is replaced by Naoto Kan.

7 **Israel/Palestine:** Four Palestinian militants in diving gear, members of the al-Aqsa Martyrs Brigade, are killed by the Israeli navy off the Gaza coast.

9 **Iran:** UN Security Council votes for a fourth round of sanctions on Iran because of its nuclear programme. Twelve of 15 members back resolution but Brazil and Turkey vote against and Lebanon abstains.

10 **Kyrgyzstan:** Ethnic violence between Kyrgyz and Uzbeks in city of Osh leaves up to 2,000 people dead and tens of thousands displaced.

19 **China:** Central bank ends currency peg to US dollar, allowing a gradual rise in the value of the renminbi.

20 **Colombia:** Former Defence Minister Juan Manuel Santos is elected president in a run-off poll, with 69% of the vote.

23 **United States:** President Obama relieves General Stanley McChrystal of his command in Afghanistan after *Rolling Stone* magazine quotes disparaging remarks by McChrystal and his staff about members of the Obama administration. General David Petraeus is appointed to replace him.

24 **Australia:** Kevin Rudd is ousted as Australian prime minister by the Labor Party and is replaced by Julia Gillard.

28 **United States:** Ten people are arrested in the northeastern United States and plead guilty to charges of spying for Russia. They are deported in a swap for four people serving sentences for espionage in Russia.

Chapter 1

Perspectives

Two challenges dominated international affairs in the year to mid-2010. The first was the task that the Western world had assumed of bringing order to Afghanistan – a task that seemed to be hitting its political and military limits. The second, essential to ensuring prosperity in the second decade of the twenty-first century, was dealing with the continuing aftermath of the 2008 financial crisis. Here, the recovery in global economic growth was vulnerable to the effects of high government borrowing, and to the measures that were being taken to bring it down.

An initiative set in motion by US President Barack Obama, to curb nuclear arsenals and reduce nuclear risks, gathered momentum but would be a long-term venture. Efforts to tackle another enduring threat, that from climate change, did not make as much progress as campaigners had hoped. Meanwhile, the earthquake in Haiti, the ash cloud from an Icelandic volcano, and the massive oil spill in the Gulf of Mexico were reminders that the world remained vulnerable to more immediate catastrophes.

Shifts in the global balance of power were evident, for example, in the efforts of Turkey and Brazil to intervene in Iran's long-running confrontation with Western countries over its nuclear programme. That stand-off continued, however, and international sanctions against Tehran were tightened. Nor was there any progress towards peace in the Middle East, as Israel defied American pressure to cease new settlements in occupied Palestine. Two attempted terrorist attacks in America were evidence of the continuing threat from violent jihadists. The course of all these issues indicated that, in spite of the more open and conciliatory approach adopted by Obama, Washington's ability to achieve its international objectives remained limited. While the United States remained by far the world's strongest power in terms of economic strength, military muscle and political clout, in relative terms its dominance had been eroded over the past decade.

Afghanistan: an intervention too far?

It was in Afghanistan that the objectives and strategy of the United States and its partners appeared to be most in question. Few signs of success were visible to the outside world, while the setbacks in terms of insurgent attacks and Western military casualties were all too evident. Success, however defined, seemed elusive and distant, and it was increasingly questionable whether foreign governments and electorates had the stomach for a long struggle. President Hamid Karzai and his government were viewed with suspicion, especially following the blatant rigging of his August 2009 re-election. Building the levels of governance required to create a functioning state began to seem unachievable, especially in the midst of an insurgency that threatened any Afghan seen to be cooperating with international forces.

The campaign in Afghanistan had become the ultimate test of the post-Cold War military interventionism of the Western world. This new readiness to intervene had been seen first in the Gulf War of 1990–91, to reverse Iraq's invasion of Kuwait. That was followed by substantial NATO military operations in Bosnia beginning in 1995 and Kosovo in 1999, and the US-led invasions of Afghanistan in 2001 and Iraq in 2003. There were also many smaller interventions. While the cases made for each of these missions were individual and specific, all involved a basic assumption that Western military power could successfully act as an instrument of change – in Western eyes at least, change for the better.

In Kuwait, Bosnia and Kosovo, the operations were successful, achieving their objectives with limited casualties. Saddam Hussein's Iraq was sent packing from Kuwait in a campaign that, while it lacked the nation-building ambitions of later projects, formed part of the same zeitgeist in that US President George H.W. Bush spoke at the time of forging a 'new world order'. In Bosnia, while the political settlement remains vulnerable today, peace was achieved by NATO action, Serbian aggression ended and independence assured. In Kosovo, the NATO military presence prevented large-scale Serbian aggression against Kosovar Albanians and paved the way eventually to a declaration of independence from Serbia. The Balkan missions, in which military involvement was aided by new, precision-guided, stand-off weapons, were examples of a successful mixture of military and political action. The countries of the western Balkans, including Serbia, are now well on the road to integration into Europe's institutions.

In Iraq, although the invasion ordered by US President George W. Bush easily toppled Saddam Hussein's regime, the ability of Western military intervention to succeed first came into question. The US-led coalition was ill-prepared for the multifaceted insurgency that developed, and the country descended into violence to such a degree that, in the dark days of 2006, no end to the foreign military mission was visible. Yet light did appear at the end of the tunnel, as an increase in the number of American troops and a change in tactics coincided with changes in the relationships between the factions and forces within Iraq. The confluence of events permitted a political solution. An Iraqi government was elected. It was able to assume responsibility for security, and to sign an agreement under which foreign troops were taken off the streets and will leave the country by the end of 2011. At mid-2010 the number of American troops in Iraq, at 74,000, was about half the peak reached in the 2007 'surge'.

By the middle of 2010, views in the Western world about the mission under way in Afghanistan appeared to be approaching the pessimism which had been prevalent about Iraq in 2006, even though the overall levels of violence and of foreign military casualties were lower than they had been in Iraq. In 2001, there had been universal support for the US-led attack on Afghanistan, which came weeks after the 11 September 2001 attacks on New York and Washington in which 3,000 people were killed. Al-Qaeda, which had carried out the 9/11 atrocity, had been allowed to base itself in Afghanistan by the ruling Taliban government, and it was accepted that Washington had no alternative but to attack. In 2003, support for the invasion of Iraq was far less broad. By 2010, however, the positions were reversed: in Iraq the mission seemed, after a number of false steps, successful; in Afghanistan, it had become hard to see how success could be achieved in any meaningful timeframe.

This was not because the strategy being pursued in Afghanistan was generally thought to be grossly mistaken. Indeed, the approach devised by US Army General Stanley McChrystal as commander of the NATO-led International Security Assistance Force (ISAF) had been widely welcomed when it was first advanced in mid-2009. This shifted tactics away from aerial attacks on insurgents (which risked killing innocent civilians) towards an emphasis on protection of the Afghan people against Taliban insurgents, clearing the Taliban out of population centres, and building trust, governance and Afghan capacity. A year later, however, Obama relieved McChrystal of his command because the general and his inner circle of advisers had spoken incautiously to a reporter for *Rolling Stone* magazine. In McChrystal's place he appointed General David Petraeus, who had masterminded success in Iraq. While assurances were given that the strategy was unchanged and the campaign would not 'miss a beat', it seemed inevitable that the arrival of Petraeus would trigger another review of strategy.

This was clearly necessary given the lack of obvious success for the McChrystal approach so far. *Operation Moshtarak* (Together), launched in February 2010, was the largest military offensive yet against the Taliban, intended to pacify an area of Helmand province centred on the town of Marjah, a Taliban stronghold. This was to be a key test of the 'clear, hold and build' tactics that, in turn, were a plank of the US counter-insurgency doctrine written by Petraeus himself. But the deployment of thousands of troops to the area had failed to establish security by the end of June, let alone to enable the rolling out of 'government-in-a-box' that McChrystal had promised. A plan to mount a similar but much more challenging effort in the city and province of Kandahar, birthplace of the Taliban, had been put off. Patience was required, and it was possible that progress was being made but was simply not yet visible. However, the lack of clear success in these operations seemed to throw the viability of the whole enterprise into doubt.

Rationale and objectives in Afghanistan

Three fundamental questions seemed to present themselves to Western leaders. Did the rationale that had driven Western military intervention still apply? If so, what were reasonable objectives? How could they be achieved? In the United States, all of these issues were subjected to intensive debate inside and outside the Obama administration as it conducted two policy reviews during 2009, culminating in the president's decision on 1 December to send 30,000 more troops but simultaneously to announce that a drawdown would begin in mid-2011. While this was a finely tuned decision intended to head off criticism from both sides of the American political divide, it clearly established Obama's ownership of the Afghan war and his intent to bring it to an end.

In making his announcement at the US Military Academy at West Point, Obama said he had made his decision to send more troops to Afghanistan – which followed three months of debate within the administration – because America's security was at stake in Afghanistan and in Pakistan. 'This is the epicentre of violent extremism practised by al-Qaeda. It is from here that we were attacked on 9/11, and it from here that new attacks are being plotted as I speak.' Gordon Brown, then the British prime minister, gave a similar explanation. Speaking at the International Institute for Strategic Studies (IISS) in September 2009, he said: 'Our aim in 2009 is the same as in 2001 … Preventing terrorism coming to the streets of Britain, America and other countries depends on strengthening the authorities in both Pakistan and Afghanistan to defeat Al-Qaeda and also the Pakistan and Afghan Taliban.' Brown's successor, David Cameron, said in June 2010 that 'we are there because the Afghans are not yet ready to keep their own country safe and to keep terrorists and terrorist training camps out of their country'. Angela Merkel, chancellor of Germany, which contributes the third largest number of troops, told the Bundestag in April 2010 that 'our security to live in freedom is being endangered by events that take place far from our borders. The security of Germany, the security of Europe, the security of our partners in the world is being defended in the Hindu Kush.'

The rationale for the Western military presence was thus essentially founded on fear about jihadist terrorism in the West, originating in the 9/11 attacks. Out of those attacks had sprung a wealth of discussion within governments and academia about the dangers of 'failed states', which Afghanistan was deemed to be. The concern that Western security could be threatened from distant ungoverned spaces had come to form a part of foreign- and defence-policy statements across the western world. Those policies, and the rationale for interventionism and the defence capabilities that developed out of them, depended on the argument that it was better to go out and meet the threats at source before they arrived in the West. This carried a risk, however, that interventions could actually provoke the very terrorism that governments were seeking to prevent. After the Afghanistan mission is over, the entire line of thinking about 'failed states' is likely to be reopened for discussion, especially given that there are a number of hardly governed spaces in the world – and even in Afghanistan itself – that apparently do not demand a foreign military presence.

The problem about Obama's specific rationale was that it could not avoid pairing Afghanistan and Pakistan. However, the West could only send troops to one of these countries. Leaders of most of the main groups masterminding resistance to NATO forces in Afghanistan were based in or had strong links in Pakistan. Al-Qaeda's leaders, Osama bin Laden and Ayman al-Zawahiri, were still believed to be hiding in Pakistan's tribal areas. Leaders of the Afghan Taliban, including Mullah Mohammed Omar and the 'Quetta Shura', were believed to be based in the Pakistani province of Baluchistan. The Haqqani network, believed to be responsible for many attacks in eastern Afghanistan, had strong historical links with the Pakistani army's intelligence agency, Inter-Services Intelligence, and a power base in the Pakistani tribal area of North Waziristan. In addition, many terrorist plots uncovered in the West in recent years – including a failed attack on Times Square, New York in May 2010 – involved links not with Afghanistan but with Pakistan, which many suspects had visited for terrorist training. It was therefore becoming more difficult to argue that the Western presence in Afghanistan was protecting American and European populations unless the Pakistani authorities were also truly cooperating in efforts to halt the activities of militant groups.

During 2009 the Pakistani government, itself facing mounting violence and territorial encroachment from the Pakistani Taliban groups, launched major offensives in the regions of Swat and South Waziristan.

While these were successful in terms of re-establishing control and suppressing militant activity, Pakistan has stoutly resisted American pressure to take convincing action against those responsible for fuelling violence in Afghanistan. With a large ethnic Pashtun population and a long border with Afghanistan's Pashtun-dominated southern and eastern regions, Pakistan has an obvious strategic interest in maintaining relations with Pashtun leaders. Remembering its bitter experience of being befriended by the United States to help counter the Soviet occupation of Afghanistan and then – in Pakistani eyes – abandoned, Islamabad has an eye to the long-term future of the region, one in which there is no longer a Western military presence. The military and economic aid that the United States and other donors have ploughed into Pakistan must, therefore, be of questionable value in securing extensive and long-term cooperation from Islamabad. Although a number of senior Afghan Taliban figures were arrested in Pakistan early in 2010, it was not clear that this represented a major change of heart on the part of the Pakistani authorities. Indeed, the arrests seemed to have the effect of stopping a dialogue that had been under way with the Taliban, and the suspicion was aired that this was Pakistan's purpose. The truth of the matter was left unclear.

> Islamabad has an eye to the long-term future of the region

The Afghanistan–Pakistan axis has therefore been a flaw in the Western rationale for a presence in Afghanistan. It gave rise to the argument of US Vice President Joe Biden, who proposed in 2009 that American troops in Afghanistan should be reduced and, in effect, withdrawn from combating the Taliban. Instead, the combat effort should be focused on attacking al-Qaeda cells, from the air and using special forces, especially in Pakistan. Meanwhile, American forces would train and support Afghan forces in their fight against the Taliban. When McChrystal addressed the IISS in October 2009, he appeared to be referring to such a plan when he said dismissively: 'A paper has been written that recommends that we use a plan called "Chaosistan", and that we let Afghanistan become a Somalia-like haven of chaos that we simply manage from outside.' When asked specifically whether he favoured the Biden plan, the general said: 'The short answer is no ... A strategy that does not leave Afghanistan in a stable position is probably a short-sighted strategy.'

On this argument, if foreign troops were withdrawn, Afghanistan would quickly sink back into the Taliban-dominated factionalism of before 2001, in which al-Qaeda would again be given free rein to foster violent jihadism, operate training camps and mount attacks on the West. It was not clear whether al-Qaeda, weakened by being scattered and by the loss of many senior figures, still had the capacity to do this. But it could also be argued that the al-Qaeda mentality had spread to other jihadist groups who persuaded recruits that there was a Western conspiracy against Islam and encouraged them into terrorism. Still, speaking at the IISS in June 2010, Karl-Theodor zu Guttenberg, German defence minister, suggested that the anti-terrorism case for a presence in Afghanistan was becoming harder to argue, and that it might be better to ask what the implosion of Afghanistan would mean for the region, and hence for global security.

Attainable objectives?

Governments with troops in Afghanistan thus remained wedded to the rationale that they had developed – in effect, they were trapped by it. The next question was what objectives they were now seeking to achieve in Afghanistan. In his West Point address, Obama said that to meet the 'overarching' goal of disrupting, dismantling and defeating al-Qaeda, the United States would pursue these objectives: 'We must deny al-Qaeda a safe haven. We must reverse the Taliban's momentum and deny it the ability to overthrow the government. And we must strengthen the capacity of Afghanistan's security forces and government so that they can take lead responsibility for Afghanistan's future.' Brown cast the mission in similar terms when he said the objectives were 'above all for the advance of Afghan responsibility and autonomy for their own affairs. The more Afghans can take responsibility in the short term, the less our coalition forces will be needed in the longer term.'

The objective as set by the main troop-contributing governments, therefore, was to deliver setbacks to the Taliban so that it would be a less credible force in the eyes of Afghans and less able to undermine Karzai's government. In tandem with this, the Afghan government would be assisted in building up its institutions, including the armed forces and police, so that it could take responsibility for the country and foreign combat troops could be withdrawn. As Obama, Brown and other leaders expressed these goals in 2009, they had in front of them the initial assessment and strategy proposals – including the request for more troops – written by McChrystal in August following his appointment as ISAF commander in June. That document, which was leaked to the *Washington Post*, did not analyse the objectives as such. In his opening words, the general said previous strategy documents had 'laid a clear path of what we must do. Stability in Afghanistan is an imperative.' In his eyes, the aim was to achieve stability and to prevent the Afghan government from falling to the Taliban. His document quoted ISAF's mission statement, which was to 'reduce the capability and will of the insurgency, support the growth in capacity and capability of the Afghan National Security Forces, and facilitate improvements in governance and socio-economic development, in order to provide a secure environment for sustainable stability that is observable to the population.' Success was achievable if there was a big change in ISAF culture and strategy, McChrystal said, but it was not assured.

The key question was whether these objectives were achievable in any reasonable timeframe, and if so, how? On the one hand, the task was a military one: to take territory from Taliban control and to try to prevent insurgents from returning and having influence over local communities. The 'clear, hold and build' approach was a logical advance on previous military efforts which, partly for lack of resources, had not sufficiently emphasised maintaining a persistent presence in areas where the Taliban had been beaten back. With additional resources, it seemed a reasonable proposition to be able to gain the upper hand militarily against insurgent groups. However, as in all such asymmetric conflicts the Taliban had long-term advantages. It could melt into the mountains and re-emerge later. It could re-infiltrate villages, and threaten and kill their inhabitants. Even in the face of extensive surveillance technologies, it could successfully plant bombs and mount ambushes on foreign soldiers. Since ISAF's success would depend on building presence and trust, on being the opposite of the Taliban, it could do none of these things except in the field of special operations. Indeed, McChrystal's strategy of protecting the Afghan people entailed restrictions on the use of lethal force so as to reduce the risk of civilian casualties. Thus, while it was feasible to deliver military setbacks to the Taliban, and to reduce their influence in certain areas, it was not possible for ISAF military action permanently to neutralise the insurgency. Military commanders repeatedly cautioned that success in Afghanistan could not be achieved by military means alone.

A further part of the military task was to facilitate the introduction of civilian expertise, aid and government in the areas where the ISAF presence ensured security. But as the experience of Marjah showed, it was very challenging to establish a secure environment and difficult to imbue confidence among the local population. At best, it would be a long-term process to introduce the governance that would help to strengthen the community and the economy – and this is not even to mention the difficulties of building prosperous, licit economies in areas where poppy cultivation for the narcotics trade held sway.

Here was where Western objectives in Afghanistan seemed most in question at mid-2010. The purpose of the ISAF military effort, however extensive, gallant and enterprising, was to improve the conditions under which a political solution could be reached. That broader solution depended, in turn, on many things that seemed beyond the reach of Western governments. It depended, for a start, on building an Afghan government, a mammoth task given that such a government had perhaps never really existed in Afghanistan, at least in the way that was being envisaged. It would be needed not just in Kabul, the capital, but also in the provinces. This ambition was rooted in the 'failed states' doctrine and in previous nation-building efforts which had had varying degrees of success. Yet to many it seemed to fly in the face of the way in which power had traditionally been wielded in Afghanistan's troubled history of conflict between warlords. In Karzai, the West was supporting a Pashtun who did not seem to command sufficient authority among Pashtuns. He was a querulous ally, running a government riddled with corruption. His half-brother, Ahmed Wali Karzai, a prominent political figure in the southern city of Kandahar, was repeatedly accused of being a major drug-runner – an allegation he denied. While the parliament showed some muscle in rejecting some of the president's ministerial appointments, and while government ministries were developing, it would be a long time before Afghanistan could be said to have a fully functioning democracy.

Meanwhile, in spite of intensive ISAF efforts to train the Afghan National Army and the police force, it seemed questionable whether they could reach their targets in terms of manning levels and capabilities. Since success would depend on ISAF handing over responsibility for security to these forces, they were an essential part of the process.

Large amounts of foreign aid were being directed to a government which was widely seen to be highly corrupt. And it was not only to the government and to aid projects that foreign money was being directed. In June 2010, a US Congressional staff report said that a $2 billion trucking contract to supply US military bases was subcontracted to 'warlords, strongmen, commanders and militia leaders who compete with the Afghan central government for power and authority'. Their interests, it said were 'in fundamental conflict with US aims to build a strong Afghan government'. These warlords, it said, made 'protection' payments that were 'a significant potential source of funding for the Taliban'. In other words, American taxpayers' money was essentially fuelling the conflict.

At mid-2010, it was therefore becoming increasingly questionable whether the West's objectives – beating back the Taliban, building an Afghan government and security forces, and building the confidence of Afghans in their institutions – could be achieved in the foreseeable future. It was not surprising that foreign governments and electorates were beginning to doubt that the sacrifices they were making were worthwhile. The deployment of troops to Afghanistan was politically controversial in many of the 46 countries that were contributing to ISAF, and two of them – Canada and the Netherlands – had decided to pull out. In the Netherlands, the coalition government had collapsed over the issue. The United States itself, in Obama's West Point speech, had announced plans to begin a drawdown of troops from mid-2011. And Cameron, asked whether British troops would be home before the next election due by 2015, replied: 'I want that to happen, make no mistake about it. We can't be there for another five years, having been there for nine years already.'

Exit ramp from combat?

Were there alternative means to achieve Western objectives? The dramatic sacking of McChrystal did not represent a rejection of his strategy, to which Obama had only recently committed 30,000 more US troops. McChrystal, after all, was executing the US counter-insurgency doctrine which had become highly voguish in the Pentagon since it was written by Petraeus, who had employed it to good effect in Iraq. McChrystal was taking it to new limits in his heavy emphasis on protecting the people, winning their trust and restricting the use of lethal force. ISAF officers needed to understand the communities in which they were operating, he said, and they needed a unified approach. It would be hard to argue with the thrust of many of McChrystal's assertions, especially given the marked lack of ISAF unity in previous years, when national contingents had seemed to pursue their own individual tactics in the areas for which they were responsible.

The appointment of Petraeus apparently signalled American determination to see the military mission through to the end. A soldier-statesman, Petraeus immediately sought to re-establish unity among the people who, in addition to Obama, had an important say in policy and had been disparaged in the *Rolling Stone* article that caused McChrystal's downfall. These included Biden, special envoy Richard Holbrooke, and Karl Eikenberry, the US ambassador to Kabul. In November 2009, as Obama deliberated on McChrystal's request for more troops, Eikenberry had sent memos to Secretary of State Hillary Clinton advising against sending more troops, arguing that this would increase Afghan dependency and would 'delay the day when Afghans will take over, and make it difficult, if not impossible, to bring our people home on a reasonable timetable'.

In spite of the assurances of continuity, McChrystal's departure did give pause for thought about the future of Western involvement in Afghanistan – and an opportunity to revisit the concerns expressed by Eikenberry.

The pressing issue for Western leaders was how to create the conditions in which a drawdown of combat troops could be undertaken. In September 2009, Sherard Cowper-Coles, then the UK regional special envoy, speaking in a personal capacity, said it was necessary to 'get on the exit ramp from combat'. Power needed to be distributed away from Kabul so that all Afghan districts could secure and govern themselves – as he put it, 'putting the elders back in charge'. Meanwhile, there needed to be a 'more political approach to the insurgency', with efforts at reconciliation and reintegration 'in the Pashtun way'.

During the year to mid-2010 there were some moves towards such reconciliation. One insurgent group leader who was not affiliated to the Taliban, former prime minister Gulbuddin Hekmatyar, indicated a willingness to talk. Kai Eide, who was the UN special representative in Afghanistan until March 2010, disclosed that he had held promising talks with senior Taliban representatives beginning in spring 2009, but these had ended when Pakistan arrested some Taliban leaders. A 'peace jirga' held by Karzai in 2010 made very limited progress, since no Taliban representatives attended – and underlining the lack of a secure environment, the meeting in Kabul was targeted by suicide bombers.

> The 'peace jirga' was targeted by suicide bombers

Yet the future clearly lay in negotiations with or among the participants in the conflict. Since military commanders said there was no military solution in Afghanistan, and since efforts to build a convincing Afghan government would take a very long time, it seemed obvious that if there was to be an end to combat involving foreign troops within a reasonable timeframe, it must come through a political accommodation.

If Iraq in 2007–09 was a guide, Petraeus would seek methodically to hand over responsibility for security in individual regions to Afghan forces. The difficulties in building and training these forces, in which there were inadequate numbers of Pashtuns, were likely to persist. The only way in which they could credibly assume such responsibilities was if the security challenges were lowered. In more peaceful areas of Afghanistan, handovers could probably be effected without difficulty. But in other areas, the only way in which insecurity could be reduced so that Afghans could take over would be through accommodations with militant leaders – since otherwise, combat could continue indefinitely.

The question of who precisely would be the parties to such deals was an open one. Since the McChrystal strategy did not appear yet to be having a significant impact, Taliban groups perhaps felt that they were under little pressure to negotiate with anyone, and indeed that they could only benefit by waiting. Yet if Washington and other capitals really wanted to reduce their military commitment, they needed to foster arrangements that could end the combat. Only then could they stick to their undertaking to hand over responsibility for the security of Afghans to Afghan security forces.

The repeated response of the United States and its coalition partners to a situation which evidently demanded more than a military solution has been to send more soldiers: when Obama took office in January 2009, there were 36,000 American troops in Afghanistan, and by mid-2010 there were 94,000, with 45 other countries contributing a total of about 41,000. But the desire of governments, as expressed by Obama, Cameron and others, will increasingly be to make an orderly withdrawal of combat troops – even though assistance to Afghanistan will certainly continue in other forms, including training. For this to happen, it seems clear that the rationale for a presence in Afghanistan, the objectives and the means to achieve them need to be re-thought and agreed by Western governments. More rough-and-ready solutions will need to be contemplated. It might be argued that a rapid pull-out of troops would cause an implosion of Afghanistan, much violence and regional insecurity. But it could equally be argued that to persist with the mission as currently defined risks being carried forward by outdated thinking into a long-drawn-out disaster.

Economic growth, financial vulnerability

While they continued to agonise about the mission in Afghanistan, leaders of the world's largest countries could boast of a major success in 2009–10. The financial crisis that had come to a climax in October 2008 did not cause a prolonged recession, did not destroy the financial system and did not bring an end to capitalism. This fortunate outcome was the result of the massive actions taken by governments and central banks – acting individually and in cooperation – to provide emergency support to the financial markets and to stimulate economies. After 2009 saw the first contraction in the global economy since the Second World

War, growth in the industrialised world resumed, albeit slowly and tentatively. In large emerging economies such as China and India, no recession occurred and growth again rose to healthy levels.

The crisis did, however, have significant longer-term effects – indeed, it seemed in some ways that it was still in process, and that it still carried large risks. In particular, there was concern that some governments' moves towards monetary and fiscal tightening – essentially, withdrawal of the emergency injection of funding in order to restore anti-inflationary and budgetary discipline – could stifle fragile demand and tip the world back into recession and even depression. The International Monetary Fund reported in July 2010 that 'recent turbulence in financial markets—reflecting a drop in confidence about fiscal sustainability, policy responses, and future growth prospects—has cast a cloud over the outlook'. However, it was still forecasting global growth of 4.6% in 2010 and 4.3% in 2011, with rapid growth in the major emerging Asian economies, moderate expansion in the United States, and slow growth in Europe.

Worries about debt problems were seen most obviously when the ballooning fiscal deficit of Greece led to a crisis of investor confidence in the debt instruments of several European countries. Since Greece was a member of the eurozone – 16 countries which use the euro as a common currency – its debt crisis posed a major challenge for all the members. It exposed the dangers of divergent economic policies in a single-currency area. Many members had ignored the pledges they had made to restrict budget deficits to 3% of GDP and their national debts to 60% of GDP. The new Greek government's disclosure in October 2009 that it would have a fiscal deficit of 12.7%, more than twice the previous government's estimate, set off a chain of events that escalated over the following six months.

Sovereign debt problems are a common phenomenon after banking crises. They occur partly because the decline in credit causes a fall in economic activity – a recession – which reduces government tax revenues. It also increases payments on entitlements, for example unemployment benefits. In this case, governments' financial commitments were increased by emergency spending to counter the crisis. Also in this case, the banking crisis hit just as some countries had built up large fiscal deficits for policy reasons – contributing factors, for example, included higher military spending in the United States and higher social spending in the United Kingdom. According to historical studies by economists Carmen Reinhart and Ken Rogoff, central government debt typically increases by 86% during the three years following a financial crisis. This, in turn, would suggest that the government debt burdens of most major Western economies would rise to between 80% and 110% of GDP. According to the IMF's *World Economic Outlook*, the combined fiscal deficit of industrialised countries rose to 9% following the crisis, and their debt-to-GDP ratio was expected to exceed 100% of GDP in 2014, some 35 percentage points higher than before the crisis.

The expansion of fiscal deficits was a major factor enabling economies to recover from recession. However, the attention that the Greek crisis focused on government debt (with Spain, Italy, Portugal and Ireland also seen as being at risk) triggered a debate among industrialised countries about the correct balance between fiscal discipline and economic stimulus. To European governments, there seemed little doubt that they needed to bring down their borrowing. They could not risk the investors' strike that had afflicted Greece. For eurozone members, it was a question of preserving the single currency, which in turn was a pillar of the European Union – though Germany and France differed widely on how this should be done, and Berlin was a reluctant participant in the common effort. If economic growth was constrained as a result, this was a necessary price to pay. During 2010, many European governments therefore announced plans to narrow their fiscal deficits through lower spending and tax increases. The plans announced by successive British governments were particularly ambitious.

The US administration, with unemployment at around 10% and midterm elections looming, preferred to keep the rhetorical emphasis on stimulus and did not project the same determination to cut government costs.

To some prominent economists, however, the policies being pursued carried extreme risk of tipping the world back into recession. They believed that it had parallels with the Great Depression of the 1930s which followed the 1929 Wall Street crash. Paul Krugman, writing in the *New York Times*, predicted that the world would now enter the 'Third

Depression' (after those in the nineteenth and twentieth centuries). 'Both the United States and Europe are well on their way toward Japan-style deflationary traps', he wrote in June 2010. The alternative view from Europe, however, was that it was important for governments to establish credible programmes towards lower borrowing, and that these would help to keep borrowing costs low and stimulate investment. Proposed spending cuts would certainly cause significant public-sector job losses, but these would take place over a period of years and would in any case have to win political approval, which was not a given.

The difference of emphasis between Europe and the United States was awkward for the fourth summit meeting of the G20 in Toronto in June 2010. The enhanced role of the G20 was itself an outcome of the financial crisis. It had held its first three summits within a year from November 2008, and at the third it had decided that henceforth it would be the premier forum for international economic cooperation, replacing the G8. This was recognition of the growing role of emerging economies such as China, India and Indonesia, and of the need for a new mechanism of global cooperation to address the world's biggest challenges. An indication of the shift in the global balance was the fact that nine members of the Asia-Pacific Economic Cooperation grouping were included in the G20, and only four European countries (though the EU was also a member).

> " The enhanced role of the G20 was an outcome of the financial crisis "

There was plenty of scepticism about whether such a large group of countries, often with competing priorities, could achieve anything. But the G20 proved to be an important instrument in navigating the world out of the financial crisis. Leaders agreed on the basic idea that widespread economic stimulus was required, on plans for reforms of financial regulation, on strengthening of the IMF and the World Bank, and on 'peer-review' of each others' economic policies.

In Pittsburgh in September 2009, leaders agreed that they would 'avoid any premature withdrawal of stimulus'. But the financial markets' worries about the budget deficits of some European countries had changed the picture by the June 2010 meeting in Canada. The G20 again expressed its commitment to 'taking concerted actions to sustain the recovery', and said that 'there is a risk that synchronised fiscal adjustment across several major economies could adversely impact the recovery'. But the leaders also acknowledged that lack of fiscal consolidation could undermine confidence, and that 'those with serious fiscal challenges need to accelerate the pace of consolidation'. This mixed message seemed to underline the fact that the G20 would always include members whose economies were in widely different states. The Toronto summit, lacking any major new agreements or commitments, raised a question about the future importance of the G20 grouping in the absence of a compelling crisis. The fifth summit was due to be held in Seoul in November 2010.

One area in which countries were edging forward was in efforts to reform financial markets so that a 2008 crisis could not occur again. In the United States, Congress passed a mammoth reform bill which would, among other measures, remove the implicit guarantee of a government bailout for financial institutions deemed 'too big to fail', by putting in place other steps that the authorities could take. The new law would ban banks from taking big risks in financial markets on their own account, as opposed to those of their customers. Meanwhile, international regulators were preparing new capital standards for banks to ensure that they were better cushioned against risks, and some European governments were introducing new taxes on banks and on bonuses. These steps did not, however, mean that the world would in future be immune from financial crises.

A further important effect of the financial crisis was to put renewed downward pressure on defence budgets, at least in the Western world. In May 2010, Robert Gates, US defence secretary, noted that the 9/11 attacks had 'opened a gusher of defence spending'. But now, he said, 'given America's difficult economic circumstances and parlous fiscal condition, military spending on things large and small can and should expect closer, harsher scrutiny. The gusher has been turned off, and will stay off for a good period of time.' Gates's counterparts in Europe were facing a similar need to make reductions as part of new austerity programmes. While American military capabilities will remain enormous by comparison with those of any other country, defence cuts in Europe are expected to cause significant reductions in both personnel and equipment. Europe's ability to deploy troops on multinational operations – much increased by comparison with previous decades, but still modest – was likely to be curtailed. Decisions in this area would be closely bound up with governments' consideration of the possibilities of exit from Afghanistan.

Political challenges

It was not surprising that, following a sharp recession and with unemployment high, Western governments faced multiple political difficulties over the past year. In the United States, Obama had come to office on the catchword of 'change'. Among the things he was seeking to change was the nature of political debate, away from the bitter partisan animosity which has characterised America for some years. He made repeated efforts to seek bipartisan approaches, but was rebuffed at every turn. His Republican opponents, lacking leadership, became increasingly fractious and vituperative, with the rise of so-called Tea Party activism which, apparently, had little common agenda beyond hatred of Democrats and a reluctance to pay taxes.

Against this background, it was remarkable that Obama managed to score one of the biggest victories in domestic politics in many years when Congress passed a law to reform the health-care system. Among the changes will be the extension of health insurance coverage to more than 30 million Americans, and the banning of such practices as refusing cover on the grounds of pre-existing medical conditions. After a tortuous path during which it seemed for a time that Democrats would not unite behind the legislation, the reforms were passed without a single Republican vote in either house. The financial reform bill would represent another achievement, but it seemed inevitable that, with unemployment high and economic prospects not assured, the Democrats would suffer setbacks.

In Europe, a shift to the right of centre was seen in elections in Germany and the United Kingdom. But neither move was decisive, and the new German coalition – under the continuing leadership of Angela Merkel – swiftly found itself under political fire over the degree of assistance that Germany would provide to Greece. By mid-2010, in spite of the recent election victory, Merkel's hold on power did not seem assured.

In Britain, the floundering Labour government of Gordon Brown was ousted, but the Conservative Party headed by David Cameron did not win a parliamentary majority and had to form a surprising coalition with the Liberal Democrats. For these two governments, just as for other Western countries, the difficult policy choices involved in economic challenges and in Afghanistan seemed likely to continue to loom as large in the coming year as they had in the last.

The world's emerging great power, China, did not face the same difficulties and was able to rebound from the 2008 financial shock more quickly than most other countries. While it enjoyed rapid economic growth, it could not however afford to ignore the broader consequences of the financial crisis as it remained the leading financier of America's fast-growing debt. Still, the events of the past two years had clearly bolstered its confidence on the world stage and made it more assertive. Its enhanced standing led to heightened international expectations for its role in addressing world challenges. How to balance these global expectations with its own national priorities was likely to be an increasingly tricky problem for Beijing in the years to come.

Chapter 2

Strategic Policy Issues

US Nuclear Policy Transformed

US President Barack Obama promised in a seminal speech in Prague in April 2009 to put nuclear disarmament at the centre of the national-security policy of the United States. This undertaking took longer to find traction than he hoped. The first element of his strategy – a new arms-reduction pact with Russia – was not agreed until four months after the Strategic Arms Reduction Treaty (START) it was to replace expired in December. The delay, and the president's troubles with an obstreperous Republican minority, pushed back the timing for a treaty-ratification vote in the US Senate dangerously close to the November 2010 midterm election. Senate consideration of the Comprehensive Test-Ban Treaty (CTBT) – another key goal – was subsequently postponed to a later year. Meanwhile, a third Prague speech promise, the start of negotiations on a treaty to ban production of fissile material for weapons purposes, remained stymied by a Pakistani veto.

Obama's nuclear agenda has not been without achievement. He led a UN Security Council session in September that focused new attention on the threat of nuclear terrorism. This was followed up by his convocation in April 2010 of 38 heads of government and the deputy leaders of nine other countries for a nuclear-security summit that coalesced support for his ambitious goal of securing all fissile material within four years. The summit, and the quintennial Non-Proliferation Treaty (NPT) Review Conference that followed in May, produced announcements by several states that they would take national actions to counter nuclear dangers. Obama's own contributions to the nuclear-security cause were high-lighted by a Nuclear Posture Review that went further than expected in meeting his promise in Prague to reduce the role of nuclear weapons in American security policy.

Obama's nuclear strategy reflected neither the pacifism of which he was accused by right-wing critics nor the George W. Bush-era stasis perceived by sceptics on the left. The new policy reaffirmed America's reliance on nuclear deterrence as long as nuclear weapons existed elsewhere. Yet Obama boldly set out the goal of a nuclear-weapons-free world, while noting that it might not happen in his lifetime. He argued that US steps towards disarmament were vital to re-establishing a consensus behind the global non-proliferation regime. Nobody expected that reductions in the US and Russian arsenals would give North Korea and Iran reason to rein in their nuclear ambitions; indeed, these two countries remained as recalcitrant as ever in defying Security Council demands. The Obama administration did hope, however, that renewed recognition of the connection between disarmament and non-proliferation would help to persuade other countries to take part in strengthening the global non-proliferation regime.

At mid-2010, the outcome of this strategy remained uncertain. The rest of the world had been united in condemning North Korea's nuclear testing, yet Pyongyang felt no need to resume multinational negotiations on ending its weapons programme. The world has been far less unified in calling Iran to account for its nuclear transgressions, and Tehran has moved closer to putting the pieces in place to produce a nuclear weapon if it should decide to cross that line. The NPT Review Conference produced a lengthy document that modestly succeeded in restoring international consensus on the goals of the treaty, but did little to significantly strengthen non-proliferation measures or to move closer to a nuclear-weapons-free world.

The Prague promise

Countering nuclear dangers quickly became a major theme of Obama's foreign policy. In his 5 April 2009 speech in Prague, he recommitted the

United States to the goal of eliminating nuclear weapons, emphasising that it would maintain its nuclear deterrent as long as nuclear weapons existed elsewhere. In addition to reducing the role of nuclear weapons in America's national-security strategy, he outlined several disarmament steps he would pursue. Obama pledged to negotiate a follow-on agreement to the START Treaty, to seek ratification of the CTBT and pursue diplomacy to bring about its entry into force, and to seek a new treaty that would verifiably end the production of fissile materials for nuclear-weapons purposes. Finally, he set a goal of securing all vulnerable nuclear material within four years.

By emphasising arms-control steps and the threat of nuclear terrorism, Obama sought also to strengthen global measures to stem the proliferation of nuclear weapons. He recognised that disarmament and non-proliferation were mutually reinforcing. In pledging to take the disarmament goal seriously and in taking concrete steps in that direction, he hoped to remove the charge of double standards from the non-proliferation debate. His message was that all responsible nations must work together if the world was to be protected from the threat of nuclear weapons.

For setting out this agenda, Obama was awarded the Nobel Peace Prize, premature though that seemed to many. His call for global nuclear disarmament and the atmosphere of hope he engendered also led the *Bulletin of the Atomic Scientists* in January 2010 to move its iconic clock a further minute away from midnight – the hour marking the symbolic risk of nuclear holocaust.

There was no doubting the president's personal commitment. In September he arranged for a special high-level UN Security Council meeting on nuclear non-proliferation and disarmament, the first time an American president had led a Security Council session. The historic summit unanimously adopted Resolution 1887 emphasising that the council had a primary responsibility to address nuclear threats, and that all situations of non-compliance with nuclear treaties should be brought to its attention. The resolution set out no new obligations, mentioned no specific problem countries and omitted mention of nuclear-weapons-free zones, such as the one pursued by Arab states in the Middle East. Yet it drew global attention to his nuclear goals and set the stage for follow-up action in the spring.

Global momentum towards disarmament

Obama spurred and was himself spurred by growing global momentum in favour of a nuclear-weapons-free world. In July 2009 a Nuclear Weapons Free Zone entered into force for the continent of Africa, following similar zones elsewhere that together declare the land masses and national waterways of the entire southern hemisphere to be nuclear-weapons free. In November the International Commission on Nuclear Non-Proliferation and Disarmament led by former Australian and Japanese Foreign Ministers Gareth Evans and Yoriko Kawaguchi put out a comprehensive set of 76 practical recommendations to eliminate nuclear threats. With somewhat less attention to practicality, the media-savvy Global Zero Commission ambitiously promoted the goal of nuclear disarmament by 2045. Other private-sector groups sought to galvanise public attention by focusing on the threat of nuclear terrorism. The US-based Nuclear Threat Initiative, for example, produced a documentary film, *Nuclear Tipping Point*, featuring interviews with US statesmen – George Shultz, Sam Nunn, William Perry and Henry Kissinger – who were rightly credited with reviving the nuclear-weapons-free vision in a series of op-ed articles in the *Wall Street Journal* beginning in 2007. UN Secretary-General Ban Ki-moon promoted his own 2008 five-point plan for nuclear disarmament, including the negotiation of a convention to ban nuclear weapons. In 2009, 124 governments backed a General Assembly resolution calling for such a convention.

New START

Russian leaders may have assumed that Obama's personal commitment to the disarmament agenda and the popular attention that it received in the West would make him over-eager to conclude an agreement to replace START before it expired on 5 December, a few days before he was to accept his Nobel Peace Prize. As these dates approached, Russia held out for favourable conditions, including linking offensive-weapons reductions to limits on ballistic missile defence. In April 2009, Obama and Russian President Dmitry Medvedev had agreed that the new treaty would recognise the interdependence between strategic offence and defence, but US negotiators insisted this linkage be mentioned only in the treaty preamble, making it non-binding. Accepting restrictions on

US missile-shield deployments would have severely endangered Senate support for ratification. When the deadline passed, the verification measures of START I expired. There was not even an informal extension, and the two sides pledged only to act 'in the spirit' of the treaty.

Throughout the winter, as each side offered repeated public assurances that the treaty was nearly complete, agreement was held up by niggling differences on verification issues such as exchange of telemetry data for missile tests (which only Russia currently conducts). To break through the impasses, the two presidents personally intervened in negotiations to an unprecedented extent, discussing the treaty 14 times between themselves before negotiations concluded in late March. To complete an arms-control agreement in less than 45 weeks (from the start of negotiations on 19 May 2009) was amazingly fast. Negotiating START I, by contrast, took nine years. 'New START' was signed on 8 April 2010, fittingly in Prague, almost on the anniversary of Obama's disarmament speech there.

Upon ratification, the treaty will also replace the Moscow Treaty of 2002 (SORT), which was scheduled to run until the end of 2012. New START sets a 1,550 limit on the number of offensively deployed warheads, a 30% reduction from the maximum of 2,200 allowed by SORT. The treaty also sets a limit of 800 deployed and non-deployed strategic nuclear-delivery vehicles (intercontinental ballistic missiles, submarine-launched ballistic missiles and nuclear-capable heavy bombers), 700 of which can be deployed. These two overlapping figures thus provide for some limit on the number of ballistic missiles the United States can employ for any future 'Prompt Global Strike' missions employing conventional warheads.

The real reductions under the new treaty are more modest than these figures suggest. Given the growing obsolescence of arsenals built during the height of the Cold War, current deployments are already less than the START I and SORT limits. In the case of the United States, which released actual numbers, the reduction of launchers will be 10%, which need not be completed for seven years. Similar to previous arms-control pacts, New START places no constraints on non-deployed nuclear weapons, including those removed from deployed systems under the terms of the treaty. Such non-deployed warheads (in storage, or awaiting dismantlement), amount to several thousand for each side. Nor does the treaty address sub-strategic weapons, including the approximately 200 gravity bombs at US bases in Europe and Russia's estimated 2,000 deployed tactical nuclear weapons.

Notwithstanding the omissions and modest nature of the reductions, New START was significant in several important ways. It returned to the principles, largely abandoned by the George W. Bush administration, that arms reductions should be effectively verifiable and irreversible. Inspection and notification arrangements that expired with the end of START I will be restored, albeit simplified to take into account the greater trust and transparency that now characterise US–Russia relations. The resumption of an arms-control partnership provided a tangible manifestation of the 're-set' in relations that the two sides had promised the previous summer. By ensuring transparency and predictability in weapons deployments, it will promote strategic stability. Russia's status as a superpower on equal footing is thus restored. This provides a better basis for further negotiated reductions, including Washington's goal of including non-deployed and tactical nuclear weapons. By addressing NPT obligations to negotiate disarmament steps, the treaty also reinforces the NPT bargain. A successful new US–Russia arms-control treaty was judged to be the vital prerequisite for a favourable outcome at the May NPT Review Conference.

When ratification hearings began in the US Senate in May 2010, several Republican opponents seized on the language of the preamble about linkage to missile defence and on a non-binding Russian statement that Moscow might withdraw from the treaty if missile defences became a threat to its strategic deterrent. In language harking back to the Cold War, one right-wing Senator even claimed that the purpose of US missile defences should be to render Russian nuclear weapons 'useless', something that the George W. Bush administration had emphatically stressed was not the purpose. Other Republicans sought to tie ratification to efforts to resurrect the 'reliable replacement warhead' programme, which both the Democratic-led Congress and the Obama administration had rejected.

To counter complaints that his arms-control agenda was undermining American security, Obama promised to spend $80 billion over ten years to maintain and modernise the nation's nuclear arsenal. This extended a previous pledge to spend $7bn in fiscal year 2011, an increase of $600 million, to modernise the nuclear infrastructure. The increased funding secured support for both the treaty and the administration's broader nuclear agenda from the directors of the US national nuclear laboratories. The four senior statesmen who were leading the drive for nuclear disarmament – Shultz, Nunn, Perry and Kissinger – joined this strategy, by arguing in the 2010 edition of their now annual January op-ed in the *Wall Street Journal*, that 'maintaining high confidence in our nuclear arsenal is critical as the numbers of these weapons goes down. It is also consistent with and necessary for US leadership in non-proliferation, risk reduction and arms reductions goals.' Some critics wondered, however, whether the $80bn price tag was necessary, and what kind of signal it sent to the rest of the world about the sincerity of Obama's commitment to nuclear disarmament.

> " Moscow decided to synchronise ratification with the US Senate "

The White House hoped the treaty would be approved by summer 2010. Russian ratification appeared more certain, given the pro-government party's majority in the two houses of the Federal Assembly. But Moscow decided to synchronise ratification with the approval process in US Senate.

Complementing New START, the United States sought in other ways to improve strategic relations with Russia. A major step had been taken in September 2009, when Obama reconfigured plans for a missile shield in Europe that, while driven by technical realities and a revised intelligence assessment about Iranian missile capabilities, also addressed some of Russia's major concerns about the previous deployment plan. In April 2010, the two sides signed a deal that had been languishing since 2000 under which each of them would dispose of 34 tonnes of weapons-grade plutonium by burning it in nuclear reactors. Separately Medvedev announced the shut-down of Russia's last reactor dedicated to producing weapons-grade plutonium. Then, in May, Obama resubmitted to Congress a civil nuclear cooperation agreement with Russia that Bush had cancelled two years earlier after the war in Georgia. Obama told the Congress that the situation in Georgia 'need no longer be considered an obstacle' to the agreement and that Russia was cooperating with the United States in pushing for new sanctions against Iran.

Test-ban treaty

Ending all nuclear testing is seen as the most important next step in moving towards a nuclear-weapons-free world. The CTBT would codify self-imposed moratoriums on testing that the major nuclear powers have observed since the 1990s. Tests by India and Pakistan in 1998 and by North Korea in 2006 and 2009 reinforced the perceived need for a global test ban, and for the United States in particular to demonstrate leadership by ratifying a treaty it had been the first to sign in 1996.

Although the Prague speech had labelled CTBT ratification a priority goal, the delay in negotiating the START follow-on treaty and the legislative timetable necessary for Senate consideration of it meant there would be no time left in 2010 for ratification of the CTBT. Given expected Democratic Party losses in the November election, the delay did not bode well for CTBT ratification. Not only was Obama out of time, he was rapidly running out of arrows. The administration's efforts to win Republican support for New START left him with less leverage to employ in seeking Senate consent for ratification of the CTBT. Indeed, this appeared to be part of the Republican strategy: to obtain maximum concessions in exchange for letting New START go through, so that there would be nothing left that the president could offer in exchange for support for the test ban.

Obama did have logic on his side. The Senate rejected ratification in 1999 on grounds that have largely fallen by the wayside, mainly questions over the verifiability of low-yield tests and the long-term reliability of the US arsenal in the absence of future testing. Advances in seismic detection technology and the expansion of the CTBT on-site monitoring system mean that sensors are able to detect any tests in most regions as low as 100 tonnes. The US stockpile-stewardship programme has demonstrated that existing weapons could be refurbished and recertified without test explosions. A September 2009 report by the independent group of prominent scientists known as JASON confirmed that the lifetimes of US nuclear weapons could be extended for decades without testing 'with no anticipated loss in confidence'.

The merits of the CTBT case, particularly in light of the higher budget for the nuclear laboratories that Obama has proposed, appeared to persuade Defense Secretary Robert Gates, who in the same position under George W. Bush had expressed doubts about forever forswearing nuclear-weapons testing. However, many Republicans remained sceptical about international treaties in general, and inclined to reject any imposed constraints on US military capabilities. Opposition to CTBT was also grounded in partisan efforts to portray Obama as weak on national security. More credibly, treaty opponents argued that US ratification would not constrain countries that had not yet ratified the treaty.

Under the terms of the treaty, the CTBT will not go into effect until ratified by the 44 states that have nuclear reactors (and thus can produce plutonium, one of the two paths to a nuclear weapon). As of June 2010, three of these countries – India, Pakistan and North Korea – had not signed the treaty and six others – China, Egypt, Indonesia, Iran, Israel, and the US – had yet to ratify it. The latter number will soon decrease. Indonesia announced at the start of the NPT Review Conference that it would soon approve the treaty, saying that Obama's promotion of nuclear-disarmament steps had prompted Jakarta to change its earlier stance against joining the pact ahead of Washington. China has hinted that it will ratify the treaty if the United States does. US ratification is essential to bringing Israel on board and would also increase pressure on India and Pakistan to accept the treaty. This would leave Egypt, Iran and North Korea, all of whom would likely seek a steep price for ratification.

Fissile material

No progress at all has been made towards one of the goals Obama spelled out in Prague: to negotiate a treaty banning the production of fissile material (highly enriched uranium or separated plutonium) for weapons purposes. A 1993 UN General Assembly resolution called for such negotiations to begin at the Conference on Disarmament (CD) in Geneva, but the 65 nations represented there have been deadlocked from the beginning. The biggest roadblock has been posed by Pakistan, which has been supported by some other countries in insisting that controls must cover existing stockpiles. In May 2009, Pakistan allowed the CD, for the first time in a decade, to adopt a programme of work that included negotiating a Fissile Missile Material Cut-off Treaty (FMCT). But before any discussions could begin, Pakistan raised procedural objections and in 2010 it rejected the plan of work altogether, citing national-security interests.

Pakistan's concerns are driven by the desire for strategic parity with India. Although the two sides today have roughly equivalent fissile-material stockpiles and production capabilities, the Pakistan Army, which is in charge of the nuclear-weapons programme, worries that India's much larger holding of reactor-grade plutonium, if put to weapons use, would put Pakistan at a disadvantage. Pakistan is also concerned that the US–India nuclear cooperation deal, finalised in 2008, will enable India to produce significant additional quantities of fissile material by freeing up the limited supplies of domestic uranium that India today devotes to civil nuclear energy generation. This concern is exacerbated by India's superiority in conventional weapons and much greater economic strength – nuclear weapons are Pakistan's equalising factor.

Islamabad has thus sought a similar civil-nuclear deal with the United States and similar exemption from the Nuclear Suppliers Group's (NSG) prohibition on nuclear commerce with states outside the NPT, which today means India, Israel, North Korea and Pakistan. Washington has little interest in such a deal, given Pakistan's recent failure of nuclear stewardship in allowing nuclear sales to North Korea, Iran and Libya from 1987 to 2004 by nuclear-laboratory director Abdul Qadeer Khan. In notes made public by the *Washington Post* in March 2010, Khan claimed that he provided this assistance with the knowledge of the Pakistani government. China, which has fewer compunctions about Pakistan's record, pledged in 2008 to supply it with two new nuclear reactors. With questionable logic, China argued that the additional reactors should be regarded as grandfathered on the basis of deals struck before China joined the NSG in 2004.

Meanwhile, although the United States has lobbied Islamabad at senior level to remove its veto on beginning FMCT discussions in Geneva, the Obama administration has more pressing foreign-policy and security priorities regarding Pakistan – such as the fight against al-Qaeda as well as Taliban insurgents in both Afghanistan and Pakistan. Washington is more concerned about the prospect of nuclear terrorism in Pakistan than about Pakistan's stranglehold on the FMCT.

Nuclear Posture Review

Obama achieved greatest success in meeting his nuclear goals when he was able to act unilaterally. His most consequential action was refinement of America's nuclear strategy through the much-anticipated Nuclear Posture Review (NPR) that was finalised in early April. The new strategy started with a revised premise that the most dangerous nuclear threat to the US came not from the risk of large-scale nuclear attack as during the Cold War but rather from the threat of nuclear terrorism and from the spread of nuclear-weapons technology to adversaries. It recognised that preventing the use of nuclear weapons was a compelling US national interest. Departing from the long-held notion that nuclear deterrence was the primary means of protecting against nuclear threats, the NPR argued that cooperation with other nations was just as important in preventing the common danger of nuclear use, and that the United States could contribute most effectively to these objectives by reducing both the size and purpose of its nuclear arsenal. Changes in the world meant that the United States could meet almost all security threats against it without recourse to nuclear weapons.

The NPR stated that the United States would maintain a safe, effective and credible deterrent for as long as nuclear weapons existed, but it ruled out the development of new nuclear weapons and new nuclear missions and capabilities. It significantly changed America's declaratory policy with regard to the role of nuclear weapons. His two predecessors had emphasised 'calculated ambiguity' by specifying that nuclear weapons could be used to pre-empt and respond to attacks by any type of weapon of mass destruction, or even in some cases by conventional weapons. The NPR narrowed this to say that the 'fundamental role of US nuclear weapons … is to deter nuclear attack' on the United States and its allies and partners. Many arms-control advocates had wanted the declaratory policy to go further by ruling out US first use of nuclear weapons, or at least by stating that the 'sole purpose' of maintaining nuclear weapons was to deter their use by others. A no-first-use pledge, which is central to the declaratory policies of China and India, is politically impossible in the United States, where it is remembered that the Soviet Union had given loud lip service to no-first-use while secretly planning first-use missions. The NPR did consider a variation of this declaratory policy, however, and held out the 'sole purpose' language as a future goal. In the meantime, the NPR included a hedge that 'there remains a narrow range of contingencies in which US nuclear weapons may still play a role in deterring a conventional or CBW [chemical and biological weapons] attack'. An additional qualification, added at Gates's request, was that the United States 'reserves the right to make any adjustment in the assurance that may be warranted by the evolution and proliferation of the biological weapons threat'.

The new declaratory policy also clarified and updated the circumstances in which the United States was pledged not to use nuclear weapons, including by updating the so-called 'negative security assurances'. The NPR said the United States would not use nuclear weapons against any non-nuclear-weapon state that was party to the NPT and in compliance with its nuclear non-proliferation obligations. Previous versions of this assurance had allowed for nuclear use against countries that were in alliance with nuclear-armed states (the so-called Warsaw Pact exemption). In explaining the new policy, Obama and Gates specified that Iran and North Korea would not benefit from the updated negative security assurance because of their NPT violations. This led both to charge that they were being threatened with a US nuclear attack. The US denied that any threat was implied, saying only that it wanted to give states a further reason to fully comply with the NPT. The NPR also said the United States would only consider the use of nuclear weapons 'in extreme circumstances' to defend vital interests.

The NPR, the third such review mandated by the US Congress, was unprecedented in several ways, including its release as an unclassified document. It was the result of an intensive interagency review that for the first time included both the full participation of the Department of State and the personal involvement of the president. However, the review did not undertake a detailed re-assessment of factors that go into determining nuclear force structure and size. A follow-on study mandated by the NPR is to address goals for future arms-control objectives after New START and options for increasing warning time 'to further reduce the risks of false warning or misjudgements relating to nuclear use'.

The NPR also signalled US interest in arms-control negotiations with China, in order to maintain strategic stability. Beijing, however, showed no immediate enthusiasm for pursuing nuclear discussions with Washington, and maintained that US and Russian nuclear forces must come down much further before China's arsenal – unspecified but believed to be in the range of 200 weapons – could realistically be included in multilateral disarmament talks.

The NPR themes were reinforced by Obama's National Security Strategy, which he announced in late May. Highlighting the danger of nuclear proliferation and of unsecured nuclear material, the strategy document emphasised international engagement and collaboration and a rules-based international system. Downplaying the role of nuclear weapons, it omitted language that had been central to the two previous such documents that the United States would use all tools of its military arsenal necessary to defend its national interests.

Tactical US weapons in Europe

Obama's new nuclear posture made no decisions on the disposition of the US forward-deployed tactical nuclear weapons in Belgium, Germany, Italy, Netherlands and Turkey. These questions were left to discussions within NATO, where the issue had been newly raised in October 2009 when Germany, under the influence of new Foreign Minister Guido Westerwelle, began to push for withdrawal of nuclear weapons from its territory. Germany and four other NATO countries, including the Netherlands and Belgium, then wrote to NATO Secretary-General Anders Fogh Rasmussen calling for a debate on the future of the tactical weapons. At a discussion among NATO foreign ministers in April 2010 in Tallinn, Estonia, US Secretary of State Hillary Clinton said Washington was not against reducing the number of forward-deployed battlefield nuclear bombs, but that such a move should be dependent on similar action by Moscow regarding the estimated 2,000 tactical nuclear weapons which were stationed on its western flank. An advisory group of NATO experts led by former Secretary of State Madeleine Albright issued a similar recommendation in a May report that intended to help shape a new NATO

Strategic Concept due to be adopted at a NATO summit in Lisbon in November 2010. The Tallinn meeting decided that no tactical arms would be removed unless there was consensus from all 28 member states.

Russian military doctrine

Two months before the US NPR, Russia released a quasi-equivalent document in the form of a new military doctrine. Contrary to statements the previous October by Security Council Secretary Nikolai Patrushev, the new doctrine did not elevate the role of nuclear weapons in Russia's national-security policy. Rather than lowering Russia's nuclear threshold as Patrushev had forecast, the document reserved nuclear weapons for 'preventing the occurrence of nuclear wars' and large-scale and regional conventional wars. Slightly tighter than the criterion spelled out in a 2000 doctrine that allowed use of nuclear weapons in situations critical to national security, the 2010 version said nuclear weapons could be used in response to aggression waged with conventional weapons against Russia that 'threatens the very existence of the state'. De-emphasising nuclear weapons in another way, the new doctrine spoke of the use of precision conventional weapons for the purpose of strategic deterrence. A Russian desire to improve relations with the United States and a more realistic assessment of the utility of nuclear weapons were probably responsible for the new doctrine coming out less threatening to the West than had been expected.

But Russia's European neighbours took no comfort in the listing of 11 main external military threats specified in the new doctrine. The first was 'the goal of NATO to arrogate to itself the assumption of global functions in violation of international law' (a reference to NATO's 1999 bombing campaign against Serbia during the Kosovo conflict) and 'to expand the military infrastructure of NATO nations to Russia's borders including through expansion of the bloc'. Russia's 2000 doctrine had not named NATO as a threat and the concern it had expressed about 'the expansion of military blocs' had followed in priority several other threats.

Nuclear Security Summit

The greatest success in Obama's nuclear campaign was his 12–13 April 2010 hosting of a Nuclear Security Summit. All nations – save Iran and

North Korea – that have significant nuclear facilities participated in what Obama described as 'an unprecedented gathering to address an unprecedented threat'. The summit produced a joint communiqué in which all states agreed that nuclear terrorism was 'one of the most challenging threats to international security', and pledged to strengthen nuclear security, most prominently by securing all vulnerable fissile materials within four years. A seven-page accompanying work plan was agreed, detailing practical steps to implement the communiqué's goals. In addition, states brought a variety of 'house gifts' to demonstrate their resolve to tackle the issue, including Russia's announcement of an end to plutonium production, a report from five states of plans for removing all fissile material from their soil, and Malaysia's passing of long-overdue national export-control laws.

Among the non-binding, political commitments that were made, summit participants agreed on the need to implement all existing nuclear-security commitments and to work towards bringing in those who had not yet joined. Special attention was given to the amended Convention on the Physical Protection of Nuclear Materials, which lacks sufficient ratifications to come into force, and the International Convention for the Suppression of Acts of Nuclear Terrorism. The United States is among the countries yet to ratify both treaties. Characterising the summit as a 'forcing event', the Obama administration used the occasion to begin the ratification process with the Senate. In another key point, the communiqué reaffirmed the 'essential role' of the International Atomic Energy Agency (IAEA) in the international nuclear-security framework, and the need to ensure it receives the requisite resources and expertise to carry out its nuclear-security activities. For several non-nuclear-weapons states, such a role is not uncontroversial, as they fear that the IAEA will be diverted from what they perceive to be its main responsibility: providing technical assistance to develop the peaceful use of nuclear energy.

Given the difficulty and expense of converting highly enriched uranium (HEU)-fuelled reactors to safer technologies, and the more than 100 facilities worldwide that still use HEU as fuel, it is highly unlikely that the four-year target of securing all vulnerable materials across the globe can be met. Washington argues, however, that such challenging deadlines lend much-needed urgency to international efforts. Apart from the four-year goal, Obama did not introduce any new initiatives but sought, rather, to strengthen the wide range of nuclear instruments already in place that depend on enforcement and widespread acceptance. Through his international political magnetism, he succeeded in raising the profile of a topic which previously had been mainly confined to technocrats. In addition to achieving unanimity on the communiqué and work plan, he was able to maintain a close summit focus on preventing nuclear terrorism and to prevent it from degenerating into a political debate. To sustain the momentum generated by the meeting, a second nuclear security summit will be hosted by South Korea in 2012.

NPT Review Conference

Although the achievements of April set a positive tone for the NPT Review Conference that followed in May, transforming atmosphere to substance proved elusive. Some press reports led their accounts by noting that at least the conference did not end in failure. More charitably, the conference can be said to have put the NPT back on track. In sharp contrast to the failed 2005 review conference, the 189 countries participating in the 2010 event reached consensus on a 'final document'.

The document's 28 pages reviewed past commitments and set out a forward-leaning action plan covering each of the three pillars of the treaty: disarmament, non-proliferation and peaceful uses of nuclear energy. But the actual content was thin. The Obama team lowered its expectations from the start of the conference, but got even less than expected with regard to its non-proliferation objectives of strengthening IAEA verification instruments, enhancing enforcement measures, and tightening treaty-withdrawal provisions. Most disappointing to the United States and its allies, the document failed to name Iran, because of the rule of consensus that prevails at the review conferences. Had Iran been named, it would have vetoed the document.

By contrast, Israel was named, in a gambit by Egypt and other Arab states that nearly led the United States to itself block consensus. The wording was seemingly innocuous; the document recalled 'the reaffirmation of the 2010 Review Conference of the importance of Israel's accession to the Treaty and the placement of all of its facilities under comprehensive IAEA safeguards'. Rather, it was the location of this sentence in the document that caused offence. Naming Israel in a section that laid out measures for moving towards implementation of a 1995 resolution on the establishment of a Middle East zone free of nuclear weapons and other weapons of mass destruction gave the impression that such efforts would be directed mainly at Israel. The most concrete outcome from the 2010 Review Conference was a call for the convening of a conference by 2012 to be attended by all states of the region on the establishment of such a zone, and of the appointment by the UN secretary-general of a facilitator for this process. Egypt and other Arab states had been demanding that such a conference be charged with negotiating a Middle East nuclear-weapons-free zone. Instead, in a compromise brokered by Vice President Joe Biden, Egypt accepted that the 2012 conference would not have a negotiation mandate. But the meeting with Biden left open the issue of naming Israel, and when the final text went through with the offending reference, the United States nearly disavowed its support. The United States said it would work to help organise a successful conference on creating a nuclear-free Middle East, but lamented that its ability to do so was 'seriously jeopardized' by the singling out of Israel.

Washington had hoped that an additional measure of nuclear transparency on its part would help gain traction for its non-proliferation objectives. On the opening day of the month-long conference, the United States made public for the first time the size of its nuclear stockpile: 5,113 (plus several thousand more retired warheads awaiting dismantlement), and the number dismantled since 1994: 8,748. The UK followed suit in the last week of the conference, by announcing that its total nuclear arsenal consisted of 225 weapons. In announcing the numbers, new Foreign Secretary William Hague said the UK would also reconsider its declaratory policy about the circumstances of use of nuclear weapons, as the US had done in its NPR. Two years earlier France had stated that its arsenal would not exceed 300. As it turned out, these transparency measures did not appear to have any measurable impact on the Review Conference results. Whether they would induce Russia and China to make similar announcements remained to be seen; there was no indication that they would.

In explaining why they vetoed tougher non-proliferation steps in the final document, Non-Aligned Movement (NAM) countries led by

Egypt and Iran referred to the refusal by the five nuclear-weapons states to accept a time-bound process for negotiating nuclear disarmament. France and Russia were the most firm in not accepting such disarmament obligations, and towards the end of the conference they were joined in this stance by the UK delegation under new orders from the newly formed Conservative–Liberal Democrat coalition government. Officials from nuclear-weapons states were heard to grumble that the NAM had simply pocketed all of Obama's steps towards disarmament without providing anything in return.

Problems ahead

Obama's tenure presents the most opportune time in many years for real progress in reducing nuclear dangers. An unintended consequence of the Prague speech, however, was the weighty set of expectations it created about how far the United States could move towards nuclear disarmament. Obama did not have the domestic support necessary to do more, and he was not helped by the uncompromising stance of his foreign adversaries. For all of Obama's efforts to restore the consensus of the NPT and the linkage between disarmament and non-proliferation, the first year and a half of his term had brought few results on the non-proliferation front. North Korea, which tested a nuclear device in May 2009, insisted on being recognised as nuclear-armed and continued to boycott the Six-Party Talks process aimed at denuclearisation of the Korean Peninsula unless Washington agreed to negotiate a peace treaty without South Korea as a participant. Syria since June 2008 has refused access to IAEA inspectors seeking to explore evidence that pointed to an unreported nuclear programme centred on a facility that Israeli bombers destroyed in September 2007. Pakistan increased its fissile-material production capabilities and, like India and Israel, continued to rule out joining the NPT as a non-nuclear-weapon state. Unconfirmed reports of clandestine nuclear development projects in Myanmar and of undisclosed cooperation with North Korea were gaining credence. Most ominously, a January 2010 report by Rolf Mowatt-Larssen, former head of the US Department of Energy intelligence unit, warned that al-Qaeda had not abandoned its goal of attacking the United States with a chemical, biological or even nuclear weapon.

Meanwhile, Iran continued to accumulate low-enriched uranium (LEU), which if further enriched could provide the feed material for one or two nuclear weapons. A tentative deal in October 2009 to exchange most of the LEU stockpile for research-reactor fuel from Russia and France fell through because of distrust in Tehran. When the deal was revived in May through intervention by Brazil and Turkey, it failed to meet the demands of a distrustful Washington. Meanwhile, as detailed elsewhere in this book (pp. 211–14), Iran took other steps that brought it closer to being able to produce nuclear weapons. These steps included enriching uranium at 20% concentration and announcing plans for additional enrichment facilities. Various multinational efforts to provide a guaranteed source of enriched-uranium fuel for nuclear reactors so that states would have no need to embark on this sensitive technology themselves met resistance from many developing nations that feared such approaches would restrict their NPT-enshrined rights to full access to the peaceful uses of nuclear energy.

On the disarmament front, Moscow shared little of Obama's enthusiasm for further reductions in nuclear weapons, because they are Russia's means of maintaining shared superpower status with the United States. Moscow insisted that any follow-on arms control agreement must take into account the linkage between offensive and defensive weapons, so that Russia's nuclear deterrence will never be undermined by US missile-defence systems. Moscow also sought some way of addressing America's huge and growing advantage in conventional weapons.

Notwithstanding these difficulties, however, there is scope for further deal-making. It is conceivable that Russia would be willing to accept significant cuts in its huge tactical nuclear weapons arsenal, if America, in addition to removing its air-dropped nuclear weapons from Europe, were willing to trade off its numerical advantage in non-deployed strategic weapons that are kept as a hedge for possible future contingencies. Improvements in the reliability of America's weapons stockpile could make it more willing to make such a trade-off. As for other nuclear-armed countries, the preamble to the New START treaty foreshadows bringing them into a multilateral arms-reduction approach. This is not expected to happen, however, until Russian and American arsenals are reduced to levels closer to the numbers possessed by France, the UK and China, not to mention the less certain arsenals held by Israel, India, Pakistan and North Korea.

US Defence Policy: Preparing for Change

While defence policy under President Barack Obama has been marked by a good deal of continuity from the previous administration, it has also foreshadowed substantial longer-term adjustments to the structure of the United States' armed forces. The degree of continuity was perhaps not surprising given that Secretary of Defense Robert M. Gates, who headed the Department of Defense through the last two years of the George W. Bush administration, continued at the helm under Obama. His presence was a strand of consistency between two administrations that in many other ways were quite different. However, the ambition to bring significant change to the Pentagon is also not a new one; Gates has long wanted to rebalance US forces to meet the challenges of a more complex and uncertain world. He first articulated his approach in the 2008 National Defense Strategy, approved during the Bush administration; the focus of the Obama administration's 2010 Quadrennial Defense Review (QDR) was implementing that strategy.

This was not to say – despite this general sense of continuity – that, the change of president did not entail important policy shifts. These included Obama's emphasis on reducing, and eventually eliminating, nuclear weapons. Change also was apparent in the new administration's expressed desire to repeal the Congressional ban on homosexuals serving openly in the military, as well as its intent to assign women to crew submarines. However, the broad thrust of policy derived principally from Gates' strong opinions on the need for a realignment of force structures.

The views of Obama and Gates were not the only factor forcing shifts in US defence policy. Indeed, the most consequential moves may be yet to come. It appears increasingly unlikely that the United States will be willing and able to sustain the current level of defence spending, which was sharply increased in the years following the 11 September 2001 terrorist attacks – years which have included the wars in Afghanistan and Iraq. The growing possibility of defence cuts as a result of strains on the US budget will put greater pressure on the government to set priorities: between the modernisation of forces and manpower; between ground, sea and air forces; and between fighting today's wars and preparing for future conflicts. The domestic political limits to American defence spending were manifesting themselves even though there was little sense in the US defence community that threats to American and global security were abating.

The search for balance

The hallmark of US defence policy under Gates has been 'balance'. As the secretary noted in an article in *Foreign Affairs*, 'the United States cannot expect to eliminate national security risks through higher defense budgets, to do everything and buy everything. The Department of Defense must set priorities and consider inescapable tradeoffs and opportunity costs.' Gates noted that the Pentagon 'strives for balance in three areas: between trying to prevail in current conflicts and preparing for other contingencies, between institutionalizing capabilities such as counterinsurgency and foreign military assistance and maintaining the United States' existing conventional and strategic technological edge against other military forces, and between retaining those cultural traits that have made the US armed forces successful and shedding those that hamper their ability to do what needs to be done.'

On 1 February 2010, the Defense Department released the 2010 QDR, intended to put Gates's strategy into practice. The review displayed a great deal of continuity not only with the 2008 National Defense Strategy, but also with the previous QDR of 2006, conducted under Defense Secretary Donald Rumsfeld. The resemblance was not surprising, given that all three documents were written after the 9/11 attacks and the beginning of the wars in Iraq and Afghanistan.

The QDR continued the trend, established by earlier post-Cold War reviews, of moving American strategic thinking away from planning for smaller versions of Cold War-era conventional conflicts and towards the need to cope with a much more diverse range of challenges not only from states, but also from non-state actors and transnational movements. A fundamental tenet was that no future adversary was likely to confront US conventional military capabilities directly. Instead, any competitor, whether a violent non-state actor like al-Qaeda or a technologically advanced near-peer competitor like China, would try to exploit US weaknesses through asymmetric means. A related tenet was that the spectrum of conflict, ranging from insurgents to sophisticated national armies, was becoming blurred, with terrorist groups using advanced technologies and large states likely to use indirect means of attack. As a result, planners were discussing 'hybrid threats' that could combine different means of attack ranging across the whole spectrum of conflict in almost any confrontation.

Since the end of the Cold War, the United States has measured the adequacy of its forces against the standard of being able to defeat adversaries in two geographically separate theatres nearly simultaneously. Between 1993 and 2006, this requirement evolved from the desire to maintain the capability to defeat two conventionally armed aggressors to the need to conduct a campaign against a conventional adversary while also waging a long-duration irregular warfare campaign and protecting the homeland against attack.

The 2010 QDR reflected Gates's view that the two-war construct was too confining and did not represent the complexity of the security environment. Indeed, the QDR did not endorse any metric for determining the size and shape of US forces. Rather, it put diverse, overlapping scenarios, including long-duration stability operations and defence of the homeland, on a par with major regional conflicts in assessing the adequacy of US forces.

Reflecting the experience of Iraq and Afghanistan, a key conclusion of the review was that operations short of major regional conflict might be at least as demanding as high-intensity wars. The report emphasised that long-duration stability and counter-insurgency operations, even if they involve fewer troops than a major conflict, can be especially demanding. Operations such as those in Iraq and Afghanistan required a very large standing force capable of providing a rotation base for deploying forces abroad without overly straining personnel. What were once seen as less demanding missions have now become core responsibilities with major implications for force planning and investment.

The review called for new investments in six joint mission areas: defending the United States and supporting civil authorities at home; succeeding in counter-insurgency, stability and counter-terrorism operations; building the capacity of partner states; countering anti-access strategies aimed at defeating US power-projection forces; preventing proliferation and countering weapons of mass destruction; and ensuring access to cyberspace.

Of most immediate importance, the 2010 QDR reflected Gates's insistence that prevailing in the wars in Iraq and Afghanistan was the first priority in military planning. It advanced a number of initiatives to boost resources devoted to current operations, including increases in helicopters, unmanned aerial vehicles, intelligence and analysis capabilities, technologies to counter improvised explosive devices (IEDs), and AC-130 gunship aircraft.

> "The US was betting that tomorrow's wars would resemble today's"

For homeland defence, the QDR called for the reorganisation of the Defense Department's chemical, biological, radiological, nuclear and high-yield explosives (CBRNE) response teams to reduce their response time and add capabilities. It endorsed plans to establish ten Homeland Response Forces across the United States, and called for enhanced efforts to develop and deploy standoff radiological detection equipment. To counter the spread of weapons of mass destruction, the review called for the establishment of a Joint Task Force Headquarters to eliminate such weapons, and for increased funding for nuclear forensics.

In addition to outlining programmatic and policy initiatives, the report called for reforms of institutional procedures that it described as 'relics of the Cold War', including acquisition, security assistance and export-control processes. Reflecting Gates's strong views on this issue, it said the Pentagon must reform its way of doing business to become more agile, innovative and streamlined, and to use constrained resources efficiently.

Gates's 'balanced' policy did not go uncriticised. Some analysts argued that the United States was betting too heavily that tomorrow's wars would resemble today's, and that policy was too heavily skewed towards responding to insurgencies like those in Iraq and Afghanistan. A further criticism was that it appeared to discount the urgency of investments needed to address emerging challenges, such as growing anti-access and area-denial threats from China, nuclear-armed regional powers, and the use and misuse of space and cyberspace. It was also argued that the QDR was too timid in readjusting the US force structure to meet the security environment, and that policy was failing to address adequately the rapidly eroding US fiscal posture. On this argument, by failing to articulate clear priorities, the QDR was not providing the basis to allocate increasingly scarce resources.

Equipment: living within one's means

One area in which Gates sought to put his policies into action was in the acquisition of equipment. Traditionally, new administrations have made only marginal changes to defence acquisition programmes in their first year in office. Obama's retention of Gates permitted bolder action. In a series of budgetary moves announced in April 2009, Gates continued to shift the focus of the Pentagon away from preparing for future high-end conflicts and towards the need to win the wars in Iraq and Afghanistan. Specifically, he announced the intent to field and sustain the capability to maintain 50 *Predator-* and *Reaper*-class unmanned aerial vehicles (UAVs) in the air at any one time by the fiscal year ending September 2011, and to increase manned intelligence, surveillance and reconnaissance capabilities, such as the turboprop aircraft operating as part of Task Force ODIN in Iraq. The DoD announced an increase in its purchase of littoral combat ships, with a goal of eventually acquiring 55 such vessels. It doubled the number of Joint High-Speed Vessels it would lease from two to four until a US production programme begins deliveries in 2011. The DoD also decided to cap the number of Brigade Combat Teams (BCTs) that the US Army would field at 45, three fewer than previously planned, while maintaining the planned strength of the Army at 547,000 – Gates had ordered an increase of 65,000 in 2006 – so as to ensure that units were better manned for deployment.

Planned additions to capabilities came at the expense of high-end systems. The Pentagon decided to halt production of the F-22 fighter at 187 aircraft. It slowed down the acquisition of new aircraft carriers, a move that would result in a force of ten after 2040, down two from the current level. The DoD decided to terminate the Air Force's Combat Search and Rescue-X helicopter programme, the Transformational Satellite programme, and the Airborne Laser and Multiple Kill Vehicle missile-defence programmes. In addition, the department eliminated the Army's large and ambitious Future Combat System programme, which had been due to replace the current generation of armoured vehicles with ones that were lighter, more fuel efficient and provided greater information awareness. In Gates's view, the programme did not adequately reflect the lessons of counter-insurgency and close-quarters combat in Iraq and Afghanistan.

The 2010 QDR contained a further round of cuts, including decisions to shut down production of the C-17 transport aircraft, delay the acquisition of the LCC command ship replacement, cancel the Navy's CG(X) cruiser, and terminate the Net Enabled Command and Control programme. This was not all. In May, Gates set his sights on the Navy and Marine Corps. In a speech to the Navy League, he announced that he did not 'foresee any significant top-line increases in the shipbuilding budget beyond current assumptions'. He questioned the Marine Corps' need for the Expeditionary Fighting Vehicle, meant to perpetuate its ability to conduct an amphibious landing under fire. He took on the Navy's aircraft-carrier programme, asking: 'Do we really need eleven carrier strike groups for another thirty years when no other country has more than one?' The tenor of the speech led many to speculate that additional cuts might be in the offing.

Gates also became the latest in a line of defence secretaries to seek reforms of equipment-procurement practices to make them more responsive and efficient. In Congressional testimony in January 2010, he criticised the Pentagon bureaucracy's tendency to 'spend five or six years' to develop and field an 'exquisite system'. In cases where American troops had needed new systems urgently, such as the Mine-Resistant Ambush Protected (MRAP) family of armoured vehicles, the Pentagon leadership had had to go outside the established acquisition system to ensure that vital systems quickly reached troops in theatre.

Growing anti-access challenges

Those who thought that Gates's emphasis on balance and winning today's wars should not be at the expense of dealing with longer-term dangers tended to point to the rise of China. The administration stressed its desire for a multi-layered strategic dialogue with China – and Gates reiterated in response to a Chinese questioner at the IISS Shangri-La Dialogue in Singapore in June 2010 that China was not an enemy of the United States. Nevertheless, military analysts pointed to fresh signs that Chinese military modernisation was proceeding apace, and had exceeded expectations. The Commander of US Pacific Command, Admiral Robert F. Willard, told reporters in October 2009: 'In the past decade or so, China has exceeded most of our intelligence estimates of their military capability and capacity, every year ... They've grown at an unprecedented rate in those capabilities. And they've developed some asymmetric capabilities that are concerning to the region, some anti-access capabilities and so on.'

In January 2010, China appeared to have conducted a second successful test of its direct-ascent anti-satellite (ASAT) system, under the guise of a ballistic missile defence experiment. In addition, Willard revealed in March that China had tested a conventional anti-ship ballistic missile (ASBM) based on the DF-21/CSS-5 medium-range ballistic missile (MRBM), which is designed specifically to target aircraft carriers. If deployed, the Chinese ASBM would be the world's first such system capable of targeting a moving carrier strike group from long-range, land-based mobile launchers. The system's configuration would make defence against it extremely difficult.

China's ASBM is part of a much larger pattern of developing so-called anti-access or area denial capabilities. While US operations in the Pacific appear most threatened by such systems, similar challenges are emerging in the Persian Gulf. The emergence of these systems, and the need to counter them, was a major theme of the QDR. The need to counter such capabilities had been identified as long ago as 1997 in a report by the National Defense Panel. To counter anti-access strategies, the 2010 QDR recommended a number of initiatives, including development of the Air–Sea Battle concept, an attempt by the Navy and Air Force to collaborate to devise innovative approaches to defeating anti-access strategies; expansion of future long-range strike capabilities; exploiting US advantages in subsurface operations; increasing the resilience of US forward posture and base infrastructure; assuring access to space and the use of space assets; enhancing the robustness of key ISR capabilities; defeating enemy sensors and engagement systems; and enhancing the presence and responsiveness of US forces abroad.

The end of the party?

The global financial crisis and the mounting US budget deficit appeared to presage considerable limits on US defence spending in the medium term. The United States has spent nearly $6.5 trillion on defence since 1998, the year that defence expenditures reached their post-Cold War low. Between 1999 and 2009, the defence budget saw a 72% increase. Part of that increase was attributable to the cost of simultaneously waging wars in Iraq and Afghanistan, and will decline as the American presence in both theatres declines. However, the growth of defence expenditures also represents more fundamental trends that are harder to reverse. For example, medical and personnel costs have been rising steeply. Over the past decade, the cost per active-duty military member of the forces grew 73% and now totals $409,000. Part of this was attributable to a series of military pay rises. Also contributing was military health care, which accounts for nearly 10% of the defence budget. The increases mean that the United States is today spending at Cold War levels to sustain a force that is 70% the size of the Cold War armed forces.

The growth in personnel costs creates a tension between providing benefits for those who are serving and have served in the past, and funding the equipment and training needed to fight the wars of the future. The US armed forces have largely been living off the modernisation of the US armed forces that occurred under Ronald Reagan in the 1980s. However, the wear and tear of wartime operations has caused equipment to wear out at an accelerated pace. This means that if they are to be maintained, large parts of the US armed forces will soon need modernisation and recapitalisation. Doing this fully would require at least 2–3% real growth in defence expenditure. Yet the need to recapitalise coincides with increasing war weariness on the part of the Congress and competing priorities at home. The stage is set for considerable political tension on the future of the armed forces and for change.

Europe's Evolving Security Architecture

All three major institutional frameworks for multinational security cooperation in Europe are in the midst of attempted renovation. The North Atlantic Treaty Organisation (NATO) is crafting a new strategic concept providing overall political guidance to the transatlantic alliance. The European Union (EU), having enacted the Lisbon Treaty to reform its institutional structure, is trying to make the new arrangements work, not least with regard to its Common Security and Defence Policy (CSDP), originally the European Security and Defence Policy (ESDP). The Organisation for Security and Cooperation in Europe (OSCE) has launched the Corfu Process to reclaim its role as a comprehensive and inclusive forum for dialogue on security matters.

The outcomes of these parallel discussions are as yet uncertain, but it has become apparent that these institutions are wrestling with the need to prove their relevance to European and American leaders in terms of their ability to address modern security challenges. The high degree of overlap between the organisations in terms of membership and increasing intersection of function – at least between NATO and the EU – have not produced a comprehensive regional security system. In fact, they have highlighted the extent to which the organisations are unable to work effectively together.

None of the organisations is short of flamboyant statements expressing wide-ranging ambitions. As NATO Secretary-General Anders Fogh Rasmussen put it, 'NATO was unlike any other alliance in the past' because it 'was not only about protecting territory. It was also about preserving our democratic values.' Even in today's environment, he continued, 'no other community of nations can generate such a powerful positive momentum. And no other community is as attractive to others who want to help shoulder the burden of common security.' The EU's security strategy argued that the organisation and its member states 'should be ready to share in the responsibility for global security and in building a better world'. The implementation report on this strategy suggests there was a distinctive European approach to foreign and security policy enabled by the EU's ability to draw on a 'unique range of instruments' across the civil–military divide. As for the OSCE, member-state foreign ministers declared that the 'vision of a free, democratic and more integrated OSCE area, from Vancouver to Vladivostok, free of dividing lines and zones with different levels of security' remained a central goal. Such declarations, however, are difficult to translate into concrete action. And while individual nations have been reforming their armed forces to be more capable of dealing with threats, and have tried to create structures and procedures to strengthen their ability for interagency cooperation, it is not at all clear that these changes have resulted in improved capacity at the institutional level to produce military or civil solutions to security problems. Events in Afghanistan appear to be a case in point.

Why is this? Perhaps part of the answer is that traditional notions of transatlantic and European security have lost much of their content. Governments and organisations often say they share aims such as dealing with present-day threats, for example nuclear proliferation and terrorism. But member countries in fact no longer have a common notion of the most important security threats, their degree of urgency and the ways in which to tackle them. There is no basic political consensus on what the three organisations are trying to achieve. It is not surprising, therefore, that there is also no consensus on their functions and geographical scope. On the contrary, divisions among countries on all of these points have become a significant centrifugal force. This presents a major challenge as each organisation addresses institutional change. In an ideal world, it would also represent an opportunity to realign them on the basis of shared goals, but there is little sign that governments are minded to do so.

Such efforts are handicapped by a lack of attention from world leaders. In the United States, NATO has increasingly been seen less as a transatlantic unifying agent and as more as a tool to mobilise European resources for American-led military operations – and when European contributions do not match up to American hopes, as a symbol of European failure. Washington eventually accepted the argument that the EU could generate a potent combination of civilian and military capabilities to deal with world problems, but it has seen little sign that this has been borne out in practice. EU operations, for example in Africa, have mostly been short term and small in scale. While the emergence of the

EU as a security actor is an important development, security and defence policy for international crisis-management is just one policy area among many, and is peripheral to the essential purpose of the organisation, which continues to lie in political and economic integration. Ironically, since the Conference on Security and Cooperation in Europe (CSCE) became formally institutionalised and was renamed OSCE in 1995, it has been in relative decline. With the fundamental division of the Cold War gone, defence questions increasingly anchored in NATO and politico-economic stability to the EU, the OSCE found it hard to identify ways to make a visible impact. This was not helped by growing Russian dissatisfaction with the organisation. As early as 2001, Moscow declared that the OSCE was headed towards 'extinction' unless it reformed drastically.

Divisions and dissonance

The landscape of international security challenges presents a wide range of risks. Government documents at the national level and strategy documents at the multinational level routinely go over the same areas of threat, including international terrorism, proliferation of weapons of mass destruction, fragile states, intra-state and regional conflicts, organised crime and residual territorial threats, as well as more recent concerns such as cyber and energy security. They also mention drivers of risk such as climate change, demographic developments, resource challenges, extremism, and pandemics. However, such assessments have taken on the character of laundry lists with very little attempt to establish a hierarchy of risks and threats. Among European countries, there is no shared perception of the key threats and as a result no unifying narrative.

European governments thus do not have the same sense of urgency when discussing threats in detail. In the absence of a unifying threat, specific national contexts regain importance. For example, while several countries have suffered terrorist attacks, many have had no direct experience of this type of threat for decades. By the same token, Russia's European neighbours still value membership of international security institutions because of their concerns about Moscow's intentions, while countries further West no longer feel such a danger. In addition, electorates find it difficult to establish a direct link between their daily lives and the catalogue of risks presented by their governments. Threat perceptions are becoming more short term and driven by events, making sustained strategic conversations about security and defence difficult.

Governments – especially those that have sent troops to Afghanistan – argue that today's security challenges demand global engagement because events far away can have an impact at home. The mantra that threats need to be met at their source so that they can be contained and do not spill over into other regions is part and parcel of many speeches by senior leaders. But national debates about participation in Afghanistan show this concept is by no means universally accepted. Many governments and electorates consider that security challenges closer to home should be addressed before they consider making a contribution to more far-flung endeavours. International organisations whose remits were originally linked to specific geographic areas will continue to face the argument that a global footprint amounts to diluting their core business.

Having several organisational frameworks available to deal with security issues is both a blessing and a curse. Ideally, NATO, the EU and the OSCE would play complementary roles, keeping functional overlap to a minimum. The comparative advantage of the OSCE is its political inclusiveness due its wide membership, which includes Russia and other post-Soviet states; the EU can bring a wide range of political, economic, civilian and military tools to bear on a security problem; and NATO embodies the transatlantic link and provides the ultimate security guarantee to its members through unparalleled American military might and the Article V commitment to mutual defence in case of attack. Most contemporary security problems, whether emerging risks or concrete threats, are too complex or diffuse for any one of these organisations to be the obvious, unequivocal framework to address them. Political disagreements and different preferences have inhibited both cooperation and an efficient division of labour.

Long-standing political impediments to closer NATO–EU cooperation, for example, remain. While a shift in US policy helped by France's reintegration into NATO military structures has meant that Washington no longer sees a strong CSDP as having negative implications for NATO, the continuing dispute between Cyprus (an EU but not NATO member) and Turkey (a NATO but not EU member) blocks meaningful coopera-

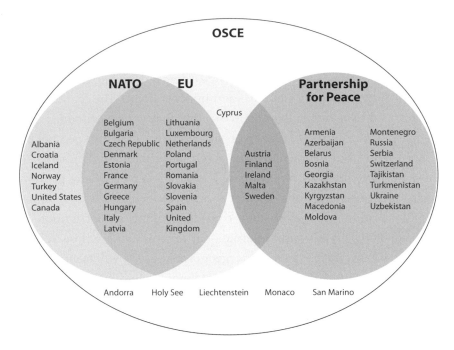

tion. Since Cyprus joined the EU in 2004, Turkey has refused to allow EU–NATO meetings to touch on matters of substance. Exceptions are limited to operational matters where the EU has made use of the Berlin Plus agreement, which allows access to NATO assets, as is the case in Bosnia.

There are also markedly different perspectives on the resources that should be allotted to defence. To the continued frustration of the United States, most countries in Europe are unwilling to significantly increase their security and defence expenditure – in fact, the trend is firmly in the opposite direction. As a result, European capabilities lag behind declared ambitions. Although the operational demands on military and civilian personnel have been steadily increasing, glaring gaps in capabilities identified more than a decade ago continue. While some are likely to be filled (in transport aircraft, for example, with the eventual entry into service of the A400M airlifter), many will probably endure, especially in light of the dramatic increase in budget pressure arising from the global financial and economic crisis. Moreover, as US Secretary of Defence Robert Gates put it to an auditorium full of NATO officials and experts in February 2010, 'the demilitarisation of Europe – where large swathes of the general

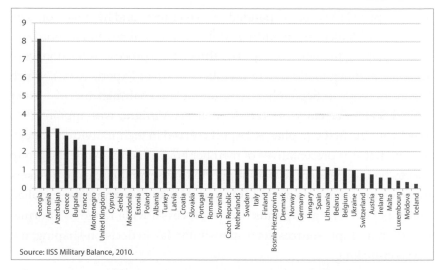

Source: IISS Military Balance, 2010.

Figure 1. **European defence expenditure as a percentage of GDP by country, 2008**

public and political class are averse to military force and the risks that go with it – has gone from a blessing in the 20th century to an impediment to achieving real security and lasting peace in the 21st.'

These factors add up to an enormous potential for dissonance among the countries involved in NATO, the EU and the OSCE. Closer cooperation between these bodies and their members is necessary, but the uncertainty and fragmentation which characterises the international security landscape makes it more difficult and less likely. The internal reform processes in which each of these institutions is engaged are therefore particularly important.

NATO and the new strategic concept

In April 2009 the heads of government of the NATO member states tasked the Alliance's secretary-general with developing a new Strategic Concept in time for a NATO summit to be held in Lisbon in late 2010. NATO's Strategic Concept expresses the organisation's purpose and core functions in the context of the international security environment and provides overall guidance for NATO's development. Since the last Strategic Concept was written in 1999, both the Alliance and the international environment have changed considerably, making a revision necessary. Security challenges have become more diffuse, transnational and complex; NATO has expanded to 28 members and has taken on new operational challenges, including Afghanistan, well beyond its borders.

Developing the new concept is a three-stage process: reflection, consultation and negotiation. A 12-member Group of Experts (GoE), which began its work in September 2009 under the chairmanship of former United States Secretary of State Madeleine Albright, was appointed to assist with the first two phases. Experts served in their individual capacities and not as representatives of member governments. While the group was to be independent, it was supported by several circles of advisers from within and outside NATO, and NATO governments supplied policy papers. The group thus had to process a wide range of information from multiple sources. Its responsibility lay in decision-shaping, not decision-making.

During the reflection phase, which ended in February 2010, NATO organised seminars involving groups of stakeholders, including external experts, to encourage debate on specific aspects of the Strategic Concept. During the subsequent consultation phase, members of the GoE visited the NATO and other capitals. In May 2010 the group's report offered Rasmussen recommendations for the content of the concept document. Based on this input and members' reactions, the secretary-general was to write his own paper to be submitted to governments to canvass their views and solicit guidance.

Drafting and negotiation of the new Strategic Concept – Rasmussen would negotiate directly with governments – was due to begin in late summer 2010. The long build-up was billed as an exercise in transparency, but was also clearly driven by the need to reconcile divergent views into a coherent picture with higher levels of consensus than were visible initially.

One key purpose of the document will be to define clearly the ends NATO is supposed to serve and the means available to meet them. It should set out ways to make most efficient use of available resources and guide member states towards better capabilities for current tasks. At the same time, the Strategic Concept should be a rallying point for the Allies and instil a renewed sense of common purpose, confirming the fundamental principles of Alliance solidarity. Finally, it will be a crucial tool for strategic communications and public diplomacy, intended to convince sceptical publics in member states that the Alliance matters to their security.

One problematic area is that of NATO's core functions. As the Alliance has become increasingly active in pursuing missions overseas, several members have debated whether such engagement distracts from the mission of collective defence and the credibility of Article V of the NATO treaty, under which an attack on one member state is considered an attack against all. Some governments see a contradiction between the capability requirements for territorial defence and expeditionary operations. While an argument can be made that for most allies these capabilities overlap significantly, not all allies believe that NATO can be relied upon collectively to defend every member against any territorial threat: the political credibility of Article V is at stake. Sven Mikser, former Estonian defence minister has said, for example, that 'we would like to see the reaffirmation of Article V and collective defence as the cornerstone of the Alliance. That's the central thing.' Several governments have called for the Strategic Concept to reassert the collective commitment and back it up with contingency planning and exercises, and possibly upgraded NATO infrastructure in central and eastern European countries.

> " The topic of Russia most clearly brings out divergences between allies "

The topic of Russia most clearly brings out divergences between allies. Whereas some are looking for reassurance from the Strategic Concept that they will be protected against any potential aggression or political intimidation from Moscow, others want it to chart the way for future NATO–Russia cooperation. Russia, for its part, remains conflicted about whether it seeks a constructive relationship with NATO or whether engagement with the Alliance should serve mainly to constrain NATO. Russian policymakers point with some justification to NATO enlargement as a policy, pursued against their will, that had important effects on what they perceive to be Russia's security sphere. On the other hand, continued allusions to NATO as a security threat to Russia and a fear of Western encirclement of Russia seem exaggerated, bordering on conspiracy theory in some cases. The differences in outlook among allies will be very difficult to reconcile in the Strategic Concept, since each

NATO member sees relations with Russia through its own lens, driven by historical experiences and bilateral interests. NATO is likely only to be able to generate unity on two aspects of its relations with Russia: on a pragmatic agenda of cooperation (for example in Afghanistan, on arms-control issues and missile defence) and on a generic statement of principle on the need for constructive and cooperative relations. Beyond this, a common perspective on Russia may well remain elusive. In a report by the NATO Parliamentary Assembly (its official contribution to the Strategic Concept debate), the authors argued that 'the relationship [with Russia] is troubled by fundamentally different perspectives on many issues, including the role and nature of NATO'. Such perceptions seem to narrow considerably the scope for new 'big ideas' in the NATO–Russia relationship.

A third problem issue is the need for NATO be clear about the future of the so-called 'comprehensive approach', which aims to bring a broad range of instruments, civilian and military, to bear on individual security problems. This comprehensive approach, formally endorsed by NATO leaders at their 2008 Bucharest summit, was intended to arise out of the complementary efforts of many actors, with NATO contributing military capabilities. Given that the goal has not so far been achieved, particularly in Afghanistan, some voices within NATO have asked whether the Alliance needs to develop its own civilian capabilities. If comprehensiveness cannot in practice be achieved through cooperation with others, should NATO try to be more comprehensive itself?

Some areas of agreement can be identified and may well serve as islands from which to expand consensus. Most governments are in broad agreement that NATO needs to tread carefully in defining the roles it wants to play with regard to new security challenges, ranging from cyber and energy security to piracy and international terrorism, as well as the security implications of climate change. The fact that there is a task to be done does not mean that NATO is the right organisation to do it; the Alliance should only take on new tasks if its engagement would provide clear added value. Some have argued that the cutting off of a member country's energy supply or a large-scale attack on its cyber infrastructure could amount to an existential threat warranting invocation of Article V. However, given that NATO's capabilities are mostly military, it is unclear how it would respond to such an attack, particularly if it involved non-state actors. Most governments seem at this stage to prefer a cautious approach that acknowledges the importance of new security challenges without locating them specifically within the remit of Article V. Given the complexity of contemporary security challenges, a widely held view within the Alliance stresses the need for NATO to build effective partnerships with non-member countries and international organisations.

The NATO-led campaign in Afghanistan is the biggest in which the Alliance has been involved, and is by far the most challenging. It has often been suggested that if the operation should not be deemed a success (however defined) the very future of NATO is in question. This may be incorrect or exaggerated, but developing new overall strategic guidance does have to be viewed in the context of Afghanistan. There is no doubt that the campaign has exposed the limits of what NATO may be able to achieve. Shortcomings in NATO's political consultation

> " At times each national contingent has appeared to be following its own strategy "

processes and in its ability to generate adequate levels of forces with appropriate equipment have given rise to a renewed debate within the Alliance over burden sharing. While the coherence of the International Security Assistance Force (ISAF) may have improved, at times each national military contingent deployed to Afghanistan has appeared to be following its own strategy rather than adhering to one set by the Alliance. Success for individual large-scale operations to establish control over specific areas, such as those launched in 2009 and 2010, has been elusive, especially in establishing stable and effective governance following a military push. Whether NATO's objective of securing a transition to Afghan control and moving towards an orderly exit can be achieved is increasingly unclear.

If, as the Afghan campaign continues, it becomes obvious that it cannot, NATO members will have to face the fact that the political will and military capabilities they can muster are insufficient to achieve their ambitions. Just as after the Kosovo campaign in 1999, some have begun to doubt that NATO can ever repeat the Afghan experience.

The report presented by the Group of Experts in May 2010 reflected the divergences among the Allies. While the document was not as visionary as some commentators had hoped, it nonetheless incorporated important themes. Even the title, 'Assured Security; Dynamic Engagement', reflected the need to balance different perceptions of NATO's purpose with regard to homeland defence and expeditionary commitments. The group frankly testified to a central problem: 'Although NATO is busier than it has ever been, its value is less obvious to many than in the past.' Reassurance was to be achieved by the rather predictable methods of contingency planning, exercises and readiness. As far as operations beyond NATO territory are concerned, the report underlined that NATO remained a regional organisation, but one that needed guidelines about when and where to act in a broader setting. As in the past when countries have debated possible criteria for intervention, the conclusion was that case-by-case decisions would have to be made based on a variety of cost–benefit factors. Partnerships with other countries and organisations would be important, as NATO would be unlikely to operate alone in the future: the comprehensive approach could see NATO providing a military component of a broader solution or acting as a facilitator to bring different instruments together. The Group of Experts also pointed to the need fully to exploit the potential benefits of Article IV, which allows for political consultations on security problems among members. Making more thorough use of this provision could enable NATO members to prepare the ground for action before a problem turns into a full-blown crisis or threat.

Alliance consensus on strategic priorities thus seems fragile overall. Since the end of the Cold War, NATO has remained relevant by partially reinventing itself through decisions such as intervention in the Balkans, enlargement to Eastern Europe, tackling security challenges out of area, and successfully engaging a wide range of countries through partnership programmes and cooperation initiatives. However, the institution's capacity for expansion seems close to reaching its limits. Against this rather troubled background, the rewriting of the Strategic Concept offers an important opportunity to re-establish consensus and establish a convincing, positive path for the future, but it is far from clear that Alliance members will seize this opportunity.

European Union: making Lisbon work

Over the course of the last decade, the EU has developed decision-making structures and instruments to deal with security problems beyond its own borders. It has defined the outlines of an EU strategic outlook and has attempted to guide member states in their development of civilian and military capabilities for external crisis-management tasks. It did so quite rapidly following agreement between France and Britain in 1998 that the EU should acquire a defence identity and develop the ESDP. This – now re-styled the CSDP following the Lisbon Treaty – has seen the launch of some two-dozen civilian and military-crisis management missions. However, there remains a marked disconnect between the EU's ambitions and its capacity to deliver them. (The IISS analysed this subject in a 2008 Strategic Dossier *European Military Capabilities: Building Armed Forces for Modern Operations*.)

High hopes were attached to the Lisbon Treaty, as several of its provisions explicitly aimed to make the EU more effective and coherent in the security field. Firstly, it created a post of president of the European Council, with a two-and-a-half-year mandate, renewable once, intended to rid the EU of the inconsistencies and inefficiencies created by the previous six-monthly rotating presidency. The president is tasked with generating consensus in the council, the body through which EU member governments make decisions, and which represents the Union on matters of foreign and security policy. Former Belgian Prime Minister Herman van Rompuy was appointed. Secondly, the treaty merged the post of high representative for the CFSP and that of the external relations commissioner of the European Commission. As the new post straddles the council and the commission, the hope is that it will bring greater coherence to the EU's international policies, including aid and crisis management. Catherine Ashton of the United Kingdom, previously EU trade commissioner, was appointed to the post with a five-year term. Both appointees brought reputations as effective administrators but very little security policy experience. Following complex negotiations, EU members chose people who would be managers rather than leaders. Neither is likely to undermine the supremacy of member states in foreign and security policy – and thus the significance of the creation of the new posts was limited.

A third innovation was the establishment of the European External Action Service (EEAS), a new diplomatic service speaking on behalf of the EU and consisting of officials from the council, the commission and member states. According to plans presented by Ashton, the EEAS might have up to 7,000 staff. Since much detail is still missing, it is unclear whether such a large structure is necessary, or how it will work. Currently, commission staff involved in foreign policy, including 130 commission delegations around the world, total about 4,000. Member-states are to contribute 30% of future EEAS personnel – an arrangement that heralds a struggle for dominance over the EEAS with Brussels. Critics in the European Parliament said Ashton's blueprint was inspired too much by French administrative structures. Elmar Brok, a German member, said: 'We don't want things to happen in the French style with the secretary-general [of the EEAS] as a spider sitting at the centre of the web controlling everything'.

A fourth new instrument was permanent structured cooperation on defence (PSCD), intended to facilitate more effective development of capabilities for crisis-management operations. It allows states with strong military capabilities to set up a leadership group to cooperate more closely within the EU framework. The underlying rationale should be to generate relevant capabilities for EU operations with greater efficiency. However, members were far from agreement on how this process should be organised or whether it was feasible in the first place. Several saw PCSD as a means to foster closer cooperation on defence and argued that it should be as inclusive as possible, ideally involving all member states. Others argued that it should be open only to those willing and able to commit to better capabilities. In the absence of consensus, several governments began to argue that PSCD threatened to be too unwieldy and should not be activated at all. It was a testament to the lack of resolve of EU leaders that an instrument heralded as a potential game-changer for European capabilities stood a good chance of failing before it even began.

When the EU initiated CSDP, improving capabilities for civilian and military crisis-management operations, as part of achieving the capacity for autonomous EU action, was a major goal. But member states have been slow to address long-known shortfalls such as strategic and tactical airlift, reconnaissance and force protection. Since 2008, the number of project-based agreements among different groups of EU member states has increased, suggesting a trend towards more flexible ways to generate capacity. But governments have been careful to avoid limits on their autonomy, and are willing to miss out on economies of scale to preserve this freedom.

There are similar gaps in the civilian capabilities that are supposed to be a hallmark of EU operations. Estimates based on think tank reports suggest there are 1.6 million civilian personnel across EU member states working in areas of relevance to civilian EU missions. Only 12,000 have been pledged for operations and only about 2,000 were deployed in 2009.

Thus, the innovations of the Lisbon Treaty, which were supposed to lift the EU to new levels of efficiency and effectiveness, have revealed deep divisions. Far from being willing to merge their requirements and cooperate more deeply, member states are still overwhelmingly concerned with national sovereignty in the security and defence field.

OSCE: efforts to regain status

After a brief moment in the early 1990s when the OSCE was seen as a possible future hub of security cooperation in Europe, it has been overshadowed by NATO and the EU. While the OSCE has played a useful role in conflict prevention, early warning and confidence building, grander aspirations have not been met. But the organisation has revived its ambition to serve as a comprehensive and inclusive forum for dialogue on security questions and to reclaim its former status. A discussion, known as the Corfu process, was formally launched in June 2009 and is set to be completed at an OSCE summit later in 2010, the first it has held since 1999.

The organisation was born out of East–West tensions and confrontation between Cold War blocs. The CSCE was set up as a forum to discuss opposing perspectives and to manage differences through cooperation, and was the multilateral forum for negotiations between Eastern and Western powers which culminated in the Helsinki Final Act of 1975. The Soviet Union intended to use the process to tighten its grip over Eastern Europe, whereas leading Western powers saw an opportunity

to lower tensions between the blocs while pressing for economic cooperation and arguing for humanitarian improvements for populations in
the East. Making human-rights issues a topic for conversations between
East and West (rather than treating them as internal affairs and hence off
limits) was a major breakthrough. The organisation functioned between
1975 and 1990 by way of conferences and meetings, to further develop
the political commitments entailed by the Helsinki Final Act and discuss
their implementation. The end of the Cold War triggered the creation of
permanent bodies to better equip the CSCE for the new environment.
To reflect this, it was renamed OSCE. With, as of 2010, 56 countries from
Europe, Central Asia and North America – including all EU members,
Russia and the United States – it is much more inclusive than NATO
or the EU. Its mandate is to pursue a comprehensive agenda in three
dimensions of security: politico-military, economic and environmental, and human affairs (the latter referring to normative commitments
including in the areas of human rights, the rule of law, democratisation
and the protection of minorities).

The OSCE's wide-ranging membership, however, means that it is
heterogeneous and its members do not share a common conception
of security. Its wide conception of security, mirrored in the principles
guiding relations between participating states agreed in the Helsinki
Final Act of 1975, encompasses on the one hand state sovereignty through
such principles as territorial integrity and non-intervention in internal affairs, and on the other the self-determination of peoples, human
rights and fundamental freedoms. Tension between these principles has
not been resolved, and perhaps is worsened by Europe's increasingly
fragmented ideas of what security means. It is questionable, therefore
whether the Corfu process can actually advance substantive, practical
discussions.

A key factor will be whether Russia plays a constructive role. Over
the last decade, Russian policymakers have begun to see the OSCE as
dominated by the United States and its NATO allies to the detriment
of Russian influence. Then President Vladimir Putin argued at the 2007
Munich security conference that 'people are trying to transform the
OSCE into a vulgar instrument designed to promote the foreign policy
interests of one or a group of countries'. Just in case there was any doubt

left as to what he meant, then Foreign Minister Sergey Lavrov added three years later at the same event: 'The role of the OSCE was, in fact, reduced to servicing [NATO expansion] by means of supervision over humanitarian issues in the post-Soviet space'.

Some observers have thus argued that President Dmitry Medvedev's proposal for a new European Security Treaty would create an OSCE without provisions for democracy and human-rights promotion, in essence a framework that would resolve the OSCE's inherent conflict in favour of state sovereignty and would not concern itself with the internal affairs of member states. Speaking at the IISS in London in December 2009, Russian Deputy Foreign Minister Alexander Grushko explained the rationale of the proposal: 'Pan-European military-political collaboration has yet to make that qualitative leap and create a strong and cohesive partnership ... It took the shock of the South Caucasus crisis for all of us to become aware that something is not quite right in Europe and that by themselves the political obligations that we have all gradually assumed in various fora are not enough.' He argued that the proposal aimed to make the 'principle of indivisible security' into a legal obligation under which no country 'is entitled to strengthen its own security at the expense of security of other nations or organisations'. A core objection by critics is that the Russian proposal would imply setting up an institution which in effect superseded all others – not an acceptable proposition for NATO and EU members.

> "The Russian proposal would set up an institution superseding all others"

The OSCE's Finnish and Greek chairmanships in 2008 and 2009 respectively tried to anchor any discussion on new European security initiatives, including Russian proposals, within the OSCE rather than letting them unfold outside of an institutionalised structure. This led to the Corfu process, launched in 2009 after exploratory discussions which served to build consensus among member states that a conversation about European security was necessary. The Greek chairmanship organised ten rounds of ambassadorial-level meetings between July and December 2009 to identify the issues of substance that should structure the discussions. A ministerial council in Athens in December 2009 was then designed to mark the beginning of these discussions through a ministerial declaration.

While Russia continues to be reluctant to accept the OSCE as the only venue to discuss its European security initiative, it now seems willing to work through the institution in order to have a sustained dialogue. Then Greek Foreign Minister Dora Bakoyannis said in 2009 that the objective of the Corfu process was to build 'whole and lasting security in Europe for all and [ensure] the security of Europe against common threats and challenges'. The ministerial declaration of 1–2 December 2009 stated that member states were committed to 'setting ambitious, concrete and pragmatic goals'. But this is exactly where the process has fallen short so far. Beyond agreement on the fact that the process is to build on the OSCE's notion of comprehensive security, that it should be tied to progress on issues of arms control and protracted conflict in Europe, and that it should be in general a home for a renewed European security dialogue, the old divisions that have long plagued the OSCE seem to prevent more substantive agreement.

While the Corfu process has generated momentum, it has fallen to Kazakhstan as the 2010 chair to move forward on a concrete and specific agenda. Many observers doubt whether Kazakhstan will be able to make the required effort and effectively tackle the unresolved tensions in the OSCE, not least because Kazakhstan's own track record on the human dimension of the OSCE's comprehensive security agenda is patchy at best.

Outlook

Europe's security architecture is a puzzle with many moving parts. All its major institutional frameworks have embarked on efforts to underline their relevance and become more effective. In theory, this could mark a defining moment in European history. However, divisions among the member states of each institution suggest that none of them is likely to significantly build on its comparative advantages. A comprehensive security structure for Europe, in which institutions with overlapping membership would all contribute related yet distinct aspects to a greater whole, therefore remains remote. If comprehensiveness cannot be achieved through the interplay of institutions, the question becomes whether one of them can achieve greater comprehensiveness by itself.

If the divisions among member states, which currently have a significant impact on deliberations in all three frameworks and make consensus on important questions difficult to achieve, are not bridged, multinational security cooperation in Europe may well drift towards crisis. Necessary reforms of NATO, the EU and the OSCE would take place only fitfully and partially, and the ability of each to meet today's security challenges could stagnate. This does not, however, necessarily mean a reversion to purely nationally defined security strategies – especially since the money available to defence will be cut sharply as a result of the economic crisis. It is more likely to lead to much looser bonds and more issue-specific cooperation between smaller groups of countries. Such a growing emphasis on a rising number of self-recruiting coalitions of the willing will be difficult to direct in a strategic sense with short-termism and ad hoc measures the likely result. A better outcome would be for repeated and frequent interactions to take place within the framework of the existing institutions. These could help to align preferences and lock in commitments, making members better prepared and more unified. But at present, the existing multilateral institutions are neither flexible enough nor strong enough.

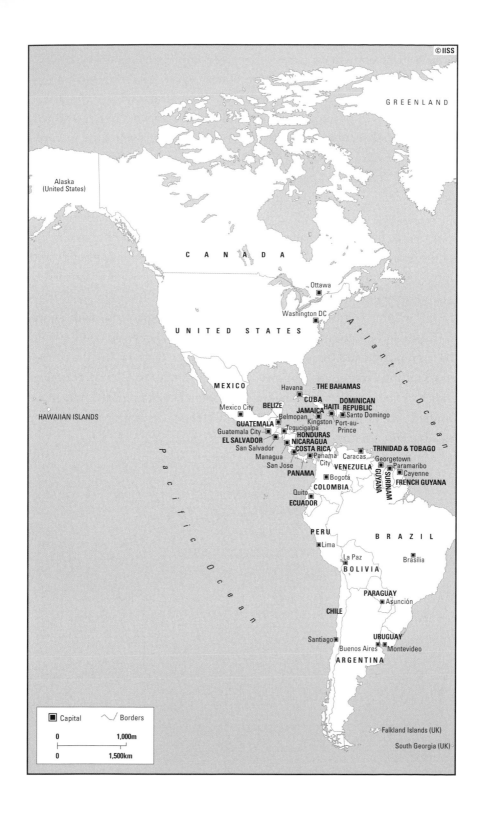

© IISS

GREENLAND

Alaska
(United States)

C A N A D A

Ottawa

Washington DC

U N I T E D   S T A T E S

HAWAIIAN ISLANDS

MEXICO

Havana   THE BAHAMAS

CUBA

BELIZE   JAMAICA   HAITI   DOMINICAN REPUBLIC

Mexico City

Belmopan   Kingston   Santo Domingo

GUATEMALA   Port-au-Prince

Guatemala City   Tegucigalpa

EL SALVADOR   HONDURAS

San Salvador   NICARAGUA   COSTA RICA   TRINIDAD & TOBAGO

Managua   Panama   Caracas   Georgetown   Paramaribo

San Jose   City   VENEZUELA   Cayenne

PANAMA   Bogotá   GUYANA   SURINAM   FRENCH GUYANA

COLOMBIA

Quito

ECUADOR

PERU   B R A Z I L

Lima

La Paz   Brasília

B O L I V I A

PARAGUAY

Asunción

CHILE

URUGUAY

Santiago   Montevideo

Buenos Aires

A R G E N T I N A

Atlantic Ocean

Pacific Ocean

Falkland Islands (UK)

South Georgia (UK)

Capital   Borders

0   1,000m

0   1,500km

Chapter 3

The Americas

The United States: Obama's New Balance

During President Barack Obama's first year-and-a-half in office, he was preoccupied by domestic exigencies, principally managing the United States' economic recovery from the collapse of 2008 and getting his signature health-care reform bill through a resistant Congress. With the US economy probably a year out of recession as of June 2010, and the health-care bill passed, he appeared to have met these priorities quite ably, despite his relative inexperience in executive office. Moreover, domestic demands had not distracted his attention from foreign affairs. He was an extroverted leader, making ten trips to 21 nations during his first year in office, maintaining worldwide approval ratings far higher than those of his predecessor George W. Bush, accepting the surprise award of the Nobel Peace Prize and repairing some of the damage done to America's image during Bush's eight-year tenure. And he got the uncontroversial moves right, mounting, for example, a robust response to the Haitian earthquake that was consonant with his own benevolent image.

Obama's election in 2008 as the United States' first black president was undeniably historic, and some Americans hopefully proclaimed it 'transformative', perhaps even the dawning of a post-racial America. But Obama was saddled with Bush's legacies of international excess, economic recession and domestic neglect, as well as the unrealistic expectations of half a nation and the untrusting resentment of most of the other half. He himself acknowledged that whatever racial progress his election might have signified in fact preceded it. It soon became clear that his first term was going to be a more typical slog.

Amidst the tentative recovery from recession, Obama's approval rating within the United States dropped from 68% at the time of his inauguration in January 2009 to just below 50% in May 2010. While new presidents virtually never maintain their honeymoon standing with the electorate, some 20 points constituted a fairly precipitous drop. The fall could be explained in substantial part by the unwillingness of conservatives and some moderates to credit the administration's cautious but effective regulatory and stimulus policies for the United States' fragile recovery, and by their dismay with the president's insistent focus on health care in a time of broader economic hardship. The latter factor caused commentators on both left and right to charge for some time that Obama and his team had lost control of the narrative and to yearn for a can-do arm-twister in the mould of Lyndon Johnson.

Obama had sought to achieve 'post-partisan' government, and had called during his campaign and early days in office for a new spirit that left behind the deeply-entrenched resentments that have long characterised American politics. Instead, America witnessed the rise of the populist 'Tea Party' movement, composed of overwhelmingly white economic and social conservatives who vituperatively paint the Obama administration as socialist and impugn its national-security policies and credentials – some members sport, among other venomous merchandise, bracelets labelled 'OBAMA REPELLENT'. In this atmosphere, Republicans in Congress blocked health-care reforms for as long as they could.

However, passage, after a long and close-run struggle, of the health-care bill in March 2010 released much of the political pressure that had threatened to paralyse the administration. Until that moment, it had been afflicted by a serious imbalance between its soaring aspirations and gritty political reality. But afterwards, the administration acquired a new balance that appeared to enable it to proceed more fluidly in making and implementing policy both domestically and internationally. Obama had run on a foreign-policy platform embracing the return of restrained pragmatic realism after Bush's militarised Wilsonian idealism and resulting strategic excesses. If Obama's supporters had lofty domestic expectations for the new president, their international ones were, or at least should have been, more down to earth. While downplaying pre-emptive and preventive action and democracy promotion, both the Pentagon's Quadrennial Defense Review (released in February 2010) and the White House's National Security Strategy (released in May 2010) were evolutionary rather than revolutionary. They continued to endorse, for example, US-led counter-insurgency and strike capabilities as major instruments of counter-terrorism.

Unsound American policies had precipitated a global economic collapse that appeared to threaten a diminution in its global influence. At a G20 summit in Pittsburgh, Pennsylvania in September 2009, chaired by Obama, each member agreed for the first time to 'peer reviews' and International Monetary Fund (IMF) monitoring. Countries pledged to take a number of steps to strengthen the international financial system, and to revive a new global trade agreement by the end of 2010. Leaders announced that international discussion of global economic issues would formally shift from the US-led G8 to the more inclusive and collaborative G20, which includes China, India, Brazil as well as other emerging nations and reflects the increased influence of developing countries in the global economy. Accordingly, Obama, who had limited room for manoeuvre owing to domestic circumstances and the Bush legacy, was thus in effect presiding over a calibrated strategic retrenchment that called for the United States' avoidance of unilateralism and acceptance of multipolarity, and therefore less rather than more American assertiveness abroad.

> **Unsound American policies had precipitated a global economic collapse**

The notable exception to this approach was Afghanistan. During the presidential campaign, Obama cast the Afghanistan conflict (and the related counter-terrorism effort in neighbouring Pakistan) as a neglected war of necessity, in contrast to the war of choice in Iraq. This distinction, which could be argued to be illusory given that Afghanistan poses no existential threat to the United States, stemmed in part from Obama's need to appear militarily tough to assuage sceptical domestic conservatives and to hold potentially exploitative international adversaries in check. Obama's characterisation of Afghanistan as a necessary war limited the administration's flexibility and prompted an escalatory policy involving more troops, robust counter-insurgency and state-building. In keeping with his realist instincts, however, when unveiling the policy on 1 December 2009 in a speech at the US Military Academy at West Point, Obama set a target date of July 2011 for the commencement of the drawdown of US and NATO forces. Many observers within and outside the United States doubted that conditions would allow the drawdown to proceed prudently on schedule. The two-pronged decision, which took some three months to make following a request from the field commander, meant that the success of Obama's foreign policy – whether it could accomplish both orderly restraint and the preservation of America's international prestige and leverage – would hinge to an important degree on developments in Afghanistan and Pakistan in 2010–11.

Domestic relief

Meanwhile, his most cherished and celebrated domestic project bore fruit. The passage in the House of Representatives by 219–212 votes of a watershed federal health-care bill on 21 March was a long-awaited breakthrough. Obama had made enacting the law, officially known as the Patient Protection and Affordable Care Act, the headline goal of his first year in office. And securing what had been the most important aim of liberals in the Democratic Party for over 50 years was a remarkable achievement. While the legislation was complex, in essence it provided health-care coverage for over 30 million Americans who had lacked medical insurance. It prohibited insurance companies from denying or ending coverage on the basis of pre-existing medical conditions, and required all Americans, in principle, to take out insurance (so as to prevent a 'death spiral' in which people might wait until they became too ill to do so). The legislation also subsidised those who could not afford to pay.

The bill produced significant disagreements both within and between the two major parties in the Senate and the House of Representatives, and Obama was criticised for not taking sufficiently clear and vigorous leadership on the issue. Nevertheless, eventual passage of some form of reform had looked likely until Scott Brown, a Republican opposed to overhaul of health-care, won a special election in Massachusetts for the seat made empty by the death of Democratic Senator Edward Kennedy (who, ironically, was perhaps the strongest advocate in Congress for expanded health coverage). The Democrats thus lost the 60-vote majority needed to break a Republican filibuster. The Senate had in fact already passed the bill, but would still need to enact changes made to secure its passage through the House.

The Obama team circumvented the problem by resorting to a process known as budget reconciliation. This required only a simple Senate majority (51 votes) to pass provisions impacting the federal budget, as most of the important ones in the health-care bill did. With the necessary majority in the Senate thus reasonably assured, the main task became securing enough votes in the House. Although Democrats had a clear majority in the House, liberals among them decried the bill's absence of a public option – that is, a government-run direct insurance provider that would serve the market alongside private insurers – while moderates harboured serious doubts about the cost of the bill and more conservative Democrats worried that the federal government could end up directly funding abortion. The president himself gathered 28 key members of Congress at a bipartisan summit on 25 February in an attempt to resolve outstanding differences and win a few Republican converts. But Republicans dismissed the summit as a desperate publicity stunt. Obama then resolved to get the bill passed only with Democrats, and embarked on an intensive personal campaign to bring House Democrats together. His overriding message was that his administration's political success and, by extension, their own political fates turned on resolving their differences and ensuring favourable votes in each house.

The health-care bill passed without a single Republican vote, underscoring the fiercely partisan nature of contemporary American politics and increasing scepticism about Obama's ability to usher in an epoch of post-partisan government. To be sure, Tea Party Republicans continued to attack the new law as socialist and vowed its repeal after anticipated Republican victories in midterm elections in November 2010, while 14 state attorneys-general filed lawsuits challenging its constitutionality.

But such blustery and divisive threats and challenges were unlikely to work, and could even backfire politically. In April 2010, Senate Republicans opted not to block debate on financial regulatory reform legislation, another key administration concern, for fear of appearing obstructionist.

Obama's display of political muscle, stamina and resilience in pushing through the most significant and controversial piece of domestic US legislation since the 1960s reinvigorated his presidency. It ended a stream of opinion pieces in the media suggesting that, in spite of his rhetoric, he was proving politically ineffectual and overly intellectual in his approach to office. This development looked likely to ease his efforts in the domestic arena. In 2010, these were expected to include pushing through financial reform and new immigration legislation aimed at tightening enforcement and monitoring, rendering legal status easier to obtain, and encouraging the admission of highly skilled immigrants.

Also on the domestic agenda was the appointment of a new Supreme Court justice to succeed Justice John Paul Stevens, who was retiring after nearly 35 years on the bench, with an eye to moving the court to the left. This process could prove acrimonious, as an increasingly conservative Supreme Court, reinforced by Bush's appointments of Chief Justice John Roberts and Associate Justice Samuel Alito, had become, in effect, an important political antagonist of the administration. The opportunity for a new appointment came on the heels of Obama's appointment of Justice Sonia Sotomayor, whom Senate Republicans stiffly and often sourly challenged before the Senate confirmed her in a 60–31 vote in August 2009. It also followed the Court's 5–4 decision in *Citizens United v. Federal Election Commission*, which strained precedent in holding that corporations had a constitutional first-amendment right to spend unlimited amounts on television campaign advertising specifically supporting or targeting particular candidates. A number of liberal jurists considered the decision a threat to American democracy. On 10 May 2010, Obama nominated US Solicitor General Elena Kagan, widely regarded as a centrist Democrat, to succeed Justice Stevens.

As they prepared for the midterm elections in November 2010, with 37 governorships, 36 Senate seats and the entire 435-seat House at stake, the Democrats were burdened by a historical trend of midterm losses incurred by the party of the incumbent president, as well as by the weak economy and Obama's struggles in office. But they were also able to identify the incoherence of Tea Party rhetoric; in particular, the mismatch between the castigation of big government and the demand for stimulation of higher employment and better economic performance, which required an active federal government (though in fact substantial government stimulus was only fitfully producing these outcomes). The Democratic strategy emerging in mid-2010 was to stay focused on concrete local problems – especially jobs – and not to be drawn into irrelevant philosophical debates, while branding Republicans as obstructionist and out of touch and promoting the Democratic Party as 'the results party'. Against this background, it was difficult to say how the midterm elections would play out beyond the general expectation of some Republican gains.

Still the economy

Obama's primary concern remained, inexorably, the American economy, which had yet to fully recover from the 2008–09 collapse. His instincts, moreover, were still cautious and incremental, and he had not given up on bipartisanship.

Notwithstanding the buoyancy of the US stock market (the Dow Jones Industrial Average topped 11,000 in April 2010, having risen roughly 70% since its low point of 6,547 on 9 March 2009), many Americans continued to struggle economically, with unemployment hovering around 10%. Economic growth, though positive, was stuttering, registering an annual rate of 5.6% in the fourth quarter of 2009 but only 3.2% in the first quarter of 2010. The residual macroeconomic problems were not of Obama's making, and his stimulus programme and, later, Treasury Secretary Timothy Geithner's measured and selective approach to regulation were grudgingly credited with helping to stave off economic disaster. Nevertheless, Obama's approval rating dropped from nearly 70% to 49% between February 2009 and April 2010, and his disapproval rating increased from 15% to 46%. Passage of the health-care bill did not give him a significant uplift.

Thus, Obama was compelled to stay focused on job creation, economic stimulus and financial reform in the short term to minimise midterm electoral losses, and in the longer term to maximise his chances for re-election in 2012. Reducing the budget deficit and cumulative debt, staving off inflation, financial sector regulation and the risk of a 'double-dip' recession were also intensifying domestic concerns. In June, Federal Reserve Chairman Ben Bernanke allayed the worst fears. Testifying to the House Budget Committee, he forecast 3.5% growth in 2010 and a somewhat faster rate in 2011, while noting that this recovery 'would probably be associated with only a slow reduction in the unemployment rate over time'. The upside was that inflation was 'likely to remain subdued', though he also commented in an ABC News interview that the Fed would probably raise interest rates to control inflation as growth picked up pace. Bernanke also reflected that, while large budget deficits were necessary in the short-term to keep the recovery on track, a 'medium term exit strategy' was needed for the United States to get its fiscal house in order – and that such a strategy was not, as of then, taking shape.

While putting off drastic action on the fiscal deficit, Obama had other highly valued agenda items to protect. These included energy reform and action on global climate change. The outcome of the December 2009 United Nations summit on climate change in Copenhagen fell short of what Obama, who anticipated that a final accord would emerge, had hoped. The three-page agreement the president negotiated with the leaders of China, India, Brazil and South Africa and then presented to the conference did not set a 2010 goal for reaching a binding international treaty. Negotiations at Copenhagen failed to forge a solid commitment by industrialised and developing nations to firm targets for medium or long-term greenhouse gas emissions reductions. The United States and other Western countries drew most of the immediate fire from developing countries and aid organisations. But accounts suggested that the prime culprit was the Chinese government. In the run-up to the conference, China, the largest emitter of greenhouse gases, had signalled that it wanted a deal. In the event, Beijing blindsided and snubbed Obama, flatly rejecting his and others' proposals for target cuts in carbon emissions, insisting on a tepid and unsatisfactory non-binding compromise and calculating – correctly – that Washington would get most of the blame.

The Copenhagen Accord set the stage for formal commitments by individual nations to act on their own to take meaningful steps to mitigate global warming. It soon became clear how fraught the politics in this area could be. The administration's March 2010 decision to allow offshore oil drilling for the first time in decades, to the delight of many Republicans and the dismay of many Democrats, demonstrated how far Obama thought he would have to go to placate Republicans to get meaningful restrictions on carbon emissions. More broadly, the move suggested that despite the health-care victory, Obama remained more inclined towards calculated compromise than triumphal imperiousness.

The administration's delicate political choreography collapsed on 20 April 2010, when an explosion at BP's mile-deep underwater drilling rig known as *Deepwater Horizon* in the Gulf of Mexico killed 11 workers, and triggered a historically massive oil spill that threatened environmental disaster for the United States' Gulf coast as well as the Gulf itself. As of 14 June, estimates of the amount of oil that had spewed into the Gulf ranged from 23.2 to 89.4 million gallons, compared to the 10.8m gallons released in the 1989 *ExxonValdez* spill in Alaska (see map, p. XX). On 27 May, Obama declared a six-month moratorium on offshore drilling at depths greater than 500 feet (152 metres), shelving 33 projects. The administration's initial response was seen as dilatory and overly deferential to BP, which was accused of cutting corners on safety requirements, understating leak estimates, and mounting risky and unsuccessful initial efforts to stop the leak. Magnifying the White House's missteps was its prior failure to overhaul the Interior Department's Minerals Management Service (MMS), which was responsible for regulating drilling and widely seen as among the most dysfunctional and compromised agencies in the US government.

> " Obama remained inclined towards calculated compromise "

By mid-May, the administration appeared to have taken control of the situation, firing the MMS director and tasking government scientists to scrutinise BP's efforts and the US Coast Guard to oversee containment and clean-up operations involving 30,000 federal personnel, while state governments took their own measures including the deployment of National Guard contingents. With congressional support, it became still more assertive in June, and secured BP's agreement to pay $20bn into a fund to pay claims arising from the spill. On 15 June 2010, in the first speech broadcast from the Oval Office since his presidency began, Obama set forth a 'battle plan' to break 'this siege', announcing the appointment of Secretary of the Navy Ray Mabus as long-term recovery coordinator, and establishing a National Commission to determine the causes of the disaster and devise appropriate safety and environmental standards for offshore drilling.

The administration was whipsawed by those who favoured an extended moratorium on deep-sea drilling for environmental and energy-policy reasons and those who supported a resumption – including Louisiana Senator Mary Landrieu (a Democrat) and Governor Bobby Jindal (a Republican) – to mitigate the economic impact of both the spill and the moratorium. With the leak unlikely to be contained before August 2010, the unprecedented oil spill had the effect of sidelining foreign-policy priorities, as Obama twice cancelled trips to Indonesia and Australia while travelling four times in less than two months to the Gulf coast. Yet despite the claims of Obama's mainly Republican critics, the *Deepwater Horizon* spill did not appear to be his Hurricane Katrina: while a mid-June Associated Press–GfK Roper poll did find that 52% of Americans disapproved of Obama's handling of the oil spill, which was only slightly lower than Bush's number on Katrina, Obama's overall approval rating remained steady at about 47% whereas Bush's had plummeted to 37% two months after Katrina had struck. Substantially more of those surveyed – some 83% – disapproved of BP's response. With a corporate giant effectively shielding Obama from the full brunt of popular outrage, as dramatic a crisis as the oil spill was, Obama's main electoral challenge remained the US economy.

A forbidding international landscape

Following the health-care victory the administration appeared more energised on the foreign-policy front. In April 2010, Obama signed an agreement with Russia on nuclear-arms reductions, unveiled a new nuclear posture narrowing the circumstances of American use of nuclear weapons with an eye towards ultimately eliminating them, and convened a nuclear-security summit aimed at minimising the threat of nuclear terrorism. The administration committed itself to resuscitating the Middle East peace process and became more openly impatient with Israeli Prime Minister Benjamin Netanyahu's refusal to completely freeze Israeli settlement activity in occupied territory. (This impatience erupted into public fury after the Israeli Interior Ministry obtusely announced the construction of 1,600 new housing units in mainly Palestinian East Jerusalem during Vice President Joe Biden's visit to Israel in March 2010.) The administration marshalled international support for strengthened sanctions on Iran, securing China's agreement to participate in negotiations, and later its positive vote – along with Russia's – on a new UN sanctions resolution. All these three areas, however, represented small steps towards long-term goals.

The foreign-policy challenges facing the United States were, as ever, substantial. The related problems of Afghanistan and Pakistan showed that Obama's early attempt to adopt a strategy encompassing both countries was fraught with difficulties, though Pakistan's army did take on militant groups in the tribal regions close to Afghanistan. Obama's 'surge' of troops and civilian expertise in Afghanistan was achieving uncertain results. His call to Iran to unclench its fist and engage in discussions with Washington fell on deaf ears: the leadership in Tehran, shaken but not threatened by internal protests, did not become more cooperative with the United States or less likely to advance its nuclear programme and geopolitical ambitions in the Gulf and Middle East. Meanwhile, Iraq's gradual transition to self-sufficiency continued to be difficult, afflicted by sectarian tensions and violence. After a good start, the Obama administration's relationship with China became frosty in parts, especially over currency valuation and US arms sales to Taiwan.

A vivid example of the limits of American power was Obama's 23 March 2009 meeting with Netanyahu. Despite the administration's open displeasure with Israel's construction of new housing in East Jerusalem, its standing advocacy of a freeze on new settlements and its intensifying diplomatic efforts to revive the Israeli–Palestinian peace process, as well as Israel's recent slighting of Vice President Biden, the meeting produced no sign that Israel would reconsider its position. To make matters worse, on 31 May 2010 Israeli naval forces boarded a ship in a pro-Palestinian Turkish NGO's aid flotilla in international waters, bound for Gaza in defiance of the standing Israeli blockade and suspected of carrying weapons for Hamas. The Israelis met resistance and killed nine Turkish people on board. Although in the aftermath Israel became more open to possible alternatives to the blockade, US–Israeli relations were strained still further. In addition, Israel's special relationship with Turkey – the closest it had enjoyed with any Muslim country – and with it Turkey's disposition to help Israel diplomatically, for example in brokering indirect talks with Syria, appeared to have come to an end. Given these developments, Netanyahu's stubbornness and the high political risk associated with Middle East peace initiatives, no major diplomatic foray on Middle East peace seemed remotely likely from Washington – especially during a midterm election year.

Managing even traditionally unproblematic relationships proved to be a challenge. The global economic crisis amplified transatlantic strains. In particular, as of mid-2010 the United States and Europe had yet to arrive at a consensus on how best to balance stimulus to economic growth, which the American side tended to emphasise, and fiscal sustainability, which was increasingly becoming Europe's priority because of concerns about mounting sovereign debt. If rescue packages agreed in 2010 worked and Greece's debt problems did not spread to other countries, there appeared from Washington's perspective to be few major worries. But if Europe's debt problems were to worsen, the American concern was that it could become paralysed, more inward-looking and nationalistic – thus halting European convergence and diminishing Europe's strategic presence. Obama did not help to blunt this possibility when he declined to attend the May 2010 US–EU summit in Madrid, apparently catering to American perceptions that he was insufficiently focused on domestic problems and views within the administration that such summits accomplished little of substance.

On matters of international security, European leaders and populations were generally fond of Obama, especially in contrast to Bush. There was a high level of common transatlantic purpose during Obama's first 18 months in office on counter-terrorism, non-proliferation, Iran, Iraq and Afghanistan, as well as the customary but generally manageable discord on intelligence-sharing matters such as the US-backed Terrorist Finance Tracking programme, which the EU had refused to support as of May 2010. But the damage done to the transatlantic relationship by the Bush administration, mainly over Iraq, was not completely fixed. There remained significant tensions, for example, over NATO's future mission, with Washington keen on a 'global NATO' and most European members more comfortable with a more Europe-focussed approach. Against this background, the NATO summit scheduled for November 2010 in Lisbon, at which the Alliance was due to agree a new 'strategic concept', appeared likely to be important.

Obama had security-related grievances to address from his putative supporters as well as his detractors. Liberals complained that Obama had partially reneged on campaign promises to curtail the Bush administration's harsh counter-terrorism policies. The continuing political need to show toughness on security matters, as well as the practical difficulties involved, made it difficult for the administration to fulfil its vow to close the Guantanamo Bay detention facility.

Afghanistan policy

If health care was the main pillar of the Obama administration's stated domestic agenda, Afghanistan was its foreign-policy counterpart. The US policy of qualified escalation sought to pacify Afghanistan through coercive and expansive counter-insurgency ('clear, hold, build') operations and a concerted state-building effort to bring order to its politics, contain regional militancy and ensure stability in Pakistan. The US planned to bring the American troop presence in Afghanistan to a peak of 100,000 by late summer 2010, which would represent an increase of nearly a third over the mid-2009 number. Obama's intention was to begin drawing down the American presence in Afghanistan in July 2011.

Yet the coalition effort in Afghanistan appeared increasingly problematic. Despite US-led offensives in early 2010 – notably in Marjah, in Helmand province – the Taliban insurgency proved to be tenacious and unrelenting. Afghan President Hamid Karzai resisted US pressure to root out corruption, and grew more distant from Washington, but his authority remained hard to sidestep. US-led training programmes for the Afghan army and especially the national police were revealed as flawed, wasteful and ineffectual. At the same time, the 'drone war' (prosecuted with unmanned aerial vehicles (UAVs) firing precision-guided munitions) against al-Qaeda and Taliban leaders in the tribal areas of Pakistan continued to be effective in containing the al-Qaeda threat, and a stepped-up effort in early 2010 appeared to discourage them from building up operational bases.

Generally speaking, Europeans appeared to be contributing militarily to the Afghanistan effort primarily to preserve transatlantic comity, rather than because of a genuine sharing of a sense of strategic threat. Defense Secretary Robert Gates's scolding February 2010 speech at the National Defense University, ominously casting Europe's collective 'demilitarization' as 'an impediment to achieving real security and lasting peace', underlined the difference between American and European views and may have been a harbinger of a rift. However, Europe's terrorist threat perceptions were shared by some in the administration, and domestic support for combat operations remained brittle. A congressionally-mandated semi-annual Pentagon report released on 28 April 2010 indicated continued public disenchantment in Afghanistan with the Karzai government, a resilient Taliban that was expanding its influence, an 87% increase in violent incidents over the course of a year, and a national dependence on foreign troops that showed little sign of diminishing.

Accordingly, a question lingered as to whether the full-blooded counter-insurgency and state-building effort embodied by Obama's Afghanistan policy was operationally necessary to protect vital American interests in establishing sufficient regional stability and denying al-Qaeda a safe haven in Central and South Asia. It remained possible that the Obama administration might judge that adjusting Afghanistan policy to less ambitious goals might prove less vulnerable to conservative political retaliation within the United States than it initially judged. Obama may then decide to stick to the tentative drawdown schedule in Afghanistan despite shortfalls in implementing the original stabilisation strategy.

A persistent Pentagon: the Quadrennial Defense Review

The flip-side to Obama's Afghan strategy was that if counter-insurgency and state-building effort in Afghanistan were to work better than expected it could produce pressure to keep a military emphasis on the global counter-terrorism effort. The Defense Department's 2010 Quadrennial Defense Review (QDR), released in February 2010, could be read to support that concern. It emphasised that 'the United States remains a nation at war' and recommended the allocation of military resources among four priority objectives: prevailing in present wars, preventing and deterring future conflicts, preparing to defeat adversaries in a wide range of contingencies, and preserving the all-volunteer force. These comprehensive aspirations suggested that the QDR was, as advertised by the Pentagon, 'strategy-driven' in the sense that it aimed to enable the United States to advance all of its national goals and defend all of its vital national interests. And the QDR's explicit acknowledgement of the need to move beyond the 'two-major-wars' paradigm and adopt a more versatile posture that accommodated a broader and more nuanced spectrum of threats made obvious sense.

The QDR cited, as two of the six key subsidiary missions, succeeding in counter-insurgency, stability and counter-terrorism operations; and deterring and defeating aggression in 'anti-access' environments – that is, countries or regions in which the United States' adversaries actively seek to prevent it from engaging in military activity. The QDR re-oriented force size and shape requirements accordingly. The document at least implicitly recognised the need for substantial non-military components (diplomacy and law enforcement, for example) among the tools required to effectively thwart terrorism, noting that 'sustainable success requires the patient and persistent application of all elements of US and international power', and military force only 'as necessary to defeat Al Qaeda and its allies'. The QDR also registered an official preference for host-nation leadership over large-scale US-led counter-insurgency campaigns.

With its emphasis on counter-insurgency and the ongoing shift away from a force-on-force focus towards smaller and more agile units attuned to asymmetric threats and irregular guerrilla warfare, and a corresponding procurement accent on helicopters and UAVs, the QDR gave the impression that the Pentagon saw counter-insurgency operations in Iraq, Afghanistan and Pakistan as salutary if limited precedents for efforts elsewhere. The implied premise was that, owing to the inadequacy of non-military counter-terrorism means, selective counter-insurgency operations were a primary tool of the global counter-terrorism campaign. Such a stance, in turn, assumed that US efforts in Iraq, Afghanistan and Pakistan had produced or were assured of producing net security gains.

This was probably due in significant part to the provisional operational success of the surge in Iraq that began in early 2007 and the widely publicised revision of the US military's counter-insurgency doctrine at the hands of General David Petraeus, who commanded the surge, and with the advice other successful US military commanders. Notwithstanding the surge's tactical success, however, it was not clear that similar deployments in other countries in which jihadist insurgencies threatened to strengthen al-Qaeda's global reach, such as Yemen or Somalia, would be operationally feasible or politically sustainable either domestically or internationally. The QDR itself recognised that 'in Iraq and Afghanistan, two theaters in which we are engaged simultaneously, we have seen that achieving operational military victory can be only the first step toward achieving our strategic objectives'.

The QDR made no attempt to change the widely held view that future setbacks in Afghanistan or Iraq could further circumscribe the United States' use of its military. Yet it broadly extolled and promoted the use of special-operations forces and high-technology assets to achieve counter-terrorism ends quickly and cheaply in areas of secondary strategic importance such as Africa. Such activities, however, threatened to freshen the sense among Africans that the American impulse on their continent is suppressive and imperialistic rather than constructive and collaborative. The Obama administration has been eager to reverse this impression. Thus, AFRICOM was given very few operational assets: manpower and equipment only as necessary to meet current threats and to train and backstop regional partners as opposed to permanent bases. AFRICOM has, moreover, been quite deliberately evolving as, primarily, a rather self-effacing diplomatic instrument, with substantial civilian staff and closely integrated with civilian agencies, focused on building regional military capacities through sustained partnerships and encouraging African solutions to African problems.

The Obama administration, in which the State Department to an extent has been rejuvenated, appeared inclined to follow this model in other locales. But in areas of more acute strategic consequence to which

US combat troops and other assets were more heavily committed, such as Central Asia, the Persian Gulf and Latin America, and with the Pentagon bureaucratically and financially stronger than the State Department, the ability to resist temptations to act militarily – especially when they were supported by documented national security policy – threatened to prove difficult. Notwithstanding the new enthusiasm for counter-insurgency, the institutional stickiness of legacy ideas and platforms still hampered the transition of the US military from a 'big war' to a 'small war' force better suited to dispersed adversaries.

Pragmatic and selective approach

Obama surprised many in declining to use his historic 2008 victory to punish Republicans, instead trying to build bipartisan consensus. The fact that he failed to do so does not mean he will abandon his pragmatic disposition. Rather, after a fitful first year, the administration appeared to have apprehended and accepted the ambivalence of the American electorate and Congress and figured out how to navigate it. By mid-2010 Obama's presidency had become a familiar battleground between New Deal liberals who look to government for solutions, and Reagan con-servatives who fear its intrusion. But observers who had seen in Obama traces of the fecklessness usually – if somewhat unfairly – attributed to Jimmy Carter had for the time being been silenced.

The passage of the health-care bill and probable success in getting financial reform legislation through Congress looked likely to free the president from having to placate as many congressmen on issues like trade policy or the Middle East, which in turn would give him greater latitude on national security and foreign policy in general. Obama, however, made it clear that, even though many Americans who voted for him may have hoped for major change in US foreign policy in the direction of liberal internationalism, which is broadly consistent with his philosophy, he did not interpret his historic ascent to the presidency as a mandate for iconoclasm. His speech accepting the Nobel Peace Prize in Oslo in December 2009, which among other things underlined the sober necessity of war, sounded in some ways not unlike the philosophy of George W. Bush. Recognising that the international tableau presents no obvious opportunities for major breakthroughs, Obama looked likely to pick his opportunities very carefully to facilitate the recovery of American interests, authority and prestige.

Latin America's Growing Global Influence

In March 2010, as Netanyahu and Obama were in the midst of a public disagreement over how to proceed with the peace process, Brazilian president Luiz Inacio 'Lula' da Silva arrived in the Middle East. Lula had meetings with leaders in Israel, Palestine and Jordan, where he called for dialogue, offered to advance the stalled peace process by conducting talks with Syria and Iran, and told local journalists that he came to the region carrying a 'virus of peace'.

Just a decade earlier, it would have seemed inconceivable to most governments that Brazil could play a role in such a high-stakes diplomatic confrontation. Although Lula's actual influence on the peace process may ultimately be small, his ambitious efforts on behalf of Brazil provided one example that the countries of Latin America, despite widespread regional fragmentation, were pursuing an increasingly assertive political agenda with global interests and aspirations.

In 2010, a number of Latin American countries perceived themselves as rising powers on the world stage, and expected to be treated as such. Signs of this confidence were present across ideological spectrums and geographical borders. Brazil and Mexico have pursued more equal partnerships with the United States and simultaneously sought to impose greater influence over regional allies, while historically marginalised countries such as Bolivia have made concerted efforts to influence the global debate on such key issues as climate change. New regional power blocs such as the Union of South American Nations (UNASUR) and the Bolivarian Alliance for the Americas (ALBA), led by Brazil and Venezuela respectively, have proliferated as Latin American governments looked to exert a greater influence over regional relations. And in February 2010, the leaders of all the Latin American and Caribbean nations announced the creation of a new, still-unnamed regional organisation that would expressly exclude the United States and Canada.

However, despite increased international influence and new regional alliances, Latin America was anything but unified, and was still marked by political polarisation and disarray. Mexico was sharply focused on an often-brutal internal war against violent drug cartels that was spilling over to its neighbours north and south; Colombia continued to feud bitterly with Venezuela and still maintained no official relationship with Ecuador; earthquakes devastated communities in Chile and Haiti; drug-trafficking cartels were reportedly infiltrating weak institutions throughout Central America; and many countries remained divided over whether to recognise the Honduran government elected following the June 2009 coup d'état that forcibly removed the president from office.

A series of presidential elections over the past year also revealed that, contrary to assertions of a leftward or rightward slant in Latin American politics, the region as a whole was far from politically monolithic. In Bolivia, Evo Morales was elected to a second term with a landslide 63% of the vote in December 2009. The leftist Morales also saw his party, Movement Towards Socialism (MAS), win the two-thirds congressional majority it needed to facilitate the implementation of the wide-ranging social and economic reforms it had promised in Morales's first term. Bolivia's neighbour Chile also went to the polls in December, but Chileans rejected the centre-left and Socialist candidates by ultimately electing the right-wing billionaire businessman Sebastian Piñera, who won a run-off with 52% of the vote. Piñera's win ended 20 years of governance by the centre-left Concertación coalition, which had dominated Chilean politics since the end of the Pinochet era.

Presidential elections in Costa Rica, Honduras and Uruguay similarly showed the absence of a consistent political trend in Latin America. Former Costa Rican Vice-President Laura Chinchilla easily won election as her country's first female president with 47% of the vote. Chinchilla, a member of the social democratic National Liberation Party (PLN), presented herself as a social conservative who would continue the free-market policies begun under the previous president, Oscar Arias. She also vowed to more effectively address the spread of drug-related violence with a campaign promise of 'security, security and more security'.

In Honduras, Porfirio Lobo of the conservative National Party won 56% of the vote in a controversial election organised by the de facto government of Roberto Micheletti. The vote was held despite the protests of many Latin American governments, which felt that Micheletti's mandate to hold an election was illegitimate because a coup had brought him to power. Lobo's victory represented an ideological break from the deposed president, Manuel Zelaya, a member of the Liberal Party who had taken Honduras into ALBA, an alliance led by Hugo Chávez, and had taken steps towards changing the Honduran constitution.

Former rebel leader Jose Mujica won 53% of the vote to become president of Uruguay. Known originally as a founder of Uruguay's radical National Liberation Movement, the Tupamaros, in the 1960s, Mujica campaigned on promises of promoting democracy, continuing the social programmes and moderate fiscal policies of popular outgoing President Tabare Vazquez, and strengthening ties with the United States. Finally, former Defence Minister Juan Manuel Santos was elected president in Colombia with a landslide 69% of the vote.

Latin Americans, according to public opinion polls, have since the mid-1990s consistently desired governments that can solve problems and deliver results. They want good performance – efficiency and honesty – in their leaders, as opposed to a specific ideological orientation. But despite this pragmatic tendency, issues of security, governance and institutional strength remain contentious throughout the region, and some ideological differences among countries stand in the way of more effective cooperation and integration.

The US and Latin America: new beginnings, old frustrations

Obama's debut on the regional stage at the fifth Summit of the Americas in April 2009 helped improve the mood in US–Latin American relations. Despite the persistence of frustrations between the United States and many countries in the region, Obama's likeability continued to contrast sharply with his predecessor's. The most recent Latinobarometro polling revealed an increase in favourable views of the United States from 58% in 2008 to 74% in 2009, the highest number ever reached by the United States since the survey began in 1995.

This shift mirrored a global upward trend and represented no meagre accomplishment for the new administration. It did not, however, obscure the fact that there had been relatively little substantive change on a number of long-standing disputes since Obama took office. Many governments in the region found that underlying differences on key agenda items (such as the status of Cuba, confronting the drug trade, and the US military presence in Latin America) interfered with the promise of increased cooperation on both ends of the relationship. Signs of disappointment were unmistakable in Washington and in many Latin American capitals, despite Obama's promise of a more productive partnership.

The pursuit of new alliances and opportunities by countries such as Venezuela (and especially Brazil), moreover, clashed with US policy and caused new strains in inter-American relations. The November 2009 visit of Iranian President Mahmoud Ahmadinejad to Venezuela, Bolivia and, most significantly, Brazil, coincided with deepening concerns in Washington about Iran's involvement with Latin America as well as worries in the international community about Iran's nuclear programme. The implications of the visit were serious enough that US Secretary of State Hillary Clinton warned Latin American countries on 11 December that 'if people want to flirt with Iran, they should take a look at what the consequences might well be for them'. Lula's visit to Tehran in May 2010 was treated delicately by the Obama administration, publicly wishing Lula success in persuading Iran to slow its nuclear programme but privately fretting that Brazil's involvement would create further delays in securing new sanctions against the country. Given the tensions between the United States and Venezuela, it was not surprising that Chávez would seek to embrace Iran. But Brazil was a different matter. Lula's meetings with Ahmadinejad highlighted the conflicting priorities in Washington and Brasilia, and provoked concern among members of Congress and some members of the Obama administration.

The unexpected challenge of the political crisis in Honduras and the fallout from a US–Colombia military pact also complicated Obama's attempts to forge a 'new beginning' predicated on equal partnerships with the region. Obama condemned the Honduran coup in June 2009, calling it illegal and a 'terrible precedent' (see Honduras, pp. 127–30). As the crisis dragged on, however, his administration pursued a middle ground and tried to work out a compromise between Zelaya and the de facto government. As a result, the Obama administration applied pressure on the de facto government but did not impose a solution or the full force of sanctions at its disposal. Calls for a more assertive, heavy-handed US approach from countries like Brazil seemed to irk Obama, who noted in August 2009 'the irony that the people that were complaining about the US interfering in Latin America are now complaining that we are not interfering enough'.

In October 2009, with the previously scheduled November presidential election in Honduras fast approaching, the Obama administration undertook a diplomatic mission that culminated in an accord between Zelaya and Micheletti. According to the agreement, Zelaya could return to power with the approval of the Honduran Congress, and the election could proceed with the recognition of the United States and its allies. This solution put in place a way for Honduras to return to Washington's good graces while leaving the question of whether Zelaya would be able to finish the remaining months of his presidency as a separate matter in the hands of the Honduran Congress.

> The accord revived suspicions about US motives in South America

This deal left Washington sharply at odds with other Latin American governments, most notably Brazil, which along with other major countries such as Argentina and Venezuela refused to recognise the election unless Zelaya was explicitly allowed to return. Among those disappointed with the results were many Latin American allies of the United States, who felt they were not adequately consulted and that elections organised by a de facto government set a dangerous, undemocratic precedent.

Lack of consultation on a pact between Washington and Bogota permitting US use of seven Colombian bases for launching anti-drug operations also strained US–Latin American relations. News of the ten-year agreement, leaked to the Colombian press in August 2009, revived suspicions about US motives in South America. Announcement of the accord was ineptly managed. Also lacking was a high-level diplomatic effort to assuage persistent concerns among Latin American countries regarding US military operations in the region. Although the accord was eventually signed in late October 2009, US allies such as Brazil and Chile publicly expressed concerns that it was incongruous with the spirit of the Obama administration's stated regional approach.

Domestic politics in both the United States and Latin America remained a major challenge to developing constructive partnerships. For Obama, reform of health care and the financial sector took precedence over issues of concern to Latin American governments, such as immigration and trade. In Latin America, Obama's personal appeal improved the image of the United States, but long-standing US policies on Cuba and anti-narcotics remained an effective rallying cry for many regional politicians. Modifications to these policies perceived as politically important in the United States (such as lifting restrictions on travel and remittances to Cuba by Cuban-Americans) strike many Latin Americans as inconsequential, and puzzling in light of Obama's professed boldness.

In 2010, the Obama administration attempted to repair some of this damage and set the stage for better relations. Hillary Clinton made a high-profile trip to Uruguay, Argentina, Chile, Brazil, Costa Rica and Guatemala in March, while Assistant Secretary of State for Western Hemisphere Affairs Arturo Valenzuela and US Defense Secretary Robert Gates both visited the Andean region in April 2010. Clinton and Gates also travelled to Mexico in March 2010. Clinton again travelled to Latin America in June 2010 for the Organisation of American States (OAS) General Assembly meeting in Lima, after which she visited Ecuador, Colombia and Barbados. The Obama administration's notably swift and forceful response to the Haiti tragedy, and its proclaimed interest in working in concert with Latin American neighbours, helped the United States recover some lost ground.

Brazil and Mexico are seen by the Obama administration as vital to advancing US priorities in the region, and have received special focus. Brazil and the United States have a bilateral agenda that includes issues such as energy, climate change, non-proliferation and the Doha round of trade negotiations, and Washington has mostly refrained from publicly criticising Brasilia. The relentless crime and violence plaguing Mexico have deepened that country's ties with the United States, beyond the pre-existing broad bilateral agenda encompassing issues such as trade, immigration, drugs, human rights and the environment.

Brazil: the year of Lula

In the final full year of his second term as president, Lula forcefully asserted the role of Brazil on the international stage, continuing its evolution as a global player on issues ranging from climate change to managing Iran's nuclear ambitions. Lula was seemingly everywhere, a result of this push as well as a confluence of events that saw Rio de Janeiro win the 2016 Summer Olympics, Lula named global statesman of the year at the World Economic Forum in Davos, and Time magazine proclaiming him the most influential leader in the world.

Brazil used the increasing strength of its economy to secure recognition as an emerging global power. In June 2009, in the midst of the global economic crisis, it announced that, for the first time, it would lend money to the International Monetary Fund (IMF) with the purchase of $10 billion of bonds. With a population of nearly 200 million people, Brazil is the world's fourth-largest democracy, and had been seen for decades as a market with immense potential. Lula has sought to take advantage of this potential by increasing economic and political cooperation with other large countries including Russia, India and China, fellow members of the BRIC group of emerging nations. In April 2010, Lula hosted a two-day BRIC summit.

At the same time, Lula maintained his image as a man of the people. He was rapturously received at the left-leaning World Social Forum in January 2010, where he vowed to hold rich nations responsible for the excesses that contributed to the global financial crisis. Lula's balancing act was credible in part because of domestic progress. Inequality dropped 5.5% since the beginning of his first term in 2003, with an estimated 21m Brazilians reaching income levels above the poverty-line during that time. A $344bn long-term infrastructure programme, as well as increases in the minimum wage, pensions and family stipends, contributed to this growth and to his popularity. One aspect of the programme, Bolsa Familia, won acclaim for providing monthly stipends to low-income families who met conditions such as consistent school attendance by children.

Lula's popularity, however, did not necessarily extend to Brazilian political institutions generally. In mid-2009, opinion polls revealed that more than 50% of Brazilians favoured closing either or both houses of

Congress, reflecting anger over persistent accusations of corrupt dealings, including payoff scandals, against his Worker's Party. One poll showed that fewer than 3% of Brazilians trusted the country's legislators.

Frustration over the perceived impunity of politicians reached fever pitch in July 2009, when a Senate ethics committee stopped pursuing a corruption inquiry into Lula ally José Sarney, a former president of Brazil and the head of the Brazilian Senate. Sarney, who was accused of embezzlement and arranging lucrative jobs for friends and family members, denied the most serious of the allegations, and received support from Lula, who called the charges 'a fantasy'. Lula dropped his support as anger grew when it appeared an investigation would not be completed. The episode reinforced disenchantment with the political system and fuelled criticisms of what some viewed as Lula's permissive stand on corruption.

Winning the 2016 Summer Olympics was a major accomplishment. Brazil will be the first South American country to host the games. While the victory was heralded as a crowning achievement of Brazil's progress, it focused renewed attention on festering problems of violence and instability, especially in Rio itself. Widespread power outages shut airports and plunged whole neighbourhoods into darkness, affecting more than 60m people throughout the country in November and renewing questions about Brazil's capacity to host an event such as the Olympics. Less than two weeks after landing the games, a weekend battle between rival gangs in Rio's favelas (slums) claimed 33 lives and refocused attention on the battle against violent drug trafficking. After over 200 gang members attacked rivals in a favela in northern Rio, police descended on the neighbourhood. In the subsequent battle, gang members downed a police helicopter, killing three officers. Lula promised emergency funding to 'do anything it takes and make all necessary sacrifices so we can clean up the mess that [drug traffickers] are imposing on Brazil'.

The conduct of the police in Brazil's major cities came under increased scrutiny following a report published by Human Rights Watch in December 2009 that accused police officers of frequently executing suspects and covering up the killings as self-defence. The report examined cases in Rio and São Paulo where alleged criminals were reported killed when resisting arrest. The organisation found many discrepancies between police reports and forensic evidence, such as autopsies showing that people had been shot at point-blank range despite claims that those killed were felled by bullets during shoot-outs with the police. Drawing on government statistics, the report concluded that police had killed more than 11,000 people in São Paulo and Rio combined since 2003, the first full year of Lula's presidency, although it is impossible to tell how many of these may have been self-defence rather than extrajudicial killings.

On the international front, Brazil became embroiled in the fallout from the coup in Honduras. It initially joined with the rest of the region and world in denouncing the ouster of Zelaya. Lula condemned the coup in strong language, threatening Honduras with 'total isolation' should Zelaya not be returned to power. In September, with no resolution to the political crisis in sight, the Lula administration sought to use its regional clout by increasing pressure on both the de facto government of Honduras and other powers (such as the United States) to take more decisive action that could end the standoff. Brazil's demand that Zelaya be reinstated without conditions, however, gained little traction in the reconciliation talks headed by Costa Rican President Oscar Arias.

On 21 September, following reports that Zelaya had secretly returned to Honduras after three months in exile, the Brazilian embassy announced it was sheltering the ousted president in its offices in Tegucigalpa. The decision to give Zelaya refuge turned the focus of the entire region to Brazil, as a wall of Honduran troops surrounded the building and forcibly scattered the Zelaya supporters who had gathered to show their support. At the United Nations General Assembly, Lula demanded the immediate reinstatement of Zelaya and warned the de facto Honduran government not to enter the embassy. Zelaya remained sequestered in the embassy until January 2010, when he went into exile on the day his term was supposed to have ended. As of June 2010, Brazil still refused to recognise the Lobo government, and had deflected repeated attempts by the Obama administration aimed at changing this policy.

Equally controversial has been Lula's prominent reluctance to support sanctions against Iran. In 2010–11 Brazil is a non-permanent member of the current UN Security Council, making it an important participant in the debate over how to address Tehran's nuclear-arms programme.

During Ahmadinejad's visit to Brazil in November 2009, he received a warm welcome from Lula and the two leaders announced a series of bilateral accords on issues such as energy and agriculture. They highlighted the growing links between the countries: in Lula's presidency, annual trade doubled to nearly $2bn and Brazil's national oil company Petrobras began assisting Iran in developing its oil fields. Responding to pressure from the United States and other Security Council members to impose fresh sanctions on Iran, Lula urged continued diplomacy, arguing that Iran had a right to a non-military nuclear programme and that 'there's no point in leaving Iran isolated'. Lula visited Tehran in May 2010, and negotiated (along with Turkey) a potential deal for Iran to ship some of its nuclear fuel to Turkey for storage (see page 210).

> " The fuel-swap agreement did not prevent the sanctions "

Lula inserted Brazil into the ongoing international discussion of how to address Iran's nuclear programme, negotiating a fuel-swap deal with Ahmadinejad in May 2010. The agreement, reached with the help of Turkish Prime Minister Recep Tayyip Erdogan, called for Iran to deposit 1,200kg of low-enriched uranium (representing about half of its stock) in Turkey. In return, Iran would receive higher-enriched reactor fuel suitable for non-military uses. Given that Turkey also holds a temporary seat on the UN Security Council, Lula's push to negotiate with Iran was seen as having the potential to undermine the US campaign for sanctions. The fuel-swap agreement added further distance between Washington and Brasilia, but did not prevent the sanctions. The United States ultimately won approval of new sanctions, with only Brazil and Turkey voting against.

Lula's push to carve out a role for Brazil extended beyond the question of Iran. Under his stewardship, the country positioned itself as an outside arbiter capable of mediating international disputes in a fair, principled manner, although with mixed outcomes. The quest for peace in the Middle East was one of Lula's targets. In an attempt to project evenhandedness, he hosted Israeli President Shimon Peres and President of the Palestinian Authority Mahmoud Abbas in separate meetings during the weeks prior to Ahmadinejad's November visit. Then, in March 2010,

Lula embarked on a high-profile tour of Jerusalem and Palestine, visiting both the Yad Vashem Holocaust Memorial and the tomb of Yasser Arafat. He struck a conciliatory tone throughout, but did call for an end to Israeli settlement construction and Israeli army violence directed towards the civilian population in Gaza. As a result, Israeli Foreign Minister Avigdor Lieberman, a hardline member of the Netanyahu administration, boycotted Lula's speech to the Knesset.

Lula's efforts to establish a distinct identity for Brazilian diplomacy throughout the world required a delicate balance between assertiveness and partnership. Despite previously registering vocal criticisms of a military pact between Colombia and the United States, the Lula administration confirmed a US–Brazil defence agreement in mid-April 2010 that would involve joint training, military exchanges and logistical collaboration on anti-drug efforts. Unlike the Colombian agreement, the accord would not allow the US military to use Brazilian bases. Brazil previously announced a military cooperation deal with France in September 2009 that would exceed $12bn in purchases of military equipment and infrastructure.

Meanwhile, Brazil devoted time and political capital to managing relations with less-powerful neighbours. In July 2009, Lula came to an agreement with Paraguayan President Fernando Lugo to pay $240m a year (three times the previous amount) for electricity generated by the Itaipu dam on the border of the two countries. The Brazilian commitment to increase its payments was a sign that Lula favoured regional integration, and was willing to use Brazil's economic advantage to shore up a poorer, less stable neighbour.

With presidential elections scheduled for 3 October 2010, the race to succeed Lula, who has served the maximum permitted two terms, was in full swing for much of 2009 and 2010. The ruling Workers Party endorsed government chief minister Dilma Rousseff, a 62-year-old economist and former energy minister. Her main opponent was to be José Serra, the governor of the state of São Paulo since 2007. Serra, who lost the 2002 presidential election to Lula, initially led in most opinion polls, although by April 2010 the race appeared to be a dead heat, and in May Rousseff pulled ahead. Lula endorsed Rousseff and planned to campaign extensively on her behalf. Rousseff and Serra both promised to maintain

Lula's popular economic policies, but it remained to be seen how much Rousseff could benefit from her association with Lula.

Rousseff, Lula's cabinet chief, has little electoral experience and began the campaign without much voter recognition. As an acolyte of Lula, Rousseff was expected to favour more extensive government intervention than Serra, and she was likely to promise continued social spending. Serra, who officially began his campaign using the slogan 'Brazil can do better', was more sympathetic to privatisation, and was expected to highlight the need to improve Brazil's public infrastructure. Continuity with Lula on foreign policy was also expected, as both candidates would maintain support for UNASUR and connections with other BRIC countries. Rousseff would more strictly maintain Lula's core agenda and alliances, while Serra would be expected to take a more critical stance on countries like Venezuela, and especially Iran.

If no candidate were to win more than 50% of the vote, a runoff for the two top finishers would take place on 31 October.

Venezuela: Chávez confronts mounting challenges

With 30 seats up for election in critical National Assembly elections scheduled for 26 September 2010, Hugo Chávez and his United Socialist Party of Venezuela (PSUV) were confronted with some of the biggest challenges they had faced in his 12-year presidency. Skyrocketing criminality, high inflation, decaying infrastructure and prolonged electricity rationing disrupted Chávez's strong base among Venezuela's urban and rural poor, a segment of the electorate that had loyally supported Chávez in return for government subsidies and services. A fall in support for 'chavismo' resulted in a resurgent, more organised opposition looking to further undermine the Chávez administration's tight grip on power and diminish the president's personal standing.

Chávez had capably manoeuvred through previous challenges to his leadership, and despite a visible drop in support he remained Venezuela's most popular politician, with opinion polls finding his approval rating between 43% and 50%. The intersection of multiple problems, however, lent credence to past criticisms of Chávez's ambitious and often controversial agenda. It also diminished support for the PSUV, whose members did not retain the same levels of support as Chávez. The resulting vulnerability of the PSUV increased the stakes in the September elections, as Chávez's long-stymied political opposition saw an opportunity to shift the balance of power in Congress and to position itself to challenge the president himself in 2012.

Violent crime has soared during Chávez's tenure. Along with the economy, it was the principal concern for Venezuelans of all political and socio-economic backgrounds in the past year. There were 4,550 homicides in the country in 1999, Chávez's first year in office; in 2009, 16,047 murders were recorded. Caracas, the capital, has the highest murder rate in South America and one of the highest in the world. Of the homicides in 2009 that were prosecuted by the police, less than 5% resulted in conviction and sentencing. 'Express kidnappings', where victims are held for short periods while ransom money is gathered from ATMs and relatives, have become frequent in Caracas and other major cities. Chávez speculated that his political enemies were exaggerating the crime problem and blamed social issues such as unequal distribution of wealth for the rise. However, faced with a persistent public outcry over crime and corrupt law-enforcement practices (Interior Minister Tarek El Aissami publicly estimated that as much as 20% of crime was committed by the police), Chávez created a new national police force that was expected eventually to deploy 5,000 officers across the country.

Venezuela's economic outlook was equally challenging for Chávez, who depends on a robust economy to provide the public services that in turn generate support for the PSUV. In April 2010, the IMF reported that Venezuela was the only major Latin American economy that would shrink in 2010, with a predicted contraction of 2.6%. Venezuela entered a recession in 2009: the economy contracted by 3.3%, and a January 2010 devaluation of the Venezuelan bolivar focused renewed attention on the country's 25.1% inflation rate, the highest in Latin America. The devaluation set two government rates for the bolivar which are dependent on whether a transaction is classified a priority (such as food) or nonessential; it dropped the bolivar's value by 17% and 50%, respectively. The bolivar is also traded on a black market widely used throughout Venezuela, meaning that with the devaluation three tiers of exchanges existed for Venezuelans. While Chávez estimated inflation in 2010 would remain as high as 22%, many analysts predicted that the devaluation would drive it to 40%, even with government restrictions on vendors of non-essential items. Declining profits from oil sales also contributed to the economic slide.

Questions about Venezuela's financial stability were highlighted in November and December 2009 when then Finance Minister Ali Rodriguez Araque nationalised eight banks, raided stock brokerages and arrested ten top financial executives. Many of those arrested were Chávez loyalists whose business interests thrived in part due to close ties with the administration. Often referred to as 'boligarchs', a pejorative combination of 'oligarch' and the namesake of Chávez's socialist revolution, Simon Bolivar, these bankers' massive accumulation of wealth during Chávez's tenure was seen by many Venezuelans as antithetical to the president's staunch anti-capitalist rhetoric. Among those arrested were Ricardo Fernandez Barrueco, a billionaire majority shareholder in four of the nationalised banks; Antonio Marquez Sanchez, former president of the National Stock Exchange Commission; and Arne Chacon, a direc-

> **“Venezuelan bankers were often referred to as 'boligarchs'”**

tor at Banco Real and brother of a government minister who resigned soon after the arrest. Arrest warrants for 30 other executives thought to have fled Venezuela were also issued. The National Assembly passed a reform law to allow more state regulation of the banks in December 2009, and the following month the government seized three more banks, bringing about 25% of the industry under its control.

Venezuela's energy infrastructure also came under increased scrutiny as a worsening electricity crisis led to rolling blackouts and government-mandated energy rationing. Venezuela, the highest per capita consumer of power in Latin America, saw a 6% annual increase in power consumption over the past decade as a result of government subsidies. But the worst drought in 50 years led to historically low levels of water in the reservoirs that power the country's hydroelectric dams. The Chávez administration's responses to the overburdened power grid – rationing and blackouts – generated widespread criticism and focused attention on the scores of unrealised projects meant to improve Venezuela's energy capabilities. The Guri hydroelectric dam, for example, is counted on to generate almost 70% of the country's electricity while alternatives to hydroelectric power have seen little development since the energy sector was nationalised in 2007.

In January 2010 Chávez was forced to suspend rolling blackouts throughout Caracas after flawed implementation caused traffic-light malfunctions and darkened major avenues. Vacillating between underplaying the severity of the crisis and introducing major restrictions, he admonished Venezuelans to take three-minute showers, stating that 'three minutes is more than enough. I've counted, three minutes, and I don't stink.' By February 2010, however, the administration was taking a more active approach as blackouts continued: the hours of the official work day for government employees were cut; nationwide energy rationing was instituted, with allotments of electricity to shopping malls, businesses and large residential complexes reduced; state-run steel and aluminium plants were closed; and a $1bn National Electricity Fund was announced to pay for new energy projects.

The political fallout from the energy shortage, which Chávez declared a national emergency in February, was sufficiently damaging that Ali Rodriguez, now electricity minister, discussed purchasing power temporarily from Colombia, a country with which Venezuela has deeply troubled relations. Chávez speculated that the energy shortages were in part attributable to 'sabotage', and in April eight Colombians were arrested on suspicion of spying on Venezuela's electricity apparatus, although four were released for lack of evidence. Electricity rationing was again extended by 60 days in April 2010.

The rising perception of major crime and infrastructure problems was compounded by a tense political standoff between Chávez and the opposition. After boycotting the National Assembly elections in 2005, the opposition made advances in the 2008 regional elections and has since tried to capitalise on PSUV infighting and the resignations of key Chávez allies. Five ministers in the Chávez administration have resigned since December 2009: Science and Technology Minister Jesse Chacon; Electricity Minister Angel Rodriguez; Defense Minister and Vice-President Ramon Carrizalez; Environmental Minister Yubiri Ortega (the wife of Carrizalez); and Minister for Public Banking and President of the Bank of Venezuela Eugenio Vasquez Orellana. All cited personal or health reasons for leaving, but the rash of resignations led to speculation about disorder within the PSUV as other public figures connected to Chávez began to publicly question his administration. In January 2010 a group of former Chávez military colleagues led by former Foreign Affairs Minister Luis Alfonso Davila called on Chávez to resign. In February 2010, well-known Chávez ally Henri Falcon, the governor of Lara, quit the PSUV, citing lack of dialogue and direction. He joined Patria Para Todos, a party that typically voted with the PSUV but expressed criticism of Chávez. Following Falcon's defection, however, the PSUV broke the alliance.

Tensions continued to rise as Chávez attempted to reassert his ideological and revolutionary credentials, while the opposition tried to capitalise on the increased attention to the administration's weaknesses. In January 2010 the media regulatory board Comisión Nacional de Telecomunicaciones (CONATEL) blocked six cable-television channels for not playing government messages as required by the July 2009 extension of the Law on Social Responsibility in Radio and Television. Among those blocked was the nationally popular Radio Caracas Television (RCTV), known for broadcasting opposition views and for playing a major role in promoting anti-government protests following the 2002 coup that briefly removed Chávez from power.

In protests against the RCTV ruling across the country, two student protesters were killed and over 80 police officers were injured. Chávez further challenged critics with the closure of 33 independent radio stations and the detention of Guillermo Zuloaga, the president of Globovision TV, for comments he made about the 2002 coup. The arrest came a day after Oswaldo Alvarez Paz, the former state governor of Zulia, was jailed on charges of incitement, conspiracy and spreading false information for an interview he gave to the anti-Chávez Globovision, in which he claimed Chávez had made Venezuela a haven for criminal activity.

The closures and arrests increased international criticism of the Chávez administration for its treatment of political opposition. Such criticism had been stoked by a February report of the Organisation of American States' Inter-American Commission on Human Rights (IACHR) that said the government routinely violated human rights by punishing citizens for their political beliefs. While recognising improvement in economic rights and social advancement, the IACHR report noted high levels of violence, and maintained that the lack of independent media and courts had caused great limits on freedom of expression. Chávez called the report 'pure garbage' and categorised it as a US-led attempt to destabilise his administration.

Amidst the problems with infrastructure, the media, the economy and violence, Chávez made a foreign-policy push to develop bilateral relations with China and Russia. In April 2010, he secured a major victory when China agreed to lend Venezuela $20bn over ten years for infrastructure, agriculture and energy projects. In return, it received access to Venezuelan oil via a deal with the country's national oil company to explore the Orinoco oil belt, which could eventually produce 400,000 barrels a day. The agreement also included provisions to address Venezuela's immediate energy needs, with China providing technology, training and three new thermoelectric plants.

Venezuela also solidified ties with Russia during Russian Prime Minister Vladimir Putin's trip in early April 2010. The visit, more symbolic than substantive, underlined the growing partnership between Moscow and Caracas and followed a September 2009 deal with Russian oil companies worth more than $20bn. The two countries announced the creation of a bilateral atomic-energy commission in September to potentially assist Venezuela in developing a nuclear-energy programme. Chávez has visited Russia eight times since taking office and Putin has predicted Venezuela's arms purchases may total $5bn. In 2009 only three countries bought more weapons from Russia. Among Venezuela's purchases were tanks, anti-aircraft missile systems, helicopters and over 100,000 Kalashnikov assault rifles.

Chávez continued his engagement with Iran while strengthening his personal alliance with Ahmadinejad. The Venezuelan president made his eighth official visit to Iran in September 2009, when he agreed to raise fuel exports to counteract international sanctions against energy imports that had hurt Tehran's fuel supplies. During the visit, the two presidents announced that each country would invest $760m in the other's energy sectors. Chávez later announced that Iran would help Venezuela process its vast unexplored uranium deposits. During Ahmadinejad's November 2009 visit to Venezuela, a joint development fund was inaugurated.

Chávez has become the principal point of entry to Latin America for the Ahmadinejad regime, as he has seemingly facilitated Iranian visits and incipient economic relationships with ALBA members such as Nicaragua, Bolivia and Ecuador. Much about the relationship between the two countries, however, remains unknown; their alliance is primarily based upon antagonising the US, a country both presidents have identified as a common enemy.

Colombia: controversy in Uribe's final year

Colombia's Constitutional Court ruled that a referendum allowing President Alvaro Uribe to run for a third consecutive term was unconstitutional, setting the stage for a closely watched battle to succeed the popular two-term president. After an abbreviated campaign, former Defence Minister Juan Manuel Santos won a landslide victory, largely because Colombians trusted him to continue to aggressively tackle the country's security concerns. Even with Uribe's considerable success on this front, Santos looked to be tested by the same pressing issues that dominated the final year of Uribe's presidency, including relations with neighbours such as Venezuela, the influence of narcotrafficking, and the persistent strength of the country's domestic insurgency.

The often tense relationship between Colombia and Venezuela escalated repeatedly throughout 2009. In July, Colombia announced that it had recovered anti-tank weaponry that Sweden had originally sold to the Venezuelan government in the 1980s from a Revolutionary Armed Forces of Colombia (FARC) camp. This discovery gave weight to Colombian suspicions that Venezuela had been providing assistance to FARC, an accusation that Chávez had long denied. In response to Colombia's implicit linking of FARC and Venezuela, Chávez abruptly recalled his ambassador from Bogotá and threatened to end the trade relationship between the countries, estimated to be worth over $6bn a year.

Relations deteriorated further when news of a military cooperation pact between the United States and Colombia was leaked to the Colombian press in August 2009. The US–Colombia Defense Cooperation Agreement, signed in October, granted the United States access over ten years to seven Colombian bases to combat drug trafficking and help fight Colombia's internal insurgency. The accord essentially maintained the previous US policy laid out under Plan Colombia, the counter-narcotics campaign funded by Washington beginning in 2000 that has since sent over $6bn in aid to Colombia. Under the agreement, US military personnel stationed at the bases and civilian contractors permitted in Colombia were capped at 800 and 600 respectively.

The agreement revived suspicions in South America about US military motives in the region. Chávez strenuously criticised Colombia and the United States, calling the base deal 'a threat against [Venezuela]' and repeatedly claiming that it was a precursor to a US invasion of his country. The deal was also criticised by the more moderate leaders of Brazil, Argentina and Chile, as well as the leaders of ALBA countries such as Nicaragua, Bolivia and Ecuador. In response to the growing furore, Uribe embarked on a seven-country visit to explain the rationale for the deal and calm concerns about the influence of the American military throughout the region.

The agreement caused the already tenuous relationship between Uribe and Chávez to deteriorate quickly. In advance of a 28 August special meeting of UNASUR to discuss the deal, Chávez obliquely warned that it had provoked 'the winds of war'. The meeting, attended by the 12 South American heads of state, featured a contentious debate over the implications of the accord. Uribe argued that it was Colombia's sovereign right to have agreements with the United States to fight drugs and terrorism, while Chávez insisted that a growing US military presence would threaten regional peace. Lula helped calm the tensions, but relations continued to worsen.

A series of incidents along the Colombia–Venezuela border in the final months of 2009 raised tensions to their highest levels in years. Eight members of a Colombian amateur soccer club were kidnapped and later shot dead in the Venezuelan state of Tachira, which borders Colombia. The Venezuelan government denied knowledge of the assailants but accused the Colombians of being paramilitaries, while the governor of the state speculated that a Colombian terrorist organisation was responsible. Later, eight Colombians were arrested in Tachira after Venezuelan authorities accused them of being paramilitaries and attempting to intimidate the local population. In November four unidentified men killed two Venezuelan National Guard troops stationed at a checkpoint entrance to Tachira, and Colombia briefly arrested four other National Guard troops who allegedly entered Colombian territory by boat. The border incidents led the Chávez administration to close some border crossings, deploy thousands of additional troops to western Venezuela, and warn that the Venezuelan army must be ready to go to war with Colombia. Venezuelan troops destroyed several makeshift bridges between Colombia and Venezuela used by citizens of the border towns.

Colombia refused to attend a UNASUR meeting called for late November to address the rising tensions. In February 2010, the two presidents argued openly at a summit of Latin American leaders, with Chávez allegedly telling Uribe to 'go to hell' after Uribe yelled at him to 'be a man'.

> "Chávez told Uribe to 'go to hell' after Uribe yelled at him to 'be a man'"

In addition to the bitter relationship with Venezuela, Uribe has been challenged by internal security concerns after years of notable improvement and apparent weakening of FARC. The Colombian military aggressively pursued FARC and carried out a number of attacks on the group over the past year. In December 2009 FARC and the National Liberation Army (ELN) issued a statement threatening to join forces against the Colombian government after decades of waging separate battles due to ideological differences. The announcement underscored that it had become increasingly hard for both groups to maintain their operations in the face of the Colombian counter-insurgency efforts.

At the same time, FARC mounted a series of attacks that reminded Colombians of its ability to strike at the heart of the country's institutions. Nine Colombian soldiers were killed in a FARC ambush in November 2009 as they attempted to prevent the insurgents from taking a town in the southwestern state of Cauca. In December, Luis Francisco Cuellar, governor of Caqueta state in the Colombian Amazon, was kidnapped in a brazen operation by FARC operatives and later found shot to death. Dressed in Colombian army uniforms, FARC members entered Cuellar's home and killed a guard before forcing the governor into a car. His body was found in a remote area, surrounded by explosives.

On New Year's Eve, the Colombian army responded with an attack on a FARC camp, killing 18 rebels and arresting another 13. In February, however, FARC killed five people in an unsuccessful attempt to kidnap José Alberto Perez, a gubernatorial candidate in Guaviare state. In March, a car bomb exploded in front of the attorney-general's office in the port city of Buenaventura, killing nine people and injuring 59 others. Though the attack was not necessarily the work of FARC, it seemed to suggest a worsening security situation in Colombia coming on the heels of the previous attacks against Cuellar and Pérez.

Amid these high-profile attacks, the durability of Uribe's 'Democratic Security' strategy came into question due to the conduct of the principal groups and agencies charged with carrying it out. In September 2009 Uribe was forced to dismantle the Department of Administrative Security (DAS) following accusations that DAS officials had used the agency's spying capabilities to illegally wiretap Colombians. DAS, which functioned in both a counter-intelligence and domestic security capacity, was long a source of controversy within Colombia; two of its last four directors have been investigated in abuse-of-power scandals.

The wiretapping controversy, however, appeared to indicate widespread wrongdoing within the agency, with 18 current and former officials said to be under investigation for illegal spying. Among those alleged to have been secretly monitored were reporters critical of the government, human-rights activists and Supreme Court justices. Former DAS officials were accused of providing information to Colombian paramilitary groups in exchange for bribes. Uribe, who had advocated reform of the agency, responded to the new accusations by calling for its abolition and the development of a new, more transparent body.

Although Uribe was not directly implicated in the scandal, the targets of the wiretapping and concurrent investigations of connections between Uribe's political patrons and illegal paramilitary groups created a cloud of suspicion around the president's administration. Concerns about the environment fostered by Uribe's aggressive security plans became more prevalent after the 'false positives' scandal, in which Colombian soldiers were accused of killing 11 youths from Soacha in 2008 and then attempting to pass them off as dead guerrillas gunned down in combat. The original accusations jump-started a national examination of similar extrajudicial killings thought to number in the thousands, leading to the investigation of over 1,200 Colombian soldiers.

These investigations, closely followed in Colombia, have been hampered by legal technicalities, with almost 40 suspects in the Soacha case being released by judges because they had not been brought to trial within the statute of limitations. Uribe, however, repeatedly promised full support for the investigations.

While these scandals and investigations tarnished his administration to a certain extent, Uribe remained an immensely popular president and all polling indicated that if he were allowed to run for a third term he would easily win. This appeared to be his intention, but would have required a national referendum to modify the constitution to allow a president to run for re-election two times in a row. The legal process to amend the constitution began in August 2009, about eight months before the scheduled elections, when the Senate and House approved a bill that called for the referendum. Uribe signed it in September, automatically sending it to Colombia's Constitutional Court for review. On 26 February, the court ruled 7–2 against the bid. Concerns had been raised about the impact that changing the constitution would have on Colombia's democratic institutions, especially given that Uribe had already successfully amended the constitution in 2006 so that he could run for a second term. The court cited this issue in the ruling, saying that the amendment would amount to 'substantial violations to democratic principles' and that the legislative approval process had been marred by irregularities.

The decision initiated a frenzied three-month presidential campaign featuring candidates from all of Colombia's political parties. By May 2010 the race had narrowed to a fight between presumed frontrunner Juan Manuel Santos, Uribe's former defence minister, and former Bogotá Mayor Antanas Mockus, who surged from single-digit support in February to a virtual tie with Santos. However, Santos won the first round by a wide margin with 46.6% of the vote, followed by Mockus with 21.5%. Mockus' poor showing put a major dent in his momentum, and Santos went on to win the 20 June run-off by a landslide with 69% of the vote. Santos, who is expected largely to continue Uribe's policies, said he would seek to enhance Colombia's partnership with the United States and continue to fight against Colombia's internal armed insurgency. At the same time, Santos will have to define himself apart from Uribe, both to ensure sustained domestic support and to placate regional partners wary of the foreign policy pursued by Uribe that has left Colombia politically isolated on security issues.

Chile's new government

Chileans ended two decades of rule by the centre-left Concertación, a coalition of Socialists and Christian Democrats, electing billionaire businessman Sebastian Piñera as president with 52% of the vote in a run-off election on 17 January 2010. Piñera, who ran on a platform of creating jobs and strengthening the country's economy, defeated former President Eduardo Frei by four percentage points. Despite being the first right-wing candidate to be democratically elected in Chile in over 50 years, Piñera promised to strengthen the social programmes for women and children championed by his popular predecessor Michelle Bachelet. He portrayed himself as a pragmatic reformer who could rejuvenate Chile's economy following the global recession and create one million new jobs by increasing investments and instituting efficient government management. His government, however, lacks a majority in Congress, making collaboration with Concertación necessary to enact major legislation.

Bachelet's popularity, which hovered close to 80% during her final months in office, did not easily transfer to Frei, whose attempt to reclaim the presidency seemed to highlight the lack of new ideas and faces being presented by the Concertación. A third candidate, Socialist congressman Marco Enríquez-Ominami, challenged Frei for the second spot but ultimately finished third despite galvanising support from Chileans (especially the young) disappointed with the mainstream candidates. Chile's constitution prohibits consecutive terms for presidents, so a Bachelet candidacy in 2014 is possible.

Preparations for the handover of power on 11 March were disrupted on 27 February by a magnitude 8.8 earthquake. The temblor was the biggest to hit Chile since 1960 and the world's fifth largest since 1900. It damaged over 500,000 homes, demolished freeways and sent destructive tsunamis towards the southern coastline. The quake killed 521 people, 87 of whom were in Constitución, a coastal town hit by the tsunamis. Twenty-two people died in the capital Santiago. The government estimated the cost of the damage at $30bn.

Bachelet declared a state of emergency in the hardest-hit central and southern areas of the country, which allowed the military to take control of disaster-relief operations. She faced criticism, however, for waiting almost two days to designate the 'catastrophe areas', with some charging that she wavered when faced with deploying the military in cities for the first time since the Pinochet era. The government faced accusations that distribution of food aid was slow and restoration of order took too long following reports of looting and other crime. Santiago, for example, sustained little damage in comparison to coastal towns and cities like Concepcion, but a poll in *El Mercurio* newspaper found that 72% of the city's residents saw government efforts to restore order as coming too late. Past experience and earthquake-conscious building codes left Chile relatively prepared to handle the devastation, although the aftermath of the earthquake posed challenges for the new government. An estimated 200,000 families were left homeless in the days following the earthquake, and over 800,000 schoolchildren were temporarily unable to return to school.

The loss of infrastructure and productivity tempered Chile's predicted economic growth following a contraction of 1.5% in 2009, causing the country's central bank to reduce the 2010 growth forecast while raising the possibility of inflation. The earthquake was blamed for the sharpest economic contraction in 14 years, with the central bank reporting that economic activity declined 6.6% in March from the previous month. However, reconstruction efforts were expected to stimulate spending and job creation, and the government forecast that the economy would continue to grow 6% annually over the next four years. Chile was invited to join the Organisation for Economic Cooperation and Development (OECD), becoming the first South American country to do so.

Relations with other South American countries remained mostly cordial over the past year. The Chilean Air Force hosted a major joint military exercise with Argentina, the United States, Brazil and France. Foreign Minister Mariano Fernandez announced that Chile would publish a list of all its military purchases to encourage transparency in the region following worries that weapons acquisitions throughout the continent were fuelling a minor arms race.

Chile and Peru were involved in a tense dispute over allegations of espionage that turned publicly bitter. Peru arrested an officer in its Air

Force in November 2009 on suspicion of spying for Chile and accused Chilean military officers of being involved in the alleged spy ring. Peruvian President Alan García cancelled a trip to a summit in Singapore where he was scheduled to meet with Bachelet and called for the Chilean president to respond to the allegations of what he called 'repulsive acts'. Bachelet denied any Chilean involvement and called García's accusations 'offensive and haughty'.

Bachelet used her final year in office to address long-standing problems with Chile's National Indigenous Development Board (CONADI), tasked with managing indigenous issues. The government agency had been faulted for its bureaucracy and politicisation. Governmental conflicts with indigenous citizens have not been as prominent in Chile as other South American countries, but a series of confrontations that turned violent in July and August 2009 added increased urgency to reforming CONADI. While only 4.6% of Chileans are indigenous according to the 2002 census, the country's largest indigenous community, the Mapuche, has higher levels of poverty and health problems, and lower levels of representation, than the population at large. In addition, the illegal appropriation of Mapuche land has been well documented by the Chilean government, which began efforts to return parts of the land in the early 1990s.

The Mapuche community, dissatisfied with the progress of this reimbursement, increasingly turned to protests to press claims to the land. The protests turned violent in August 2009, following a series of land occupations in the southern Araucanía region. One Mapuche was killed and others injured when government forces removed the protesters from the land in August 2009. In October, Bachelet announced the creation of a Ministry for Indigenous Affairs to replace CONADI, with the aim of directing more political resources towards implementing policies beneficial to indigenous citizens. Piñera stated his support for the new ministry.

Bolivia: Morales wins decisive victory

Bolivian President Evo Morales easily won re-election to a second term in December 2009 with over 63% of the vote, furthering his mandate to implement pending elements of the country's new constitution. Resistance to Morales's self-proclaimed 'revolutionary' agenda from opposition forces concentrated in Bolivia's eastern Media Luna region was strong throughout the president's first term, but the landslide victory revealed an increase in support for Morales since the 2005 election. His party Movimiento al Socialismo (MAS) won a significant majority in the Bolivian legislature: 26 out of 36 seats in the Senate and 89 of 130 seats in the Chamber of Deputies. This two-thirds majority was lacking in Morales's previous term, when the MAS was the minority party in the Senate and thus had to compromise on or discard key legislative priorities.

The MAS exercised its new majority in February 2010 with the passage of a law in the Senate that granted Morales the power to make interim appointments to high levels of the Bolivian judiciary without legislative approval. The law, called the Ley Corta, allows Morales to appoint judges to empty seats on the Supreme and Constitutional Courts. The judges will then face a nationwide vote in December 2010. The law was decried by the opposition, which argued that it violated the independence of the judiciary. The MAS countered that it was a short-term fix needed to fill empty court posts that Morales had been blocked from filling by opposition in the Senate throughout his first term.

Morales's electoral win left Bolivia's main opposition parties without a clear path forward as they remained divided over tactics and without a unifying leader. Manfred Reyes Villa, who finished a distant second behind Morales, fled to the United States following the election to escape charges of fraud that he claimed were politically motivated.

Morales made major changes to his 20-member cabinet, allowing only six ministers to maintain their previous positions. He appointed an equal number of men and women, to demonstrate the equal-opportunity demands of the new constitution, but he was criticised by prominent indigenous leaders who felt that the six indigenous cabinet members did not adequately represent Bolivia's majority-indigenous population. The government's key priorities were to be judicial reform, land redistribution and the extension of social programmes.

Morales faced another electoral test during departmental and local elections held in April 2010. Despite its strong showing in December, the MAS made only modest gains, winning governorships in the important states of La Paz, Cochabamba and Pando but losing in Tarija, Beni and the opposition stronghold of Santa Cruz. The governors' races were important because Morales's social programmes depended on cooperation in recouping natural-gas royalties from state governments. The MAS also performed unevenly in mayoral races, winning in only two of the nine state capitals. The opposition portrayed their victories as integral to defending regional autonomy in the face of Morales's attempts to reform Bolivian society.

Morales has pursued an assertive foreign-policy stance that attempts to balance his long-standing distrust of capitalism with the requirements of improving Bolivia's infrastructure and economic capabilities. He has struck a consistently negative tone towards the Obama administration. Bolivia and the United States have not had ambassadors in each other's countries since Morales expelled US Ambassador Philip Goldberg in 2008 for allegedly assisting opposition groups. The Obama administration suspended trade benefits to Bolivia in July 2009 to punish what it perceived as a lacklustre effort to fight drug trafficking, leading Morales to refer to Obama as a liar for pledging to treat Latin American countries as equal partners. Counter-narcotics has remained a major bone of contention. In September 2009 the United States again criticised Bolivia for its anti-drug efforts, writing in an annual report that (along with Venezuela's and Myanmar's) Morales's counter-narcotics policy had 'failed demonstrably'. By early 2010 the final remaining US Drug Enforcement Administration (DEA) agents had left Bolivia, almost two years after Morales first demanded the DEA cease operations during his dispute with Goldberg. The Bolivian government also demanded that the US Embassy close various democracy-promotion programmes, citing suspicions that money was being diverted to opposition groups.

Amidst this testy relationship with the United States, Bolivia and China signed an agreement for collaboration on construction of a $300m communications satellite intended to link remote areas of Bolivia to better technology as a means of spurring development. Morales purchased six Chinese military aircraft for anti-narcotics efforts at a cost of $58m. In March 2010, China committed a loan of $67m for building mineral-extraction infrastructure in the Oruro region on top of a $60m loan to buy natural-gas drilling rigs. Russia also agreed to lend Bolivia $100m for the purchase of Russian helicopters to help battle drug traffickers.

Iranian President Ahmadinejad visited La Paz for the second time in November 2009, and signed an agreement to assist Bolivia's development of lithium-extraction infrastructure. Morales told him that his country, like Bolivia, had a 'mandate to liberate ourselves from the empires'. Morales received further infrastructure support in December from Spanish oil conglomerate Repsol, which pledged $1.5bn to improve Bolivia's natural-gas output. The Morales administration has also announced plans to invest up to $400m in developing lithium infrastructure in the Uyuni region, which contains one of the world's largest lithium deposits.

Honduras: trying to go beyond the crisis

A coup d'état on 28 June 2009 ousted Honduran President Manuel Zelaya, sending him into forced exile and throwing the country into a months-long political crisis. From the time of the coup until January 2010, Honduras was ruled by the constitutional successor to Zelaya, the former Speaker of Congress Roberto Micheletti. Porfirio Lobo was elected president of Honduras in elections held on 29 November and inaugurated on 27 January.

Although Lobo's election was thought to have ended the crisis, a number of Latin American countries, including Brazil, Argentina and Venezuela, refused to recognise him because the government that organised the November election came to power illegally. The coup and resulting political crisis cost the Honduran government, according to the Business Council of Latin America in Honduras, over $200m in lost investment and led to the country's suspension from the Organisation of American States (OAS). Many questions remain about the events that preceded and followed Zelaya's exile. The establishment of a truth commission to analyse the political crisis was part of a US-brokered agreement between Zelaya and Micheletti, and was formally inaugurated in May 2010. Its findings were expected to be released by January 2011.

Zelaya had been elected president in 2005 and took office in January 2006. Although he ran as a centrist politician who promised to improve security and reduce poverty, his politics took a more radical turn as his term progressed. In 2009, he announced a plan to convoke a Constituent Assembly for the purpose of rewriting the constitution. His motives were unclear, but many analysts interpreted the proposed assembly as a first step towards removing the constitutional limit on presidents of a single term. Zelaya was thought to be moving in this direction in part because of his burgeoning alliance with Venezuelan President Chávez and ALBA, which Honduras joined in 2008. Restrictions on term limits had been changed or removed by other ALBA members, including Ecuador, Bolivia and Venezuela, as well as by non-ALBA members. The Honduran constitution had been amended over 25 times since its approval in 1982.

Zelaya's attempts to establish a Constituent Assembly generated opposition throughout Honduras's legislative and judicial branches, and the president's persistence directly precipitated the coup: he had proposed that a non-binding poll be held on 28 June to survey the public about whether they wanted the option of voting for a Constituent Assembly during the November 2009 elections.

The Supreme Electoral Tribunal and the National Attorney General's Office both ruled the 28 June referendum unconstitutional and illegal. Zelaya also faced opposition from major political parties and the Congress, which passed a law prohibiting him from carrying out the poll. After facing stiff resistance from the military, which supervises electoral logistics, Zelaya attempted to fire the head of the military command and bring the poll ballots under the control of the executive branch to ensure the military would not destroy them. Two days before the scheduled poll, the Supreme Court issued a secret warrant for Zelaya's arrest to prevent it from taking place.

On 28 June, soldiers stormed the presidential palace and Zelaya was taken at gunpoint from his bed and forced onto a plane, which took him to San Jose, Costa Rica. On the same day, the Congress voted to remove him from office, and Micheletti became de facto president, charged with completing the remainder of Zelaya's term.

The coup was widely condemned, and thousands of people protested in front of the presidential palace. Electricity was shut down throughout the city, soldiers massed in front of government buildings and tanks patrolled the streets. The OAS issued a 72-hour ultimatum for the return of Zelaya to power, and OAS Secretary-General José Miguel Insulza travelled to Honduras in an attempt to persuade the government to accept the demand. Micheletti refused, and the country's membership in the OAS was suspended, only the second time such an action had been taken in the organisation's history (Cuba in 1962 was the first). Zelaya attempted to return to Tegucigalpa airport on 5 July in a plane also carrying Insulza and several Latin American presidents, but the Honduran army blocked the runway and he was unable to land.

In the weeks following the coup, Zelaya retained the public support of every Latin American government. The coup particularly touched a nerve in those Latin American countries that have suffered from military rule in the past and have struggled to keep the armed forces under civilian control. Ambassadors from most countries were recalled from the country, organisations such as the World Bank suspended aid, and the international community worked to isolate the Micheletti administration in hopes of forcing the de facto government to the negotiating table. No country officially recognised the Micheletti government.

Costa Rican President Oscar Arias attempted to broker a solution between Zelaya and the de facto government. Arias proposed a seven-point plan that would reinstate Zelaya and offer amnesty to all parties involved in the coup. He floated the idea of holding early elections and creating a power-sharing plan for a provisional government in which Zelaya would retain the presidency until the end of his term in January 2010. A stalemate ensued in international negotiations, while large protests both for and against Zelaya continued. On 21 September, it emerged that Zelaya had entered the country and taken refuge in the Brazilian Embassy. He demanded to meet representatives of the de facto government to end the impasse. Honduran soldiers encircled the embassy, trapping Zelaya, his wife and a small group of supporters inside.

In October 2009, with the presidential elections approaching and the two sides still unable to reach an agreement, a US-brokered deal under which the decision on whether to restore Zelaya as president was left to the Honduran Congress was signed by Zelaya and Micheletti. Washington agreed to recognise the results of the November elections. Although the accord opened the possibility of Zelaya's return, it did not guarantee his restoration. Zelaya stated that he was 'satisfied' with it. Within a week, however, he was calling it 'dead'. It did not specify a deadline for Congress to vote on whether to restore him, allowing his opponents to delay the vote indefinitely. In addition, the agreement mandated that Micheletti announce a unity government to govern until the inauguration of the new president. Micheletti did, but without Zelaya's collaboration, rendering the principle of a unity government moot. The Congress ultimately voted against Zelaya's restitution by a vote of 62 to 8.

Porfirio Lobo of the conservative National Party won the 29 November elections with 56% of the vote, with turnout just below 50%. Zelaya remained at the Brazilian Embassy until 27 January, the day of Lobo's inauguration. Lobo himself escorted Zelaya to the airport, where the former president proclaimed that he would return before flying to the Dominican Republic.

Lobo faced the task of restoring Honduras's international standing and regaining recognition by countries in the region that have important ties with Honduras. The Supreme Court found six generals who had ordered soldiers to remove Zelaya from the presidential palace innocent of abuses of power, and Congress approved an amnesty for all military participants in the coup, as well as Zelaya. The United States resumed aid and the World Bank resumed assistance programmes. By the end of February, some Central American countries, along with Peru and Colombia, had recognised Lobo's election. Brazil, Venezuela, Argentina, Chile, Bolivia and Ecuador, however, continued to see the election as illegitimate and forced Lobo to withdraw from an international conference in Spain in May 2010 by threatening a boycott.

Under Lobo, Honduras faced continued challenges exacerbated by persistent anger over Zelaya's forced removal and the heavy hand of the de facto government. Increased drug trafficking and violence were reported in the wake of the instability caused by the political crisis. In April 2010 Reporters Without Borders named Honduras the most dangerous country in the world to be a journalist, alleging that over 20 reporters had been killed since the coup.

Haiti: earthquake and aftermath

The most powerful earthquake to hit Latin America's poorest country in a century struck on 12 January 2010, killing an estimated 230,000 people, injuring 300,000 more, and leaving over a million Haitians homeless. The

7.0 magnitude quake was centred about 10 miles southwest of Port-au-Prince, the capital. Two aftershocks measured 5.9 and 5.5. The damage to the capital and surrounding area was immense: more than 250,000 homes and 30,000 commercial buildings were destroyed, causing billions of dollars in damage. The earthquake obliterated many of the country's key institutions, severely complicating relief efforts and killing scores of senior government officials. Among the buildings destroyed were the presidential palace, the headquarters of the UN peacekeeping mission, and the National Assembly. The buildings housing 13 of Haiti's 15 ministries collapsed, and the city's main jail was destroyed, allowing its 4,000 prisoners to escape.

President Rene Préval survived the quake, although his control over the country was tenuous at best in the hectic weeks that followed. Préval and his cabinet worked out of the police headquarters as they attempted to respond to the disaster. Many organisations, including the UN and the US government, took part in relief efforts to rescue trapped Haitians and distribute aid. Operations were severely hampered by widespread destruction of infrastructure and institutions responsible for assisting in emergencies. Despite a global commitment to assisting in relief efforts, the poor state of the airport and seaport delayed the arrival of personnel and materials. Préval ceded control of the airport to the United States, which repaired a runway and began to speed up flight operations.

Relief operations managed to rescue some Haitians trapped in fallen buildings, and medical personnel from around the world arrived to treat the injured. Sporadic violence was reported throughout the city, which had been plagued by gang warfare for years, but the majority of incidents stemmed from Haitians desperate for medical attention and food aid. Food-relief trucks were overwhelmed by hungry people. The United States dispatched of thousands of marines to assist in rescue operations and maintain order in the chaotic capital. At the peak, the United States had deployed almost 22,000 military personnel to the country, with 7,000 troops in Port-au-Prince and the rest on ships offshore. Washington withdrew the last of its troops in June 2010, although 500 National Guardsmen will remain to assist with humanitarian aid work.

Préval indefinitely postponed legislative elections scheduled for 28 February, but presidential elections scheduled for November 2010 were expected to go ahead. Préval's five-year term ends in February 2011, and he is constitutionally barred from seeking re-election. In May 2010, however, he announced that he intended to extend his term by three months if elections were not held before the end of November, to ensure a smooth transfer of power. This announcement was strongly condemned by the political opposition, which promised a Supreme Court challenge to any extension of his term. The conduct of elections will be complicated by to the destruction of polling places, as well as the displacement of hundreds of thousands of voters.

The Dominican Republic, which shares the island with Haiti, played a major role in assisting relief efforts despite historically strained ties between the two nations. Due to the diminished capabilities of Port-au-Prince's airport and seaport, the Dominican Republic functioned as one of the principal entry points for relief workers, and President Leonel Fernández facilitated the use of Santo Domingo, the capital, for coordinating aid efforts.

A 30 March UN donor conference secured aid pledges of $9.9bn from over 130 countries, of which $5.3bn was due to be delivered within two years to support construction of infrastructure such as schools and hospitals. The European Union pledged $1.7bn and the United States $1.15bn. Préval appointed a commission to oversee the aid, co-chaired by Haitian Prime Minister Jean-Max Bellerive and former US President Bill Clinton.

Mexico: how to stop the drug-fuelled violence?

On 9 January 2010, Mexico recorded 69 murders in one day, setting another gruesome record in the country's three-year battle with violent drug cartels. The figure underscored the mayhem confronted by Mexicans on a daily basis. Violence and intimidation rose after President Felipe Calderón declared war on the cartels, with more than 6,500 people dying in drug-related killings in 2009, a record that looked likely to be broken again in 2010.

The violence was mostly between cartels, but also involved the security forces and ordinary civilians. It traumatised the country and put into question the government's ability to maintain order. Despite the capture and killings of key cartel leaders in the past year, there was increased concern that Calderón's strategy was not working and could in fact be counter-productive. Major cities such as Ciudad Juárez became virtual war zones, while the instability of cartels targeted by the security forces led to devastating battles for supremacy and the prime drug routes, frequently causing the deaths of innocent bystanders.

Reports of fights over territory and spiralling revenge killings dominated the Mexican media for much of the past year. In July 2009, 12 people were found on the side of a road in the western state of Michoacan, Calderon's home state, after being tortured to death. The president had sent 6,500 federal troops and police to Michoacan as part of his opening salvo against the cartels in 2006, and it remained a centre of drug trafficking. Also in July, gunmen suspected of having loyalties to the La Familia cartel killed 16 federal police officers, five local police officers and two soldiers in an assault on law enforcement throughout the state. Some of the attacks were thought to be reprisals for the arrest of Arnoldo Rueda Medina, a leader of the cartel. Federal police had also jailed eight mayors of towns in Michoacan in May 2009, after accusing them of allowing La Familia members to operate without interference from local authorities. In response, Calderón ordered 5,500 soldiers and police to the state. Over 1,000 troops had already been deployed there in previous months. Despite criticism of the use of the army in fighting drug trafficking, Calderón has sent over 50,000 troops and federal police to trafficking strongholds like Michoacan state and Ciudad Juárez since the war began.

The government pursued innovative measures to curtail the seemingly unabated influence of the cartels. In August 2009 it fired 700 customs agents from airports and borders, and replaced them with more than 1,400 new agents who received special training in detecting weapons and drug smuggling. They were required to pass psychological evaluations and drug tests, and unlike the previous agents were not eligible if they had criminal records. The government meanwhile decriminalised the possession of small amounts of marijuana, cocaine, heroin, LSD and methamphetamines for 'personal use'.

Calderón also sought to fortify the anti-drug alliance with the United States, the main consumer of drugs trafficked through Mexico. The key component of this alliance is the three-year, $1.4bn Merida Initiative, started under the George W. Bush administration to train and equip

Mexican law-enforcement agencies. Obama continued to back the programme, and reiterated US support for Calderón's aggressive fight. The
full disbursement of the Merida funds was delayed by the US Senate,
however, following concerns about human-rights abuses perpetrated by
the Mexican army in its persecution of the drug war. The withheld funds,
totalling $214m, were released in September 2009. However, Secretary of
State Hillary Clinton sought to direct the Merida funds more towards
community-building and less towards military purchases, because of a
perception that the aggressive deployment of the Mexican military was
not addressing the needs of affected communities, and had in some ways
exacerbated the violence.

In December 2009 the Mexican authorities tracked one of the country's most wanted cartel leaders, Arturo Beltrán Leyva, to an apartment
in the city of Cuernavaca, where he was killed during a battle with 400
special-forces troops. Hours after the funeral of the only soldier killed
in the shootout, however, gang members killed four people at his home.
Such murders underscored the capacity of the cartels to intimidate the
populace and reduced the perception of progress. In January 2010 the
authorities captured Teodoro Garcia Simental, a drug kingpin infamous
for having members of rival cartels tortured and dissolved in acid. His
cartel was thought to be behind a rash of violence in the border city of
Tijuana. In the same month, however, suspected cartel members killed 13
high school students, with no known ties to drug gangs, as they attended
a party in Ciudad Juárez. By the end of January, the army announced
that it would cede control of Ciudad Juárez to the federal police. The
government was forced to admit that militarisation of the city had not
produced the intended results. Despite the shift in strategy, however,
Ciudad Juárez remained problematic for Calderón as he tried to convince
Mexicans that the drug war can be won. In March 2010 a US consulate
employee and her husband were killed by gunmen while driving near
the bridge that connects the city to El Paso.

The demands of fighting the drug war reduced attention to other
areas of Calderón's agenda, which included reforming Mexico's tax
system, labour regulations and energy sector. Calderón and his National
Action Party (PAN) faced strong opposition to many proposals from
the Institutional Revolutionary Party (PRI), which wielded power for 70

years until losing the presidency in 2000. Calderón has not had a majority in Congress since winning the presidency in 2006. The PAN's standing was further diminished following the July 2009 midterm congressional elections, where it lost close to 50 seats and saw the PRI win 100.

Implications of a transformed region

The days in which Latin America was part of the United States' 'backyard' have long passed. From China to India to Russia to Iran, countries with a wide range of interests have increasingly taken notice of Latin America's gradual transformation and enhanced confidence in global affairs. This process accelerated in 2009 and 2010.

The continuing irritations and historic resentments that mark relations between the US and Latin America have sometime made it difficult to take full advantage of opportunities and pursue common interests. The challenge facing Washington is to engage in intensive diplomatic efforts with largely friendly governments and willing partners in the region to make progress on a shared agenda. However, the most salient change in the region has not been the reduced influence of the United States, or the heightened activity of actors from outside the hemisphere, but rather the rising power and expanding role of countries in the region. As Brazil advances towards a role as a global power, Lula has made it an important player in the dispute over Iran's nuclear programme, although his diplomatic push on a wide range of issues has met some criticism. And while the effectiveness of Chávez's ALBA bloc is debatable, the ALBA countries can project some influence within and beyond the region if they work in concert.

Most Latin American countries appeared to react to Brazil's more assertive role with some ambivalence. While they welcomed a rising force that can convene regional forums (as has been the case with UNASUR) and ensure a relatively peaceful neighbourhood, many wanted space to chart their own, more independent, foreign policies. In a complicated, multi-polar world, an ascendant Brazil will need to take care to avoid the imperial impulses that, as the United States can testify, have tended to create problems for a hemispheric power.

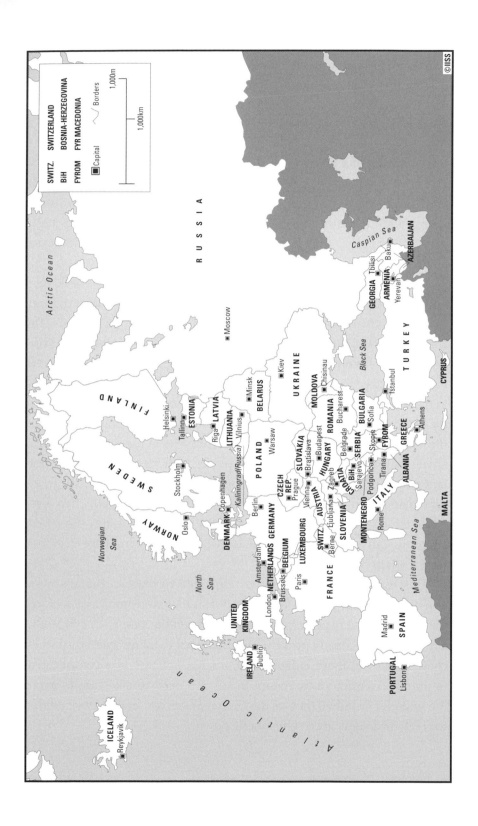

Chapter 4

Europe

Months after the 27 member states of the European Union (EU) signed up to the Lisbon Treaty, agreeing to reform and streamline the Union's structure so that it was better fitted for the future, Europe was struck by a crisis that threatened to destroy one of its bulwarks. The euro, adopted as a single currency since 1999 by 16 countries which form the 'eurozone', had always been vulnerable to divergences in economic policy between them. The revelation in October 2009 that Greece's budget deficit would be more than double the previous official estimate caused a crisis of confidence that afflicted European markets for the next six months. Although the economy of Greece was small, the country's pressing financial troubles exposed differences of approach among its larger neighbours that threatened to blow the common currency apart – an event that would throw the very existence of the EU, and therefore the future of Europe as a whole, into question. Eventually, a €750 billion bailout fund was agreed by EU members, together with the International Monetary Fund (IMF), that may have deferred a financial crisis in the eurozone but on its own did not address the euro's fundamental structural weaknesses.

The financial crisis of 2008 had prompted many European governments to ease fiscal policy to soften the blow to their economies. This resulted in a sharp expansion of budget deficits that rapidly expanded the debt burdens of many European countries. The increasing concerns of investors about the ability of these states to continue to fund themselves in the financial markets were reflected in a series of down-gradings by credit-rating agencies. Greece, with a high budget deficit, was most at risk – Iceland having already been an early casualty of the crisis – and Spain, Portugal and Ireland were also singled out. In this atmosphere, all European countries had to look to the size of their budget deficits lest they too should become targets of negative speculation in the financial markets.

The debate about how to respond to the Greek crisis revealed a philosophical gulf between the euro's two largest members, France and Germany. (The United Kingdom, not being a member of the eurozone, did not have as direct a stake or voice in the outcome.) French President Nicolas Sarkozy was activist in arguing for a bail-out for Greece and in pursuing France's long-standing objective of establishing some form of economic governance for the eurozone – essentially, procedures for political oversight and policy coordination by and among the member states. This clashed head-on with the attitude of German Chancellor Angela Merkel, who resisted both the bail-out itself – she insisted that Greece must adopt draconian austerity measures – and the notion of common economic governance.

Her approach was viewed as part of a growing German tendency to put national interests ahead of European considerations. Merkel and her cabinet feared a public backlash against bailing out Greece given the significant contribution that Germany would have to make to any rescue. Merkel wanted Greece's problems to be dealt with by the Greek government – the agreement on European monetary union had included a 'no bailout' clause.

But in any case, growing caution about a more federal Europe was already evident not only in Germany but elsewhere on the continent. Most notable in this respect was the outcome in November 2009 of negotiations over who should hold the top two positions in the EU following the Lisbon Treaty's reforms. EU members were to appoint a new EU Council President, intended to replace the previous system in which the presidency rotated among member states every six months. They were also to appoint a new 'foreign minister' who would combine the previous positions of EU High Representative for Foreign and Defence Policy and the European Commission's External Relations Commissioner, and would set up and run a new EU diplomatic service. The names of many prominent politicians were mentioned for these posts. But in the end, government leaders opted for people who would not – at least not through pre-existing prestige and clout – take limelight or sovereignty away from national capitals. Herman van Rompuy, a former Belgian prime minister, was chosen as the EU Council president and the new foreign-policy supremo was Catherine Ashton, previously the European trade commissioner and before that a junior government minister as a member of Britain's upper House of Lords.

Merkel's intransigence over Greece prompted considerable opprobrium across Europe. It was suggested by many critics that Berlin should adopt a more expansionary approach and boost domestic demand in order to assist global economic recovery and its European partners. In March 2010 both French Finance Minister Christine Lagarde and European Commission President José Manuel Barroso suggested that Germany had to do more to boost domestic demand, even if that entailed deficit spending. Critics also argued that, since the German economic model depended on exports, including to other European countries, it was incumbent upon Berlin to help in the finance of such exports by contributing to European rescue measures. However, opinion in Germany remained strongly against such views. Merkel's position reflected German belief in the need for fiscal discipline not only in Germany but also in other European countries. The fear in Germany was that too much fiscal stimulus could tip Germany and Europe into an inflationary spiral. This view seemed unlikely to change, and on the day of the eventual bailout, 9 May, the electorate's worries about the degree of likely German participation in European bailouts contributed to Merkel's Christian Democratic Union (CDU) party suffering election losses in the country's largest state, North Rhine–Westphalia.

From November onwards, Greece launched successive measures to reform its economy, reduce its fiscal deficit and restore investors' confidence in its debt. These provoked violent protests. The need for an international rescue was obvious, but weeks were lost while Germany delayed coordi-

> " The need for an international rescue was obvious, but weeks were lost "

nated action as policymakers attempted to define a narrative that would make it acceptable to their domestic audience. On 2 May, a €110bn bailout was agreed by eurozone member governments and the IMF, forcing a new round of reform measures on the government in Athens. While this was effective in terms of stemming speculation against Greece, it was not sufficient to calm worries about other countries that could run into similar difficulties. Sarkozy insisted that the very existence of the eurozone was at stake and that it was the responsibility of Europe's leaders collectively to defeat the speculators. During the weekend of 8–9 May, after a long, tense meeting between Merkel and Sarkozy (the chemistry between the two leaders has never been good), the German chancellor effectively performed a U-turn and embraced virtually all of the French proposals. At a meeting of European finance ministers, a €750bn package of measures was agreed to shore up other vulnerable economies in the eurozone.

The bail-out fund included €440bn of loans and guarantees, mainly from eurozone governments, and up to €250bn of support from the IMF. In addition, the role of the European Central Bank (ECB), previously limited basically to interest-rate action to preserve the stability of the euro, was expanded and it began purchasing European government bonds in debt markets. Germany contributed a total of €148bn to the Greek and European guarantee pot, including €123bn to the general eurozone package.

Merkel had insisted on three conditions: countries seeking access to funding would have to undertake considerable efforts to address structural problems and introduce tough austerity programmes; the IMF would need to be involved; and before any bail-out it would need to be clearly assessed that there was no alternative. These conditions were reflected in the justification she advanced for the bail-out. By early May, she was arguing that a bail-out was necessary to deal with an 'emergency situation consisting of the factual inability of Greece to gain access to the financial markets, which would have implications for the stability of the euro'. This assessment, she said, was supported by the ECB and the IMF. She added: 'This is about nothing more and nothing less than the future of Europe and hence also the future of Germany in Europe'. And in her statement before the parliamentary vote in the Bundestag, Merkel insisted: 'If the Euro fails, then Europe fails'.

In spite of these efforts to put a positive spin on the decision, the events were widely interpreted in Europe as putting a question mark over Germany's commitment to further European integration. The fact was that, over the last decade, Germany had come to view integration in more utilitarian terms, weighing the costs and benefits instead of automatically equating German interests with European interests. It was likely that German leaders would in future have to work harder if they wanted to convince the electorate of the benefits of a more federal Europe.

Even after the bail-out, economists thought it possible that Greek debt payments might in time need to be deferred and rescheduled, but following the rescue package there was a far higher likelihood that any financing crisis for at-risk countries could be dealt with in an orderly manner. In addition, it was clear that in the longer term the survival of the euro as a common currency would require closer mutual monitoring of economic policies and greater harmonisation of fiscal policies.

Meanwhile, the financial markets' focus on sovereign debt led to a new set of austerity programmes across Europe. Germany announced in May 2010 that it would aim to cut €80bn from government spending by 2014. Italy aimed to save €24bn by 2012, France €45bn by 2013. The United Kingdom planned a combination of £113bn of spending cuts and tax rises in order to all but eliminate its high budget deficit over five years. Economists voiced concerns that this substantial fiscal tightening across Europe – which followed a period of fiscal stimuli introduced to mitigate the recessionary effects of the financial crisis – could kill off economic recovery.

Among other important developments in Europe in the year to mid-2010, the first peacetime coalition government since the 1930s emerged in the United Kingdom, displacing the Labour Party after 13 years. David Cameron, the Conservative prime minister, and Nick Clegg, the Liberal Democrat deputy prime minister, swiftly oversaw a dramatic fiscal tightening to reduce government borrowing. In Germany, Merkel's CDU and its Christian Social Union (CSU) partner had retained power in elections and she was able to strike a coalition with the Free Democratic Party (FDP), the preferred partner, after four years of an uneasy 'grand coalition' with the Social Democratic Party (SPD). In the Netherlands, the coalition government collapsed following the withdrawal of a member party over the deployment of Dutch troops in Afghanistan. The president of Poland, Lech Kaczynski, was killed along with many senior officials in a plane crash in Russia as he flew to attend a ceremony to commemorate the Katyn massacre of Poles by Soviet forces in 1940.

Germany: New Coalition Tested

The general election on 27 September 2009 ushered in a centre-right coalition government composed of the CDU/CSU and the FDP, with Angela Merkel continuing as chancellor. Because of the FDP's strong showing and significant losses for the SPD, she was able to end the previous unwanted grand coalition with the SPD and exercise her preferred option of forming a government with the FDP.

Led by Guido Westerwelle, who became foreign minister and vice chancellor, the Free Democrats ran on a platform emphasising tax cuts and were able to improve their share of the vote from 9.8% in 2005 to 14.6% in 2009. Merkel's party actually lost support, attracting 33.8% (down from 35.2% in 2005), however, the SPD won just 23% of the vote (down from 34.2%). With the two other parties represented in parliament, the Left and the Greens, also able to increase their share of the vote to 11.9% and 10.7% respectively, the 2009 results produced the most fragmented German Bundestag in recent history. Hopes were high that the new government would prove more dynamic, since the grand coalition was seen as having been able to agree on only lowest-common-denominator policies.

However, the domestic agenda of the new coalition was hindered by the financial and economic situation, which placed constraints on the FDP's tax-cutting agenda and revealed splits between Merkel and powerful factions within her own party, with some commentators speculating the coalition government might fall. This was despite the fact that the German economy was recovering well, if slowly: after shrinking by 5% in 2009, GDP was expected to grow in 2010 by 1.5–2%. Unemployment was falling due to the use of measures such as asking workers to work reduced hours; in April 2010, it stood at 8.1%, down from 8.6% a year before. The government, although it resisted international pressure to adopt a more expansive policy and act as a locomotive for global recovery, targeted only a modest reduction in the budget deficit. Through €80bn of spending cuts over four years, it planned to reduce the deficit from 5% to 3% of GDP. In the early months of 2010, economic and political debate was dominated by the question of Germany's future role in the bail-out of Greece (see above).

Afghanistan role

Discussion about Germany's commitment in Afghanistan was almost as intense. During the night of 3–4 September 2009, the head of the German military's Provincial Reconstruction Team (PRT) in Kunduz province ordered an air-strike on two fuel trucks stuck in the Kunduz river which had earlier been hijacked by insurgents. US pilots dropped two 500lb bombs, destroying the trucks and killing up to 142 people in the immediate vicinity. After the strike it emerged that the German commander's assessment that all the individuals in the river bed were insurgents was wrong and that an unknown number of ordinary civilians had been killed. It also became apparent that several rules of engagement had been broken. The judgement of the PRT chief that the fuel trucks represented a direct danger to the German military headquarters at Camp Kunduz (because they might be turned into rolling bombs) was also questioned, given that the trucks were stuck in the river.

The death toll that resulted from orders given by a German officer and the manifold doubts about the process leading to the decision to strike triggered a parliamentary inquiry, launched with the support of all political parties. The defence committee of the Bundestag investigated the air-strike, the information and investigation efforts of the government, and the appropriateness of the actions taken in light of national and multinational political, judicial and military guidance.

Even before the inquiry was launched, the Kunduz bombing had ended three careers. Chief of Defence General Wolfgang Schneiderhan and State Secretary for Defence Peter Wichert were asked to resign on 25 November 2009 by new Defence Minister Karl-Theodor zu Guttenberg on the grounds that information had been withheld from him. (Schneiderhan and Wichert both denied any wrongdoing.) In addition, Franz Josef Jung, who had been defence minister at the time of the air-strike and subsequently became labour and social affairs minister, had to resign from the cabinet on 27 November in response to emerging evidence that he had denied the existence of civilian casualties, despite reports from within his own ministry. And although the incident occurred before he became defence minister, zu Guttenberg himself ran into trouble because he had first called the air-strike 'appropriate', a judgement he later retracted. The reputation of zu Guttenberg, seen as a rising star of German politics, suffered from the fact that he, Schneiderhan and Wichert produced fundamentally different versions of the story that led to the dismissals, centring on the question of whether or not information had been withheld. However, the colonel who had ordered the air-strike was cleared of criminal charges by the German federal prosecutor in April 2010, a decision greeted with relief in the armed forces, despite their acknowledgement that mistakes had been made.

This was by far the most controversial incident so far in Germany's nine-year deployment to Afghanistan, during which (as of June 2010) there have been 43 German fatalities. Seven soldiers were killed in attacks in Baghlan province south of Kunduz in April. The new chief of defence, General Volker Wieker, said the situation in Kunduz had deteriorated significantly since April 2009, and suggested that the complexity of attacks across time and space pointed to 'central command and a close coordination of the attackers', which was new for the Kunduz area. Furthermore, insurgents had begun to single out Germans for attack to cause casualties and fuel the political discussion in Germany, with the aim of undermining domestic support for the operation.

With Germans killing and getting killed in Afghanistan, the operational realities intruded into the political debate at home. Leaders had previously been keen to frame the mission as one of reconstruction and stabilisation, and on this basis won parliamentary approval for deployments. A series of operational caveats have restricted German soldiers' activities but invited much criticism from Allies. Gradually, however, in recognition of the deteriorating security situation in the North and shifts in Allied strategy – for example, requiring German mentors to deploy with Afghan contingents – these caveats have been reduced.

German soldiers have been quoted in the media reacting positively to the reduced limits, because they found that more options were available to them. In parallel, zu Guttenberg began to speak of the 'war-like conditions' in Afghanistan in an effort to put the official rhetoric on a more solid footing. In February 2010, the government formally declared that Afghanistan was a 'non-international armed conflict' suggesting that at the core it was a struggle between the security forces of the Afghan government and insurgent groups, despite the large ISAF presence. Aside from the semantics, this step provided greater legal clarity for the soldiers in the field.

Recognising that domestic support for the Afghanistan deployment was likely to become even weaker if casualties, both taken and inflicted, rose further, German leaders argued that NATO and the international community had increasingly begun to align with German preferences, for example through a heightened focus on civilian reconstruction. At the same time, they downplayed the greater risks to German troops arising from the new strategy of working much more closely with Afghan forces and among the population, and taking part in operations that were previously off limits.

Financial constraints on defence

The new government mandated a commission to review the organisational structures of and processes in the Bundeswehr to identify ways to increase efficiency. The commission, set up in April 2010, was due to report by the end of the year. With zu Guttenberg asserting that 'in part we still have structures that breathe the spirit of 20, 25, 30 years ago', the goal was to find ways to get more out of personnel, structures and resources without radical down-sizing. The commission was chaired by Frank-Jürgen Wiese, head of the Bundesagentur für Arbeit (the Federal Labour Agency), which provides services to the unemployed and has seen substantial reform. The sole military representative on the six-member commission was General Karl-Heinz Lather, chief of staff, SHAPE. The commission was expected to streamline administrative processes and review acquisition processes to avoid delays and cost overruns.

Plans mooted in the finance ministry in May and June, however, suggested that the defence ministry would be hard hit in 2011 and 2012 by efforts to rein in federal spending levels, and changed the dynamic towards more comprehensive measures – savings of €600m, 1.1bn and 1.3bn were demanded by Finance Minister Wolfgang Schäuble for the years 2011–13 respectively. The government programme outlining priorities for the austerity period called on the minister of defence to outline by September 2010 the implications of cutting the strength of the Bundeswehr by up to 40,000 from its current level of around 252,000.

As the ministry conducted an internal analysis of shortfalls, Wieker suggested that planning for the period 2011–13 was problematic because current financial resources were aligned neither with the task of the Bundeswehr, nor with the equipment and force structures that would be required to carry out what was being demanded of it. The resource crunch meant the Bundeswehr would have to accept at least temporary capability gaps, for example by phasing systems out earlier than planned and delaying replacements – the navy had to retire six of its ten submarines in 2010, five years earlier than planned, to reduce costs. A ministry task force was reviewing procurement projects to establish priorities that could balance military needs and financial feasibility. According to zu Guttenberg, it was 'self-evident that there will be a stop of one or the other armaments programme' and that bases below a certain number of personnel would have to be cut was well.

Part of the problem was that the restructuring of the armed forces into force categories with different levels of capability, a mainstay of a 2006 Defence White Paper, had not yielded the envisioned increases in force-projection capacity. By early 2010, the Bundeswehr still seemed to be limited to sustaining a maximum deployment of 8,500–10,000 troops abroad. Reportedly, the army argued in internal discussions that, at current resource levels, the 2006 level of ambition was not sustainable as far as the scope and concurrency of operations was concerned. The division of the military into categories, initially thought to offer an opportunity to modernise the force at an affordable cost, turned into an obstacle because the army did not have sufficient capabilities to slot into the different force categories at the required levels. For example, the air force still had to deal with limited transport capabilities caused by the delay of major programmes such as the A400M aircraft and the NH90 helicopter. Germany often had to rely on commercial solutions or allies for its transport needs. To deal with some of the financial pressures, the government agreed to make 37 of the Eurofighter *Typhoon* fighters Germany was buying available for export.

As part of the effort to reduce costs, the period of conscription was to be further reduced to six months from January 2011. Conscription, which still has significant political support, is seen by many defence commentators as inefficient and unable to meet the demands of a military engaged in modern operations. However, the coalition agreement struck between the CDU/CSU and the FDP in 2009 had confirmed that the government 'remain[s] firmly committed to the principle of general military service obligation'. Arguably, holding on to conscription but shortening its duration makes it even harder to justify. Six months is too short a period to have conscripts do anything other than basic training; yet the approximately 50,000 conscripts will continue to tie up considerable resources in terms of infrastructure and training provided by professional soldiers. Financial pressure had a direct impact on this aspect of the German defence debate as well. As zu Guttenberg pointed out, the budget crunch demanded structural reform of the armed forces and the continuation of conscription had to be debated anew.

Merkel's new coalition thus suffered a period of tests as it confronted the euro crisis and came under pressure over events in Afghanistan. Questions emerged about her government's durability, especially as it has been in the uncomfortable position of having its decisions questioned by both domestic and international audiences. There was little indication, however, that Germany would abandon long-held positions and adopt a more expansive, stimulatory economic policy so as to help other European countries suffering from debt problems.

France: Domestic Challenges, International Activism

President Nicolas Sarkozy had a tumultuous third year in office, facing major challenges from the European economic crisis, growing opposition to his economic and social policies, declining poll ratings and severe setbacks in France's regional elections. In an attempt to divert public opinion from the harsh economic reality, he launched two domestic initiatives which proved both controversial and divisive: a debate on national identity and a law banning the wearing of the burka in public. On the international scene, France pursued a highly activist approach to resolving the crisis afflicting the euro, a conciliatory line in Africa and a traditional policy of embracing all major partners in complex and potentially contradictory bilateral initiatives. Sarkozy was still reckoned the favourite to win re-election in 2012, amid continuing divisions within the opposition Socialist Party.

The year was dominated by the global – and European – economic crisis, and Sarkozy took a prominent role in securing the comprehensive rescue package for Greece and other European countries that could run into financial problems (see above). France itself emerged from the 2008 crisis in better shape than most of its European partners. The state intervened rapidly to shore up a banking sector which was far less exposed than its European peers. France did not suffer from the real-estate bubble which hit Spain and the United Kingdom. The government's emphasis was on ensuring the strength of the overall economy, which already benefited from a strong cushion in the form of a sizeable public sector and generous welfare provisions. France, far less dependent on exports than its major European partners, was protected to some extent from weakness in the United States and the emerging economies.

France's domestic stimulus measures had included a car-scrappage scheme, tax relief for small companies taking on new staff, tax credits for public–private partnerships, tax reductions for lower incomes and various investment credit schemes. A new welfare scheme, the Revenu de Solidarité Active, targeted the most disadvantaged with monthly payments of between €500 and €1,000. These measures produced the desired result of buoying household consumption, and a massive increase in new car sales resulted in late 2009. France emerged from the recession in the second quarter of 2009, and overall its GDP declined by only 2.5% in 2009, compared with figures of 4% to 5% for most major European competitors.

However, the government remained cautious about reducing the stimulus to improve public finances. In October 2009, Finance Minister

Christine Lagarde proposed a 2010 budget with a projected deficit of 8.2% of GDP, up from 3.4% in 2009. Public debt stood at over 80% of GDP. Tax cuts of €2bn following Sarkozy's 2007 election campaign had fuelled the deficit. They were temporarily balanced out by a new carbon tax, but in December 2009 the Constitutional Court ruled the tax unconstitutional on the grounds that it failed to meet its own declared objectives of curbing global emissions – over 90% of industrial emissions were unaffected. This meant that, as was the case for many industrialised countries, economic policy seemed caught between the need to reduce the deficit and the need to foster economic growth, on which government revenues depended. As stimulus measures were gradually phased out, falling from €39bn in 2009 to €7bn in 2010, the target of reducing the deficit to 3% of GDP by 2013 was looking unattainable.

> " Most economists considered the growth projection to be unrealistic "

Most economic forecasts predicted that France's growth performance would fail to maintain its comparative European advantage through 2010. Inflation was rising and unemployment was heading for 10% from 7% in 2008. It was estimated that to meet its budget-deficit target, the government would have to find some €100bn in savings through spending cuts and tax rises, as well as achieve a 2.5% annual growth projection (considered by most economists to be unrealistic, especially following a freeze on public expenditure announced in May 2010). The government said it would take measures to cut spending and raise revenues.

While the fate of the euro raised important long-term issues for France, Sarkozy's biggest domestic reform challenge was his policy on pensions. In February 2010, he announced a long-awaited process leading to a major reform of pensions to be submitted to parliament in September. The lengthy time-frame was an immediate indication of the sensitivity and complexity of the task. The pension deficit was expected to reach €11bn in 2010 and could rise to €50bn in 2020. Both the socialist opposition and the unions recognised the inevitability of reform, but there was considerable disagreement over the most effective measures. The right was focusing on an increase in the working life, while the left wished to ensure that those with 65,000 working hours were entitled to a state pension. An initial orientation document was made public in mid-May 2010 in which the government unveiled two major proposals, without specifying details: a rise in the age of eligibility for state pensions, and a new form of contribution for high earners and also for income derived from capital. This represented a reversal of Sarkozy's opposition to removing the so-called *bouclier fiscal,* the 'fiscal shield' which caps at 50% the maximum tax that can be imposed on any individual. The opposition criticised the lack of detail and the unions expressed their intention to oppose any increase in the pensionable age. Political analysts were agreed that this reform could well make or break the Sarkozy presidency. To pull off a reform which a majority of French citizens perceived as equitable and necessary would be a huge challenge.

Domestic distractions

Two domestic policy distractions were introduced by the government. In October 2009 the minister for immigration and national identity, former socialist Eric Besson, launched a debate on national identity. The initiative, officially designed to produce a definition of 'Frenchness', was denounced by the socialists as a smokescreen designed to help Sarkozy's Union pour un Mouvement Populaire (UMP) party in regional elections by playing on fears of immigration, and by the right-wing National Front as a government plot to acclimatise French people to values and cultural norms from the Islamic world. The debate, which took the form of opinion pieces and discussions in the media, as well as public discussions in town halls and 58,000 contributions to a dedicated website, rapidly degenerated into a discussion about the merits and demerits of Islam. The government proved incapable of steering it back to a wider rehearsal of the cultural bases of Frenchness. By January, only 40% of the population thought the discussion worthwhile, and only 20% thought it had addressed fundamental issues. A large majority was convinced that it was purely an electoral ploy. The culmination of over three months' discussion was intended to be a colloquium held under government auspices. In view of the verbal fireworks sparked by the initiative, this event was cancelled and replaced by a 'government seminar' on 8 February at which each minister was expected to come up with policy proposals in his or her field. The harvest was minimal and Prime Minister François Fillon was visibly embarrassed when announcing that it had been decided to hang the tricolour flag from every French school and to make sure that the full text of the 1789 Declaration of the Rights of Man and the Citizen was made available in every classroom. A last-ditch effort to insist that the debate should continue was laughed out of court. The episode was a humiliation for the government and for Besson.

The other initiative, the drafting of a law to ban the burka, proved only marginally less controversial. Having initially sided with Obama's opinion, expressed in a speech in Cairo, that dress should be a private matter, Sarkozy switched tack when a cross-party group of parliamentarians, including 40 from his own UMP, demanded the establishment of a commission to investigate the spread of burka-wearing in France. In June 2009, he told parliament that the full face covering for Muslim women was 'unwelcome in France' and set up a commission of inquiry. The idea of a ban acquired traction when Sarkozy's two high-profile Muslim politicians, Rachida Dati and Rama Yade, spoke out in favour. Opinion polls suggested a majority of French people agreed. But human-rights organisations, as well as Muslim leaders around the world, condemned the idea and opinion rapidly polarised. The Socialist Party rejected the comprehensiveness of the proposed ban and suggested the burka should only be disallowed inside official buildings. The Algerian-based group al-Qaeda in the Islamic Maghreb called for violent resistance. In April 2010, despite an opinion from the Conseil d'Etat, a high judicial and advisory body, that a ban might prove unconstitutional, Sarkozy announced that a bill would be put to parliament in the summer.

The proposed law rapidly led to dramatic confrontations. A female motorist who was fined €22 for driving while wearing a burka became the trigger for a stand-off between her male partner and Minister of the Interior Brice Hortefeux. The partner, Lies Hebbadj, who was married to one woman and kept several others as mistresses, had fathered 12 children and collected €5,000 per month in welfare cheques. He was accused by the minister of polygamy and threatened with withdrawal of his citizenship. As Hebbadj noted, if keeping a mistress was now a crime in France, large numbers of French men risked losing their citizenship. Elsewhere, a woman lawyer, involved in an altercation with a young burka-clad shopper in a clothing store, physically ripped off the offending headgear and the two engaged in a fist-fight. At the same time, an armed robbery took place in a small-town bank carried out by two men who had disguised themselves under burkas. Government officials, eager to defuse the 'anti-Islamic' charge, argued that the proposed ban had nothing to do with Islam. It simply reflected the fact that 'the visibility of the face in the public sphere [is] essential to our security and a condition for living together'. The proposed law was unequivocal: its first article stated that 'nobody, in a public place, may wear clothing designed to conceal the face'. The main police union, Unité SGP-Police, was unhappy about the prospects of intervening to enforce the removal of the apparel. The controversy looked set to continue, and it was unclear whether it would redound to the president's political credit or debit.

Contrasting election results

The past year saw two electoral battles in France, with diametrically opposite results. In June 2009, the Socialist Party hoped to turn the European elections into a referendum on Sarkozy's record. The tactic backfired badly. Not only did the president's UMP win the elections with 27.87% of the vote, but the Socialist vote collapsed to 16.48%. This reflected the electorate's disenchantment with a party unable to put its own house in order. With 16.28%, the Greens, under the colourful gadfly Daniel Cohn-Bendit, who had been a student leader in the May 1968 disturbances, almost pushed the Socialists into third place. In March 2010, however, the Socialist Party pulled off a spectacular rebound in the regional elections, winning 54% of the vote against 35.4% for the UMP, after campaigning in opposition to pensions reform. The party seemed increasingly unified under its leader Martine Aubry, and controlled 21 of the 22 regions of metropolitan France. Sarkozy shrugged off the defeat, arguing that regional issues and outcomes did not affect the broad national picture and vowing to forge ahead with the pensions plan, which he formally entrusted to Prime Minister Fillon, whose popularity ratings have remained consistently higher than his own.

This electoral drubbing was seen as a wake-up call for the president, whose term ends in 2012. However, turnout was below 50%, reflecting voters' disaffection with politics. Projections for the 2012 presidential election were clouded in unknowns, such as the intentions of IMF Managing Director Dominique Strauss-Kahn, the former finance minister who, despite progress made by Aubry, is consistently seen in opinion polls as the only Socialist candidate able to defeat Sarkozy. On the right, former Prime Minister Dominique de Villepin emerged vindicated from a high-profile court case brought against him largely at Sarkozy's instigation, and was vying for a challenge in 2012. If Sarkozy's approval ratings remain low, Fillon himself could emerge as a credible candidate in 2012.

While opinion polls revealed profound public lack of confidence in economic and financial prospects, this did not mean that the Socialist Party could automatically expect to benefit. Following the regional election success, it was sharpening knives for a major attack on the government's policies in the autumn. But polls indicated that, while 50% of the population still expressed confidence in the government's performance, only 35% felt the Socialists would do better.

Activist international posture

The French president continued to be extremely active in international affairs. Sarkozy was outspoken in his call for radical reform of the international institutions created in the aftermath of the Second World War. He championed the cause of new permanent members of the UN Security Council: Germany, Japan, Brazil, India and at least one African country. He argued for radical reform of the IMF and the World Bank to reflect the reality of the rising powers. With France assuming the presidency of both the G8 and G20 in 2011, he argued that the G8 was effectively defunct. He demanded draconian new regulations for the international financial and banking system, an end to tax havens, oversight of credit-rating agencies, stabilisation of raw-materials prices and robust intergovernmental agreements to constrain the markets.

Sarkozy continued to assert that there was a total meeting of minds between France and the United States on virtually every issue. The claim was somewhat rhetorical since there was clearly more than a nuance between Paris and Washington over the conduct of policy in Afghanistan and the Middle East, as well as towards Russia, China and even South America.

France significantly deepened relations with Russia, which was overtly supportive of French efforts to reform the international financial and institutional system. France has also been the Western country most open to discussion of President Dmitry Medvedev's plan for a new European security architecture and has incurred the wrath of senior American officials by negotiating the sale to Russia of advanced *Mistral*-class amphibious-assault vessels. French energy companies EDF, GDF, Total and Suez were involved in intensive discussions over investment in the strategically sensitive North Stream and South Stream oil pipelines, fuelling Moscow's hopes of gaining an additional political advocate inside the EU. Relations with China were equally positive, with major state visits in both directions in 2010. China, like Russia, was outspokenly supportive of France's activism in the area of international financial reform. President Hu Jintao endorsed Sarkozy's talk of a new 'multipolar monetary world order'. Sino-French cooperation intensified in the fields of nuclear technology (a joint venture to build two third-generation pressurised-water reactors in Taishan, Guangdong province), aeronautics (France is helping build the engine for the first Chinese-constructed large aircraft, the C-919, and has partnered China in constructing the medium utility helicopter Z-15), the environment, agriculture and agribusiness. Both sides spoke of a new departure in Sino-French cooperation.

On the Middle East, France continued to press for resumption of direct peace talks between Israel and the Palestinian Authority, emerging as the sternest critic of both continued Israeli settlement expansion and Iranian nuclear defiance. The French position on a peace settlement was crystal clear: two states, living within the 1967 borders; Jerusalem as the capital of both states; an exchange of territory; and discussions on refugees. In February 2010, Foreign Minister Bernard Kouchner went so far as to imply that if, as had been suggested, Palestinian Prime Minister Salam Fayyad were simply to proclaim the existence of a Palestinian state irrespective of the outcome of negotiations, France would recognise that state. France has been extremely active across the Middle East, engaging in regular top-level talks with Syria. President Bashar al-Assad visited Paris in November 2009, Fillon travelled to Damascus in February 2010 and Kouchner followed this visit up in May. The aim was to stimulate direct negotiations between Syria and Israel as well as to help engineer an effective government of national unity in Lebanon. In this regard, France was risking the displeasure of the United States, which still had severe reservations about Assad.

France was also increasingly active in Iraq following Sarkozy's visit to Baghdad in February 2009, the first ever by a French head of state. A French commercial centre, a French agricultural mission and a centre for archaeology and social sciences were opened in Baghdad. In November President Jalal Talabani made a state visit to France, again the first by an Iraqi head of state. France was seeking to restore Franco-Iraqi relations to their high point of the 1970s and 1980s. There has been a growing French presence in the Gulf following the May 2009 opening of a permanent French military base in the United Arab Emirates. In October 2009, negotiations began over the sale to Kuwait of up to 28 *Rafale* fighters. France has been keen to appear as a firm supporter of the Gulf Cooperation Council states in their nervous attempts to counter Iran's growing regional hegemony. It also took the firmest international position on increasing sanctions against Iran, while nevertheless refusing to extradite to the United States an Iranian citizen, Majid Kakavand, accused by Washington of illegally supplying Tehran with military equipment. The release of Kakavand was clearly not unconnected with the return to Paris in May of Clotilde Reiss, a French student who had been detained following anti-government protests in July 2009. The release of Reiss was followed several days later by the return to Iran of Ali Vakili Rad, who had been in prison in France since 1991 when he was sentenced for the murder of former Iranian Prime Minister Shapour Bakhtiar.

> "France was risking the displeasure of the United States"

France's relations with Africa shifted somewhat. Sarkozy embarked on a tour in February 2010 designed to repair frayed ties with several former allies. In Gabon, despite France's current investigations into the financial holdings of the Bongo family, he was able to establish a good rapport with President Ali-Ben Bongo, whose controversial succession to his father Omar in 2009 created tensions with Paris. In Rwanda, he overcame 15 years of bad blood between Paris and Kigali by acknowledging that France had made 'grave errors of judgment' in its handling of the genocide in 1994. It was clear, however, that despite Sarkozy's early calls for a comprehensive new relationship between France and Africa, transcending the tradition known as 'Francafrique' which was based on close personal ties between French presidents and African leaders, Sarkozy was essentially continuing the same tradition.

Finally, France made serious efforts to emerge as a significant partner with Brazil, of which it is a neighbour through the 700km frontier between Brazil and the French overseas department of Guiana, 70% of whose electorate voted in a January 2010 referendum to reject independence from France. Sarkozy visited Brazil three times in 2009, cheerleading the familiar discourse about a new institutional and financial world order in which Brazil must play a major role. But above all the trips were dominated by military transactions. Brazil agreed to purchase four *Scorpène* diesel-electric attack submarines from France and to retrofit a fifth with nuclear propulsion. Brasilia was to supply Paris with a dozen KC-390 *Embraer* transport aircraft, with helicopters and army equipment also part of the deal. But the real negotiations revolved around the prospect of Brazil emerging as the first-ever client for France's *Rafale* fighter, which has been unsuccessful in the international export market. Talks opened in September 2009 for a fleet of 36 *Rafales*, a contract worth $6.3bn. However, no final decision had been taken by summer 2010 and the approach of elections in October 2010, in which President Luiz Inácio 'Lula' da Silva could not stand again, was causing consternation in Paris. To increase the attractiveness of the French offer compared with the American F-18 and the Swedish *Gripen*, Sarkozy agreed to significant technology-transfer arrangements.

France continued, through 2010, to be a major player on both the European and the international scene. In June, as the rescue package for Greece was agreed, Sarkozy and Merkel appeared to patch up their differences by agreeing that 'economic governance' of the eurozone should involve all 27 EU member states rather than just the eurozone members, as Sarkozy had proposed. They also staked out a joint position on reform of international institutions in advance of the G20 summit in Toronto at the end of June.

The United Kingdom: Coalition Experiment

The year to mid-2010 was one of political transition for the United Kingdom. It was dominated by the campaign leading up to the 6 May 2010 general election, which produced the first peacetime coalition government since the 1930s. While it had seemed likely that no party would win an overall majority, it was a surprise that a coalition could be formed by the right-of-centre Conservative Party and the centre-left Liberal Democrats. Thirteen years of government by the Labour Party thus came to an end, and David Cameron, the Conservative Party leader, became prime minister.

Labour's tenure in power had begun triumphantly in 1997 after 18 years of Conservative rule. Styling the party 'New Labour', Tony Blair had shifted it to the centre to win power, and had benefited politically from the damage done to public-sector services by the right-wing philosophy of Margaret Thatcher. Labour poured money into state-funded health and education. But following an initial spell of fiscal discipline, Blair's government steadily increased borrowing to fund its programmes. After Gordon Brown succeeded Blair in 2007, Britain found its finances horribly exposed when the credit crunch of 2008 tipped the world into recession, drastically reducing tax revenue and forcing additional spending to counter the recession's effects. Since Brown had been finance minister for ten years, he was discredited. The Labour Party became disaffected and divided, and Brown was unable to rise above this, in part because of his gloomy, uncomfortable demeanour in office. Having plotted against Blair for years to become prime minister, he was grimly determined to hang on to the top job. But on 11 May, five days after the election, he resigned and quit the party leadership.

The switch to a Conservative–Liberal Democrat government did not, however, have the air of a decisive shift in Britain's political atmosphere. Cameron had also had to move his party towards the centre after it had easily lost the elections of 1997, 2001 and 2005. Even then, and with the advantage of Brown's lack of popularity and with recovery from recession only tentative, the Conservatives were not able to win an outright majority in 2010. This could be partly attributed to deficiencies in their electoral strategy: the party, still recovering from splits that tore it apart in the 1990s, had not clearly enunciated what it stood for. Indeed, Cameron was clearly conscious that general belief in strong public-sector services was still prevalent in Britain, and acknowledged some of Labour's successes. He understood this was not the time for him to be setting a more right-wing agenda in an election campaign – but the result was that it was difficult for his party to articulate clearly how it would differ from Labour.

The most remarkable outcome of the election was to catapult the Liberal Democrats into government, with five positions in Cameron's cabinet, including that of deputy prime minister for Nick Clegg, their leader. He had suddenly shot to prominence in Britain's first televised leaders' debate in April, presenting himself and his party as a fresh alternative after decades under the 'old parties' – an irony given the prominence of the Liberals and their 'Whig' forebears in the eighteenth and nineteenth centuries. His party's platform was a mixture of leftist policies – in some cases to the left of Labour – and an assertion of civil liberties that was more in tune with the Conservatives. For years it had been assumed that if the Liberal Democrats were ever to take part in government, it would be in an alliance with Labour. The ability of the Conservatives and the Liberal Democrats to agree a substantive coalition platform of common policies and plans was therefore a big surprise. It was also fortunate, for they were the only two parties who could command a parliamentary majority between them – it had seemed more likely that the Conservatives would try to govern as a minority. However, this victory of pragmatism left traditionalists and ideologists in both parties bruised and confused, sowing seeds of future discontent.

Economic platform

The new government inherited an economic situation in some ways worse than in other European countries, but in some ways better. Its advantage was that Britain was not a member of the euro. It therefore escaped the need to involve itself directly in European rescue efforts for Greece, and was also able to benefit in terms of economic competitiveness from the substantial depreciation of the pound since early 2008. The disadvantage, however, was the wide budget deficit, which at 11% of GDP in the financial year ended March 2010 was one of the largest in the industrialised world. While the government was having no difficulty in funding its borrowing requirement, and its total stock of debt was much less than that of some other large European countries, the government was acutely conscious of the risks of being hit by further financial turbulence and of a downgrading in its triple-A credit rating. Therefore, Cameron and his finance minister, George Osborne, deliberately talked up the dangers of the fiscal deficit in preparing the nation for a stringent emergency budget on 22 June. As they did so, respected economists warned of the risks of over-reacting to the budget problem and pitching the country back into recession and even of deflation and depression.

In the event, the budget dramatically accelerated the fiscal tightening that had been planned by the previous government, taking an additional £40 billion out of the economy over the next five years through spending cuts and tax rises on top of the £73bn previously planned. There was a strong risk that economic growth could be hit by measures such as a 2.5 percentage-point increase in value-added tax to 20% on most purchases, and by planned cuts of some 25% over four years in spending by most government departments. If Britain were to tip back into recession, the budget's plans to reduce the deficit almost to nothing would not be achieved, and it would appear in hindsight to have been reckless rather than bold. However, it was accepted by most that drastic measures were required, and Osborne combined stringency with business-friendly moves to stimulate private investment. While this – and reductions in welfare spending – made it a typical Conservative budget, several ideas advanced by the Liberal Democrats were also included, in particular a rise in the threshold for paying income tax. Osborne also announced a levy on banks, in agreement with the French and German governments. Overall, the new government chose to subscribe to the prevailing European view that strong fiscal discipline was required to promote future prosperity, ignoring Keynesian warnings about the effects of such an approach in the 1930s.

Iraq, Afghanistan and defence

The past year has seen Britain's two most recent major expeditionary ventures – the Iraq War and the campaign in Afghanistan – come under the microscope. Blair's decision to send more than 40,000 troops to take

part in the US-led invasion of Iraq in 2003 remained extremely controversial. It had been supported by a parliamentary vote. But regardless
of the rights and wrongs of the matter, the former prime minister is routinely referred to in the media as a 'liar' and 'war criminal', accused of
falsely inventing the case for war based on faulty intelligence about Iraqi
weapons. Aside from such crude personalisation, many in Britain continued to have misgivings about the lead-up to the war, about the planning
of the mission and about Britain's relationship with the United States
during the period. Even though there had already been two inquiries on
the use of intelligence, the view that the Iraq venture had inflicted a scar
on the nation that needed to be healed was widely held across the political spectrum, and in June 2009 Brown announced that a fuller inquiry
would be held.

A five-person committee was formed, consisting of three former
senior officials and two historians – convincingly independent and
non-political, and with no lawyers and no military representation. John
Chilcot, the inquiry chairman, said its terms of reference were to consider 'the UK's involvement in Iraq, including the way decisions were
made and actions taken, to establish, as accurately as possible, what happened and to identify the lessons that can be learned'. From November
onwards, politicians, military officers and senior officials who had been
involved were called to give evidence, mostly public and televised. The
hearings were not confrontational, but included pointed questioning.
Blair's own testimony would clearly be crucial. In 2003, he had made his
case forcefully in the face of aggressive questioning on live television,
and those who expected his answers to be any different in 2010 were
inevitably disappointed. He argued that the 11 September 2001 terrorist
attacks on the United States had altered the 'calculus of risk' in dealing
with Saddam Hussein's Iraqi regime over its weapons programmes, and
that Iraq was in breach of United Nations resolutions and had to be dealt
with. He blamed Iran and al-Qaeda for problems that caused the mission
nearly to fail. Blair said: 'I genuinely believe that if we had left Saddam in
power, even with what we know now, we would still have had to have
dealt with him, possibly in circumstances where the threat was worse
and possibly in circumstances where it was hard to mobilise any support
for dealing with that threat.' Britain and the world were safer as a result.

Asked by Chilcot if he had any regrets, he said: 'Responsibility but not a regret for removing Saddam Hussein.'

While Blair thus gave very little ground to the war's critics, other witnesses used their appearances before the inquiry to vent long-held feelings about the entry into the war, and its execution. Publication of the inquiry's report in late 2010 or early 2011 will be a key moment. Just how important such reviews could be was seen in June 2010 when a judicial inquiry reported after ten years of investigation into the deaths of 13 people in Northern Ireland on 'Bloody Sunday', 30 January 1972. Over 38 years after the event, the judges reported that the deaths were caused by British soldiers and that all those killed were entirely innocent, and Cameron issued an apology on behalf of the government. While Northern Ireland is now at peace, the Chilcot inquiry will be published at a time when the role and value of British expeditionary force is very much at the heart of debate about foreign and defence policy. A full-scale defence review was getting under way in mid-2010, and the mission of British troops in Afghanistan was increasingly under scrutiny.

The number of UK troops in Afghanistan has increased steadily to about 10,000, most deployed in Helmand province and engaged in active combat against Taliban insurgents. Following the sharp increases in deployments ordered by US President Barack Obama, the number of US soldiers in Helmand rose rapidly, with the result that in June 2010 the British soldiers came under American command. Amid growing disquiet in military and political circles about the chances of success of the NATO-led mission in Afghanistan, the new UK government – conscious that Obama had announced that US troops would begin to be withdrawn in mid-2011 – appeared to be preparing the country for an eventual exit. On 21 June, after the death of the 300th member of British forces since the deployment began, Cameron said: 'We are paying a high price for keeping our country safe, for making our world a safer place, and we should keep asking why we are there and how long we must be there.' The argument that had been advanced by the Brown government, that it was necessary to be in Afghanistan in order to keep Britain safe from terrorism, was being heard much less. But Cameron said British troops had to be there 'because the Afghans are not yet ready to keep their own country safe and to keep terrorists and terrorist training camps out of their country'. They would leave as soon as Afghans could take care of their own security.

With the Iraq War over and the Afghan deployment perhaps within sight of being wound down, the stage appeared to be set for significant cuts in the defence budget. That spending plans for new equipment far exceeded available resources had been clear for several years. The commitment to a defence review would force the government to make the difficult choices that its predecessor had put off. These were likely to involve a reduction in the size of Britain's 176,000-strong armed forces.

In other key areas of international affairs, however, British policy seemed unlikely to change significantly. The UK continued to take a hard line, alongside France and Germany, on Iran, and on counter-proliferation in general. There was no doubt that a Conservative-led government would maintain the close relationship with the United States, although following the Iraq War experience Foreign Secretary William Hague was careful to say that the relationship would not be 'slavish'. Equally, Cameron insisted that there would be no further cession of sovereignty to Brussels – in keeping with long-standing Conservative suspicion of European federalism. But here, the ground was changing: Britain was not a member of the euro, and so could resist pressure to be involved in closer mutual monitoring of economic policies. And in any case, the march towards closer European federalism appeared to have halted.

Post-agreement disillusion?

In planning cuts to defence and other parts of the public sector, the coalition could argue that much the same would have had to have been done by Labour if it had held on to power. But this would not offer much protection from the political heat that it would have to endure – like the American and other governments – for tackling economic and fiscal problems inherited from its predecessor.

How strong was the coalition government likely to be in the face of such pressures? This was not yet known. The early signs emanating from the coalition were reassuring – it brushed off the early resignation of a Liberal Democrat minister who was alleged to have committed a financial peccadillo. Oxford-educated Cameron and Cambridge-educated Clegg seemed to strike a rapport and both seemed easily suited to holding the reins of power. The Conservatives had experience in their cabinet in the form of Hague and Ken Clarke. The early days saw a marked shift away from the personality-driven politics of Labour's tenure.

The coalition's legislative programme for the coming year included bills to give schools greater freedom over their curricula and discipline, to make the National Health Service more responsive to patients' views, to improve energy efficiency, and to restrict government intrusion into private lives. These and other bills constituted a rich agenda that reflected the goals of both parties. In addition, the parties were able to reach a mutually acceptable compromise on the issue of electoral reform, the top priority for the Liberal Democrats, who under the first-past-the-post system polled 23% of the popular vote in 2010 but won only 8.7% of parliamentary seats. Conservatives feared reform would erode their power base considerably. However, they agreed on a referendum on an alternative vote system, on fixed-term five-year parliaments, and to reduce the number of parliamentary seats from 650 and equalise their size.

Agreement on this agenda – and the very holding of power – gave Cameron and Clegg ammunition against those in their parties for whom such an alliance was anathema. In a country unused to coalitions, it raised questions for voters about for what exactly they had been voting. Those who chose the Liberal Democrats had certainly not expected to be signing up to a Conservative manifesto. The rough-and-tumble of events, economic and politics seemed bound to throw up difficult situations for both sides, and it would take strong leadership from Cameron and Clegg to navigate through them.

Developments in European Defence

Budget stringency forced governments across Europe to cut into already-stretched defence budgets in the year to mid-2010, with the prospect of further reductions in coming years, triggering a plea from NATO Secretary-General Anders Fogh Rasmussen for leaders to 'resist the temptation to use the economic crisis as an excuse for letting the transatlantic defence spending gap widen'. While Rasmussen urged countries to continue to invest in 'more flexible, mobile and modern armed forces', the ability of governments across Europe to do so was reduced.

Among larger countries planning or contemplating cuts, Italy announced that 2011 defence spending would be cut by about 10%. Funding for equipment-acquisition programmes, including armoured vehicles and frigates, was set to run out in 2011 and it was not clear to what extent it would be renewed. France was considering defence cuts of €2–5bn over the next three years, according to press reports. Germany's plans to cut public spending, announced in June 2010, were set to force escalating defence cuts in 2011 and beyond. Defence Minister Karl Theodor zu Guttenberg indicated that such reductions could only be managed if they were accompanied by structural reform of the armed forces, including a possible reduction in manpower, bases and possibly even the end of conscription (see Germany, pp. 145–7).

In the United Kingdom, the coalition government announced in an emergency budget statement in June 2010 that spending in most government departments, including defence, would be reduced by a total of 25% over the next four years. Liam Fox, defence minister, said that 'resources will be tight for the country as a whole and defence is no exception'. Since the previous government's equipment-acquisition programme was already under-funded by an estimated £15bn, the stage was set for sweeping cuts in Britain's armed forces. Details of departmental spending cuts were not set to be revealed for several months, and a defence review was under way.

Since governments have always found it difficult to make inroads into personnel costs, it was probable that the axe in most countries would fall first on procurement programmes and on research and development. After cuts to Spain's defence budget were announced, Spanish Defence Secretary Constantino Mendez Martinez said that the armed forces would find it difficult to invest in new systems while maintaining existing force structures: 'Industry has to be aware that a cycle of modernisation is over and it will be a long time before investments of a similar scale are considered again'. In Austria, already one of Europe's lowest defence spenders in relation to GDP, Defence Minister Norbert Darabos said cuts were 'reasonable in economically difficult times' and that 'some acquisitions will have to wait'. Austrian Chief of the General Staff Edmund Entacher responded by arguing that this would pose a structural challenge for the armed forces, because available resources would not permit them to take part in territorial defence and international crisis-management missions at the same time.

Many countries saw their capabilities affected. Lithuania, which cut defence spending by 9% in 2009, announced a moratorium on procurement. Estonia likewise postponed procurement decisions, even on basic items such as trucks and ammunition. Slovenia and Slovakia were set to cut at least 10% from defence budgets. Poland, which reduced its 2009 budget by 9%, announced that its contributions to operations in Lebanon, Syria and Chad/Central African Republic would have to end because of financial constraints. One of the few countries able to buck the trend was Norway, which announced a 4% rise in the defence budget for 2010 and a focus on new equipment.

This developing defence-spending crunch was set to generate fundamental questions for governments across Europe. They will have to consider whether they should lower levels of ambition, for example by reducing the number of troops available for international operations. Lack of money could have a positive effect if it acts as a catalyst for transformation of European armed forces for modern operations, forcing them to eliminate legacy capabilities that have lost relevance. It will also create increased pressure to expand cooperative methods such as pooling and sharing, role specialisation and joint acquisition. However, many countries still worried about placing limits on national autonomy (see *The Military Balance 2010*, pp. 107–108).

A further consequence could be to encourage further consolidation of Europe's defence industries. This could occur if governments opt for more common spending and procurement. Collaborative defence procurement in Europe remains problematic, the latest example being the project to build the Airbus A400M transport aircraft, which was affected by project-management failures and technical problems. In March 2010, customer nations decided to allow a price increase of €2bn to €22bn for 180 aircraft, and also agreed to provide €1.5bn in export finance to EADS, the contractor. Meanwhile, EADS took losses of €4.2bn and announced cost savings of €3.6bn. In spite of the problems, governments decided not to abandon the project because of the jobs involved and the damage to EADS and Airbus that cancellation would have caused.

Counter-piracy operations

Over the past year, Europe's armed forces continued to be engaged in missions in Afghanistan, Lebanon, Kosovo and elsewhere. Naval forces, operating within both EU and NATO frameworks, were able to point to operational success as attacks by Somali pirates were reduced significantly in the Gulf of Aden. However, to some degree activity was displaced further south in the waters off Somalia. Pirates adapted tactically and began to conduct operations further off shore and with greater use of mother ships. The EU's *Operation Atalanta* involved, as of April 2010, 1,800 personnel and up to 12 vessels along with several maritime patrol aircraft. The EU had begun to integrate non-EU elements into its operation, with contributions from Croatia, Norway, Montenegro and Ukraine. Between December 2008 and April 2010, EUNAVFOR conducted 70 escorts and protected World Food Programme vessels delivering some 340,000 tonnes of food. To complement its naval presence, the EU launched a mission to strengthen Somali security forces by providing military training in Uganda. Meanwhile, NATO continued its counter-piracy efforts with *Operation Ocean Shield*. The Alliance added new elements to its approach, offering capacity-building to regional states, for example helping to build coast guards.

The EU strengthened agreements with regional states that allowed for the transfer and prosecution of apprehended pirates. Like Kenya, the Seychelles allowed the transfer of suspected pirates to its jurisdiction. The Tanzanian parliament passed amendments to the country's criminal code to make it possible to join in the effort. Negotiations with Mauritius, Mozambique, South Africa and Uganda were reported to be under way. However, the Kenyan government indicated it had concerns about security guarantees and cost-sharing arrangements with the EU and would only organise new trials of pirates on a case-by-case basis.

Allied Command Transformation – coming of age?

While NATO was in the midst of developing its new strategic concept (see Essay, pp. 69–74), there were new developments in the evolution of its US-based command, Allied Command Transformation (ACT). General

Stéphane Abrial of the French Air Force took over from General James Mattis, US Marine Corps, as Supreme Allied Commander Transformation in September 2009. ACT, co-located with the US Joint Forces Command in Norfolk, Virginia, had stood in the shadow of the latter, especially since Mattis had commanded both until Abrial was appointed. ACT was intended as a forward-looking organisation guiding NATO through its transformation process, a task that was vital but lacked the urgency of its counterpart in Belgium, Allied Command Operations. Many commentators had detected the detachment of ACT from core discussions in the Alliance and had begun to question the utility of the command.

Abrial set out to change the situation. He defined four core ACT priorities: firstly, to establish ACT as NATO's in-house think tank, making innovative contributions to NATO's responses to the evolving nature of warfare; secondly, the more established role of identifying and prioritising capability shortfalls; thirdly, coordinating national transformation processes; and fourthly, to take on a role in expanding NATO's cooperation with the EU and the UN. Overall, these priorities were meant to position ACT 'as a catalyst for making the comprehensive approach operational'. For the putative think tank role, issues such as the global commons, strategic communications, assured access to space, and the budgetary impact of the economic crisis were identified. However, establishing such a role seemed likely to be challenging within a hierarchical military command. Meanwhile, the commander's attempt to win backing for new priorities drew attention to the fact that ACT's role within NATO needed further definition.

The need for new thinking within the Alliance was evident from the unfolding impact of the economic and budgetary crisis on defence spending – the most significant development in European defence over the past 12 months. The austerity programmes initiated by many governments were set to affect all aspects of defence directly. Financial constraints seemed likely to force a number of governments into structural reform of their armed forces, which might well lead to cuts in manpower. NATO and the EU faced the inevitability that countries would scale back their contributions to international crisis-management operations, and that managing short-term and long-term risk to the security of European nations would thus become more difficult.

The Balkans: Integration Hopes Advance

Balkan politics often resemble a roller coaster and the last year was no exception. Full integration into Europe remained the goal of all western Balkan states, and some countries made progress along this road, though there were also setbacks. A key obstacle was the prevalence of organised crime, and the dismantling of a major drugs gang indicated that some governments were becoming serious about tackling it, but also revealed its extent. Meanwhile, countries of the Western Balkans made slow recoveries from recession, overshadowed by the weakness of the euro-zone, the main market for their exports. But the much feared spill-over from the Greek financial crisis remained limited, despite the prominence of Greek banks and companies across the region.

Serbia's progress

For Serbia the high point on the roller coaster was December 2009 when, after much preparation including the introduction of biometric pass-ports and a new border-management system, Serbians regained the right to travel visa-free to the 25 Schengen-zone countries. (The same right was given to citizens of Montenegro and Macedonia, and in May 2010 the European Commission proposed that citizens of Bosnia and Albania also receive it.) In addition, the EU began to implement Serbia's Stabilisation and Association Agreement (SAA), which had been granted in February 2008 but was immediately frozen. Ratification of this step towards EU membership had been held up by the fact that two indicted war criminals, Bosnian Serb wartime leader Ratko Mladic and Croatian Serb wartime leader Goran Hadzic, remained at large. However, Serge Brammertz, chief prosecutor of the International Criminal Tribunal for the Former Yugoslavia (ICTY), indicated that he believed Serbia was doing enough to try and capture them to justify ratification.

Emboldened by these two advances, the Serbian government decided to apply for membership of the EU. Normally a country would have an SAA fully in place before applying, but as Serbian officials pointed out, there was nothing in the rules mandating this. However, by June 2010 EU foreign ministers had not moved on the application. Italian Foreign Minister Franco Frattini implied that while the decision to begin ratification of the SAA had been an 'incentive' for Serbia, the next step would depend on continued cooperation with the war-crimes tribunal and on restraint over politicising the issue of Kosovo.

Kosovo, which declared independence from Serbia in February 2008, had by mid-2010 been recognised by 69 countries, only nine more than a year earlier. The EU remained divided; 22 states had granted recognition and five – Greece, Spain, Cyprus, Slovakia and Romania – refused, as did Russia, China, Egypt, Brazil and India. The International Court of Justice (ICJ) in The Hague was expected to hand down an advisory opinion before the end of 2010 on the legality of Kosovo's unilateral declaration of independence. European diplomats offered contradictory opinions on whether Serbia would be able to join the EU without recognising Kosovo, or at least coming to some sort of modus vivendi with it. Some said that, as the EU did not want a 'new Cyprus', it was inevitable that Serbia would have to recognise Kosovo as the price of accession, while others disagreed. Some mooted the example of Ireland and Britain, which entered the EU together in 1973 though the Irish constitution included clauses asserting sovereignty over Northern Ireland.

With a few ugly exceptions Kosovo remained quiet over the last year. The NATO-led force there was reduced from 13,289 in June 2009 to some 10,000 at the end of the year. In June 2010 plans were discussed to reduce the number to some 5,000 and then to 2,500. After a meeting of NATO defence ministers, however, NATO Secretary-General Anders Fogh Rasmussen said that they had 'not yet decided to take the next step in that transition process', but that he was confident that it would happen soon, 'when our military assesses that the conditions are right'.

In December 2009 significant numbers of Serbs living in enclaves in the centre and south of Kosovo voted in its local elections, suggesting that many Serbs south of the Ibar river, which divides Mitrovica, were coming to terms with the reality of Kosovo's independence. But Serbs in northern Mitrovica and the region of Novo Brdo elected local councils as part of the Serbian local elections in May 2010. Many believed that a deal would eventually be struck in which Serbia would recognise Kosovo, which in turn would give up its claim to the north. Some ethnic Albanian leaders in Serbia's Presevo valley argued that their territory should join Kosovo in exchange. Suggestions of partition or exchange of territories were, however, denounced by visiting Western dignitaries and international officials in Kosovo, who feared it would open the Pandora's box of division, with serious consequences for Bosnia and Macedonia.

Serbia's minority communities voted in June 2010 for a revamped system of national minority councils, which are supposed to have considerable power or influence both within their communities and with government. Apart from Albanians and Bosniaks, the majority of Serbia's minorities live in the northern province of Vojvodina. In the former Yugoslavia Vojvodina, like Kosovo, had a considerable degree of autonomy from Serbia, and in December 2009 a new statute for the province confirmed the return of certain powers from Belgrade to Novi Sad, its capital. Although Serbian nationalists saw this as a step towards secession, the grant of a far more limited form of autonomy than Vojvodina had once had was greeted with widespread apathy by its 2m people. Some dismissed fears of secession by pointing to the fact that, in the 2001 census, 65% of Vojvodina's population had been Serb, and that the number was since thought to have risen above 70%.

There was debate amongst Serbian politicians as to whether the country, which had been bombed by NATO in 1999 during the Kosovo conflict, should now seek to join the Alliance. Amongst those most in favour were military officers: the Serbian military has been undergoing radical changes, and was due to turn fully professional in 2011. It has also been quietly making up with old enemies. In June 2010 Serbia and Croatia signed a military cooperation agreement. There was also discussion of cooperation with Croatia and other former Yugoslav states in the defence-industry field. Branko Vukelic, the Croatian defence minister said this was important because 'our military industries ... are quite complementary. It is possible they will appear jointly on foreign markets.' Serbian defence minister Dragan Sutanovac confirmed this, saying that he expected defence contracts would be won which would 'require cooperation at the regional level for specific products that used to be produced in the former Yugoslavia, and we will then offer cooperation not only to Croatia but also to Bosnia and Herzegovina and Slovenia'.

Under constant pressure from Brussels to do more to crack down on organised crime, the Serbian authorities scored a major success in breaking up a massive drugs gang. At the end of 2009 *Operation Balkan Warrior* netted 2.7 tonnes of cocaine in Uruguay and Argentina prepared for shipment across the Atlantic. The bust was made in cooperation with the police and intelligence services of the two South American countries as well as the US Drug Enforcement Administration and the UK's Serious Organised Crime Agency. Serbian police indicted Darko Saric, a 40-year-old Serbian citizen from the northern Montenegrin town of Pljevlja, and 19 others for drug trafficking and seized up to €20m worth of Serbian property belonging to him or his associates. Officials believed the property may represent only a tenth of the gang's holdings, and in April the state moved to seize shares in travel firms also believed to be owned by them. Saric, last seen in Montenegro, vanished, and the gang reportedly made threats against Serbian President Boris Tadic and other senior officials.

Bosnian stalemate

Serb, Bosniak and Croat leaders failed to find a way of breaking the perennial political deadlock in Bosnia-Herzegovina. A push by Brussels and Washington to get them to agree to modest reforms aimed at streamlining the unwieldy structure of the state bequeathed by the Dayton peace accords of 1995 fizzled out after a few months.

This left the Office of the High Representative (OHR), led by Austrian diplomat Valentin Inzko, to continue to address the impasse. It was in open conflict with Milorad Dodik, prime minister of the sub-sovereign Republika Srpska (RS). In February 2010 Dodik pushed through legislation which could theoretically allow him to hold a referendum on secession, but this was immediately subjected to legal challenges by Bosniaks. In March Dodik talked openly about the possibility of the 'peaceful dissolution' of the Bosnian state. But as the year progressed Serbian President Tadic made several statements in which he committed Serbia to the territorial integrity of Bosnia, and by mid-2010 a chill beset relations between the RS and Serbia. Dodik was particularly displeased by Tadic's initiative to push through the Serbian parliament a landmark resolution condemning the 1995 massacre of some 8,000 Bosniaks by Bosnian Serb forces at Srebrenica.

Turkey significantly stepped up diplomatic efforts in the western Balkans, especially in Bosnia. There were important trilateral meetings involving Turkey, Bosnia and Croatia and Turkey, Bosnia and Serbia, in which Ankara attempted to use its influence, especially amongst Bosniaks, to help find solutions for political problems. These meetings survived the surprise move by Serbia to ask the UK to arrest Ejup Ganic, who had been a leading Bosniak politician during and after the Bosnian War. He was arrested at London's Heathrow Airport on his way back to Sarajevo after a brief visit to the UK in March and, although he was released on bail, he was ordered to remain in the country while the authorities considered Serbia's request for extradition on war-crimes charges relating to an ambush of Yugoslav troops in 1992. In an attempt to defuse tensions, Tadic subsequently said that he did not mind if Ganic was extradited to Bosnia rather than Serbia.

In December 2009, when NATO invited Montenegro to join its Membership Action Plan (MAP), seen as a stepping stone to membership, Bosnia failed to make the grade. However, after lobbying from friends and neighbours who argued that a MAP would help solidify the country politically, it was granted MAP status in April 2010. Some 2,000 EU-led troops remained in Bosnia and there were no imminent plans to reduce their numbers.

Croatia closer to the EU

Croatia took a major step towards EU membership in November 2009 when Slovenia lifted its obstruction of the process. For ten months Slovenia had prevented progress because of a dispute between the two countries, mainly over their maritime border. Under pressure from EU members, Slovenia agreed to a deal that would permit accession talks to re-start and send the dispute to international arbitration. This was approved by a close vote in a referendum in Slovenia in June 2010.

Although Croatia hoped to join the EU by 2012 or 2013, it still however faced a major problem with the ICTY. Brammertz had requested the so-called 'artillery diaries' from August 1995 – when Croatia re-took the rebel Serbian Krajina region – which might show whether civilian areas had been targeted. The Croatian authorities insisted that the documents had long been removed from the archives and that, despite their best efforts, they had been unable to find them. This left the prosecutor unimpressed, and he argued that 'key investigative avenues remain unexplored'. Croatian cooperation with the tribunal is a condition for the country's eventual accession to the EU.

The government made further efforts to clean up crime and corruption. After Prime Minister Ivo Sanader's sudden and unexplained resignation in July 2009, his successor Jadranka Kosor moved rapidly against high-level corruption, and in October Deputy Prime Minister Damir Polancec was forced to step down. In March 2010 Polancec was arrested while further investigations were carried out. The issue was whether certain transactions with large companies had been carried out with or without Sanader's knowledge. The former prime minister and Polancec denied knowledge of or involvement in illegal activities. In December 2009, however, Sanader announced that he had made a mistake in resigning and was returning to politics. There was speculation that fear of where the trail might lead was behind his bizarre move. He was immediately stripped of his membership of the ruling Croatian Democratic Union (HDZ) party.

Sanader's comeback attempt came days after the HDZ candidate came third in the first round of the presidential election. In January 2010 Ivo Josipovic of the opposition Social Democratic Party (SDP) beat an independent in the second round to become Croatia's new president. Josipovic was relatively unknown to the Croatian public, but this was seen as an advantage, as Croats widely perceived their politicians to be corrupt.

In April 2010, Josipovic told the Bosnian parliament in Sarajevo that he regretted Croatia's policies during the Bosnian War, because they had led 'to human sufferings and to divisions that still plague us today'. Many in the Croatia saw this as a broadside against the HDZ, which had been in charge during the war, and the start of a long campaign to prise the HDZ out of office in the 2011 elections.

Josipovic also made a serious effort to reach out to Tadic, whom he began to meet at regular intervals, and Serbian–Croatian relations warmed considerably. The two presidents declared they would work together to withdraw their countries' mutual accusations of genocide before the ICJ. Croatia had launched its case in 1999, four years after its forces routed the Serbs in Croatia, and one of the main authors of the case was Josipovic. When Croatia ignored a Serbian request to withdraw the case, Belgrade launched a countersuit in 2010 alleging that Croatia had committed genocide against Serbs.

In Albania, which like Croatia had joined NATO in 2009, the narrow victory by incumbent Prime Minister Sali Berisha and his Democratic Party in the June 2009 general election was contested by the Socialists, leading to a year of political paralysis, boycotts of parliament and hunger strikes. In May 2010 the heads of the socialist and conservative blocs in the European Parliament threatened to recommend that Albania's accession bid to join the EU, formally launched in 2009, be suspended if it was unable to sort out its problems.

Turkey: Assertive Ambitions

In late 2009, Turkey appeared poised to fulfil its long-held aspiration of becoming a regional power. Ahmet Davutoglu, the former chief foreign-policy adviser to Prime Minister Recep Tayyip Erdogan who became foreign minister on 1 May 2009, was aggressively implementing his policy of 'zero problems' with Turkey's neighbours, criss-crossing the region, holding talks, initiating dialogues and lifting visa restrictions. He even undertook an unprecedented diplomatic drive in Africa, announcing the opening of new Turkish embassies in 15 African states. If Turkey's EU accession remained stalled, the country had at least managed to avoid a major crisis in December 2009 over its continued refusal to open its ports and airports to Greek Cypriot ships and planes. There were tensions with the United States over Ankara's reluctance to support tougher sanctions against Iran on account of its nuclear programme, but they appeared merely to demonstrate Turkey's increased confidence that it could pursue an independent foreign policy and assert itself as a regional power.

By mid-2010, however, Davutoglu's energetic diplomacy appeared overstretched and instinctive rather than calculated. The Turkish Ministry for Foreign Affairs struggled to keep pace with the increased demands on its limited resources, and the foreign minister's relentless activity seemed apt to endanger rather than facilitate the achievement of his ambitions by spreading his attention thin. Davutoglu did not appear to have considered how to reconcile his ideal of 'zero problems' with situations in which Turkey's neighbours – in particular, Armenia and Azerbaijan – had serious differences with one another. Nor did he seem to have thought through the full repercussions of Turkey's vote against a US-sponsored motion at the UN for increased sanctions against Iran over its nuclear programme.

Perhaps more seriously, although the ruling Justice and Development Party (JDP) had enthusiastically supported Davutoglu's policy of international engagement and dialogue, it seemed to be following the opposite course in domestic affairs, allowing party supporters in the security forces and lower echelons of the judiciary to intimidate and harass the government's opponents. Most significantly, the JDP's abrupt abandonment of an apparently sincere but poorly planned initiative to reach out to Turkey's Kurdish minority merely intensified the growing resentment and distrust between ethnic Turks and ethnic Kurds at a time Turkish society was already dangerously divided over the role of Islam in public life.

Region and religion

In Davutoglu's 2001 book on Turkey's foreign policy, entitled *Strategic Depth*, he argued that Turkey's traditional pro-Western strategic alignment had lost sight of the countries in its immediate neighbourhood, particularly the majority-Muslim countries of the Middle East. An unabashed Ottoman nostalgist, he believed Turkey should reclaim its previous regional pre-eminence – not by restoring political hegemony over the former Ottoman territories but by leading an informal grouping of Muslim countries bound to Turkey by closer bilateral ties. In his vision, Turkish leaders would focus the region's Muslims and speak for them to the rest of the world. But Davutoglu stressed that Turkey should still try to maintain good political and economic ties with Europe and the United States. Although critics claimed that he was seeking to move Turkey away from the West towards the East, his main objective was not to align the country with either but to establish it as a power centre in its own right.

After the JDP first came to power in November 2002, Davutoglu's vision served as a blueprint for Turkey's relations with the Middle East, as closer regional engagement ran parallel to the JDP's attempts to secure a date for the formal opening of EU accession negotiations. In recent years, as enthusiasm for EU membership has faded, that vision has dominated Turkish foreign policy, and has been pursued with even greater energy since Davutoglu became foreign minister.

In 2009, Turkey established a series of bilateral 'High Level Strategic Cooperation Councils' with Iraq, Syria, Jordan and Lebanon, and drafted a provisional agreement to establish another with Libya. The councils were designed to provide an institutional framework in which ministers from each country could meet at least once a year to discuss ways of improving bilateral cooperation. In late 2009, visa requirements were abolished for travel between Turkey and Syria, Lebanon, Jordan, Qatar and Libya with an eye to boosting trade and tourism. Turkey also upgraded its commercial relationships with Syria and Iraq. In February 2010, the railway linking Turkey, Syria and Iraq was reopened, and work continued on a fast train between Aleppo in northern Syria and Gaziantep in southeast Turkey. There were also plans to open a second border crossing between Turkey and Iraq. Turkey remained the main supplier of processed foodstuffs and consumer goods to northern Iraq as well as a major source of foreign investment in the region. By early 2010, Turkey's policy of engagement with other Muslim countries had changed the structure of its foreign trade. Although the EU still accounted for over 40% of Turkey's foreign trade and around two-thirds of its foreign investment, its economic ties with other Muslim countries were growing at a faster rate. The global recession, which hit markets in the EU harder than those in the Middle East, accelerated the trend. In 2009, Turkey's total exports contracted by 22.6%, while Turkish exports to Muslim countries rose by 9.9%.

Turkey's heightened engagement with the Middle East also had a strong ideological component of Muslim solidarity, which underpinned practical considerations. This was especially clear in the continuing deterioration in Turkey's relationship with Israel. Already strained, it reached a new low in January 2009, when Erdogan stormed out of the World Economic Forum summit meeting in Davos, Switzerland, in protest of Israel's military incursion into Gaza, bluntly accusing Israeli President Shimon Peres of 'knowing very well how to kill'. Through 2009, JDP officials continued to harshly condemn Israel's policy towards the Palestinians and reiterate their support for Hamas both against Israel and in its bitter domestic rivalry with the secular Fatah faction of the Palestine Liberation Organisation. In October 2009, Turkey abruptly announced that it would not allow Israel to participate in Turkey's annual *Anatolian Eagle* military exercises, which had been held nearly every year since 2001 and normally involved Turkey, Israel and Turkey's NATO allies. NATO, which had spent months planning its participation, withdrew in protest, while the Turkish General Staff issued a statement holding Davutoglu responsible.

> " Relations plummeted to outright hostility after Israeli commandos stormed the ship "

On 31 May 2010, relations between the two countries plummeted to outright hostility after Israeli commandos stormed one of a flotilla of aid ships, led by an Islamist Turkish NGO, which were trying to break Israel's embargo on Gaza. Eight Turkish citizens and one Turkish-American were killed in the assault and more than 20 injured (see Middle East, pp. 227–9). The JDP government immediately withdrew the Turkish ambassador to Tel Aviv and demanded an independent international inquiry into the incident. It warned that relations between the two countries could not return to normal until Israel issued a public apology and agreed to pay reparations. Israel rejected all of the JDP's demands.

The incident – and Washington's muted criticism of Israel's actions – accelerated the shift in emphasis in Turkey's foreign relations away from Europe and the United States to the Muslim countries of the Middle East. On 10 June 2010, speaking at a meeting of the Turkish–Arab Cooperation Forum in Istanbul, Davutoglu announced plans for a free-trade zone encompassing Turkey, Jordan, Syria and Lebanon. He predicted that the zone would form the foundations for what would eventually become a single political and economic bloc consisting of the Muslim countries of the Middle East and North Africa.

The same sense of Muslim solidarity could be seen in the JDP's pursuit of close ties with Sudan in the absence of any obvious practical benefits and despite the ongoing international condemnation of Khartoum for its role in the Darfur conflict, generally considered genocide in the West. Turkey rejected the EU's call to withdraw an invitation to Sudanese President Omar al-Bashir to attend a summit meeting of the Organisation of the Islamic Conference in Istanbul on 9 November 2009. The EU noted that the International Criminal Court (ICC), of which Turkey is still not a member, had issued an arrest warrant for Bashir for war crimes in Darfur. Erdogan angrily responded that Turkey could host whomever it wished and declared Muslims incapable of genocide. The statement came four months after Erdogan had accused the Chinese authorities of genocide in their suppression of political agitation by the Uighur Muslim minority in Xinjiang. Bashir himself cancelled his trip to Turkey for fear that his plane would be intercepted by countries that were members of the ICC.

Turkey also continued to resist US plans for increased sanctions against Iran amid growing international concern that Tehran was developing a nuclear bomb. As with Syria and Iraq, Turkey's economic and political ties with Iran had grown rapidly since the JDP came to power. From 2002 to 2009, bilateral trade between the two countries increased sevenfold and Tehran became Turkey's second-largest supplier of energy (mostly natural gas) after Russia. In recent years, the two countries also shared intelligence on, and occasionally coordinated military operations against, Kurdish insurgents – the Kurdistan Workers' Party (PKK) in Turkey and its affiliate the Kurdistan Free Life Party in Iran. Iran remained the only country that had extradited PKK militants to Turkey.

On 13 September 2009, Erdogan defended Iran's lack of transparency over its uranium-enrichment programme, dismissing growing evidence that it was accelerating its quest for weapons-grade material as 'gossip' and suggesting that the West should focus instead on disarming Israel, the only country in the Middle East known to possess nuclear weapons. Privately and publicly, Davutoglu continued to insist that diplomacy rather than increased sanctions or military action was the best way to prevent Iran from developing a nuclear capability. In early 2010, Davutoglu travelled frequently to Tehran to try to broker an agreement. Eventually, on 17 May, acting together with Brazil, Turkey announced that Iran had agreed to a deal under which it would ship

1,200 kilograms of low-enriched uranium for storage in Turkey in return for foreign nuclear fuel for a research reactor. The agreement was similar to one brokered in October 2009, which eventually collapsed when Iran backtracked. However, since October 2009, Iran had continued with its enrichment programme. As a result, unlike the previous agreement, the deal brokered by Turkey and Brazil would still have left Iran with enough uranium to make one nuclear weapon. More critically, the new agreement did not require Tehran to halt uranium enrichment or be more open about its nuclear programme. The deal was promptly dismissed by Washington, which pushed ahead with plans to seek approval from the UN for a new package of sanctions against Iran.

Despite intense pressure from the United States to abstain, when the sanctions package was presented to the UN Security Council on 9 June 2010, Turkey joined Brazil in voting against. Although the package was still passed by 12 votes to 2, with Lebanon abstaining, Turkey's 'no' vote was interpreted both inside and outside the country as a gesture of defiance against the United States; and triggered a palpable cooling in Ankara's relationship with Washington.

Outsized ambition

Davutoglu's surplus of energy over acumen was most striking in Turkey's attempted rapprochement with Armenia. Turkey's land border with Armenia had been closed since April 1993, when Ankara severed all ties with Yerevan to protest its support for the ethnic Armenian uprising which resulted in Armenia's de facto control of the Azerbaijani enclave of Nagorno-Karabakh. Although a ceasefire was reached in May 1994, the status of Nagorno-Karabakh remains unresolved. In recent years, the restoration of bilateral ties between Turkey and Armenia has been further complicated by the campaign by the Armenian diaspora for international recognition that the massacres, forced marches and deportations of ethnic Armenians in 1915 constituted genocide, which Turkey has long vehemently denied.

In 2008, Turkish and Armenian diplomats began meeting in third countries and on the margins at international forums to explore how to improve relations. On 6 November 2008, Turkish President Abdullah Gul became the first Turkish head of state to visit Armenia when he attended a World Cup qualifying match between the two countries in Yerevan. On 22 April 2009, under pressure from the United States, Turkey and Armenia announced that they had drawn up a roadmap for improving bilateral ties, although it excluded any commitments on the genocide or Nagorno-Karabakh. Privately, Turkish officials admitted that they had agreed to the roadmap to discourage US President Barack Obama from fulfilling a pre-election promise to recognise Turkish actions as genocide on 24 April 2009, the 94th anniversary of the beginning of the deportations and massacres of Armenians. Persuaded that using the word 'genocide' could infuriate Turkey and endanger the rapprochement between Ankara and Yerevan, Obama released a statement referring only to 'great atrocities'.

For several months, neither Turkey nor Armenia attempted to advance the roadmap. On 10 October 2009, however, under US pressure, Turkey and Armenia signed a protocol in Switzerland setting a timetable for the normalisation of their bilateral relations, to include the establishment of diplomatic relations and the opening of their shared border. Although the protocol did not mention genocide or Nagorno-Karabakh, its signing triggered an angry reaction from Turkish ultranationalists and an even angrier one from Azerbaijan, which threatened to triple the price of the natural gas it supplied to Turkey and re-route any new oil and gas pipelines around it, thus frustrating Turkey's long-cherished ambition of becoming a regional energy hub. Davutoglu appeared not to have realised that agreeing to normalise ties with Armenia, which Azerbaijan regarded as effectively occupying Nagorno-Karabakh, would infuriate Baku. Davutoglu flew immediately to Azerbaijan to reassure the Azerbaijani government that Turkey would not ratify the protocol until the Nagorno-Karabakh issue had been resolved. Azerbaijani officials issued public statements of approval, but privately indicated it would take time for their confidence in Turkey to be restored.

As the protocol foundered, the Armenian diaspora continued to lobby for international recognition of the Armenian genocide. On 5 March 2010, Turkey recalled its ambassador to the United States after the Foreign Affairs Committee of the US House of Representatives approved a resolution calling for the US government to recognise the genocide, and on 11 March 2010 recalled its ambassador to Sweden after the Swedish parliament passed a similar resolution. Both ambassadors subsequently returned to their posts, but the resolutions continued to infuriate Erdogan, who blamed Armenia. On 17 March 2010, Erdogan publicly threatened to expel 100,000 Armenian citizens working illegally in Turkey – apparently oblivious to overtones of racism in singling out Armenians from myriad other illegals, or to the ominous resonance of the policy with the deportations that preceded the massacres of 1915. On 22 April 2010, Armenian President Serzh Sargsyan signed a decree indefinitely suspending the presentation of the protocol to parliament for ratification.

Armenia's suspension was perhaps a tactical error, sparing Turkey the international opprobrium that could have materialised if Ankara had unilaterally abrogated the agreement. Nevertheless, Davutoglu's failure to predict Azerbaijan's reaction or consult with Baku before signing the protocol led to accusations that his energetic diplomacy had more breadth than depth, and that, in trying to juggle numerous issues, he was achieving less than if he had focused on a few. Doubts also arose about the calibre of his support staff, which included a very young team of advisers, including several PhD students, whose dynamism and idealism seemed to come at the cost of experience and prudence. Questions arose as well about whether the Turkish state had the resources to establish Turkey as a major power. In May 2010, Turkey had around 1,000 career diplomats, approximately one-quarter of the average in the major Western powers that Davutoglu sought to emulate. The decision to open 15 new embassies in Africa placed a huge burden on Turkey's already overstretched diplomatic corps.

The EU: fading interest

The vigour that Davutoglu devoted to cultivating close ties in the Middle East and Africa contrast sharply with the JDP's fading interest in Turkey's EU membership, which the EU has reciprocated. In early autumn 2009, there was fleeting speculation that Turkey might attempt to revive its reform programme in contemplation of EU accession in the run-up to the EU summit in December 2009. The summit was slated to review the decision in December 2006 to freeze eight chapters of Turkey's accession process pending its implementation of the Ankara Protocol of 30 July

2005, under which Turkey had pledged to open its ports and airports to Greek Cypriot ships and planes. Turkey refused to implement the protocol unless the EU took measures to ease the economic isolation of the Turkish Republic of Northern Cyprus, the Turkish Cypriot enclave in northern Cyprus that only Ankara has recognised. In the end, the JDP government made no attempt to revive its reform programme and, when it met in Stockholm on 10–11 December 2009, the EU decided merely to extend the suspension of the eight chapters for another year.

Although Ankara greeted the decision with relief, it once again demonstrated how dependent Turkey's hopes of EU accession had become not only on domestic reforms but also on progress in US-brokered negotiations to reunify Cyprus, which has been divided since 1974. The Greek and Turkish Cypriots had embarked on another round of direct talks in September 2008. But in March 2010, when the process was temporarily suspended for presidential elections in the North, the two sides remained far apart on a number of key issues – in particular, the distribution of property and the division of power between the two communities in a unified state. The elections themselves, on 18 April 2010, produced another setback. The incumbent Mehmet Ali Talat, an outspoken supporter of the island's reunification, was roundly defeated by Dervis Eroglu, a hardliner who had long advocated a two-state solution, anathema to the Greek Cypriots.

Although Eroglu promised to continue negotiating with the Greek Cypriots, in May 2010 the prospect of a solution appeared to be receding. By then, both Ankara and Brussels appeared more concerned with merely keeping Turkey's accession process alive than with moving it forward. Of the 13 chapters of the accession process that had been opened since membership negotiations officially began on 4 October 2005, only one had been closed. No more appeared likely to be closed in the foreseeable future. The JDP seemed to have little appetite for implementing the long list of required reforms, and the issue of EU membership had almost disappeared from Turkish public discourse. A December 2009 poll commissioned by the BBC found that only 29% of Turks had a positive opinion of the EU, down from 34% in December 2008 and 70% in 2003–04, when many Turks believed that there was a genuine chance of speedy accession.

Domestic tensions

As the local elections of 29 March 2009 approached, the JDP sought to offset its overall decline in popularity by picking up votes in the predominantly Kurdish southeast of Turkey, where it believed its Islamist credentials would boost its support in what has traditionally been the most conservative region of the country. In the event, the JDP lost ground both nationwide, winning 38.4% of the vote compared with 46.6% in the last general election in 2007, and in the southeast, losing control of several municipalities to the Kurdish nationalist Democratic Society Party (DSP). In response, in June 2009, the JDP initiated what it termed a 'Democratic Opening'. Through summer 2009, the JDP held a series of meetings and consultations with political parties, NGOs and professional associations in an attempt to identify and address the problems faced by Turkey's Kurdish minority. In addition to securing Kurdish votes for the next general election in 2011, the JDP hoped to find a peaceful solution to the Kurdish insurgency, which has claimed over 40,000 lives since it began in 1984. The Democratic Opening ran in parallel to discreet, indirect negotiations with the PKK for a cessation of violence.

Yet the Democratic Opening failed to secure the support of any opposition parties. Even the DSP regarded it with suspicion, particularly when JDP officials said they would not allow the use of Kurdish as a language of instruction in schools or a comprehensive amnesty for PKK militants. In October 2009, frustrated by the lack of progress and anxious for some return on its efforts, the JDP announced that eight PKK militants would arrive at Turkey's Habur border crossing on 19 October 2009 from the organisation's main bases in northern Iraq. The PKK remained militarily much weaker than it had been in the early 1990s, when it controlled large swathes of the countryside in southeast Turkey after dark. But it had also become aware that it could not achieve its goals through military victory, and had in recent years used violence tactically, to bludgeon the Turkish authorities into recognising the organisation as a legitimate interlocutor and conceding greater political and cultural rights to the country's Kurds. When the PKK militants walked unmolested through the Habur border gate, they declared that they had come not to surrender but to serve as emissaries from the organisation's leadership. They were greeted by thousands of supporters, who celebrated what they regarded as the successful culmination of the PKK's 25-year campaign and paraded the militants through southeast Turkey as conquering heroes.

The JDP's apparent calculation was that other PKK militants would be inspired to lay down their arms. But it had neglected to create a legal framework for reintegrating returning militants or to secure an unequivocal commitment from the PKK to abandon violence. In the event, the repatriation produced a furious Turkish nationalist reaction. Tens of thousands of demonstrators took to the streets to protest what they regarded as the state's capitulation to terrorism. In many cities, including cosmopolitan ones such as Istanbul and Izmir, ethnic resentment exploded, as Kurdish-owned premises were trashed and Kurds were attacked on the street. Alarmed, the JDP promptly cancelled any more militant repatriations, handing the PKK another propaganda victory by enabling it to claim that the government had rejected its peace overtures. The JDP made no attempt to revive the Democratic Opening, and on 11 January 2010, the Constitutional Court formally outlawed the DSP on the grounds that it had become a locus of Kurdish separatist activity. In response, starting from spring 2010, the PKK stepped up its attacks against the Turkish security forces in the predominantly Kurdish southeast of Turkey and threatened to broaden its insurgency to include a bombing campaign against soft targets in the west of the country.

Though poorly thought out and implemented, the JDP's Democratic Opening was the most ambitious attempt by any Turkish government to address the concerns of the Turkey's Kurds. The JDP has taken a considerably less conciliatory approach to the other major fault line in Turkish society: Islamist supporters of the government versus their secularist opponents. In the most controversial development, 194 critics of the government were charged with membership of a terrorist organisation called Ergenekon, which was allegedly plotting to use violence to destabilise the government and trigger a military coup. Despite egregious abuses of legal procedures – and the dearth of tangible evidence that Ergenekon even existed – in early 2010 additional allegations of coup plots appeared in pro-JDP newspapers. Another round of arrests, including the detention of over 70 serving and retired military personnel, ensued. Again the evidence appeared unconvincing and frequently contradictory. Moreover, critics of the investigations were subjected to smear campaigns in the pro-JDP press, and transcripts of private telephone conversations of some were published on the Internet. Several were arrested and themselves charged with attempting to overthrow the government.

Compounding concerns about the politicisation of judicial processes were a string of tax fines imposed on the Dogan Group, the largest media outfit not aligned with the JDP. This action following a speech by Erdogan in September 2008 calling on JDP supporters not to purchase Dogan Group newspapers, which had published corruption allegations involving some of his close associates. By late August 2009, the penalties levied against the Dogan Group came to $3.3bn. In late December 2009, rumours surfaced that the fines would be dropped, and the Dogan Group quietly dismissed several of its editors. From January 2010 onwards, its newspapers adopted a more conciliatory tone towards the JDP.

Unavoidable introversion

In May 2010, domestic divisions appeared to pose a greater threat than Turkey's questionable diplomatic capabilities and resources to Davutoglu's goal of positioning Turkey as a regional power. In April 2010, the JDP presented to parliament a series of constitutional amendments which would, amongst other things, increase the government's control over appointments to the higher echelons of the judiciary. The JDP's parliamentary majority ensured that the amendments were passed on 7 May 2010. Although they failed to secure the two-thirds majority necessary to be enacted automatically, the government planned to put them to a public referendum in September 2010. With the once-powerful Turkish military's waning political influence further reduced by the Ergenekon case and the arrests in early 2010, most Turkish secularists regarded the higher echelons of the judiciary as the JDP Islamists' next – and perhaps last – major target. They vowed to challenge the constitutional amendments in the courts and, if that failed, to launch a vigorous campaign to have them overturned in the referendum.

In May 2010, secularist hopes of toppling the JDP government at the next general election, which was scheduled to be held in July 2011 at the latest, received a major boost when Deniz Baykal, the long-time leader of the main opposition Republican People's Party (RPP) was unexpectedly forced to step down following a sex scandal. For the previous decade, Baykal had combined a tight control of the party apparatus with a singular lack of political charisma, with the result that he had often appeared as irremovable as he was unelectable. On 22 May 2010, Baykal was replaced as RPP leader by the party's deputy head, Kemal Kilicdaroglu. An ethnic Kurd from the eastern province of Tunceli, Kilicdaroglu had long enjoyed a reputation for modesty, honesty and an ability to communicate with the mass of the population. His appointment revitalised the RPP. By June 2010, opinion polls suggested that it was running neck and neck with the JDP. Although it was unclear whether the RPP would be able to sustain its momentum through to the next general election, in late June 2010 the JDP nevertheless appeared to be facing the first credible challenge to its grip on power since it initially took office in November 2002.

The revitalisation of the RPP came at a time the JDP was coming intense public pressure over its handling of the PKK insurgency. By the end of June 2010, the escalating death toll had triggered a rise in ethnic tensions between Turks and Kurds. With a general election only a year away, the JDP did not appear able to attempt a new initiative to end the conflict without risking a nationalist backlash at the polls. The anti-Kurdish sentiments that had erupted in October 2009 showed no sign of abating. Funerals of the soldiers killed in PKK attacks regularly turned into anti-government and anti-Kurdish protests, and there was a marked increase in ethnic violence in Turkish cities and university campuses. Although Davutoglu continued to press ahead with his ambitions to transform Turkey into the dominant power in its region, in June 2010, there appeared little doubt that in the ensuing year, for the rest of the JDP government, the main priority would be not enhancing Turkey's international standing but addressing deepening divisions inside the country in the run up to the 2011 general election.

Chapter 5
Russia

The past year did not see dramatic developments in Russia by comparison with the previous two years, in which Vladimir Putin had retained the reins of power while passing the presidency to his hand-picked successor, Dmitry Medvedev, and Russia had sent its forces into Georgia. There were no political upheavals, and Moscow was much less activist and assertive on the international stage. Following a severe recession, the early months of 2010 saw a return to moderate economic growth, backed by the rise in world oil prices.

Yet beneath the surface of this more subdued and 'normal' Russia, an important introspective process was gaining momentum. Political and economic elites were engaged in heated debates about the country's future prospects and strategic direction. For some, this debate was akin to former President Mikhail Gorbachev's glasnost, which preceded the perestroika years and eventually brought down the authoritarian Soviet regime. Few would dispute that in today's Russia there was more freedom than at any point in the past decade to question the political status quo and the 'glorious' legacy of Putin's era of consolidation and autocratic state capitalism.

But others viewed such discussions as nothing more than window dressing: the apparent ability to question the country's direction was a Potemkin village, a false construct put up by the Putin–Medvedev duopoly to silence critics at home and abroad. It would not facilitate any real change to the power and privilege enjoyed by the elite. Critics pointed

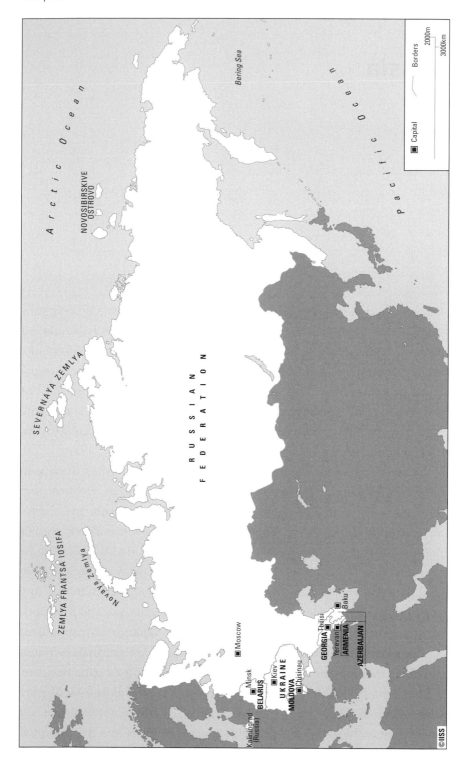

Arctic Ocean

Bering Sea

Pacific Ocean

NOVOSIBIRSKIYE OSTROVO

SEVERNAYA ZEMLYA

ZEMLYA FRANTSA IOSIFA

Novaya Zemlya

RUSSIAN FEDERATION

Moscow

Minsk
BELARUS

Kiev
UKRAINE
MOLDOVA
Chişinău

GEORGIA Tbilisi
Yerevan
ARMENIA
AZERBAIJAN
Baku

Kaliningrad
(Russia)

Borders
2000m
3000km

Capital

©IISS

out that debates tended to involve only a small group of Internet-savvy technocrats with little real power. Although Medvedev had promised more freedom, application of the rule of law and a crackdown on corruption, they noted, he had done little to put these promises into action.

Debating modernisation

If one phrase could sum up the impression gleaned from Russian leaders, experts and people, it was that Russia was once again at a historic crossroads: it could either continue, through inertia, with Putin's model of economic development, which was increasingly seen as synonymous with stagnation; or it could attempt fundamental reform to diversify and revitalise the economy, modernise society and ultimately introduce more democracy into the political system.

The period of soul-searching was encouraged by Medvedev himself in an article published in September 2009 on the gazeta.ru website under the title 'Forward, Russia!'. The president offered a sobering diagnosis of the country's problems. 'The global economic crisis has shown that our affairs are far from being in the best state', he wrote. The economy remained dependent on exporting natural resources, and failed to meet citizens' demand for high-quality goods. Russia's democratic institutions were sub-standard, civil society was weak, and the population was falling. 'Alcoholism, smoking, traffic accidents, the lack of availability of many medical technologies, and environmental problems take millions of lives.' Medvedev bemoaned 'endemic corruption, and the inveterate habit of relying on the state, foreign countries or some all-powerful doctrine to solve our problems – on anyone except ourselves'. He asked: 'Should we continue to drag into the future our primitive raw-materials economy?' Modernisation, however, would be undertaken cautiously: 'We will not rush. Hasty and ill-considered political reforms have led to tragic consequences more than once in our history ... Changes will take place, but they will be gradual, thought-through, and step-by-step.'

In a parliamentary address in November, Medvedev was more specific about the changes he wanted. Opposition parties should be given opportunities to be elected into regional legislatures. The 'state corporations' created by Putin should be part privatised. Corrupt officials would be prosecuted. A new approach would be developed to reduce instability in the North Caucasus, plagued by unemployment, poverty, corruption and clan-based violence.

These two major statements by Medvedev, identifying many problems with the economic and political system, inspired critics of Putin's resource-led state-capitalist autocracy to speak out more assertively in support of change. The debate unfolded online in comments on Medvedev's gazeta.ru article and among more liberal think tanks, some of them associated directly or indirectly with Medvedev. In September over 800 comments were posted on gazeta.ru and the presidential blog site in response to the 'Forward, Russia!' article. Although many were supportive, others were either critical or mistrustful of the real intentions of the president and the ruling elite.

In February 2010 the Institute of Contemporary Development (INSOR), an influential think tank with Medvedev as chairman of the board, published a report entitled 'Russia in the 21st Century: Vision for the Future'. The authors presented a medium-term vision of a Russia with a functioning multi-party system, elected regional governors and reformed law-enforcement and security services. Russia would join the EU and NATO. The report, which called on the government to clearly articulate long-term goals for Russia's domestic and foreign policies, had the effect of extending the debate beyond the moderate ambitions that had so far been articulated by Medvedev.

The third major symbol of the president's push for modernisation came in June 2010 when he visited Silicon Valley in California to discuss ways to attract investment. He had established Russia's own research and innovation centre at Skolkovo, outside Moscow, with funding and special privileges in order to attract investment and expertise. Viktor Vekselberg, a leading business 'oligarch', was appointed to oversee the project, which was envisioned to house 30,000 to 40,000 personnel from Russia and abroad by 2014. However, the project met scepticism about its chances of success in the absence of fundamental reforms.

Several conclusions could be drawn from the debate. Firstly, it indicated a growing realisation within the ruling elite that the status quo was both unsustainable and undesirable. The financial crisis had shown that Putin's model, which a decade ago had been credited with saving Russia from collapse, was no longer able to deliver sufficient economic growth to guarantee the country a place among leading emerging nations such as China, India and Brazil, let alone among the most developed nations. Without systemic change, Russia would have problems addressing challenges such as population decline, the growing gap between rich and poor, uneven regional development, lack of technological innovation, declining military capabilities, falling gas and oil production and aging Soviet-era infrastructure. Failure to undertake major reforms could plunge Russia into stagnation and decay.

Secondly, while there was broad agreement about the challenges, there were disagreements on the best ways to overcome them. The key contentious issues could be summed up in five questions. Could economic modernisation be accomplished without political modernisation? Should the state or the private sector take the lead? Could the system be reformed gradually or were drastic measures needed to fight corruption and to implement the rule of law? Could modernisation be implemented in such a vast country using Putin's top-down model, or would devolution of power to the regions be necessary? What would be the foreign-policy implications of spending the next several years concentrating primarily on domestic reforms?

The third conclusion was that the society created by Putin, featuring a strong bureaucracy, centralised authority based on personal loyalties, and a weak civil society with an even weaker political opposition, was the major impediment to reform. Moving towards a more entrepreneurial and open society would require Medvedev to undo many of Putin's legacies. But not only was Putin now the prime minister, but Medvedev was himself a part of this legacy, having stood side by side with Putin throughout his political career. He had pledged to Putin and to the electorate that he would preserve Putin's legacy and continue his policies.

Obstacles to modernisation

There were other barriers to change. The first was the lack of incentives to undertake reforms for a government which had mentally returned to its pre-financial-crisis comfort zone as a result of the recovery in commodity-export revenues. In 2009 Russia was the world's largest exporter of natural gas, the second largest exporter of oil, and the third largest exporter of steel and primary aluminium. Oil prices averaged $75 per barrel in the first quarter of 2010, 70% higher than in the first quarter of 2009. Oil and gas export revenues accounted for 25% of GDP, and Russia earned $2 billion in extra revenue for each $1 rise in the price of oil. The economy was bouncing back from the sharp 7.9% decline in GDP in 2009. In the first quarter of 2010 it grew at annual rate of 2.9%, and for the whole of 2010 the government was projecting 3.1% growth. The budget deficit was projected at about 5% of GDP, and in the first quarter of 2010 Russia attracted over $13bn of foreign investment, 9.3% more than in the first quarter of 2009.

The second obstacle was uncertainty about the 2012 presidential election. Many in the elite, still loyal to Putin, were betting on his return to power. Since Medvedev had made it clear that he would not run against Putin, the decision on who would return to the Kremlin lay with Putin. According to a Levada-Center poll in May 2010, only 4% of Russians believed Medvedev was pursuing a different policy from that of Putin. Convincing voters that he was independent of the prime minister and winning their support for change would be a tall order in two years.

The third obstacle to modernisation was the dominance of state corporations. Putin had funnelled a massive amount of state funds into them, with little result. For example, more than R200bn was given to Rosnano, which was charged with making Russia the world leader in nanotechnology. Rostechnology, headed by Putin's close friend Sergei Chemizov, was given control over more than 400 state companies, but more than a third of them were on the edge of bankruptcy. State corporations were often accused of being vehicles for diverting state resources into corrupt practices. Their books were opaque and there was little oversight of their use of state subsidies.

Fourthly, the notoriously inefficient public sector was hardly in a position to modernise itself. Despite several attempts at administrative reform under Putin's presidency, the size of the state bureaucracy had increased. Tensions were emerging between the Medvedev and Putin teams within the bureaucracy. Medvedev decided on 21 June 2010 to publicly reprimand officials for not implementing his decisions and asked his staff to draw up lists of those most obviously at fault. A final obstacle was the shortage of qualified public servants in the regions. Some provincial chiefs had been in their posts for over a decade. Medvedev made several attempts to rejuvenate the regional governments and remove the most notorious regional 'tsars', such as Meitemer Shaimiev, prime minister of Tatarstan, and Murtaza Rakhimov, president of Bashkortostan. He remained opposed, however, to the direct election of regional governors, fearing that this could threaten Russia's territorial integrity and make it more likely that elected officials would foster special interests that could fund their election bids.

Positive signs

Yet amidst the prevailing scepticism, there were tentative signs that things might be changing. Cracks started to appear within the ruling United Russia party, with a growing number of politicians identifying themselves as part of Medvedev's pro-modernisation team. Meanwhile, members of the middle class who had been severely affected by the financial meltdown staged protests against the privileges enjoyed by officials. Mid-ranking officials, including police in the regions, posted appeals to Medvedev on the Internet alleging corruption in their departments. However, despite Medvedev's encouragement of such action, many who spoke out found themselves under investigation and harassed. A Moscow lawyer, Sergei Magnitsky, who testified about police corruption was imprisoned and died in custody. In some regions, protests came from the most vulnerable sectors of society, including miners who closed roads in protest at poor working conditions, and traders in places such as Kaliningrad and Vladivostok, whose businesses were badly affected by Moscow's protectionist policies. In many demonstrations Putin and his government were singled out for criticism.

Meanwhile, Medvedev took steps to prepare the ground for modernisation and for the privatisation of some state corporations. In June 2010 the Duma adopted a law to turn Rosnano into a joint stock company. The number of so-called 'strategic enterprises' in which foreigners could not invest or which were to be kept under state control for reasons of national security was reduced from 213 to 41. Medvedev said the state 'should not pick the apples from the tree of the economy, but should help the garden to grow full of apple trees'. He asked the prosecutor's office to check whether state corporations had spent state funds efficiently and lawfully. The office started 22 criminal investigations on alleged misuse of resources. In addition, the president approved in April 2010 a national anti-corruption plan, and supported anti-corruption investigations against senior law-enforcement officials.

One important step Medvedev took was to put the problem of the North Caucasus back on Russia's political agenda. Putin had preferred to keep the issue out of the headlines, ignoring spreading violence in Ingushetia, Dagestan and Chechnya. Medvedev, by contrast, acknowledged that Russia was facing a major challenge and that the region required special attention. According to independent sources, in 2009 the number of violent incidents in the North Caucasus was around 1,100, compared with 795 in 2008, and fatalities numbered 900 compared with 586. The number of suicide bombings nearly quadrupled in 2009, from 4 to 15. Medvedev criticised the suppression-based strategy of the past decade and said effective managers were needed to control financial flows from the centre to these regions. In January 2010 he established a special federal district covering all the republics of the North Caucasus and appointed Alexander Khloponin, former governor of Krasnoyarsk region, to head it. Khloponin developed a strategy combining education, economic development and a fight against corruption, organised crime and clan politics.

Khloponin's arrival, however, produced little visible improvement. Regional bosses, including the powerful Chechen president, Ramzan Kadyrov, resented outside efforts to influence their use of federal funds and resisted Khloponin's attempts to remove their supporters from regional governments. Weeks after his appointment, two women from Dagestan blew themselves up on the Moscow metro, killing 40 people. Many viewed this attack as a warning against interference, though it was also seen as a reaction to the killing of a jihadist leader in the North Caucasus.

Pragmatism in foreign relations

Perhaps the most visible change credited to Medvedev, strongly reinforced over the past year, was a more pragmatic and cooperative foreign policy. While Putin occasionally intervened, on the whole Medvedev was in charge of managing Russia's relations with the United States and Europe. For many Western leaders, Medvedev – a new-generation, Internet-savvy lawyer and self-professed liberal with no KGB background – was a more welcome interlocutor than Putin. Medvedev's foreign-policy objectives were linked closely to his domestic modernising agenda. Relations with the United States, NATO and the European Union, and specifically with Poland and Ukraine, improved.

Following US President Barack Obama's visit to Moscow in July 2009, the atmosphere in bilateral relations warmed. Obama's policy to 'reset' relations delivered concrete results. Washington removed two serious irritants: it abandoned plans to site parts of its missile-defence shield in Poland and the Czech Republic and downgraded its engagement in post-Soviet countries. When a political crisis engulfed Kyrgyzstan in 2010, for example, Washington signalled its support for close cooperation with Russia on crisis management and even encouraged Russia to take the lead in addressing the humanitarian crisis.

The United States engaged Russia in negotiations on a new strategic arms control treaty, though hopes of a quick agreement turned out to be over-optimistic. The two sides failed to meet the symbolic deadline of 5 December 2009, when the START I treaty expired, and final agreement was reached following intervention by Obama and Medvedev, who signed the new treaty on 8 April (for details, see pp. 40–44). The key area of disagreement was missile defence. While Russia sought to include provisions limiting US capacity to deploy national missile-defence systems, the United States fought to exclude such limits, aware that any explicit linkage could derail ratification in the US Senate. The two sides settled for ambiguity in the text, which did not prevent either side from having 'limited' missile defences. Russia issued a unilateral statement warning that it could withdraw from the treaty if the United States deployed a missile-defence system that could threaten its nuclear deterrent.

The signing of the New START treaty was an important milestone in the transformation of US–Russian relations, though it had still to be ratified – Medvedev indicated that Russia would seek to do so simultaneously with the United States. US senators were likely to raise the statement on missile defence, the relaxation of verification procedures and the lack of inclusion of Russia's tactical weapons. A spy scandal that erupted in July 2010 – resolved with a rapid Cold War-style spy swap – added to the difficulty. Nevertheless, the balance of expectation was on the side of ratification.

There was also better cooperation over Iran's nuclear programme. The first signal that Moscow might have become ready to support new sanctions against Iran came in April 2010, when Medvedev, visiting Washington for the Nuclear Security Summit, said such sanctions 'could be unavoidable'. On the day US Secretary of State Hillary Clinton announced preliminary agreement on new sanctions, several Russian entities, including its main arms-export agency Rosoboronexport, were removed from the list of entities against which the United States had been applying unilateral sanctions for alleged cooperation with Iran. On 9 June, Russia voted alongside the United States and China in the UN Security Council to impose new sanctions.

NATO and the EU

Soon after the Obama administration's statements that it intended to reset relations with Moscow, NATO leaders agreed at their April 2009 summit to restart the work of the NATO–Russia Council, whose proceedings had been suspended by NATO following the 2008 Russia–Georgia War. On 27 June, the council held a foreign-minister level meeting and agreed to restart military cooperation. Relations further improved with Russia's agreement to allow the resupply of the NATO-led mission in Afghanistan over land and through its airspace, and to provide financial assistance for reconstruction and Afghan National Army training projects.

This more positive atmosphere was assisted by the decision of the incoming NATO secretary-general, former Danish Prime Minister Anders Fogh Rasmussen, to make improvement in relations between NATO and Russia one of his top priorities. In his first major speech in September 2010, Rasmussen presented his concept of a partnership with Russia that envisioned practical cooperation, joint review of security challenges, and rejuvenation of the NATO–Russia Council. In February 2010, the Group of Experts on NATO's new Strategic Concept visited Moscow, marking the first time that Russia had been consulted in this way. The group's report recommended that the Strategic Concept should underscore NATO's desire for a better relationship and should ensure that 'from the Alliance's perspective, the door to cooperation [with Russia] at all levels is and will remain open'. Meanwhile, Russia proposed a treaty regulating relations with NATO. Medvedev's previous proposal of a European security treaty had not been received enthusiastically by European leaders, as it was seen as directed at weakening NATO and blocking enlargement and other decisions.

Russian–EU relations also improved, with an agreement establishing an early-warning mechanism to enhance cooperation to solve commercial or technical problems that might threaten oil, gas and electricity deliveries. Russian notification of a likely interruption would trigger consultations and joint prevention efforts. The new mechanism was successfully employed during a Russia–Belarus gas dispute in June 1010 which caused a brief interruption of supplies to the Baltic states. At a summit that same month, a 'Partnership for Modernisation' intended to support Medvedev's reform goals (including investment in technology and innovation, although the EU was keener to view it as a vehicle to support political and judicial reforms) was launched. Germany and Russia also proposed an EU–Russia Political and Security Committee to be chaired by EU High Representative Catherine Ashton and Russian Foreign Minister Sergey Lavrov. The committee would exchange views on international security issues and develop guidelines for joint civil–military operations. While other EU member states and EU officials expressed concern that they were not initially consulted on the proposal, there seemed to be growing support for it.

The improvement in EU–Russian relations owed something to a reduction in divisions within the EU regarding Russia. Among such changes, the most remarkable was the reconciliation between Russia and Poland. As recently as 2008 relations had been very poor, as Moscow protested Warsaw's decision to host interceptors for the US missile-defence system, and resented Poland's strong support for Georgia during the Russia–Georgia War. Less than two years later, they were more constructive and friendly than they had been for decades. The transformation was a result both of deliberate efforts on both sides, and of tragic circumstances beyond their control.

The reconciliation was led by Prime Ministers Donald Tusk and Vladimir Putin. Putin travelled to Poland on 2 September 2009 to take part in ceremonies marking the 70th anniversary of Nazi Germany's invasion of Poland. In his speech, Putin termed the Molotov–Ribbentrop non-aggression pact between Germany and the Soviet Union, signed in August 1939, 'immoral'. On 7 April 2010 the Russian and Polish prime ministers took part in a joint ceremony honouring 22,000 Poles murdered in 1940 by Soviet forces in Katyn Forest. Until recently, some

Russian officials had claimed that the victims had been killed by the Nazis.

Three days later, an aircraft carrying Polish President Lech Kaczynski and a high-level delegation crashed in Russia near the site of the massacre when trying to land in thick fog. All on board were killed. They had been travelling to Katyn to hold another ceremony commemorating the massacre. The tragedy brought the two nations together. Putin, who offered personal support to Tusk when he visited the crash site, took charge of the investigation. The Russian government arranged for the film *Katyn*, by Polish director Andrzej Wajda, portraying the killings of Polish officers by Soviet soldiers, to be shown on the main Russian state television channel. Poles were touched by Russia's compassion, and a Polish contingent was added to the American, British and French soldiers who had been invited for the first time to march alongside Russian soldiers on 9 May in the Victory Day parade in Moscow's Red Square.

Russia and its neighbours

The qualities that made Medvedev a welcome partner for the West made it harder for him to earn the loyalty and respect of Russia's closest allies among former Soviet states. In the majority of these countries the old Soviet generation remained in charge and Putin was seen as the real leader of Russia, so it was not surprising that relations were less harmonious. In Medvedev's pragmatic foreign policy, there was little room for special economic privileges for allies who, in his view, were trying to abuse their bilateral relationships. But a new trend, in which Russia was increasingly prepared to cooperate with the United States and the European Union on matters relating to its neighbourhood, seemed to be emerging.

The first example involved the normalisation of Turkish–Armenian relations (see pp. 179–81). Even though protocols to establish diplomatic relations were signed on 10 October 2009, they remained unratified by both countries. But an important feature of the process was the close involvement of both Russia and the United States. Russia encouraged Armenia to take the first step: Armenian President Serzh Sargsyan's invitation to the Turkish president to attend a football match in Yerevan was issued while Sargsyan was on a visit to Moscow. Before the protocols were signed the Obama administration worked hard to bring Turkey to the table. Lavrov,

Clinton and EU foreign policy chief Javier Solana attended the signing ceremony in Zurich, while Lavrov intervened with the Armenian delegation at the last moment to prevent the deal from falling apart.

Another example of US–Russian cooperation in the neighbourhood related to the crisis in Kyrgyzstan. On 8 April 2010, protests forced President Kurmanbek Bakiyev to step down and opposition leader Roza Otunbayeva became transitional head of state. The situation threatened to escalate into civil war (see pp. 316–18). The leaders of Russia, the United States and Kazakhstan (which held the chair of the Organisation for Security and Cooperation in Europe for 2010) met in Washington and agreed to back the interim government. This helped reduce tensions. When ethnic violence erupted in the Kyrgyz city of Osh in June, the United States encouraged Russia to intervene to help relieve the suffering, and on 24 June, Obama and Medvedev issued a joint statement affirming their common interest in avoiding further violence and restoring democracy.

Russia's hesitation over intervening to stop the bloodshed in Kyrgyzstan left a perception in Russia and the region that it was no longer interested in carrying the burdens associated with a 'special zone of influence'. Russian experts claimed that the restructuring under way in Russia's armed forces meant that it did not have forces to send quickly to deal with contingencies such as the situation in Osh. The lack of Russian action also threw into question the supposed rapid-reaction forces of the Collective Security Treaty Organisation (CSTO). Despite several meetings, the CSTO's members (Armenia, Belarus, Kazakhstan, Kyrgyzstan, Russia, Tajikistan and Uzbekistan) were unable to reach a consensus. The Shanghai Cooperation Organisation (SCO) also failed to offer help to solve or contain the problem, despite the fact that an SCO summit in Uzbekistan coincided with the violence in Osh.

There was a significant rapprochement between Russia and Ukraine following the 7 March 2010 election of President Viktor Yanukovich, who quickly moved to fulfil his main election pledge to improve ties with Moscow. Medvedev and Yanukovich reached two major agreements: Russia would discount the price of natural-gas exports by 30%, and Ukraine would extend the lease on Russia's naval base at Sevastopol, home of the Black Sea fleet, for 25 years to 2042. Yanukovich officially denounced plans for Ukraine to seek NATO membership. Ukraine's move towards Russia was not a capitulation, but was based on Ukraine's national interest as understood by Yanukovich, who inherited a country on the brink of economic collapse. He drew clear red lines: a proposal from Putin to merge the gas companies Gazprom and Naftohaz Ukrainy was rejected, and Ukraine made clear that it had no plans to recognise the independence of Abkhazia and South Ossetia. Russia's efforts to win international recognition for these territories, which had broken away from Georgia, had very limited success overall. Only Nicaragua had previously recognised them, and only two more states granted recognition in the year to mid-2010: Venezuela and Nauru.

In South Ossetia, reconstruction after the 2008 conflict moved slowly due to corruption and political infighting. In Abkhazia, Russia expanded its economic and military presence. Relations with Georgia remained hostile, with no diplomatic relations and dialogue only taking place within the framework of Geneva discussions co-chaired by the EU, the OSCE and the UN. There were some small signs of progress, however: the two countries opened a border checkpoint at Verkhni Lars, and Georgian and Russian airlines were given permission, at least temporarily, for direct charter flights between the countries.

Conclusion

In Russia's debate over its future, the truth seemed to lie somewhere between the optimists and the pessimists. Opinion polls indicated growing support for reform. Grassroots initiatives were emerging across Russia's vast territory to expose police corruption and challenge the privileges enjoyed by the political elite. A new atmosphere of openness was bringing to light previously suppressed problems in the economy, public sector and military, and in the North Caucasus. A more pragmatic foreign policy was shifting Russia towards more 'transactional' relationships with both Western and Asian countries. Russia's aim was not so much to assert great-power status, as it had been inclined to do in recent years, but to attract investment and modernise its economy. These developments were tangible and significant. What was less clear, however, was whether they were sufficient to stimulate real modernisation. Sceptics pointed out that there were no clear signs yet that Russia would be transformed.

Strategic Geography 2010

Legend

——————— subject country international boundaries

——————— other international boundaries

················· province or state boundaries

ANBAR province or state

■ capital cities

● state or province capital cities

● cities/ towns/ villages

GLOBAL ISSUES: Emerging from the global recession

The G20 emerged from the 2008 financial crisis as a broad and powerful decision-making body, establishing itself as the 'premier forum for international economic cooperation'. Superseding the G7/G8 groupings, the G20's membership is truly representative of global economic power. Looking at the current circumstances of its member states, it is clear that the recovery process has begun across the globe, albeit at varying rates.

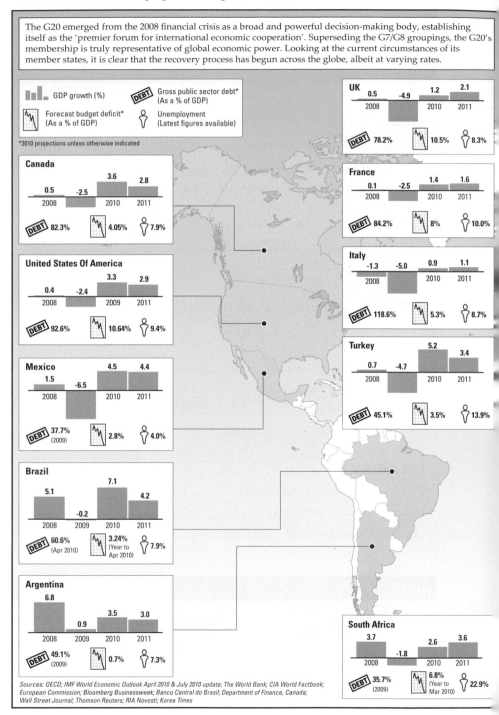

GDP growth (%)

Forecast budget deficit* (As a % of GDP)

DEBT Gross public sector debt* (As a % of GDP)

Unemployment (Latest figures available)

*2010 projections unless otherwise indicated

UK
0.5 | -4.9 | 1.2 | 2.1
2008 | | 2010 | 2011
DEBT 78.2% | 10.5% | 8.3%

Canada
0.5 | -2.5 | 3.6 | 2.8
2008 | | 2010 | 2011
DEBT 82.3% | 4.05% | 7.9%

France
0.1 | -2.5 | 1.4 | 1.6
2008 | | 2010 | 2011
DEBT 84.2% | 8% | 10.0%

United States Of America
0.4 | -2.4 | 3.3 | 2.9
2008 | | 2009 | 2011
DEBT 92.6% | 10.64% | 9.4%

Italy
-1.3 | -5.0 | 0.9 | 1.1
2008 | | 2010 | 2011
DEBT 118.6% | 5.3% | 8.7%

Mexico
1.5 | -6.5 | 4.5 | 4.4
2008 | | 2010 | 2011
DEBT 37.7% (2009) | 2.8% | 4.0%

Turkey
0.7 | -4.7 | 5.2 | 3.4
2008 | | 2010 | 2011
DEBT 45.1% | 3.5% | 13.9%

Brazil
5.1 | -0.2 | 7.1 | 4.2
2008 | 2009 | 2010 | 2011
DEBT 60.6% (Apr 2010) | 3.24% (Year to Apr 2010) | 7.9%

Argentina
6.8 | 0.9 | 3.5 | 3.0
2008 | 2009 | 2010 | 2011
DEBT 49.1% (2009) | 0.7% | 7.3%

South Africa
3.7 | -1.8 | 2.6 | 3.6
2008 | | 2010 | 2011
DEBT 35.7% (2009) | 6.8% (Year to Mar 2010) | 22.9%

Sources: OECD; IMF World Economic Outlook April 2010 & July 2010 update; The World Bank; CIA World Factbook; European Commission; Bloomberg Businessweek; Banco Central do Brasil; Department of Finance, Canada; Wall Street Journal; Thomson Reuters; RIA Novosti; Korea Times

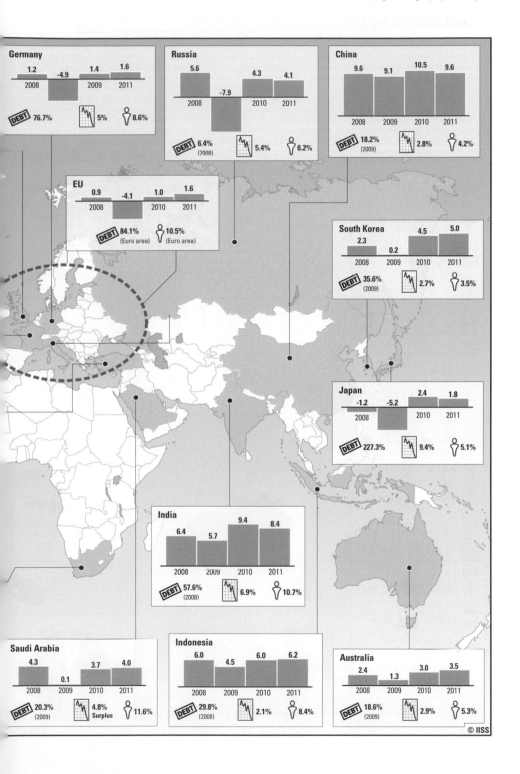

Germany
1.2 | -4.9 | 1.4 | 1.6
2008 | 2009 | 2011
DEBT 76.7%   5%   8.6%

Russia
5.6 | -7.9 | 4.3 | 4.1
2008 | 2010 | 2011
DEBT 6.4% (2008)   5.4%   6.2%

China
9.6 | 9.1 | 10.5 | 9.6
2008 | 2009 | 2010 | 2011
DEBT 18.2% (2009)   2.8%   4.2%

EU
0.9 | -4.1 | 1.0 | 1.6
2008 | 2010 | 2011
DEBT 84.1% (Euro area)   10.5% (Euro area)

South Korea
2.3 | 0.2 | 4.5 | 5.0
2008 | 2009 | 2010 | 2011
DEBT 35.6% (2009)   2.7%   3.5%

Japan
-1.2 | -5.2 | 2.4 | 1.8
2008 | 2010 | 2011
DEBT 227.3%   9.4%   5.1%

India
6.4 | 5.7 | 9.4 | 8.4
2008 | 2009 | 2010 | 2011
DEBT 57.6% (2008)   6.9%   10.7%

Saudi Arabia
4.3 | 0.1 | 3.7 | 4.0
2008 | 2009 | 2010 | 2011
DEBT 20.3% (2009)   4.8% Surplus   11.6%

Indonesia
6.0 | 4.5 | 6.0 | 6.2
2008 | 2009 | 2010 | 2011
DEBT 29.8% (2008)   2.1%   8.4%

Australia
2.4 | 1.3 | 3.0 | 3.5
2008 | 2009 | 2010 | 2011
DEBT 18.6% (2009)   2.9%   5.3%

© IISS

GLOBAL ISSUES: The BASIC position on climate change

The BASIC group of countries – Brazil, South Africa, India and China – emerged during the United Nations climate change conference in Copenhagen in 2009 as defenders of the developing world's position on reducing carbon-dioxide emissions. These growing powers threatened to leave the talks if the rich nations they blame for climate change did not meet their demands to make cuts first. China especially wants developed countries to reduce emissions to 40% below 1990 levels by 2020, and to pay to help others adapt. The group negotiated the final Copenhagen deal with the United States, and has since worked to define a common position on emission reductions and climate aid. As per the Copenhagen Accord, the four countries announced emissions targets in January 2010. But different ways of calculating reductions (see BASIC and other examples below) make comparison difficult, and the BASIC bloc has rejected some Western calls to make targets binding.

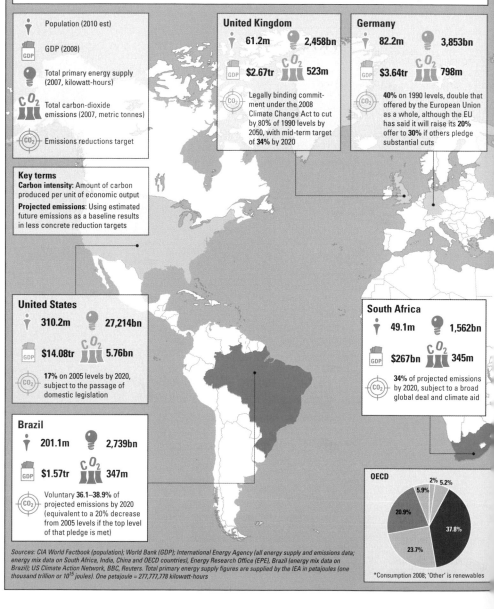

Population (2010 est)

GDP (2008)

Total primary energy supply (2007, kilowatt-hours)

CO_2 Total carbon-dioxide emissions (2007, metric tonnes)

(CO_2) Emissions reductions target

Key terms
Carbon intensity: Amount of carbon produced per unit of economic output
Projected emissions: Using estimated future emissions as a baseline results in less concrete reduction targets

United Kingdom
61.2m — 2,458bn
GDP $2.67tr — CO_2 523m
CO_2 Legally binding commitment under the 2008 Climate Change Act to cut by 80% of 1990 levels by 2050, with mid-term target of **34%** by 2020

Germany
82.2m — 3,853bn
GDP $3.64tr — CO_2 798m
CO_2 **40%** on 1990 levels, double that offered by the European Union as a whole, although the EU has said it will raise its **20%** offer to **30%** if others pledge substantial cuts

United States
310.2m — 27,214bn
GDP $14.08tr — CO_2 5.76bn
CO_2 **17%** on 2005 levels by 2020, subject to the passage of domestic legislation

South Africa
49.1m — 1,562bn
GDP $267bn — CO_2 345m
CO_2 **34%** of projected emissions by 2020, subject to a broad global deal and climate aid

Brazil
201.1m — 2,739bn
GDP $1.57tr — CO_2 347m
CO_2 Voluntary **36.1–38.9%** of projected emissions by 2020 (equivalent to a 20% decrease from 2005 levels if the top level of that pledge is met)

OECD
2% 5.2%
5.9%
20.9%
37.8%
23.7%

*Consumption 2008; 'Other' is renewables

Sources: CIA World Factbook (population); World Bank (GDP); International Energy Agency (all energy supply and emissions data; energy mix data on South Africa, India, China and OECD countries), Energy Research Office (EPE), Brazil (energy mix data on Brazil); US Climate Action Network, BBC, Reuters. Total primary energy supply figures are supplied by the IEA in petajoules (one thousand trillion or 10^{15} joules). One petajoule = 277,777,778 kilowatt-hours

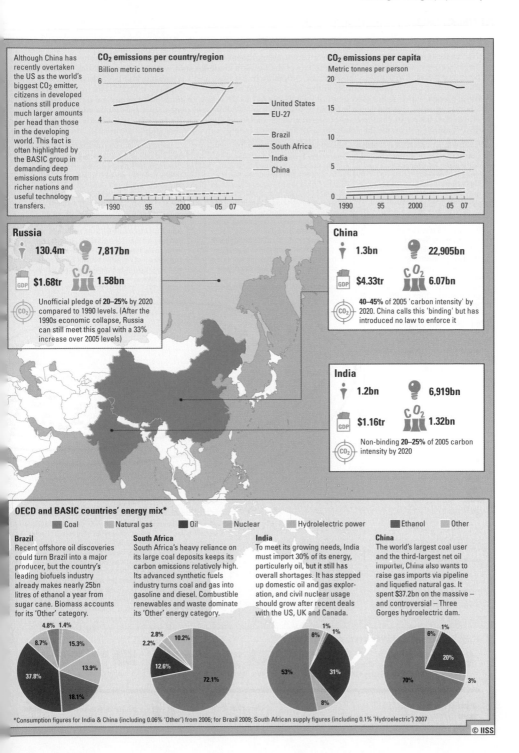

Although China has recently overtaken the US as the world's biggest CO_2 emitter, citizens in developed nations still produce much larger amounts per head than those in the developing world. This fact is often highlighted by the BASIC group in demanding deep emissions cuts from richer nations and useful technology transfers.

CO_2 emissions per country/region
Billion metric tonnes

- United States
- EU-27
- Brazil
- South Africa
- India
- China

CO_2 emissions per capita
Metric tonnes per person

Russia

130.4m   7,817bn

GDP $1.68tr CO_2 1.58bn

Unofficial pledge of **20–25%** by 2020 compared to 1990 levels. (After the 1990s economic collapse, Russia can still meet this goal with a 33% increase over 2005 levels)

China

1.3bn   22,905bn

GDP $4.33tr CO_2 6.07bn

40–45% of 2005 'carbon intensity' by 2020. China calls this 'binding' but has introduced no law to enforce it

India

1.2bn   6,919bn

GDP $1.16tr CO_2 1.32bn

Non-binding **20–25%** of 2005 carbon intensity by 2020

OECD and BASIC countries' energy mix*

- Coal
- Natural gas
- Oil
- Nuclear
- Hydrolelectric power
- Ethanol
- Other

Brazil
Recent offshore oil discoveries could turn Brazil into a major producer, but the country's leading biofuels industry already makes nearly 25bn litres of ethanol a year from sugar cane. Biomass accounts for its 'Other' category.

4.8% 1.4%
8.7%
15.3%
37.8%
13.9%
18.1%

South Africa
South Africa's heavy reliance on its large coal deposits keeps its carbon emissions relatively high. Its advanced synthetic fuels industry turns coal and gas into gasoline and diesel. Combustible renewables and waste dominate its 'Other' energy category.

2.8%
2.2%
12.6%
10.2%
72.1%

India
To meet its growing needs, India must import 30% of its energy, particularly oil, but it still has overall shortages. It has stepped up domestic oil and gas explor-ation, and civil nuclear usage should grow after recent deals with the US, UK and Canada.

1% 1%
6%
53%
31%
8%

China
The world's largest coal user and the third-largest net oil importer, China also wants to raise gas imports via pipeline and liquefied natural gas. It spent $37.2bn on the massive – and controversial – Three Gorges hydroelectric dam.

1%
6%
20%
70%
3%

*Consumption figures for India & China (including 0.06% 'Other') from 2006; for Brazil 2009; South African supply figures (including 0.1% 'Hydroelectric') 2007

© IISS

AFRICA: Al-Qaeda's new world order

Two years ago, Western officials were starting to think that al-Qaeda presented a much diminished threat to world security. Since the July 2005 bombings of the London Underground system, no 'spectacular' attacks had been unleashed in its name in the West; its leadership in Pakistan and Afghanistan had been driven back by US drone strikes; and its indiscriminate killing of civilians in Iraq lost it the support of local Sunni insurgents. But the al-Qaeda franchise has staged minor comebacks in old stomping grounds and re-emerged in new territories. Islamist fighters have particularly found new havens in failed or weak states, such as Somalia and Yemen, from where they have launched a series of recent attacks, plots and attempts. However sustainable this new lease of life eventually proves for the jihadi network, it paints a new picture of transnational terrorism.

The FBI revealed in 2009 that it was investigating the disappearances of young Somali–American men in Minneapolis (home to 60,000 Somali refugees) in 'one of the most significant terrorism investigations since 9/11'. Up to 20 young men have vanished since 2007, and recruiters are thought to have spirited them to Somalia to join al-Shabaab. An early example was Shirwa Ahmed, who became the first American suicide bomber in late 2008, killing 27 in Somaliland. The FBI feared the missing men could return to attack the US.

Before Umar Farouk Abdulmutallab, a London-educated, privileged Nigerian student, tried to bring down Northwest Airlines Flight 253 as it landed in Detroit on Christmas Day 2009, he had attended an al-Qaeda training camp in Yemen. So soon after the Fort Hood shooting (below), this second Yemeni-linked plot hastened action against militants in the Gulf country. Abdulmutallab's efforts to detonate an 80g bomb in his underpants were similar to another 'body bombing' attempt four months earlier on Saudi Deputy Interior Minister Prince Muhammad bin Nayef.

The plot to bomb three New York subway lines in September 2009 was one of the most serious threats to the US since 9/11, said Attorney-General Eric Holder. Prosecutors said Najibullah Zazi and his two associates travelled from Queens to Pakistan in 2008. There they met al-Qaeda operatives Rashid Rauf and Saleh al-Somali – both now reportedly dead – who persuaded them to launch an attack on the US. An attempted car bombing in Times Square in May 2010 was first linked to the Pakistani Taliban, and other reports suggested that would-be bomber Faisal Shahzad was also inspired by radical American–Yemeni cleric Anwar al-Awlaki.

Major Nidal Hasan, the army psychiatrist accused of killing 13 colleagues at the Fort Hood army base in November 2009, reportedly corresponded by email before-hand with American-born, Yemen-based radical Islamic cleric Anwar al-Awlaki. This link helped to galvanise Yemen into action against al-Qaeda militants within its borders. Al-Awlaki praised his 'students' Hasan and Detroit bomber Abdulmutallab in a video.

Minneapolis

Detroit   New York

US

Fort Hood

TUNISIA
ALGERIA
MAURITANIA
Nouakchott
MALI   NIG

★ Bombing/explosion

Clashes with security forces

Kidnapping

Plot

Shooting/massacre

→ Link to plot

•••► Possible link to plot

→ Militant movement

•••► Possible militant movement

In late 2006, al-Qaeda deputy leader Ayman al-Zawahri declared a 'blessed union' between his network and the Salafist Group for Preaching and Combat, an Islamist group from the 1990s civil war in Algeria. The renamed al-Qaeda in the Islamic Maghreb (AQIM) has since increased its terrorist activities across Africa's Sahel region. Its most common tactic is kidnapping, with at least 15 Westerners abducted since 2008 (see timeline below). In August 2009, the group carried out the first suicide attack in Mauritania when a member blew himself up outside the French embassy in the capital, Nouakchott.

AQIM kidnappings of Westerners since 2008

22 Jan 2009, Mali
4 tourists: Briton Edwin Dyer (later killed); Swiss Werner & Gabriela Greiner; German Marianne Petzold

29 Nov 2009, Mauritania
Spanish aid workers Albert Vilalta, Roque Pascual & Alicia Gamez

28 Dec 2009, Mauritania
Italians Philomene Kabore & Sergio Cicala

14 Dec 2008, Niger
Canadian diplomats Robert Fowler & Louis Guay

26 Nov 2009, Mali
Frenchman Pierre Camatte

22 Apr 2010, Niger
Frenchman Michel Germano

fter retreating to the
ortheastern province of
iyala in 2007, al-Qaeda in
Mesopotamia (i.e. Iraq)
nade a comeback in 2009,
with three bombings of
aghdad ministries in
ugust, October and
ecember 2009 killing 380
nd wounding 1,500. An
ndigenisation' of the
oup has meant more
cal and fewer foreign
ghters. With a phased US
oop withdrawal begun
nd ongoing political
ncertainty, al-Qaeda could
gain become a strategic
ayer in Iraq, or it may stay
highly disruptive actor on
e political sidelines.

Yemen reappeared on the counter-terrorism
radar after high-profile terror attempts in the
US were linked to it in 2009 – long after the
2000 bombing of the *USS Cole* in Aden. After
the Fort Hood and Detroit incidents (*see left*),
Sana'a was persuaded by the US to take
stronger action against a reinvigorated
al-Qaeda within Yemen. Airstrikes in
December 2009 reportedly killed 34 jihadi
leaders meeting in Shabwah province,
although attacks continued in 2010, including
an attempt to kill the British ambassador in
April. A jailbreak in 2006 led by local al-Qaeda
leader Naser al-Wahishi paved the way for
the group to rebuild, and Wahishi merged his
branch with the Saudi division in 2009 to form
al-Qaeda in the Arabian Peninsula (AQAP).
Saudi Arabia also remains an attractive
target for AQAP, where it has tried to kill the
deputy interior minister and threatened to
kidnap many of the Kingdom's royals.

Presence of insurgents/rebels in Yemen

Al-Qaeda	Al-Houthis	Secessionists
Stronghold	Stronghold	Presence
Presence	Presence	

Sharing a porous border with wealthy Saudi Arabia, and with
poor government control over much of its territory, Osama bin
Laden's ancestral homeland is a useful haven for al-Qaeda.
The Yemeni authorities also have to deal with a failing
economy, a tribal 'al-Houthi' insurgency and a secessionist
movement, and have not always prioritised the jihadi threat.

US intelligence concluded in late 2009 that there were only
100 al-Qaeda, as opposed to Taliban, fighters in Afghanistan.
But both groups appear to have been involved in the deaths of
seven CIA agents at a NATO base in Khost on 30 December
2009. Suicide bomber Humam Khalil Abu-Malal al-Balawi was
reportedly a Jordanian informant working as a double agent
for al-Qaeda, and was acting on Taliban information.

Only 100–150 Westerners travelled to Pakistan for terrorist
training during 2009, US counter-terrorism experts believe.
This is down considerably on previous years, but one of those
so trained was Najibullah Zazi, an Afghan immigrant to the US
who pleaded guilty in February 2010 to plotting to bomb the
New York subway. Meanwhile, a US unmanned drone
reportedly killed Saleh al-Somali in Pakistan's North
Waziristan region in December 2009. Several unnamed Arab
diplomats described al-Somali as 'a lynchpin in al-Qaeda's
well-considered new strategy' to move Arab militant fighters
out of the Afghanistan/ Pakistan region to Yemen and Somalia.

IRAQ **AFGHANISTAN**
Baghdad Khost **PAKISTAN**
SAUDI Waziristan
ARABIA

YEMEN

UGANDA **SOMALIA**

AUSTRALIA
Sydney
Melbourne

ar-torn Somalia has harboured al-Qaeda militants at least since
e 1998 US embassy bombings in Kenya and Tanzania. However,
ntil recently the country's home-grown Islamists, al-Shabaab,
cused on their domestic struggle with the weak, Western-
acked interim government. In 2008, the group broadened its
orizons when it verbally threatened US interests; in 2009, terrorist
ots in Sydney and Minneapolis were linked to it. That September
e group released a video 'At your service, Osama', followed by a
atement in February 2010 that 'the jihad of Horn of Africa must be
ombined with the international jihad led by the al-Qaeda network'.
aiming responsibility for the deadly bombings in the Ugandan
apital, Kampala, during the FIFA World Cup football final on 10
uly 2010, the group showed it could strike abroad.

Australian police believe they foiled a plot by al-Shabaab supporters to
bomb an army barracks in southwest Sydney when they raided 20 homes in
and around Melbourne in August 2009 and arrested a group of men of
Somali and Lebanese descent. A further sign of al-Shabaab's 'globalisation',
the plot apparently included sending Australians to fight in Somalia. In 2010,
it emerged that an Australian woman who had converted to Islam and
moved to Yemen was among 30 Westerners being held in Sana'a for alleged
al-Qaeda activity.

ces: ABC News, Aljazeera, Associated Press, BBC, CBS News, Council on Foreign
ions, Critical Threats, CTC Sentinel, The Economist, IISS Armed Conflict Database,
estown Foundation, New York Times, NPR, Politics Daily, Reuters, The Telegraph,
The Times, The Washington Post, Yemen Post

© IISS

EUROPE: Turkey's soft power

Ankara's deteriorating relations with Tel Aviv became headline news after nine Turkish activists were killed in an Israeli raid on a Gaza-bound aid ship in May 2010. However, Turkey's 'zero problems' foreign policy has resulted in warmer ties with other neighbours recently. Since taking office in 2002, the Justice and Development Party (AKP) has been trying to carve out a greater role for Turkey as a regional player, independent of its traditional Cold War allies in the West. Foreign Minister Ahmet Davutoglu, the policy's main architect, believes the country's multiple ethnic and religious links also make it an ideal mediator in such regions as the Balkans, the Caucasus, Central Asia and the Middle East. A long-term NATO member, Turkey's hand has been strengthened by G20 membership and a two-year term on the United Nations Security Council until 2011. Yet, as events with Israel and Iran show, things do not always run smoothly.

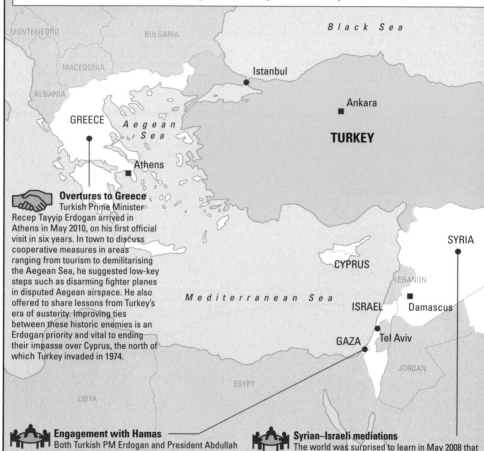

Overtures to Greece
Turkish Prime Minister Recep Tayyip Erdogan arrived in Athens in May 2010, on his first official visit in six years. In town to discuss cooperative measures in areas ranging from tourism to demilitarising the Aegean Sea, he suggested low-key steps such as disarming fighter planes in disputed Aegean airspace. He also offered to share lessons from Turkey's era of austerity. Improving ties between these historic enemies is an Erdogan priority and vital to ending their impasse over Cyprus, the north of which Turkey invaded in 1974.

Engagement with Hamas
Both Turkish PM Erdogan and President Abdullah Gul have repeatedly called for the Hamas government in Gaza to be included in US-mediated Middle East peace talks. Washington and Tel Aviv have officially excluded Hamas from the process because they consider it a terrorist organisation. However, Turkey has contacts with Hamas, and has also offered to take over from Egypt in mediating reconciliation talks between Hamas and rival Palestinian group Fatah in the West Bank. US envoy to the region George Mitchell said in 2009 that Turkey could be 'an important force for peace and security in the Middle East'.

Syrian–Israeli mediations
The world was surprised to learn in May 2008 that Syria and Israel were in peace negotiations mediated by Turkey. The indirect talks focused on the Golan Heights, which Israel seized from Syria in 1967's Six-Day War, but the process was halted after four rounds when Israel invaded Gaza in December 2008. Syria, which continued to grow closer to Turkey, said in May 2010 that it was willing to resume, but Israeli Prime Minister Benjamin Netanyahu questioned Ankara's continued impartiality as a mediator. Turkey was the first Muslim-majority country to recognise Israel, but relations were damaged by the Gaza invasion, later diplomatic spats and the Gaza flotilla incident.

Caucasus 'Stability Platform'

So far, the major beneficiary of its Caucasus Stability and Security Platform has been Turkey itself, through the goodwill it has accrued. The platform was devised after the 2008 war between Russia and Georgia, as a way of jointly resolving regional tensions. Bringing Russia and Georgia to the table with Armenia, Azerbaijan and Turkey, it demonstrated Ankara's willingness to play a constructive role in the Caucasus, which the other four participants welcomed. Turkish MPs' visits to the region raised their country's profile, and strengthened its dialogue with Armenia and Russia in particular.

Normalising ties with Armenia

Ankara agreed in October 2009 to normalise relations with Yerevan, after a century of hostility over the killing of hundreds of thousands of Armenians in the Ottoman Empire. The two nations' border remains closed, and further formal negotiations have stalled over Nagorno-Karabakh, a disputed Armenian enclave in Azerbaijan. Nonetheless, it was a historic agreement, and lower-level discussions continue. Armenians demand that Turkey recognise the 1915 massacre of their compatriots as genocide. Turkey rejects this, refused to deal with Armenia after it became independent from the Soviet Union in 1991, and closed the border in 1993. Diplomats began secret talks in 2008, culminating in the normalisation deal. But its execution has been delayed by a Turkish promise to ally Azerbaijan not to reopen the border until Armenia gives up control over the areas around Nagorno-Karabakh.

Rapprochement with Iraqi Kurdistan

Turkey has changed its tune towards the KRG, the regional government in semi-autonomous Iraqi Kurdistan. While still facing calls for greater autonomy from its own Kurdish minority, Ankara said in 2009 it would open a consulate in Erbil, the KRG's capital. Growing Kurdish nationalism in Iraq after Saddam Hussein's demise in 2003 heightened Ankara's anxieties about its own Kurds, and it often accused KRG leader Massoud Barzani of plotting against it. Relations reached a nadir after its army pursued fighters from the outlawed Kurdistan Workers' Party (PKK) into Iraqi Kurdistan in 2007. Now Turkey sees good relations with the KRG as a way of maintaining a strategic position in Iraq after the US troop withdrawal, and of building a united front against the PKK. Economic interests, especially in the energy sector, have also helped.

RUSSIA

BKHAZIA

SOUTH OSSETIA

GEORGIA ■ Tbilisi

● ARMENIA AZERBAIJAN ■ Baku

Yerevan

Caspian Sea

IRAN

Erbil
IRAQI
KURDISTAN

IRAQ ■ Tehran

Voyage of the *Mavi Marmara*

Istanbul ■ **22 May**: Leaves Istanbul

President Abdullah Gul has said that Turkey will never forgive Israel for killing activists on the *Mavi Marmara*. Bought by a pro-Hamas Turkish charity, the ship was leading a six-vessel flotilla to break a three-year Israeli blockade on Gaza, when it was boarded in international waters by Israeli commandos. For more details, see Chapter 6, pp227–29.

TURKEY

25 May: Arrives Antalya

Antalya

28 May: Leaves Antalya

SYRIA

CYPRUS

30 May: Flotilla rendezvous

4pm: Gaza-bound

International waters

Israeli
waters

LEBANON

10pm: Israel radio contact

ISRAEL

1am, 31 May: Boarded

Ashdod

31 May: Escorted to
Israeli port of Ashdod

GAZA

Iranian enriched-uranium deal

In May 2010, Turkey and Brazil brokered an 11th-hour nuclear fuel-swap deal with Iran, under which Tehran would ship much of its low-enriched uranium (LEU) to Turkey in exchange for research-reactor fuel. Designed to defuse global tensions over Tehran's nuclear programme, the agreement was another sign of Ankara's determination to establish itself as a player in the Middle East. However, many Western nations found the deal too accommodating to Tehran, and they effectively dismissed it by passing further sanctions against Iran in the United Nations Security Council in June. While Russia and China voted for the new financial curbs and expanded arms embargo, Turkey and Brazil voted against, and this lack of unanimity was seen as weakening the UN resolution.

Sources: Al-Jazeera, All Voices.com, Associated Press, BBC, Foreign Policy, Haaretz, New York Times, Radio Free Europe/Radio Liberty, Reuters, The Time, Xinhua, Zaman

© IISS

AFRICA: Communal violence in Nigeria's Plateau State

Inter-communal violence in Nigeria's Plateau State has killed thousands in the past decade. After outbreaks in 2001, 2004 and 2008, it resurfaced in 2010, when political uncertainty in the period before President Umaru Yar'Adua's death left the authorities too distracted to properly deal with it. In the 'middle belt' between the country's Christian-dominated south and largely Muslim north, the state is a microcosm of the deep social divisions that endure 50 years after Africa's most populous nation gained independence. Clashes between ethnic Hausa–Fulani Muslims and Christians from the Berom, Anaguta or Afisare tribes have political and economic dimensions. Under a nation-wide classification of citizens as 'settlers' or 'indigenes', Muslims living in Plateau for decades are still 'settlers' and find it hard to run for potentially lucrative political positions.

Jos: September 2001
Jos was long a peaceful city, but tensions grew in the 1990s over the division of political power between the majority Christian population and the significant Muslim minority. Civil unrest in 2001 killed 1,000. The catalyst was the appointment of a controversial 'settler' Hausa Muslim to the sought-after post of poverty-eradication coordinator in Jos North. Sharia law is a common cause of violence in other Nigerian states. In Plateau, some Christians fear their Muslim neighbours wish to see it introduced, but many Hausa–Fulani there have left one of Nigeria's 12 Sharia states *(see bottom, left)* to avoid it.

Dogo Nahawa, Zot & Ratsat: March 2010
Some 200–500 Christians were killed when Hausa- and Fulani-speaking Muslims attacked these three villages. The raid was apparently in retaliation for January violence in Kuru Karama and the theft of cattle from Muslim herdsmen. Acting President Goodluck Jonathan sacked national security adviser Sarki Mukhtar after the incident.

Jos: November 2008
Rumours that the People's Democratic Party, supported by most Christians, had rigged an election in Jos North triggered two days of rioting. Churches, mosques, schools and homes were targeted, and at least 700 killed. At stake in the local government election was control of the public purse and the right to determine which citizens are categorised 'indigene'. (The classification system applies nationally but parameters are set locally.) As 'settlers', many Hausi–Fulani Muslims are openly denied government jobs and academic scholarships.

Kuru Karama: January 2010
Around 150 bodies were found in wells and sewers in Kuru Karama, after Muslims were shot, burnt or hacked to death by Christian mobs. They were among a total 300–400 killed in four days of violence. Clashes began in a Christian district of Jos over the rebuilding of a Muslim home destroyed in the 2008 riots, then spread south. Before Goodluck Jonathan – then acting president, later president – called in the army, 40,000 people were displaced from their homes.

Yelwa: May 2004
Christian militias surrounded the town of Yelwa and went on a 24-hour killing spree. The attackers came from the Tarok ethnic group, long involved in land battles with the Fulani. More than 700 died in the violence, which followed a Muslim attack on a church earlier in February. There was local anger that the security forces had not done enough to protect Muslim civilians. Later revenge attacks in the state of Kano, to the north, killed 30 and forced 10,000 Christians to flee.

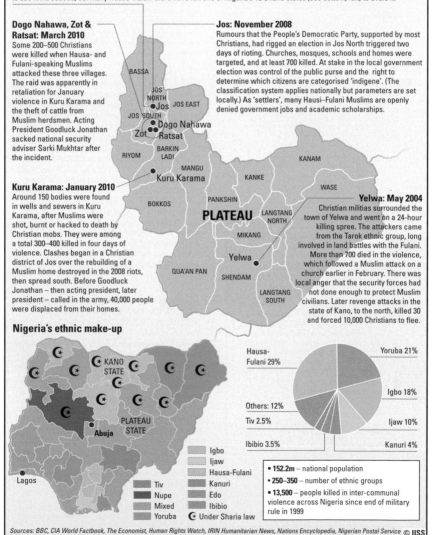

Nigeria's ethnic make-up

Hausa-Fulani 29%
Yoruba 21%
Igbo 18%
Ijaw 10%
Kanuri 4%
Ibibio 3.5%
Tiv 2.5%
Others: 12%

- **152.2m** – national population
- **250–350** – number of ethnic groups
- **13,500** – people killed in inter-communal violence across Nigeria since end of military rule in 1999

Legend:
Igbo
Ijaw
Hausa-Fulani
Kanuri
Tiv
Nupe
Edo
Mixed
Ibibio
Yoruba
☾ Under Sharia law

ASIA-PACIFIC: India's Naxalite rebellion

India's Maoist insurgency – its biggest internal security challenge, according to Prime Minister Manmohan Singh – has worsened recently. A guerrilla attack killing 76 police in Chhattisgarh state in April 2010 was the deadliest in the 'Naxalite' rebellion's 43 years. Today's movement harks back to a peasant uprising in the West Bengal village of Naxalbari, but violence has surged since 2004, when two left-wing parties merged into the latest grouping, the Communist Party of India–Maoist. The rebels, who say they are fighting to protect the rural poor, cut a large 'red corridor' across central and eastern India. Despite attempts at coordination by New Delhi, the insurgency has traditionally fallen under the law-and-order remit of state governments. But some of the worst-affected states are India's poorest, incapable of addressing the terrorist threat or the social inequality at its root.

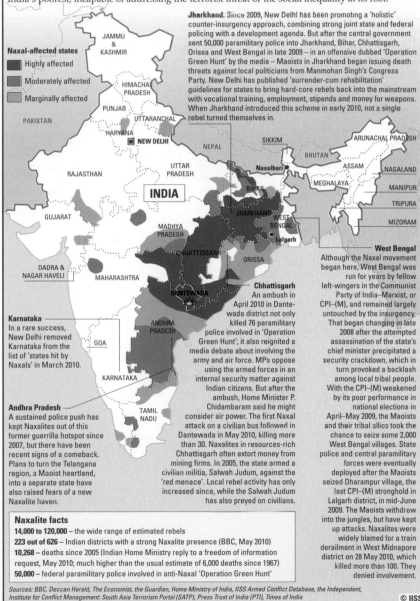

Naxal-affected states
- Highly affected
- Moderately affected
- Marginally affected

Jharkhand. Since 2009, New Delhi has been promoting a 'holistic' counter-insurgency approach, combining strong joint state and federal policing with a development agenda. But after the central government sent 50,000 paramilitary police into Jharkhand, Bihar, Chhattisgarh, Orissa and West Bengal in late 2009 – in an offensive dubbed 'Operation Green Hunt' by the media – Maoists in Jharkhand began issuing death threats against local politicians from Manmohan Singh's Congress Party. New Delhi has published 'surrender-cum rehabilitation' guidelines for states to bring hard-core rebels back into the mainstream with vocational training, employment, stipends and money for weapons. When Jharkhand introduced this scheme in early 2010, not a single rebel turned themselves in.

Karnataka
In a rare success, New Delhi removed Karnataka from the list of 'states hit by Naxals' in March 2010.

Andhra Pradesh
A sustained police push has kept Naxalites out of this former guerrilla hotspot since 2007, but there have been recent signs of a comeback. Plans to turn the Telangana region, a Maoist heartland, into a separate state have also raised fears of a new Naxalite haven.

Chhattisgarh
An ambush in April 2010 in Dante-wada district not only killed 76 paramilitary police involved in 'Operation Green Hunt'; it also reignited a media debate about involving the army and air force. MPs oppose using the armed forces in an internal security matter against Indian citizens. But after the ambush, Home Minister P. Chidambaram said he might consider air power. The first Naxal attack on a civilian bus followed in Dantewada in May 2010, killing more than 30. Naxalites in resources-rich Chhattisgarh often extort money from mining firms. In 2005, the state armed a civilian militia, Salwah Judum, against the 'red menace'. Local rebel activity has only increased since, while the Salwah Judum has also preyed on civilians.

West Bengal
Although the Naxal movement began here, West Bengal was run for years by fellow left-wingers in the Communist Party of India–Marxist, or CPI–(M), and remained largely untouched by the insurgency. That began changing in late 2008 after the attempted assassination of the state's chief minister precipitated a security crackdown, which in turn provoked a backlash among local tribal people. With the CPI–(M) weakened by its poor performance in national elections in April–May 2009, the Maoists and their tribal allies took the chance to seize some 2,000 West Bengal villages. State police and central paramilitary forces were eventually deployed after the Maoists seized Dharampur village, the last CPI–(M) stronghold in Lalgarh district, in mid-June 2009. The Maoists withdrew into the jungles, but have kept up attacks. Naxalites were widely blamed for a train derailment in West Midnapore district on 28 May 2010, which killed more than 100. They denied involvement.

Naxalite facts

14,000 to 120,000 – the wide range of estimated rebels
223 out of 626 – Indian districts with a strong Naxalite presence (BBC, May 2010)
10,268 – deaths since 2005 (Indian Home Ministry reply to a freedom of information request, May 2010; much higher than the usual estimate of 6,000 deaths since 1967)
50,000 – federal paramilitary police involved in anti-Naxal 'Operation Green Hunt'

Sources: BBC, Deccan Herald, The Economist, the Guardian, Home Ministry of India, IISS Armed Conflict Database, the Independent, Institute for Conflict Management: South Asia Terrorism Portal (SATP), Press Trust of India (PTI), Times of India

© IISS

ASIA-PACIFIC: ISAF operations in Afghanistan

In the hope of reversing the momentum of the Afghan insurgency, NATO-led forces have swelled in size as their governments commit more troops to the conflict. Operations are designed to strike a decisive blow against insurgents and to build the capacity of Afghan forces. United States President Barack Obama decided to send more troops, but also announced that a drawdown would begin in mid-2011.

Operation Moshtarak: A test for US counter-insurgency doctrine

Operation Moshtarak was an ISAF–Afghan offensive designed to assert government authority in the previously Taliban-held areas of Nad Ali and Marjah (the latter was described as an 'insurgent-narco hub' by ISAF) in central Helmand province. As the first significant operation to make use of the extra troops deployed under General Stanley McChrystal's surge plan, it represented a litmus test for the new American strategy's prospects of success.

Timeline of events

January–12 February 2010:
UK, US, Danish and Afghan forces in the central Helmand River valley conduct 'shaping' operations in preparation for the forthcoming offensive

13 February: A 1,600-man taskforce led by the UK's 1st Royal Welsh Battlegroup is deployed by helicopter northeast of Nad Ali (**A**) between 0400 and 0600. Meanwhile, a similarly sized force, led by the US 1st Battalion, 6th Marine Regiment, is deployed by helicopter into Marjah itself (**B**). They seize key locations behind the Taliban's defensive lines and begin the task of securing the area

14–15 February: Offensive continues as further coalition and Afghan units reinforce the initial landing forces

16–27 February: Operations become more piecemeal in nature, as coalition and Afghan forces clear the remaining Taliban resistance from both Nad Ali and Marjah

Operation Moshtarak's progress, as reported by ISAF in June 2010

- Coalition troops were gaining the initiative across central Helmand with a presence in every major village
- While the threat of IEDs remained, the population had benefited from increase freedom of movement and perceptions of coalition operations had improved
- District governors were in place and councils functioning, as they now had access beyond provincial centres
- Schools and clinics were reopening, as well as bazaars and shops in Marjah

Camps Bastion, Leatherneck and Tombstone

1st Royal Welsh (UK)

Infantry battalion

Mechanised infantry battalion

Battalions' helicopter deployments on the morning of 13 February 2010

A

Highway 1

1st Coldstream Guards (UK)

Nad Ali

3/6 Marines (US)

Lashkar Gah

1st Grenadier Guards (UK)

Marjah

4/23 Infantry (US)

B

KANDAHAR

HELMAND

1/3 Marines (US)

AFGHANISTAN
Area of detail

1/6 Marines (US)

Major units involved in the operation

3 US Marine Corps battalions
1 US Army Stryker mechanised infantry battalion
3 UK battlegroups
6 Afghan National Army 'kandaks' or battalions
2 Afghan National Army commando kandaks
ε6–7 Afghan National Police kandaks

Total strength
15,000, of which ε10,000 were used in the ground offensiv

Garmsir

Sources: ISAF; IISS; BBC; UK Ministry of Defence

Estimated national troop contributions to ISAF, as of June 2010

PRT lead countries

Country	Troops	Country	Troops	Country	Troops	Country	Troops
Albania	250	Estonia	160	Latvia	170	Slovakia	290
Armenia	75	Finland	115	Lithuania (Li)	245	Slovenia	75
Australia	1,550	France	3,750	Luxembourg	9	Spain (Sp)	1,415
Austria	3	FYROM	210	Mongolia	40	Sweden (Sw)	500
Azerbaijan	90	Georgia	925	Montenegro	30	Turkey (Tu)	1,710
Belgium	590	Germany (Ge)	4,350	Netherlands (Nl)	1,705	Ukraine	15
Bosnia & Herz.	10	Greece	75	New Zealand (NZ)	155	UAE	25
Bulgaria	525	Hungary (Hu)	340	Norway (No)	500	United Kingdom (UK)	9,500
Canada (Ca)	2,830	Iceland	3	Poland	2,500	United States (US)	78,430*
Croatia	280	Ireland	7	Portugal	265	**Total**	**119,500**
Czech Republic (Cz)	525	Italy (It)	3,300	Romania	1,140		
Denmark	750	Jordan	6	Singapore	40		

*A further 20,000 US troops are thought to be deployed as part of *Operation Enduring Freedom*

Force strength

Provincial Reconstruction Team (PRT)

Regional Command North
Lead country: Germany
11,000

Regional Command West
Lead country: Italy
6,000

KUNDUZ TAKHAR Faizabad (Ge)

JAWZJAN BADAKHSHAN

Mazar-e Sharif (Sw) Kunduz (Ge)

FARYAB (Tu) BALKH Pul-e Kumri (Hu) NURISTAN

SAMANGAN Nuristan (US)

PANJSHER KUNAR

Maymeneh (No) BAGHLAN

SARI PUL Panjsher (US) Asadabad (US)

Bagram (US) KAPISA LAGHMAN

BADGHIS PARWAN KABUL Mehtar Lam (US)

Qal'eh-Now (Sp) Wardak KABUL Jalalabad (US)

Meymaneh (Tu) Pol-e Alam (Cz) NANGARHAR

(No) BAMIYAN WARDAK

Chaghcharan (Li) Bamiyan (NZ)

ISAF Commands Kabul
3,500

LOGAR Gardez (US)

Herat (It) GHOR DAIKONDI Ghazni (US) Khost (US)

HERAT GHAZNI PAKTIA KHOST

URUZGAN Sharan (US)

Regional Command Capital
Lead country: Turkey
5,000

FARAH ZABUL PAKTIKA

Tarin Kowt (Nl)

Regional Command East
Lead country: United States
32,000

Farah (US) Qalat (US)

Lashkar Gah Kandahar

(UK) (Ca)

Size and shape of Afghan forces

Afghan National Army
Current strength (June 2010):
119,388

Afghan National Police
Current strength (June 2010):
104,459

Target strength (October 2011):
171,600

Target strength (October 2011):
134,000

NIMRUZ HELMAND KANDAHAR

	Number of units at 'capability milestone 1'*	Total
Corps/division HQs	2	7
Brigade HQs	6	16
Kandaks (battalions)	21	99

Regional Command South West
Lead country: United States
27,000

Regional Command South
Lead country: United Kingdom
35,000

* Needing no external support to plan and execute operations

© IISS

ASIA-PACIFIC: Thailand's political turmoil

Two months of major street protests in Bangkok led by the United Front for Democracy against Dictatorship (UDD), or 'red-shirts', came to an end on 19 May 2010, after a crackdown by the Thai authorities. Killing 85 and injuring 1,387, the protests marked the latest phase of a crisis that has gripped the country since 2006. The red-shirts were questioning the legitimacy of Prime Minister Abhisit Vejjajiva's government and calling for an election. While they are often described as the rural poor from the north and northeast of the country, loyal to former prime minister Thaksin Shinawatra and envious at the apparent injustice of the wealth of their urban cousins, support for the red-shirts can be found across all strata of society.

Timeline of events leading up to Spring 2010 protests

September 2005
Sondhi Limthongkul, media magnate and former ally of then-prime minister Thaksin Shinawatra (himself an ex-police officer and billionaire telecoms tycoon in office since 2001), starts hosting and televising anti-Thaksin rallies

19 September 2006
Thaksin is ousted by a military coup; an interim military regime known as the Council for National Security assumes power

January 2008
Following the end of military rule, a coalition of pro-Thaksin parties form the first elected government, but protests by the PAD between May and December at Government House and Bangkok's main airport bring it down by December 2008

December 2008
Following the banning of three of the parties in the governing coalition including the PPP on charges of electoral fraud in the 2007 election, an anti-Thaksin government led by Democrat Party leader and current Prime Minister Abhisit Vejjajiva takes office without an election being held. (The Democrat Party is not synonymous with the PAD, though they have supporters in common).

January–Sept 2006
Sondhi's movement culminates in the emergence of the People's Alliance for Democracy (PAD) or 'yellow-shirts', who stage mass protests against Thaksin

December 2007
The pro-Thaksin People Power Party (PPP) wins 39.60% of the vote in elections, while the Democrat Party wins 39.63%

October 2008
Thaksin sentenced to two years' jail on corruption charges. Currently living in self-imposed exile in Dubai and Montenegro

April 2009
Thaksin openly questions the legitimacy of Abhisit's government leading the United Front for Democracy or 'red-shirts' to initiate violent protests in Bangkok and Pattaya. Two are killed and 123 injured; a state of emergency is imposed on Bangkok and surrounding areas

Insecurity spreads across Thailand's northern provinces

State of emergency declared in Bangkok and surrounding areas on 7 April

State of emergency extended to these provinces on:

13 May   16 May   19 May   ⊗ State of emergency lifted in these provinces on 6 July

On 6 July, the Thai government announced that in 19 of 24 provinces the state of emergency would hold for a further three months

CHIANGRAI

CHIANGMAI   NAN ⊗

LAMPANG

THAILAND

UDON SAKHON
NONG BUA THANI· NAKHON
LAMPOO
KHON KALASIN
KAEN· ⊗ MUKDAHAN LAOS
CHAIYAPHUM MAHASARAKHAM
NAKHON
SAWAN ⊗ NAKHON ROI-ET
RACHASIMA UBON
RATCHATHANI
NAKHON AYUTTHAYA SI SA KET ⊗
PATHOM PATHUMTHANI
NONTHABURI
⊗ ■ BANGKOK

BANGKOK CHONBURI

CAMBODIA

SAMUT PRAKAN

Army area of operations

Streets occupied by the red-shirts

🚧 Red-shirt barricades

13 May – General Khattiya Sawasdipol, the red-shirts' unofficial security chief, is shot by a sniper. It is only after his death in hospital on **17 May** that the Thai army decides to launch a decisive crackdown, using armoured personnel carriers to overwhelm the remaining protesters

19 May – Central World shopping plaza set ablaze

Rama I Road

Rajdamri Road

Lumpini Park

19 May – Thai army takes control of Lumpini Park, breaks through protesters' tyre-and-bamboo-pole barricades and advances up Rajdamri Road

Ratchaprasong intersection – The centre of the protesters' encampment. Up to 10,000 were thought to have congregated here at the height of the protests, falling to around 4,000 as the Thai army began its offensive

Sources: IISS; Time; The Independent; New York Times; www.capothai.org; BBC; The Times; www.asiatimes.it

© IISS

ASIA-PACIFIC: The US military presence on Okinawa

Japanese Prime Minister Yukio Hatoyama resigned in June 2010, after having to break an election promise to remove a United States military base, Futenma, from the southwest island of Okinawa. The US presence dates back to the Second World War, when defeated Japan – initially prohibited by the allies from rearming – signed an agreement allowing the Americans to keep military bases on its soil provided the US acted as its security force. The arrangement has proved increasingly controversial, especially on Okinawa. Close to the Chinese mainland, Taiwan and the Korean Peninsula, this 'keystone of the Pacific' was an important US base during the Korean and Vietnam wars. Returned to Japanese control in 1972, it still houses one of the world's largest concentrations of US bases. However, accidents, crime, noise pollution and other environmental effects have sparked local protests and strained the US–Japanese security alliance.

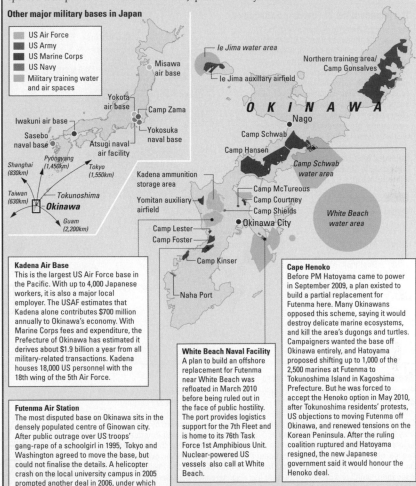

Other major military bases in Japan

- US Air Force
- US Army
- US Marine Corps
- US Navy
- Military training water and air spaces

Misawa air base
Yokota air base
Iwakuni air base
Sasebo naval base
Atsugi naval air facility
Camp Zama
Yokosuka naval base

Shanghai (830km)
Pyongyang (1,450km)
Tokyo (1,550km)
Taiwan (630km)
Tokunoshima
Okinawa
Guam (2,200km)

Ie Jima water area
Ie Jima auxiliary airfield

Northern training area/ Camp Gonsalves

O K I N A W A
Nago

Camp Schwab
Camp Hansen
Camp Schwab water area

Kadena ammunition storage area
Yomitan auxiliary airfield

Camp McTureous
Camp Courtney
Camp Shields
Okinawa City

White Beach water area

Camp Lester
Camp Foster
Camp Kinser
Naha Port

Kadena Air Base
This is the largest US Air Force base in the Pacific. With up to 4,000 Japanese workers, it is also a major local employer. The USAF estimates that Kadena alone contributes $700 million annually to Okinawa's economy. With Marine Corps fees and expenditure, the Prefecture of Okinawa has estimated it derives about $1.9 billion a year from all military-related transactions. Kadena houses 18,000 US personnel with the 18th wing of the 5th Air Force.

Futenma Air Station
The most disputed base on Okinawa sits in the densely populated centre of Ginowan city. After public outrage over US troops' gang-rape of a schoolgirl in 1995, Tokyo and Washington agreed to move the base, but could not finalise the details. A helicopter crash on the local university campus in 2005 prompted another deal in 2006, under which the base would move to the less-crowded Cape Henoko, while another 8,000 marines on Okinawa would be transferred to the US territory of Guam, east of the Philippines. Futenma is home to the Marine Aircraft Group 36 under 1st Marine Aircraft Wing of the 3rd Marine Expeditionary Force (III MEF).

White Beach Naval Facility
A plan to build an offshore replacement for Futenma near White Beach was refloated in March 2010 before being ruled out in the face of public hostility. The port provides logistics support for the 7th Fleet and is home to its 76th Task Force 1st Amphibious Unit. Nuclear-powered US vessels also call at White Beach.

Cape Henoko
Before PM Hatoyama came to power in September 2009, a plan existed to build a partial replacement for Futenma here. Many Okinawans opposed this scheme, saying it would destroy delicate marine ecosystems, and kill the area's dugongs and turtles. Campaigners wanted the base off Okinawa entirely, and Hatoyama proposed shifting up to 1,000 of the 2,500 marines at Futenma to Tokunoshima Island in Kagoshima Prefecture. But he was forced to accept the Henoko option in May 2010, after Tokunoshima residents' protests, US objections to moving Futenma off Okinawa, and renewed tensions on the Korean Peninsula. After the ruling coalition ruptured and Hatoyama resigned, the new Japanese government said it would honour the Henoko deal.

Okinawa facts
- Okinawa (pop. 1.3m) makes up 0.6% of Japan's total area
- 18.8% of the main island is covered by US bases
- 47,000 US troops in Japan are joined by an equal number of family
- 74% (nearly 35,000) of those military personnel are on Okinawa
- 90,000 protesters in April 2010 demanded Futenma's total removal

Sources: Al-Jazeera, Associated Press, BBC, Global Security, Institute for Defence Studies and Analyses, Japan Times, Kadena Air Base, Prefecture of Okinawa, Reuters, Stars and Stripes, United States Forces Japan, United States Marine Corps

© IISS

THE AMERICAS: Chile: an election and an earthquake

For the first time since the end of General Augusto Pinochet's dictatorship in 1990, in late 2009 and early 2010 Chile's voters backed a centre-right presidential candidate. But this reflected a sense of popular disillusion rather than a sea change in political inclinations. Taking office on 11 March, just 12 days after a devastating earthquake, President Sebastian Piñera of the Coalition for Change faces a formidable task in rebuilding quake-hit areas and maintaining economic stability. Outgoing Concertación President Michelle Bachelet, who was barred by the constitution from running for a second consecutive term in office, enjoyed an 80% personal approval rating at the time of her departure – filling her shoes will be a formidable task.

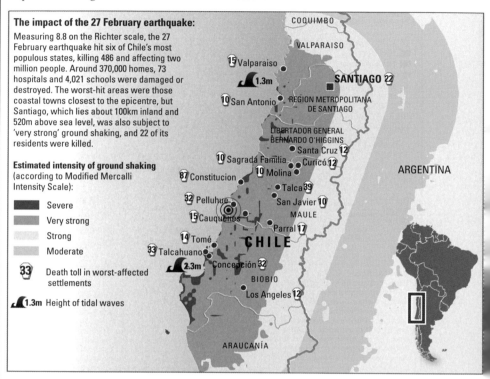

The impact of the 27 February earthquake:

Measuring 8.8 on the Richter scale, the 27 February earthquake hit six of Chile's most populous states, killing 486 and affecting two million people. Around 370,000 homes, 73 hospitals and 4,021 schools were damaged or destroyed. The worst-hit areas were those coastal towns closest to the epicentre, but Santiago, which lies about 100km inland and 520m above sea level, was also subject to 'very strong' ground shaking, and 22 of its residents were killed.

Estimated intensity of ground shaking (according to Modified Mercalli Intensity Scale):

- Severe
- Very strong
- Strong
- Moderate

33 Death toll in worst-affected settlements

1.3m Height of tidal waves

COQUIMBO
VALPARAISO
15 Valparaiso
1.3m
10 San Antonio   REGION METROPOLITANA DE SANTIAGO
SANTIAGO 22
LIBERTADOR GENERAL BERNARDO O'HIGGINS
Santa Cruz **12**
10 Sagradá Familia   Curicó **12**
10 Molina
87 Constitucion   Talca **39**
32 Pelluhue   San Javier **10**
MAULE
15 Cauquenes   Parral **17**
14 Tomé   **CHILE**
33 Talcahuano
2.3m   Concepción **32**
BIOBIO
Los Angeles **12**
ARAUCANÍA
ARGENTINA

Economic challenges facing Piñera

President Sebastian Piñera must not only steer his country out of the global economic downturn, but he must also pay for the recovery effort following the 27 February earthquake. In comparison to the dramatic fluctuations of neighbouring economies, Chile has a good record of stability and growth. This was recognised by the OECD in May 2010 when it welcomed Chile as its 31st member, the first South American country to join the group. The foundations of Chile's prosperity were laid by the Pinochet regime, and growth has been steady under the various Concertación governments in power since 1990. GDP per capita has increased from $4,542 to $14,299. Investment in education, health and civil infrastructure has also increased considerably.

The UN Office of the Resident Coordinator estimates that the cost of the earthquake to Chile's economy will be around $30 billion, equivalent to 17% of GDP. The Chilean finance ministry has diverted $730 million in public resources, set about selling off non-core state assets, issued global debt bonds and is attempting to stimulate investment in small-to-medium enterprises. It has also approved a temporary increase in corporate tax and taxes on high earners, a permanent increase in taxes on tobacco and modifications to royalty fees for mining companies (copper accounts for 50% of Chile's exports).

Growth rate (%

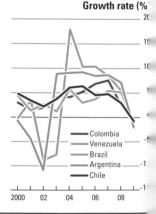

— Colombia
— Venezuela
— Brazil
— Argentina
— Chile

2000   02   04   06   08

09/2010 presidential elections

Juardo Frei's narrow defeat in the presidential
n-off at the hands of Sebastian Piñera betrayed
sense of frustration with the status quo on the
rt of Chilean voters. Having already served as
esident between 1994 and 2000, Frei failed to
ject new energy into the Concertación's
ectoral campaign and to claim any of Bachelet's
rsonal popularity for himself. Meanwhile,
ñera's Coalition for Change attempted to detach
self from the associations of the Pinochet era
nd occupy a political middle ground.

st round – 13 December 2009
al votes: 6,977,544

uardo Frei Ruiz-Tagle
ncertación de Partidos
la Democracia
65,061 votes (29.60%)

Jorge Arrate Mac-Niven
Partido Comunista de Chile
433,195 votes (6.21%)

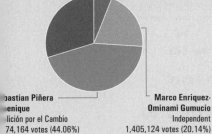

bastian Piñera
enique
lición por el Cambio
74,164 votes (44.06%)

Marco Enriquez-
Ominami Gumucio
Independent
1,405,124 votes (20.14%)

cond round – 17 January 2010
al votes: 6,958,972

ardo Frei Ruiz-Tagle
ncertación de Partidos
la Democracia
67,790 votes (48.39%)

Sebastian Piñera
Echenique
Coalición por el Cambio
3,591,182 votes (51.61%)

rces: Tribunal Calificador de Elecciones, Chile; USAID; United
ions Office of the Resident Coordinator, Chile; La Tercera; Comité
Emergencia, Chile; Economist; OECD; openDemocracy; United
es Department of Agriculture Economic Research Service

National voting patterns in the presidential run-off

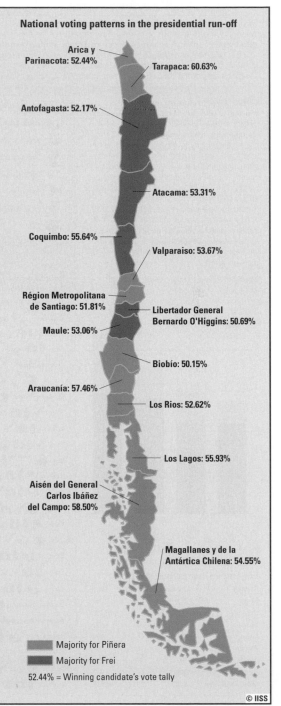

Arica y
Parinacota: 52.44%

Tarapaca: 60.63%

Antofagasta: 52.17%

Atacama: 53.31%

Coquimbo: 55.64%

Valparaiso: 53.67%

Région Metropolitana
de Santiago: 51.81%

Libertador General
Bernardo O'Higgins: 50.69%

Maule: 53.06%

Biobío: 50.15%

Araucanía: 57.46%

Los Rios: 52.62%

Los Lagos: 55.93%

Aisén del General
Carlos Ibáñez
del Campo: 58.50%

Magallanes y de la
Antártica Chilena: 54.55%

Majority for Piñera

Majority for Frei

52.44% = Winning candidate's vote tally

© IISS

THE AMERICAS: Haiti's devastating earthquake

Striking just 15km away from Haiti's densely populated capital Port-au-Prince with its notorious slums and at a relatively shallow depth of 10km below the earth's surface, the 12 January 2010 earthquake had a devastating effect on a country in an already wretched state. With a magnitude of 7.0, the earthquake claimed the lives of 222,517 (226,000 were killed by the Asian tsunami of December 2004). The international community was swift to provide financial and material assistance, but the recovery process will be long. Legislative and presidential elections scheduled for February were postponed, but may take place 'at some point' in 2010.

MINUSTAH peacekeeping force

In place since June 2004, the UN stabilisation mission in Haiti (MINUSTAH) was originally charged with restoring security after a period of civil unrest which had led to the departure of then-President Bertrand Aristide, as well as promoting democracy, strengthening the country's weak judicial system and promoting human rights. In the absence of a national army, MINUSTAH works in partnership with the Haitian national police force. Following the 12 January earthquake, in which 96 MINUSTAH personnel died including Head of Mission Hédi Annabi, the UN Security Council decided to increase the force's strength to help the recovery effort.

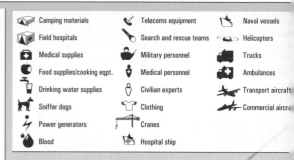

Camping materials · Telecoms equipment · Naval vessels
Field hospitals · Search and rescue teams · Helicopters
Medical supplies · Military personnel · Trucks
Food supplies/cooking eqpt. · Medical personnel · Ambulances
Drinking water supplies · Civilian experts · Transport aircraft
Sniffer dogs · Clothing · Commercial aircraft
Power generators · Cranes
Blood · Hospital ship

MINUSTAH authorised force strength since 2004
(thousands)

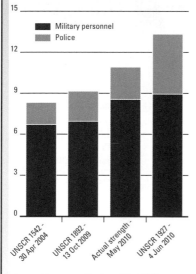

Legend: Military personnel, Police

X-axis: UNSCR 1542 - 30 Apr 2004 | UNSCR 1892 - 13 Oct 2009 | Actual strength - May 2010 | UNSCR 1927 - 4 Jun 2010

Some 60 nations provided material aid to Haiti in the aftermath of the earthquake

Listed below are some of the largest contributions

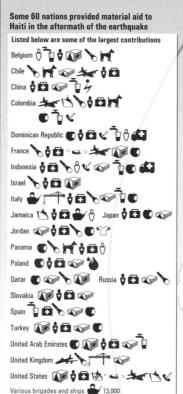

Belgium
Chile
China
Colombia
Dominican Republic
France
Indonesia
Israel
Italy
Jamaica · Japan
Jordan
Panama
Poland
Qatar · Russia
Slovakia
Spain
Turkey
United Arab Emirates
United Kingdom
United States
Various brigades and ships · 13,000
Uruguay
Venezuela

Largest troop contributions, May 2010

Country	Troops	Police	Total
Brazil	2,187	4	2,191
Uruguay	1,131	4	1,135
Nepal	1,073	208	1,281
Sri Lanka	957	17	974
Jordan	603	349	952
Argentina	562	16	578
Chile	503	15	518
MINUSTAH Total	8,549	2,367	10,916

Jeremie

50,000

GRAND ANS

Port Sal

The largest donations to the Haitian relief effort, as calculated by the UN Office for the Coordination of Humanitarian Affairs

Donor	Funding (US$), where the transfer of funds has taken place	% of grand total	Uncommitted pledges (US$), denoting non-binding announcements of an intention to donate
Private (individuals and organisations)	1,165,643,449	37.0%	70,673,505
United States	1,093,211,627	34.7%	0
Canada	137,792,229	4.4%	0
Red Cross/Red Crescent	86,181,683	2.7%	120,000
European Commission	68,255,128	2.2%	97,021,237
Spain	67,983,639	2.2%	13,275,613
Saudi Arabia	50,000,000	1.6%	0
Japan	48,127,154	1.5%	52,400,000
UN Central Emergency Response Fund	38,330,141	1.2%	0
France	35,956,408	1.1%	252,100,840
Sweden	33,307,037	1.1%	278,940
United Kingdom	33,167,336	1.1%	450,000

Grand total of global contributions, as of June 2010 (US$) **3,149,607,731**
Total of uncommitted pledges (US$) **1,191,020,550**

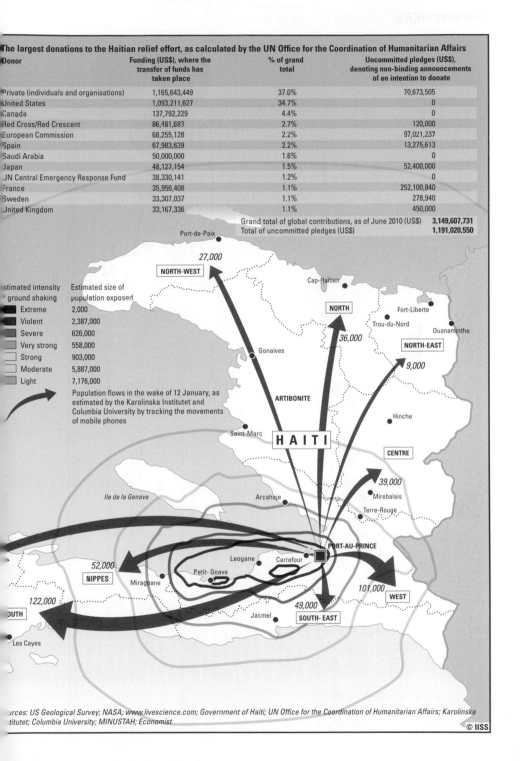

Estimated intensity of ground shaking | Estimated size of population exposed
Extreme — 2,000
Violent — 2,387,000
Severe — 626,000
Very strong — 558,000
Strong — 903,000
Moderate — 5,887,000
Light — 7,176,000

Population flows in the wake of 12 January, as estimated by the Karolinska Institutet and Columbia University by tracking the movements of mobile phones

Port-de-Paix
27,000
NORTH-WEST
Cap-Haitien
NORTH
Fort-Liberte
Trou-du-Nord
Ouanaminthe
36,000
NORTH-EAST
Gonaives
9,000
ARTIBONITE
Hinche
Saint-Marc
HAITI
CENTRE
Ile de la Genave
Arcahaie
39,000
Mirebalais
Terre-Rouge
PORT-AU-PRINCE
Leogane
Carrefour
52,000
Petit-Goave
NIPPES
Miragoane
101,000
WEST
122,000
49,000
SOUTH
Jacmel
SOUTH-EAST
Les Cayes

Sources: US Geological Survey; NASA; www.livescience.com; Government of Haiti; UN Office for the Coordination of Humanitarian Affairs; Karolinska Institutet; Columbia University; MINUSTAH; Economist

© IISS

THE AMERICAS: The Gulf of Mexico oil spill

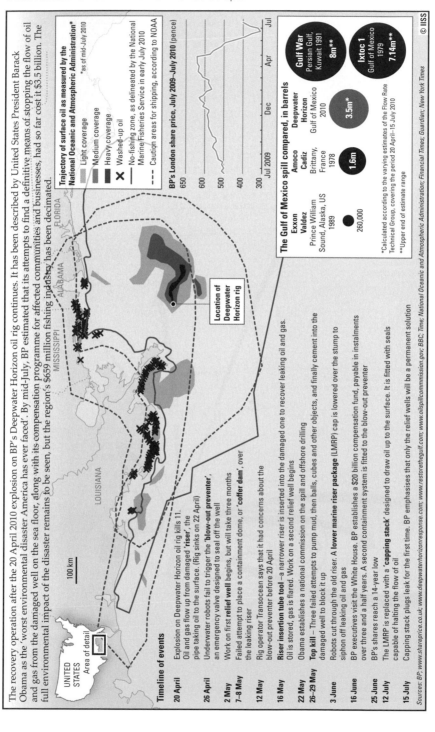

Chapter 6

Middle East/Gulf

In the year to mid-2010, Iran's continuing defiance of international pressure provoked a new round of United Nations sanctions. The Middle East saw setbacks, and no progress on the path to peace between Israelis and Palestinians. Iraq's political processes were precariously balanced, and the Gulf was beset by worries about Iran and financial stability.

Iran: Domestic Turmoil Thwarts Nuclear Deal

The political turmoil that engulfed Iran after the disputed 12 June 2009 presidential election continued for several months thereafter. Street demonstrations in Tehran and other cities that initially focused on charges of election fraud grew into a more general demand for government accountability, as ruthless government suppression polarised even the political elite. Though they were ultimately brought under uneasy control, the protests called into question the legitimacy of Iran's leadership.

The domestic tensions complicated Tehran's response to US President Barack Obama's attempts to establish dialogue. Paradoxically, Iran's hardline president, Mahmoud Ahmadinejad, was the only prominent politician in Tehran to support Obama's proposal for supply of reactor fuel for production of medical radioisotopes in exchange for Iran's export

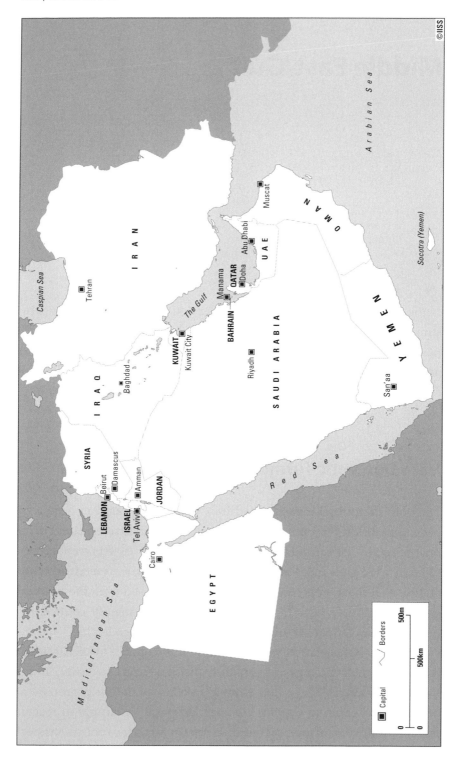

of the bulk of its enriched uranium. Political rivalries and distrust of the West led Iran to withdraw Ahmadinejad's acceptance in principle of the deal. Various Iranian counter-proposals then gave China, Russia and several other non-Western nations on the UN Security Council reason to delay and dilute adoption of sanctions that seemed inevitable after new revelations and other troubling developments concerning Iran's nuclear programme. After an ill-fated effort by Brazil and Turkey to broker a revised fuel-swap deal, new sanctions were finally adopted but not with the unanimity or teeth that Washington wanted. A year after the election dispute, Ahmadinejad could boast of having prevailed over both internal and external foes. Yet Iran's continued defiance of the Security Council boded ill for the stability of the region.

Movement against repression

Following the government's announcement on 13 June 2009 that incumbent President Ahmadinejad had won re-election by garnering nearly twice as many votes as his nearest competitor, an estimated three million people took to the streets claiming fraud. Although most outside observers concede that Ahmadinejad may well have had a slight majority of popular support, the claimed landslide seemed incomprehensible. A hasty intervention into the political fray by Supreme Leader Ayatollah Ali Khamenei to certify the announced result, calling it a 'divine assessment', added to the sense of injustice and diminished his standing. Reformist presidential candidate Mir Hossein Mousavi demanded a recount and the protests took on his green campaign colour as their symbol. But the Green Movement, as it came to be known, was largely a bottom-up expression of popular outrage, with Mousavi and fellow reformist presidential candidate Mehdi Karroubi acting as instruments of the populist movement rather than leaders of it. Heavy-handed government fetters on the reformists, including the arrest of key figures, contributed to popular anger. Claims of a stolen election were never confirmed, but came to matter less as government repression overtook election fraud as the focus of popular anger.

Determined to prevent an Iranian-style 'velvet revolution', the government arrested hundreds of protesters and employed the plainclothes paramilitary Basij to use deadly force. Mousavi supporters claimed that 72 demonstrators were killed throughout summer 2009 (double the official figure). The dying image of 26-year old Neda Agha-Soltan, fatally shot on 20 June, became a symbol of the struggle. In July, reports emerged of prison rapes of young male and female detainees, particularly in Kahrizak Prison, which was later closed by chastened officials but not before the disappearance of a doctor who reported the rapes. That month also saw the death in prison of the son of a senior adviser to conservative presidential candidate Mohsen Rezai. In August, the government began to conduct show trials of protesters, many of whom were forced to publicly confess to having received foreign help in bringing about a revolution.

The United Kingdom was particularly demonised, on unfounded grounds of foreign interference, both for historical reasons and because of the popularity of the BBC Persian service. Those detained included nine local staff of the British Embassy, one of whom, Hossein Rassam, was sentenced to four years' imprisonment for being the 'kingpin behind a British plot'. In connection with the post-election unrest, a French journalism student was detained for six weeks, a Canadian-Iranian journalist was held in solitary confinement for four months, and a US-Iranian academic was sentenced to 15 years in prison. Journalists in general were particularly targeted, and as of April 2010, 47 remained in prison. Universities were also subject to heavy pressure, and the government sought to Islamise the humanities curriculum.

As the government crackdown continued throughout 2009, many of the protesters voiced opposition to the theocracy of the Islamic Republic as embodied in the concept of the supreme leader and the person of Khamenei. Slogans that had started out fairly tame – 'Where is our vote?', 'We are Iranians too' – by autumn directly threatened the regime: 'Death to the Dictator', 'Khamenei is a murderer, his leadership is invalid' (which rhymes in Farsi). Fissures among the political elite came into stark relief, as the hardliners sought to sideline former presidents Akbar Hashemi Rafsanjani and Seyed Mohammad Khatami and arrested several family members of prominent regime figures. In light of these rifts and the surprising sustainability of the protests, the Green Movement began to be seen by many overly optimistic observers in the West as a viable alternative to the hardline clerical leaders through a 'colour revolution'-style popular uprising of the kind that replaced authoritarian regimes in Georgia, Ukraine and Kyrgyzstan earlier in the decade.

The post-election turbulence resulted in the further consolidation of the strong political influence of the Iranian Revolutionary Guard Corps (IRGC), a parallel force separate from the regular military. The IRGC is not monolithic (many of its members supported Mousavi), but its power is palpable. Veteran IRGC hardliners now occupy such key government posts as the ministers of defence, intelligence, interior and oil. They and other hardliners have increasingly prevailed over pragmatic conservatives including Ali Larijani, the speaker of the Majlis (parliament). The IRGC's political role is reinforced by the control the IRGC exercises over key economic sectors, including missile development, oil resources, the Tehran airport, dam building, telecommunications and military nuclear technology. The IRGC absorbed the Basij into its command structure, giving the corps a street presence by which to exert power in internal politics. Exaggerating for effect, US Secretary of State Hillary Clinton warned in speeches in Qatar and Saudi Arabia in February 2010 that Iran was moving towards becoming a military dictatorship.

> " A violent response by the protesters caused a backlash in popular opinion "

Later protests never matched the number of demonstrators immediately after the election, but there was a resurgence of popular anger on 21 December when up to half a million people demonstrated at the funeral of outspoken opposition cleric Grand Ayatollah Hossein Ali Montazeri. Protests turned violent a week later when the seventh day of mourning for his death coincided with the observance of Ashura, one of the holiest days in the Shia calendar. Mousavi's nephew was killed in the demonstrations and the 1,500 reported arrests on the day included a former foreign minister. Opposition leaders chastised the government for using violence on the holy day. But a violent response by the protesters themselves caused a backlash in popular opinion towards the demonstrations and contributed to a subsequent fall-off in the number of people the Green Movement was able to put on the streets.

Huge protests that were forecast for the 11 February 2010 anniversary of the Islamic Revolution failed to materialise. The government deployed massive numbers of security forces, shut down electronic communications on which the opposition had relied for coordination, and mobilised pro-government supporters to drown out scattered protests. Protest pyrotechnics that were expected on the 16 March date of an ancient Persian fire festival similarly fizzled. Mousavi and other opposition leaders vowed they would continue their struggle against the government, but it was not clear how.

In a further sign of the ebbing influence of the Green Movement, Khamenei in early 2010 was able to bring Rafsanjani back into the fold. The first sign of this was the announcement in mid-February that the Expediency Council he headed would soon be discussing a comprehensive elections bill to address shortcomings in the existing law. Then, on 4 March, Rafsanjani appeared in public with Ahmadinejad for the first time since the disputed election. This appeared to signal that Khamenei had realised a need to balance the power of hardliners by giving pragmatic conservatives a greater voice while continuing to marginalise reformists. Yet the ongoing tension between power elites contributed to a paralysis in government decision-making apparent in both the economic and diplomatic spheres.

Economic troubles

Amidst the political perturbations, Iran's sluggish economy presented a chronic problem that the government proved incapable of handling. Reliable statistics were scarce, but private estimates put both inflation and unemployment at more than 20%. The government's perennial budget deficit continued, consumers experienced shortages of natural gas and electricity and many of Iran's most educated citizens continued to emigrate – by one estimate 150,000 people leave Iran each year to live abroad.

Despite Iran's vast gas and oil reserves, for which it respectively ranks second and third in the world, output continued to decline due to inadequate refurbishing and investment. The International Energy Agency forecast that by 2015 Iran's oil production capacity will drop about 18%, or roughly 700,000 barrels a day, from current levels. Sanctions and US-led financial pressure were partly to blame for the lack of foreign investment, and increased the cost of imports by about 15%. But most of

Iran's economic woes were self-inflicted. Massive subsidies, which comprise nearly 25% of GDP, and regulatory and price controls squandered much of the nation's wealth. Rising oil prices helped, but the problems were exacerbated by rampant corruption; Iran ranked among the most corrupt countries, tied with Haiti, in the 2009 Corruption Perceptions Index compiled by Transparency International. The IRGC, for example, was a major beneficiary of sweetheart contracts.

Efforts to reduce subsidies have largely failed due to government paralysis and fear of public backlash. For much of 2009–10, the Ahmadinejad administration and the parliament were deadlocked over subsidy reform, and who would bear responsibility for the inflation hike that would result. According to former Minister of Finance Jahangir Amuzegar, the Iranian economy was facing its bleakest forecast in nearly two decades, and the worsening economic conditions would likely place considerable stress on internal politics.

Iran–US dynamics

Iran's domestic situation complicated the outreach strategy Obama had envisioned at the beginning of his term in 2009. Iran's election timetable had already required patience; Obama understood that Iran would not be able to respond meaningfully until after 12 June. That May, when Israeli Prime Minister Benjamin Netanyahu had pressed Obama to give Iran a three-month deadline, Obama said he expected to know by the end of the year whether Iran was making 'a good-faith effort to resolve differences'.

The post-election protests further delayed Tehran's response to Obama, although the protest movement itself could be seen as a form of popular response. Contrary to the government's charges, the Green Movement was not spawned by a foreign conspiracy. The demonstrations were a natural outburst of long-suppressed aspirations. Yet the protests were enabled by Obama's subtle policy. Because his open hand belied the regime's narrative of being beset by hostile foreign forces, protesters were emboldened to take to the streets and even to challenge the regime's authority. Government charges that protesters were Western lackeys held little potency when the leader of the Western world was offering the nation an embrace. Indeed, many of the protesters were disappointed at Washington's muted support for their demands. 'Obama, Obama, either you are with them or with us' (a word play in Farsi) was a popular protest chant. Many reform-minded Iranians argued that Obama should give more emphasis to enriching human rights in Iran than to opposing enrichment of uranium.

Many Western observers saw reason for hope that political change in Iran propelled by the Green Movement would be the best and maybe only long-term solution to the nuclear crisis. While realising that the prospect for a Green Revolution was still a long shot, influential American commentators argued that it was far less likely that the hardliners now in charge would give up their nuclear aspirations. Although the reformists shared the nationwide nationalist support for the nuclear programme, it was presumed that if they were in power they would be willing to engage in negotiations, at least over tactics, as was the case when Khatami was president. American proponents of regime change argued that the United States should do all it could to support the Green Movement, including refusing to lend Ahmadinejad legitimacy by engaging with his government.

As the protests, and the suppression, continued through the autumn and into the winter, the United States became increasingly vocal in expressing support for human rights in Iran. In his 10 December Nobel Peace Prize acceptance speech, Obama forcefully called for the respect of human rights and civil liberties. In publicly mourning Montazeri's death, the White House purposely sought to give moral support to Iranian opponents of the regime, something many of them had been demanding for months. But once the protests died down, the debate in Washington about whether to focus more on human rights than uranium enrichment shifted to questions of how best to employ sanctions.

Nuclear fuel swap deal

Obama's outreach strategy finally crystallised in the form of an October offer to provide replacement fuel for the Tehran Research Reactor (TRR) in exchange for 1,200kg of the low-enriched uranium (LEU) that Iran had been accumulating since 2006. By October 2009, Iran had produced about 1,600kg of LEU, enough feed material for about 1.5 bombs' worth of fissile material if further enriched to 90%. The TRR produces isotopes for x-rays and other medical purposes, but its fuel, which utilises 19.75% enriched uranium, was projected to run out in late 2010.

Iran's June 2009 request to the International Atomic Energy Agency (IAEA) for help in obtaining replacement fuel had given the United States and its partners an opening. If Iran would export the bulk of its LEU, Russia would be willing to enrich it to 19.75% and ship it to France for processing into fuel assemblies for the TRR. France and Argentina are the only countries that produce this niche product. Argentina had no interest in exporting to a country that in August had named as defence minister an intelligence officer, Ahmad Vahidi, who was implicated by Interpol for the 1984 deadly bombing of the Buenos Aires Jewish Centre. France, which is the most sceptical of Iran's Western critics, also had little interest but was persuaded to join the deal, as long as Iran shipped out all 1,200kg of LEU in one batch and by the end of 2009, to bring Iran's stockpile well below the amount needed for a weapon. Keeping the stockpile below a weapon's worth was the goal, because it would set a useful precedent for long-term solution and provide for mutual confidence.

Because each of the three reactor core loads to be provided would take France a year to produce, the deal would require Iran to part with its LEU before receiving the TRR fuel. This was a difficult condition to accept. Ahmadinejad's representatives nevertheless went along with the principle of the exchange in a meeting on 1 October in Geneva, which included a rare bilateral meeting with US officials. Iran also accepted *ad referendum* the details of the exchange plan in IAEA-led negotiations in Vienna in late October. But the deal encountered heated opposition in Tehran, where Ahmadinejad's rivals across the political spectrum, including Mousavi, denounced him for selling out, and the naturally suspicious supreme leader sided with the crowd. Reneging on the outlines of the Geneva–Vienna deal, the Iranian government insisted that the exchange would have to be simultaneous and on Iranian soil. It would permit the IAEA to take custody of a quantity of LEU, but this would not be allowed to leave Iran until the TRR fuel was provided.

Unstated by Iran was that this would take a year, by which time continued LEU production would more than replace any amount to be transferred. The West thus rejected Iran's counter-proposal for a simultaneous exchange, although Iran continued throughout the first half of 2010 to woo Brazil, Turkey and other would-be intermediaries. Meanwhile, except for the 1 October 2009 meeting in Geneva, Iran refused to discuss its nuclear programme with its erstwhile P5+1 negotiating partners (the five Security Council permanent members plus Germany).

Sanctions diplomacy

By early 2010 Obama was turning increasing attention to sanctions as a means of trying to affect Iran's nuclear calculus. In mid-May, as the Security Council neared action on a new sanctions resolution, Iran suddenly agreed to a deal brokered by Brazil and Turkey that incorporated some of the key elements of the October fuel swap deal. In the deal, Iran agreed to send 1,200kg of LEU to Turkey, in exchange for TRR fuel a year later. By May, however, 1,200kg represented less than half of Iran's growing stockpile, meaning that it would retain at least a weapon's worth. Worse, there was no provision curtailing Iran's production of 20%-enriched uranium, which Tehran insisted would continue. These and other problematic elements of the Brazil–Turkey–Iran deal made for a 'too-little, too-late' reception by the major powers, which proceeded instead to introduce the new sanctions resolution.

UN Security Council Resolution 1929, adopted on 9 June by a 12–2–1 majority over objections by Brazil and Turkey (which both voted no) and Lebanon (which abstained), was far less than the 'crippling' sanctions that the United States and its key allies had sought. China and Russia ensured that the resolution contained no measures targeting Iran's oil and gas sector and few mandatory restrictions of any sort. Washington reasoned that unity among the permanent members of the Security Council was more important than tough content. Yet the new measures imposed were not insignificant. The resolution banned specified categories of major arms sales to Iran, and while the sophisticated S-300 ground-to-air-missile system that Iran had been seeking to import from Russia was not included in the banned list of arms, Moscow said it would interpret the resolution as covering the S-300 anyway. For the first time the resolution banned ballistic-missile-development activity, setting up a confrontation the next time Iran carries out a missile test.

Most importantly, UNSCR 1929 called upon countries to restrict a number of financial activities, including transactions involving the IRGC, that could contribute to sensitive nuclear or missile programmes. Although not mandatory, these provisions gave countries a UN justification and legal basis for imposing their own controls on business with Iran. EU heads of government agreed on 17 June to go beyond the UN measures by prohibiting new investment and technology transfer in key parts of the gas and oil industry, and to concentrate additional sanctions on trade insurance, banking and transport.

The United States also imposed additional measures of its own. After persuading the US Congress to hold off until after the UN decision, Obama on 1 July 2010 signed a new set of extraterritorial sanctions imposing restrictions on foreign entities involved in refined petroleum sales to Iran or doing business with key Iranian banks or the IRGC. Even some of the most vigorous proponents of these sanctions acknowledged that they would not bring an end to Iran's nuclear programme. The hope, rather, was that tightening the economic pressure would bring Tehran back to the bargaining table in earnest. The most effective approach in this regard was through subtle pressure on foreign firms to curtail economic activity with Iranian entities that were involved directly or indirectly in supporting the nuclear programme.

New revelations of nuclear work

An impetus for new sanctions was created in September 2009, when Iran was found to have been secretly building a new enrichment plant buried within a mountain at Fardow, near the holy city of Qom. Because of its small size, the plant appeared to be designed to produce enriched uranium for weapons purposes. Obama revealed the existence of the plant to maximum publicity at a G20 summit on 25 September. Realising that its secrecy had been compromised, Iran had told the IAEA about the plant only two days before Obama's announcement. IAEA safeguards rules which have been in effect worldwide since the 1990s and were accepted by Iran in 2003, require notification of any new nuclear facility at the time a construction decision is made. Iran claims that because in 2007 it rescinded its acceptance of this rule, it needed only follow the older requirement for notification six months before nuclear material is introduced into a building. The IAEA noted, however, that there was no provision for unilateral rescission of the early notification requirement, and Director-General Mohamed ElBaradei characterised Iran's action as being 'on the wrong side of the law'. Unfazed, Ahmadinejad announced in December that his government had authorised the construction of ten additional uranium-enrichment facilities – a claim widely doubted, given Iran's difficulties in equipping its existing enrichment plant at Natanz – and would let the agency know the details if and when necessary.

Russian anger at having to learn about the Fardow plant from America made it inclined for the first time since March 2008 to consider imposing additional UN sanctions. But President Dmitry Medvedev's statement in September 2009 that 'sanctions may be inevitable' was undercut by Prime Minister Vladimir Putin's comments to the contrary. It took Russia several more months to agree to sanctions, which it insisted be limited to entities directly related to the nuclear programme. Meanwhile China maintained throughout the winter that there was still room for diplomacy. Not until April 2010 did Beijing agree to begin negotiating the text of a sanctions resolution, and then it worked to restrict the sanctions' scope.

Just as China seized on Iran's fuel-exchange counter-offers as a rationale for delaying sanctions, Israel and some European countries pointed to further Iranian provocations as reason to ramp up the pressure. In December 2009 the *Times* of London published evidence that Iran, as recently as 2007, was embarked on a plan involving uranium deuteride, which is used as an initiator for a nuclear weapon and has no civil application. Although the evidence required corroboration, it undoubtedly contributed to an ongoing reassessment by the US intelligence community of its infamous 2007 conclusion that Iran had suspended work on nuclear-weapons development. According to unconfirmed press reports, a new classified US national intelligence estimate on Iran, possibly to be concluded in the second half of 2010 but not made public, was to assess that Iran likely had resumed work on weapons design after 2004, but not necessarily the development of a bomb.

Further enrichment

International frustration with Iran deepened in early February 2010 when it began enriching small quantities of 20%-enriched uranium.

The amount of effort required to produce weapons-grade uranium is reduced by more than half when 3.5% LEU is further enriched to 20%. Iran justified this step on grounds of not being able to import TRR fuel, although Iran itself did not yet have the technology to produce the fuel plates required. The purpose of this move was both strategic and political: to seek leverage in negotiations with the West and to rally domestic opinion in support of another nuclear achievement. The new enrichment level prominently featured in Ahmadinejad's Revolution Day speech on 11 February. To enable him to proclaim success in time for the anniversary, Iranian engineers began operation without giving the IAEA time to adjust its safeguards procedures. This prompted an unusually swift report by the agency complaining about the insufficient notice.

A week later, newly elected Director-General Yukiya Amamo issued the IAEA's harshest report yet about Iran's nuclear activities. In addition to detailing areas of non-cooperation, the report summarised outstanding issues of concern, including evidence of military dimensions to the programme. The report said the information available to the Agency 'raises concerns about the possible existence in Iran of past or current undisclosed activities related to the development of a nuclear payload for a missile'. The reference to 'current' activity was widely seen as another reason the US intelligence agencies needed to reassess their 2007 conclusion that weapons-development work had remained suspended.

Varying estimates with regard to how close Iran was to producing a bomb contributed to expert commentary in Israel and the United States about possible military options if diplomacy did not succeed in stopping Iran's programme. On the one hand, the increasing stockpile of LEU, which could be re-enriched to weapons-grade material in a few months (albeit not without tipping off the IAEA), and the evidence of weapons-design work led Israel and many analysts elsewhere to contend that Iran could have a bomb by 2011. Other experts and Western policymakers noted that the exposure of the Fardow facility had rendered it unusable for clandestine weapons purposes. They said that there was, therefore, still ample time before Iran would be able to present a nuclear threat. The decreasing number of centrifuges actually producing enriched uranium in winter 2010 and the high failure rate of the centrifuges, which some reports attributed to US covert sabotage, added to a perception that not everything was going well for Iran's nuclear programme. However, those centrifuges that were enriching uranium were doing so with greater efficiency. By May 2010, Iran had produced 2,427kg of LEU, nearly sufficient for two bombs' worth of feed material, and was continuing to increase the stockpile by about 120kg a month.

Iran also continued to make progress in developing ballistic missiles that appeared to be developed with the aim of giving it the capability to deliver nuclear warheads well beyond its borders, although the government claimed that the missiles are strictly defensive in nature. Adding to its *Ghadr*-1 liquid-fuelled medium-range missile, Iran has developed a new solid-fuelled missile capable of delivering a 750kg nuclear weapon approximately 2,200km. This missile, the *Sajjil*-2, is less vulnerable to pre-emptive military action thanks to its shorter launch-preparation time. First flight-tested in November 2008, it had three more successful flight tests in 2009.

Iran's space-launch programme also raised concerns because of the technological carry-over to military applications. Following on from its 2009 success in putting a small satellite into orbit, Iran in February 2010 unveiled a mock-up of a new *Simorgh* launch vehicle. The display suggested that Iran planned to develop and use more powerful satellite carriers in the coming years. But the Iranian missile threat in the near future would come from its short- and medium-range ballistic missiles. A new US intelligence estimate assessed that the threat of potential Iranian intercontinental ballistic missile capabilities had been slower to develop than previously estimated. This estimate, which was independently reached by an IISS analysis published in May 2010, informed Obama's September 2009 decision to reconfigure the missile-shield system the United States had been planning to install in Europe into a more mobile, adaptive system.

Military option

America's military and defence leaders remained opposed to a military option to deal with the threat from Iran's nuclear programme, in light of the commitment of US forces to Iraq and Afghanistan, and the likelihood that air-strikes on Iran's nuclear facilities would only set back the programme for a relatively few years while entangling the United States in a wider regional conflict and unleashing any number of unpalatable consequences. The official US line was that 'military action has never been taken off the table' but that it is 'an action of last resort'.

Israeli strategists also saw strikes as a last option, but they seemed more willing to accept the potential consequences and the fact that the time before Iran could reconstitute its programme would only be brief. The prevailing mood among Israelis was that they could defend against counter-attacks, whether directly from Iran or via Hizbullah and Hamas, and that if Iran were to reconstitute a nuclear-weapons programme, it would just have to be attacked again (albeit with less certainty of the location of what would surely be secret facilities.)

Israelis were more divided on the need for – and likelihood of – American approval for a unilateral attack by Israel. Although Vice President Joe Biden in an unscripted July 2009 interview had seemed to give a green light to an Israeli attack, he and other US officials later made clear their opposition to such a move. A deepening rift between Netanyahu and the Obama administration over expanded Israeli settlements in the West Bank complicated the issue. Some Israelis sided with the perspective of former Deputy Defense Minister Ephraim Sneh, who said: 'We don't have permission and we don't need permission from the US'. A more cautious reaction was voiced by retired Brigadier-General Shlomo Brom, former strategic planning chief for the Israeli military's general staff, who asked rhetorically: 'What will Americans say if Israel drags the US into a war it didn't want, or when they are suddenly paying $10 a gallon for gasoline and Israel is the reason for it?'

Iranian responses to threats

Iranian officials professed to be unfazed by talk of military action, apparently calculating it to be unlikely. Yet foreign visitors to Iran reported a genuine fear of the United States, and the government trumpeted the perceived threat for purposes of rallying domestic opinion. In April, Obama's Nuclear Posture Review (NPR) clarified an American policy not to employ nuclear weapons against states that were themselves not nuclear-armed, but countries such as Iran that were in violation of their non-proliferation obligations were excluded from this assurance. Although the NPR did nothing to change Washington's military options vis-à-vis Iran, Obama and Defense Secretary Robert Gates in public remarks highlighted the Iranian exception, which prompted Tehran to react angrily to what it characterised as the threat of a nuclear attack. In Iran's view, this confirmed that Obama's outreach strategy was simply rhetoric that reflected no real change in US policy. An Ahmadinejad letter to Obama in March 2010 welcoming 'genuine change' received no response.

Iran claimed that it was already the victim of an American-led 'soft war' and a covert war. Accusing foreign groups of inciting post-election unrest, the Ministry of Interior in January 2000 made it illegal for citizens to have contact with any of 60 banned US and international non-governmental organisations, including Human Rights Watch and Yale University. Iran also blamed the United States and Israel for the assassination in January of physics professor Masoud Ali-Mohammadi, who according to some reports was connected with a secret nuclear bomb development programme. But some opposition groups claimed government involvement in his death, noting that he had publicly supported Mousavi, and claimed he might have been killed to prevent his defection or leaking of information. Iranian officials blamed the United States for kidnapping another Iranian nuclear scientist, Shahram Amiri, who had gone missing during a pilgrimage to Saudi Arabia in June 2009 and who nine months later was reported to have settled in the US. In July 2010, he flew back to Tehran and claimed that he had been abducted.

Regional relations

Western efforts to isolate Iran over the nuclear issue did not succeed in many parts of the developing world, where Iran's emphasis on its right to nuclear energy and its criticism of Western double standards continued to find a receptive audience. Parlaying its prominent position in the Non-Aligned Movement, Tehran was able to persuade six members of the IAEA Board of Governors to abstain on a November resolution that criticised Iran's failure to provide advance notice of the Fardow enrichment plant. Three other board members voted 'no' on the resolution, although one of them – Malaysia – recalled its ambassador after the vote for violating instructions. This lack of unanimity was a precursor to the 'no' votes by Brazil and Turkey and the abstention by Lebanon in the long-awaited June 2010 UN sanctions resolution vote.

In the immediate neighbourhood, Syria remained Iran's most staunch supporter. Reciprocal state visits and frequent bilateral meetings deepened already close political, diplomatic and economic ties, including advancing plans for a joint Iranian–Syrian bank. The two countries also cooperated in arms trading in violation of a Security Council ban on weapons exports from Iran. In October 2009, a German cargo ship travelling from Iran to Syria was discovered to include Kalashnikov rifle ammunition, apparently intended for either the Syrian army or Hizbullah.

Iran also strengthened relations with Afghanistan and Pakistan, both of which reportedly provided intelligence cooperation for Iran's arrest in February 2010 of the leader of the Jundallah terrorist group in Iranian Balochistan. Iran claims the group receives CIA support. Tehran's ties with Kabul were reinforced when Ahmadinejad visited in March 2010 and scolded the United States over its military presence. Yet he also called on the United States and NATO to do more to tackle Afghanistan's narcotics trade, which creates a significant problem for Iran. Implicit in this was a call for Iran–NATO cooperation to secure the porous Iran–Afghanistan border, where Iran and the West have congruent goals. One opportunity for cooperation in this regard was lost when Iran declined to take part in a January 2010 conference in London on the future of Afghanistan. Iran explained its refusal on grounds that the meeting was focused on increasing military action in Afghanistan and did not take into account the region's own capacity to solve the problem.

Iran's complex relations with its Gulf neighbours took a sour turn in April, when United Arab Emirates Foreign Minister Sheikh Abdullah compared Iranian occupation of three disputed islands located at the entrance to the Strait of Hormuz with Israeli occupation of Arab lands. The Gulf Arab states also grew increasingly nervous about the nuclear and missile threat from the eastern side of the Gulf, and most of them sought to strengthen their defence ties with the United States, including introducing Patriot anti-ballistic-missile batteries. In addition, Yemen accused Iran of arming the Shia Houthi rebels fighting against the government in northern Yemen, seeking autonomous rule. (The United States said it saw no evidence of such an arms flow.) In response, Iran warned Arab countries against interfering in its affairs and deepening sectarian rifts between Sunnis and Shi'ites in the region.

A border dispute with Iraq in December 2009 similarly exacerbated Iran's relations with its Shia-majority neighbour. The dispute flared when Baghdad sought to auction development rights to oil fields near the Iranian border and Tehran responded by occupying an Iraqi oil well in disputed territory. After a several-day stand-off, negotiators agreed to form a joint technical group to discuss border claims. While minor, the incident confirmed the Iraqi government's growing independence from the client relationship that prevailed until very recently with Iran.

Preparing for containment and deterrence

Neither sanctions nor engagement has worked yet to dissuade Iran from coming ever closer to being able to produce a nuclear weapon if so chose. Nor did any combination of diplomatic policy options look likely to succeed in the foreseeable future. The *New York Times* reported that Gates said in a January memo to the White House that the administration lacked an effective strategy to counter Iran in the event that the current set of policies failed. Responding to the leak, Gates said the memo had been 'mischaracterised' and was meant to prepare for an 'orderly and timely decision-making process'. To some observers, this meant preparing the ground for a containment policy rather than a military confrontation strategy that, Gates had said, would be damaging to America's regional position. But arguing explicitly for containment and deterrence could be seen as 'defeatism'.

Nevertheless, a sense of resignation began to emerge in the US analytical community that the world would have to live with a nuclear-armed Iran. It may be more realistic to say that the world will have to live with a nuclear-capable Iran, but not necessarily one armed with nuclear weapons. After all, Iran is already nuclear-capable in the sense that it has the technology to produce fissile material, and its leaders must calculate that any overt crossing of the line to weapons production would provoke a military attack. How close Iran can get to crossing the red line of weapons production and how large a stockpile of LEU it can accumulate before Israel takes matters into its own hands is unknown, probably even in Jerusalem. The possibility that Iran's nuclear programme might provoke an attack will keep the region on tenterhooks.

Middle East: Grim Stocktaking

Two major developments occurred in the Middle East in 2009–10. Firstly, a widening split emerged between the United States and Israel on key issues. Secondly, the Israeli–Palestinian conflict became internationalised so as to include Turkey. In other ways, prior conditions continued. The Palestinian leadership remained divided between Fatah, the main secular party that controlled the Palestinian Authority (PA) in the West Bank, and its rival Hamas, the militant Islamist group that held sway in Gaza. An uneasy standoff between Israel and Hizbullah, the militant Lebanese Shia Muslim organisation, persisted. And Israel's right-wing coalition remained solidly in control of the country's politics and policies.

US–Israel relations: the settlements issue

The most salient factor in US–Israel relations in 2009 was the Obama administration's demand that the Israeli government, a coalition of religious and secular right-wing parties with the participation of a rump Labor Party, freeze all settlement construction in occupied territories. The origins of the demand are murky, but its thrust aligned with the instincts of US President Barack Obama himself and those of his closest advisers. The view that he manifested during his 2008 presidential campaign had been that rapid progress in the peace process was essential to US interests – in particular, though not exclusively, that of stemming the decline in US prestige and popularity in the Muslim world that had occurred during the George W. Bush administration.

The choice of settlements as the focal point for Obama's effort was a deft one. A discernible majority of Israelis consider the settler movement deleterious to Israel's larger interests. According to the annual Tel Aviv University summer opinion polls in 2009, a large majority of Israelis who live within the June 1967 borders – over 70% – had not visited the West Bank in the previous year. This suggests that most Israelis had fenced the West Bank out of their mental landscape. On one level, this was an unsurprising psychological reality, given the potential for violence there. On another level, it was a practical consequence of the Israeli road network, which obviated the need to enter West Bank towns for drivers traversing parts of occupied territory. Moreover, the US Congress, despite its generally strong support for Israel, opposed Israeli settlements, especially those protruding deeply into the West Bank. Settlements were therefore a reasonably safe point of entry for a White House looking for leverage.

The Obama administration's gambit, however, was poorly played by an inexperienced White House staff that overestimated the president's influence while misreading the dynamics of Israeli coalition politics. In particular, the White House exaggerated both Obama's moral authority on the basis of his relatively large margin of victory in the US presidential election, and the pliancy of Israeli Prime Minister Benjamin Netanyahu on the basis of his record of last-minute cave-ins to American demands in the 1990s during his first stint as prime minister. The White House also failed to account for popular mistrust in Israel of the new administration. The tenacious and widespread view that Obama was a Muslim, a persistent belief held by a minority of Americans as well, combined with sinking Israeli confidence in the established land-for-peace formula and the two-state solution, undercut Obama's considerable capacity for persuasion.

The president's June 2009 speech in Cairo, which was framed by the White House as part of a larger effort to woo the Muslim world, further diminished the president's seductive powers. Israelis interpreted the fact that the Cairo visit was not coupled with a stop in Israel to speak to an Israeli audience as an indication of disdain for their interests and, perhaps, for them. The call for a settlements freeze in the speech reinforced this reading because, from an Israeli perspective, the Arab states were not being asked to take commensurate risks. Obama had inserted references to the Holocaust to counter pervasive Holocaust denial within the audiences he was trying to reach, but Israelis interpreted its mention as intended merely to ground the legitimacy of the state of Israel in the disaster of the Second World War rather than in the wider biblical claims to Palestine and a long record of Jewish residence there. For Israelis, then, an earnest American challenge to an adverse Arab idée fixe therefore turned into a patronising and delegitimising swipe at the very constituency it was supposed to benefit. Aluf Benn, a distinguished and mildly left-of-centre Israeli diplomatic correspondent, summed up the Israeli mood in a plea for the American president 'to speak to us'.

Thus, while the selection of settlements as a wedge issue was shrewd, the way it was deployed proved to be counter-productive. The freeze demand, as Israel was quick to note, ran counter to a letter that Bush had sent to then-Israeli Prime Minister Ariel Sharon in 2004, which implicitly excluded Jerusalem among other locations from freeze agreements. The shared reasoning behind this 'carve out', as it is termed in diplomatic parlance, was that there was no conceivable negotiated outcome in which Jewish Israelis could be removed from Jerusalem, the eastern part of which was annexed by Israel in the wake of the June 1967 war, and that Israel's borders would ultimately incorporate the large suburban communities that more or less hug the old border on the Palestinian side. Both of these implicit understandings derived from negotiations between Palestinians and Israelis in the waning days of the Clinton administration and the government of Israeli Prime Minister Ehud Barak. Together, they fell under the rubric of the so-called Clinton Parameters, which were long held by the United States, Israel and most Palestinians to constitute the contours of an eventual final status accord.

> **The Obama team failed to foresee the effect of the freeze on the Palestinians**

Obama's apparent abrogation of the Bush–Sharon correspondence afforded Netanyahu valuable ammunition against both Washington and his domestic opponents. Survey data suggested that Israelis, who generally expect their leaders to manage the bilateral relationship carefully and have punished at the polls premiers who have failed to so, concluded Obama had genuinely wrong-footed Netanyahu. This perception meshed unhelpfully with more broadly negative Israeli impressions of Obama. The Israeli message was that the US position was unfair as well as poorly aimed, insofar as it appeared not to recognise that the only source of serious political pressure on Netanyahu was the right. Thus, to the extent that the US initiative interacted with coalition dynamics, it was perversely to incentivise Netanyahu to reject the administration's demand in a way that would inoculate him against right-wing agitation while allowing him to appear to the Israeli public as having an authentic grievance against the United States.

The Obama team also inexplicably failed to foresee the effect of the freeze initiative on the Palestinian leadership. Since the president had gone farther in his demands regarding Israeli settlement activity than had the Palestinian leadership up to that point, PA President Mahmoud Abbas was forced to embrace a position that he knew to be unworkable in order not to be seen as willing to settle for less on behalf of his constituency than was Obama. As Abbas told an interviewer in *Asharq al Awsat*, the London-based international Arab newspaper, he felt as though he'd been 'treed' by Obama.

It took time for the White House to understand that it had overplayed its hand and that Netanyahu was, in effect, an immovable object. Once that realisation had set in, grinding diplomatic trench warfare began, with the aim of achieving a face-saving compromise for both sides. The result, reached in November 2009, was an Israeli commitment to a ten-month freeze excluding Jerusalem. This modest success was transformed into something closer to Orwellian farce when US Secretary of State Hillary Clinton characterised it as 'unprecedented' and a demonstration of Israeli 'restraint'. Most observers viewed it as neither. Within months, different interpretations of the agreement led to a second crisis in the relationship. Furthermore, the ten-month sunset provision automatically started the clock ticking for another confrontation when the terms of that agreement approached an end.

The first of these problems arose during Vice President Joe Biden's March 2010 visit to Jerusalem, which had been staged to defuse some of the tensions generated by the settlement controversy and by vocal and public disagreement about linkage between the Middle East peace process and non-proliferation efforts vis-à-vis Iran. Biden has a reputation as a friend of Israel and possesses an effusive, even emphatic style that Israelis find appealing. In the midst of what seemed to be unfolding as a feel-good event, however, Eli Yishai – the Israeli cabinet minister with the portfolio for housing, and a representative of the Sephardic religious party Shas – announced the impending construction of 1,600 new housing units in a burgeoning Jewish neighbourhood in East Jerusalem that threatened to displace Arab Jerusalemites living next door. As a technical matter, the construction programme was permissible under the terms of the US–Israeli agreement on the settlement freeze, given that Jerusalem was excluded from the pact. But the Obama administration was incensed, feeling that the announcement not only contravened the spirit of the agreement but also humiliated the vice president. The

Israelis, who focused on the specific terms of the agreement, judged American outrage to be misplaced, unfair and, some insisted, manufactured to impress the Arab audience.

The obtusely uncomprehending nature of Israel's reaction was both reinforced and revealed by Netanyahu's subsequent labours to convince Washington that, insofar as his own cabinet seemed not to have bothered to inform him that the announcement was on the cards, he could not be held responsible for the ensuing fuss. His attempt to press this argument on Obama in the White House reportedly led to Obama's brusque departure from the meeting. The overall effect was to widen a gap between Israel and the United States that if not unprecedented was still alarming to advocates of the putative special relationship on both sides.

US–Israel relations: Iran

Compounding the complexity of the bilateral situation were differing approaches to the challenge posed by Iran's pursuit of a nuclear-weapons programme. This divergence emerged starkly in Netanyahu's first joint press conference with Obama in Washington in May 2009. When the issue of Iran arose in the question and answer part of the conference, Netanyahu volunteered that for Israel the precondition for concessions necessary to move the process forward was a halt to Iran's nuclear programme. The rationale for this position was that an empowered Iran, especially one ruled by individuals and organisations with a revolutionary world view, would feel more free to interfere on behalf of Israel's local adversaries, especially Hamas and Hizbullah. Both groups were steadfastly opposed to a peace accord with Israel and both had attacked Israel after the Israel Defense Forces (IDF) had withdrawn from their territories in Gaza and Lebanon, respectively. In such an environment, Israel could not reasonably be expected to incur the risks entailed in a withdrawal of its forces from, or substantial lessening of its security control over, the West Bank. The path to Israeli compromise and Palestinian flexibility therefore ran through Tehran. Obama rejected the direction of this linkage, arguing in the press conference that progress towards an Israeli–Palestinian agreement would be essential to the task of assembling a regional coalition in support of measures to bring Iran's nuclear programme to a halt. From his perspective, the road to an Iran without nuclear weapons ran through Jerusalem.

This stand-off hardened over the course of the year, owing to several events and trends, some perhaps predictable and others not. The force of Obama's argument on linkage necessarily depended, in the first place, on the degree to which there was a regional coalition to be assembled against Iran, and secondly, whether key regional states, especially Saudi Arabia, were willing to offset risks taken by Israel in the Palestinian context through some sort of limited recognition of Israel. The White House understood this well enough and, in June 2009, Obama travelled to Saudi Arabia to meet King Abdullah to gain his cooperation on both points. The visit, which had a spontaneous feel, was ill-fated. The Saudis urged the US Embassy to persuade the White House not to announce the visit, claiming that the king had nothing to offer Obama and they did not want the king to be put in the position of publicly disappointing and possibly embarrassing the president. It is unclear whether Obama's advisers saw the stakes as so high that the risk of a bad outcome was worth taking, or simply disregarded the Saudis' reluctance on the assumption that the mere fact of the meeting would force the king into a compliant posture. In any case, the mission failed. Substantively, the king offered nothing in terms of a coalition against Iran or steps that Israel could interpret as consistent with recognition.

On the first issue, there was really very little that could have been expected. Indeed, it was never clear what precisely the White House envisaged that a regional coalition could deliver. On the second, from a Saudi perspective, reliance on Netanyahu to follow through on his commitment to a partial settlement freeze, let alone agree to expanded terms for a second-phase freeze, must have been seen as a particularly risky bet, certainly too risky to wager the king's prestige on the outcome.

Ironically, the Israeli leadership believed it had a chance of mobilising a Sunni coalition against Iran. In December 2009, Israeli Deputy Foreign Minister Daniel Ayalon, a member of the hardline Yisrael Beiteinu party, published an open letter to the Arab world in *Asharq al Awsat*. He argued that Israel and Sunni Arab states were all being challenged by a revolutionary Iran and that they all shared an interest in resisting Iranian encroachment. Israel's hopes for a limited coalescence were not entirely

unfounded. Egypt had arrested dozens of individuals of various nation-
alities on charges of trying to overthrow the Egyptian government at the
behest of Hizbullah, while the Saudis trumpeted accusations of Iranian
proselytisation in the kingdom and King Abdullah of Jordan warned
darkly of a Shia crescent hanging like the sword of Damocles over Sunni
capitals. But Ayalon's letter failed to put forward specific measures that
Israel and its Sunni neighbours might actually take, separately or in
concert, to contain or roll back Iranian encroachment.

Even if such details had been forthcoming, the Arab response to this
public appeal would likely have been the same: silence. Ayalon's effort,
however, fuelled speculation that Saudi Arabia and Israel had forged
some sort of back-channel agreement to cooperate in the event that Israel
decided to attack Iran to destroy the parts of nuclear infrastructure that
Israeli intelligence had identified. The Saudis' role in this scenario would
be to turn off its air-defence radars to ensure that Israel's overflight of
Saudi airspace en route to Iran was unimpeded. Speculation along these
lines was revived in mid-2010 when Saudi Arabia conducted air-defence
drills that were thought to have included practice in turning radars on
and off quickly. Viewed alongside the permission Egypt granted to
Israeli warships to transit the Suez Canal and steps some of the Gulf
Cooperation Council states were taking to upgrade their air defences
with US help, it did appear that some sort of tacit arrangement, aimed
at facilitating an Israeli strike rather than persuading or compelling Iran
to comply with UN Security Council resolutions regarding its nuclear
programme, was emerging.

Palestinian factors

Despite the erosion of trust between Israel and the PA, dialogue did
resume in spring 2010. Negotiations, however, were confined to prox-
imity rather than direct talks. From a Palestinian perspective, the
political costs of talking to the Netanyahu government overshadowed
any concessions the Israeli side were likely to offer, so there were no
official talks until Abbas got the cover he needed from the Arab League,
which endorsed a resumption of talks but only if they were indirect. As
of summer 2010 they had not yielded any of the contemplated concrete
results, which included a timeline for a return to direct talks. The situa-

tion was no more promising within Palestine, where unity talks between Hamas and Fatah remained at an impasse.

There were two somewhat more salutary developments. Firstly, Palestinian economic growth in the West Bank was quite robust over the course of the year, rising to 16%. Secondly, US Lieutenant-General Keith Dayton's training programme for Palestinian security forces succeeded in creating a large, well-disciplined and skilled cadre, despite Israeli scepticism and Palestinian infighting at the ministerial level. But these accomplishments were highly qualified. To return to the favourable economic situation that obtained before the second intifada broke out in 2000, the Palestinian economy would need to perform at extraordinarily high levels for years to come – a tall order given the vulnerability of the Palestinian economy to political shock, its isolation from Israel's larger economy and the lack of territorial contiguity. On the security side, knowledgeable observers worried that the formation of a competent and cohesive military force in the absence of a diplomatic end game would make a new intifada even more destructive, or endow a Palestinian strongman with the force he needed to dominate his rivals. Analysts also pointed out that the more Palestinian forces maintained order on the West Bank, the less pressure Israel would be under to strike a political deal. There were concerns, too, that Dayton's replacement lacked the experience and unique skills that fostered the surprisingly strong results achieved thus far.

> The more Palestinian forces maintained order, the less pressure Israel would be under

The year was punctuated by a bizarre event that in retrospect seemed to be part of a pattern of Israeli action divorced from any holistic approach to the country's interests, at least as seen from other capitals. On 19 January 2010 a Hamas arms-procurement official, Mahmoud Abdel Rauf al-Mabhouh, was murdered in his room at a hotel in Dubai, United Arab Emirates (UAE). Suspicion fell at first on rival Palestinians, or on whomever Mabhouh might have been dealing with. Efficient analysis of the extensive video-surveillance data gathered at the hotel, however, soon led the Dubai police to conclude that a large team had converged on the site and that at least some of its members were travelling on passports stolen from Israelis who held dual citizenship. Dubai police subsequently stated that 12 British passports, six Irish, four French, one German and four Australian were used by suspects in the assassination operation. The event, which led to diplomatic rows and the expulsion of Israeli officials from several of the countries whose passports were used by the killers, hurt Israel diplomatically. Whether Israel's relationship with the UAE suffered is unknown. There had been an Israeli trade mission in Dubai and there were rumours of discreet forms of security cooperation. But even if Israel was able to control some of the damage, given its concern about delegitimisation and isolation, the assassination seemed a poor move, especially when measured against the marginal security benefits that Israel was likely to accrue from the killing. In that light, the event could indicate a failure of policy coordination at high levels, which led to the cabinet's authorising a potentially risky action without having a full grasp of its implications. Alternatively, it could suggest that the Israeli leadership rashly believed that the removal of a single Hamas arms dealer in a sensitive third country was worth the diplomatic consequences and negative effect on international perceptions of Israel as a liberal state.

The questions raised by the Mabhouh assassination about the soundness of the Israeli government's judgement re-emerged about six months later, on 30 May 2010, when the Israeli navy intercepted a flotilla of six vessels sponsored and supplied by a pro-Hamas Turkish non-governmental organisation that had rendezvoused earlier off Cyprus and were headed towards Gaza to break the Israeli blockade by delivering humanitarian aid. The blockade had been in force for several years as part of a plan to prevent weapons from reaching Hamas from outside Gaza and to reduce the flow of goods that would indirectly buttress Hamas's rule by raising living standards in Gaza. There was also a land component to the blockade, which hinged on measures that Egypt was taking on the southern border of Gaza to stem weapons smuggling through tunnels connecting Gaza to the Sinai Peninsula. The blockade was considered essential to Israel's longer-term goal of depriving Hamas of the means to attack cities neighbouring Gaza with missiles, defend against Israeli incursions and, at some point in the future, reprise its 2006 military victory over the security forces of Fatah, Hamas's principal secular rival.

The United States had supported Israel's right under international law to maintain the blockade, but with brittle and variable degrees of enthusiasm. During the Bush administration, US officials had hoped that Hamas could be delegitimised and strangled by the blockade. The Obama team did not share that hope, but neither did it have a convincing alternative to present to Israel. Given these factors, Israel appeared to feel compelled to exercise its right of self-defence to maintain the blockade and interdict the flotilla, while Washington had little choice but to acquiesce. In the event, five of the six vessels were boarded in international waters about 125km west of Haifa and stopped without incident. However, one, a large Turkish cruise ship, the *Mavi Marmara*, proved to be a more difficult challenge. Israeli marines who descended one by one onto the deck from a helicopter in the early hours of 31 May were surrounded by people who attacked them with metal rods, slingshot and, according to the Israeli account, knives. The marines opened fire, killing nine activists.

> **The Israeli approach seemed egregiously imprudent**

It is not yet known why the takedown of the *Mavi Marmara* was carried out in the way it was. Fast-roping single soldiers into a sea of hostile activists seemed egregiously imprudent. Certainly the Israeli approach was inconsistent with the techniques that the US navy and other well-trained professional forces would have used. After the fact, it was reported that some of the activists on the ship had talked about their desire for martyrdom. The Israeli failure to coordinate intelligence and tactics was compounded by a policy-coordination miscue whereby the Israeli Foreign Ministry, which foresaw the possibility of controversy, was either not consulted or disregarded.

These errors carried severe penalties. In the first instance, Israel's relationship with Turkey – which had already been strained by the ideological imperatives of an Islamist government in Ankara and Ayalon's reckless humiliation of Turkish Ambassador Ahmet Oguz Celikkol in January 2010 over an anti-Israeli television show that had aired in Turkey – was stretched to the breaking point. Turkish Prime Minister Recep Tayyip Erdogan accused Israel of 'state terrorism', telling his parliament that Israel 'violated international law, the conscience of humanity and world peace'. For decades, the Israel–Turkey bilateral relationship had been the closest between Israel and any Muslim country. Turkey had been an informal ally of Israel since the 1950s, when the two countries along with Iran collaborated in a 'periphery strategy' meant to counter-balance Arab powers in the region. Turkey had also been a market for Israeli tactical weapons systems, a source of diplomatic support and mediation and, vis-à-vis Syria, military backing. But the fading epoch in Israeli–Turkish relations appeared to come to an end with the decision by the Turkish government to sanction the flotilla's objectives and Israel's killing of Turkish nationals.

Secondly, the international reaction to the flotilla debacle resulted in Hamas's political empowerment, at least in the short term, as Hamas resembled David battling Goliath. It was diplomatically imperative for Israel subsequently to permit more goods into Gaza. More importantly, Egyptian public opinion forced Cairo to abandon its support for the blockade. This was undoubtedly a source of frustration for Egyptian security officials, who view the empowerment of Hamas as inspiration for the extremist Muslim Brotherhood political opposition within Egypt. In addition, Israel's maladroit handling of the flotilla put the United States in a difficult situation. Washington could not afford to endorse Israel's action without appearing to validate Hamas, which was unacceptable. At the same time, however, there was a silver lining for Washington: the *Mavi Marmara* fiasco created space in which to question the viability of Israel's Gaza strategy, which before the incident could not really be debated in the absence of an American alternative, and for the time being obviated the need for fresh US thinking.

Sober assessments

By summer 2010, these events had re-ignited a debate in the United States about two fundamental issues. The first was whether a two-state solution was still feasible. Several developments in Israel had fuelled doubts about its viability. The Israelis' reversion to core demands was one. Netanyahu stressed that Palestinians must recognise Israel as a Jewish state, a requirement that previous governments had not imposed that suggested the need for a deeper acceptance of Israel than that signified by diplomatic recognition. He has also referred to the termination of the conflict, rather than a formal peace agreement, as the desired end state. And he has emphasised Palestinian economic development and Israeli security rather than Palestinian sovereignty as the goals of a diplomatic process. While the Obama administration did persuade Netanyahu at one point to employ the phrase 'two-state solution', given the nature and weight of Netanyahu's world view, there are doubts about his commitment. A reciprocal phenomenon was palpable on the Palestinian side, where the emphasis on refugees' right of return and rhetoric about time favouring the Palestinians also suggested a return to core claims and diminished interest in a two-state solution. In these respects, the state of play of the Israeli–Palestinian conflict in mid-2010 resembled 1948 more than 1998.

The other key debate was about the US–Israel bilateral relationship. As expressed by Mossad chief Meir Dagan, no shrinking violet, in a briefing to the Knesset, Israeli policies have provoked the question in the United States of whether Israel is more of a liability than an asset. This question is under serious discussion in US foreign-policy circles, and arguably has been since the publication of John Mearsheimer and Stephen Walt's shrill but unavoidable *The Israeli Lobby and US Foreign Policy* in 2007. But in Israel, some are also asking reciprocally whether the United States is an asset. In this perspective, Israel has one existential threat – Iran – and despite Washington's assertions that a nuclear-armed Iran would be 'unacceptable', it is increasingly clear to Israelis that their only true ally is not going to disarm this strategic adversary. In fact, the United States and Israel do have differing threat perceptions. A nuclear-capable Iran would make life far more difficult for Israel than it would for the United States. From an Israeli standpoint, this necessarily raises doubts about the future of the relationship that mirror the doubts of some in the United States.

The trajectory of these two closely linked debates looked likely to be the most critical single factor in strategic developments in the Middle East over the coming year. Given that those debates implicate the rebuilding of the very foundation of conflict resolution in the Middle East, little if any substantive progress on that front was to be expected.

Iraq: Political Wrangles

Iraq's political landscape was dominated over the past year by the third set of national elections to be held since Saddam Hussein was deposed by American-led invading forces in 2003. Although the elections on 7 March 2010 proceeded reasonably smoothly, with a fairly strong 64% turnout, the intense political wrangling in the run-up to the vote, the questioning of the results by key politicians and the inability of the governing elite to pick a new prime minister all pointed to the continued instability of Iraqi politics. The elections were held against a backdrop of the United States' commitment to end all combat missions in Iraq by August 2010 and withdraw all troops by the end of 2011. Meanwhile, there was an apparently corresponding rise, albeit gradual, in politically motivated violence across Iraq. The sustainability of post-Ba'athist Iraq thus remained in some doubt.

Electoral manipulation and dysfunction

The legal committee of the Iraqi parliament drafted an election law in July 2009 and sent it to the Iraqi cabinet in September. All the major political parties, however, attempted to maximise their own advantage by urging amendments that would increase their electoral support. At the centre of the extended dispute surrounding the electoral law was an argument about whether a closed- or open-list voting system should be used in the elections. In the national elections of 2005, a closed-list requirement meant voters could only choose from a comparatively small number of large multi-party coalitions. This voting system obscured the balance of power among the parties within each coalition and left voters unable to decide between them, let alone assign their vote to individual politicians. The result was a political campaign that played to the lowest common denominator – sectarian and religious division.

A 'modified list' system was used for the January 2009 provincial elections. Although voters still chose between large alliances, they could vote for specific politicians within these lists. This new system encouraged a less sectarian voting pattern and allowed policy issues, especially those involving law and order, to come to the fore. Unsurprisingly, those parties that had previously benefited from maximising the sectarian vote renewed their campaign for the re-adoption of the closed-list system after the provincial elections. The list debate, along with the disputed status of the city of Kirkuk and the voting rights of exiled Iraqis, delayed the passing of the election law for months. Thus, the constitutionally mandated date for a January 2010 election was not met and a crisis looked imminent.

Popular opinion and the Shia religious hierarchy surrounding the country's most important religious figure, Grand Ayatollah Ali al-Sistani, backed the open-list system, seeing it as a key tool for moving the country away from sectarian violence and division. Such public and religious backing for the open-list system, along with a series of last-minute parliamentary compromises, saw the Iraqi election law passed by parliament in November 2009. But Vice-President Tariq al-Hashemi vetoed the law, arguing that the system did not allocate enough votes to the large number of Iraqi refugees driven into neighbouring countries in the waves of violence after the invasion of 2003. Eventually, another compromise was hammered out and an election date was set for 7 March 2010. In addition to using a modified list system, the election law recognised Iraq's 18 governorates or provinces as constituencies, forbade the overt use of religious imagery in campaigning and expanded the number of members to be elected to the parliament from 275 to 325.

As with the previous national elections in December 2005, the electoral system favoured the formation of large, multi-party coalitions to maximise the vote. The electorate in the 2009 provincial elections had sided substantially with those running on an overtly nationalist platform, so coalition-building amongst parties seeking to represent the Arab vote in the south and centre of the country tended to stress cross-communal and nationalist themes. Furthermore, the March 2010 elections became a test of not only Iraqi popular opinion but also the ability of Iraq's neighbours to exert influence in the country. During the election campaign, suspicions abounded that Iraq's Arab Gulf neighbours were funding the Iraqiyya coalition and that Tehran was giving extensive financial support to the Iraqi National Alliance (INA).

The incumbent prime minister, Nuri al-Maliki, rejuvenated the State of Law coalition that had been successful in 2009 while attempting to broaden the number of parties within it. Maliki conducted extended negotiations with various politicians including Minister of Interior Jawad al-Bulani and his Iraqi Constitutional Party as well as the nationalist Mahmud al-Mashhadani. However, when the coalition was finally announced in October 2009, although it contained 39 different groups, its core constituents were long-time Maliki allies such as Oil Minister Hussain al-Shahristani, as well as smaller and relatively insignificant parties. Maliki, it was argued, had been too arrogant in the wake of his provisional election success to make the meaningful concessions needed to build a broad coalition. This left independent politicians like Bulani and Mashhadani to form their own, smaller alliance.

> " Maliki had been too arrogant in the wake of provisional success to build a broad coalition "

In his quest to retain the premiership, however, Maliki declined to rebuild the overtly Shia multi-party coalition that had proved so successful in 2005. Although extensive negotiations were conducted, Maliki's demand for a majority of the seats in such a coalition and the guarantee of the prime minister's job after the election proved too high a price for the other parties to pay. This left the other two major Shia parties, the Islamic Supreme Council of Iraq (ISCI) and the Sadrist Current, to form the INA, the second major electoral coalition. ISCI and the Sadrists had been involved in a violent conflict in 2006–07, which saw key members of both groups murdered in the south of the country. The fact that this long-running conflict could be set aside ahead of the national elections did not indicate any durable reconciliation between the two groups, but rather the lengths to which Iran would go to see a united Shia electoral coalition. In both 2005 and 2010, Iranian policy towards Iraqi elections focused on attempting to maximise the Shia vote. This was done by encouraging those parties seeking to represent the Shia section of the population to join as large a coalition as possible. Tehran then pushed the resultant coalition to campaign on an exclusively Shia sectarian agenda. Iran judged this to be the most efficient way to maximise its influence in Baghdad.

The third major electoral coalition, Iraqiyya, was assembled by the former interim prime minister, Ayad Allawi. He brought together Vice-President Tariq al-Hashemi's Renewal Party, with the former Ba'athist

Saleh al-Mutlaq and the Hadba list that had been formed in northwest Iraq to maximise Arab votes in territories disputed with the Kurdish Regional Government. These geographically disparate parties were united around a common commitment to Iraqi nationalism and secularism. This left the two dominant Kurdish parties, the Patriotic Union of Kurdistan and the Kurdistan Democratic Party, to form an alliance to maximise the Kurdish vote and hence the influence of the Kurdish regional government in Baghdad.

Campaigning for the elections officially began in mid-February 2010, with the Iraqi High Electoral Council publishing a list of 6,172 approved candidates. The party of the radical Shia cleric Muqtada al-Sadr, who had twice launched rebellions against the US military, adopted the most innovative campaigning style, holding nationwide hustings to let its supporters choose the movement's candidates. However, it was the actions of a government agency charged with implementing the de-Ba'athification process set in train by the Americans in 2003, the Justice and Accountability Commission (JAC), that came to shape the campaign. On 7 January 2010, the commission, chaired by former American favourite Ahmed Chalabi, issued edicts seeking to ban 511 individual candidates and 14 party lists from the elections. Both Chalabi and Ali Faysal al-Lami, the general director of the JAC, were running for election in the INA coalition, which is dominated by the ISCI. This flagrant conflict of interest indicated both the political nature of the exclusions and the fragility of the whole political system, in which governmental institutions have been colonised by political parties and run as private fiefdoms.

The lack of a legal basis for the exclusion of the 511 candidates also reflected how tenuous the rule of law was in Iraq. Only two pieces of legislation passed by the Iraqi parliament deal with de-Ba'athification. The first, Article Seven of the Iraqi constitution, forbids the glorification or promotion of 'Saddamist Ba'athism' in Iraq. The second is the Justice and Accountability Law of January 2008, which stipulates that former high-ranking ex-Ba'athists are subject to de-Ba'athification. But Lami made it clear in a public statement that the most influential politician to be banned from the elections, Saleh al-Mutlaq, and his party, the Iraqi Front for National Dialogue, were not excluded under this legislation. (Mutlaq had been expelled from the Ba'ath Party in 1977, helped draft the new Iraqi constitution and had led a party that won 11 seats in the 2005 elections.) The extra-judicial exclusion of Mutlaq, although justified by his ideological affinity with Ba'athism, was an attempt to increase sectarian voting patterns and break the coherence of a coalition seeking to build interdenominational support.

Those advocating and backing the mass exclusion of candidates must have known that, at the very least, doing so would inflame sectarian tensions and run the risk of lowering Sunni participation, encouraging politically motivated violence. In the aftermath of the bans, the 'Ba'athist threat' became a key plank of both the prime minister's and the INA's election campaign. When faced with a cynical electorate alienated by the incumbent government's inability to deliver jobs and services, the parties that dominated government chose to conjure up the spectre of Ba'athism, playing to sectarian sentiment in an attempt to solidify their vote. The Iraqi High Electoral Council, the organisation charged with delivering a free and fair election, simply rubber-stamped the de-Ba'athification orders.

The prime minister's own coalition and that run by ISCI were very lightly touched by the bans, as were the coalitions seeking to maximise the Kurdish vote. Both Tawafuq, the Sunni Islamist coalition, and the parties seeking to mobilise the Sunni tribes of Anbar province involved in the Awakening Movement were also largely unaffected. It was the coalitions seeking to build cross-sectarian support – in particular, Iraqiyya, run by Allawi – that saw the largest number of their candidates excluded. The clear implication was that state institutions had been manipulated to increase sectarian tension as an election ploy. More worryingly still, these very same institutions were used to break the political cohesion of electoral coalitions trying to win votes on a secular, non-sectarian nationalist platform. Those parties and coalitions seeking to maximise an exclusively Sunni vote and posing no threat to either the prime minister or the other Shia coalition were left alone.

The elections and their aftermath

In the election itself, 64.2% of eligible Iraqis voted, a drop from the 79.6% turnout in 2005. A general cynicism about the government saw voter turnout in the Shia majority areas of southern Iraq drop by between

5% and 23%. But Sunni indifference disappeared. Whereas in the 2005 elections Sunni majority areas largely boycotted the poll, in 2010 voter turnout in the northwest ranged from 61% to 73%. The de-Ba'athification campaign at the start of electioneering appeared to have solidified what could be termed the 'Sunni vote', motivating people to go to the ballot box to avoid being politically marginalised or excluded altogether.

The mobilisation of Sunni voters across the northwest greatly favoured Allawi's Iraqiyya coalition, giving it 2,851,823 votes and 91 seats in the new parliament. Maliki's State of Law coalition came second with 2,797,624 votes and 89 seats. With 163 seats needed for an overall majority neither of the two winning groups gained enough votes for an outright victory. That left the INA, which came third with 70 seats, and the Kurdish alliance with 43 seats, holding the balance of power. Within the alliances, the modified list system allowed voters to pick both individual candidates and specific parties. This convention greatly favoured Sadr's party, which secured 39 seats in parliament, making it a key player in the choice of prime minister.

The Iraqi High Electoral Council took 20 days to announce the final vote tally. This delay gave all the major parties a pretext for alleging voter fraud when the partial results appeared to favour their rivals. In the early stages of counting, when it looked as though Maliki's coalition was leading, Allawi's organisation lodged a number of complaints alleging widespread fraud. Maliki vigorously rebutted these allegations, stating that although no electoral process had 'zero violations', in this case they did 'not change the results'. But as the number of votes counted swung against Maliki, Allawi quickly changed his stance, arguing that 'the Iraqi people have honoured the Iraqiyya list and chosen it to be the basis of forming the new government'. When faced with electoral defeat, Maliki also dramatically changed his opinion. 'No way we will accept the results', he bluntly stated, calling for a recount in order to prevent a 'return to violence'. The fact that Maliki issued this statement as head of the country's armed forces gave it a sinister undertone. Maliki's demands for a manual recount of votes focused on Baghdad. In mid-May 2010, however, after the recount, the electoral commission, backed by the United Nations, announced that it had found no evidence of fraud and the vote and seat allocation remained unchanged.

Officially, the parliament needed to elect the president of Iraq, who was then constitutionally bound to ask the largest bloc within parliament to nominate a candidate for prime minister no later than 30 days after the president was chosen. Given Allawi's slim two-seat election victory, it was assumed he would be given the first attempt at forming a government. But the process was confounded when, just prior to the elections, Maliki obtained a ruling from the Supreme Federal Court directing the president to ask the leader of the alliance with the largest number of seats to nominate the prime minister not when the vote was ratified but once the chamber sat. The significance of this ruling became apparent in early May when Maliki agreed to merge his coalition, State of Law, with the third largest group, the INA. In effect, after coming second in the national poll, Maliki decided to reconstitute the victorious election coalition of 2005, combining the majority of parties seeking Shia votes into a new super-alliance which controlled 159 seats in parliament. Unsurprisingly, Allawi angrily refused to recognise this Supreme Court ruling, whilst some of his supporters claimed it was obtained through bribery.

> " Neither Maliki nor Allawi was willing to cede power "

The fractured voting, legal challenges and Supreme Court ruling resulted in political deadlock in Baghdad through spring and summer 2010. Neither Maliki nor Allawi was willing to cede power. In theory, the merger of the State of Law coalition with the INA gave this new political organisation the dominant voice in the new parliament and control over Iraqi politics. But the main groups within the INA – ISCI and the Sadrists – were adamant that Maliki should not be returned as prime minister. Having suffered politically and militarily as Maliki tightened his grip on government in 2007–08, they were determined not to allow any growth in what they claimed was his authoritarian power.

As the largest single party within parliament, the Sadrists continued to deploy innovative populist methods to maximise their influence. In April 2010, they held another poll amongst their members to decide whom they should back for prime minister. The rank-and-file of the movement chose Ibrahim al-Jaafari, who had been interim prime minister in 2005 and had then favoured the Sadrists. With such a large voting bloc in parliament, the Sadrists would have to be brought into government and given major cabinet posts. They intimated that they were aiming to take control of major service ministries such as health, transport and possibly even finance. Given the destructive influence they had on the ministries they controlled in 2006, this prospect added another potentially destabilising feature to an already unsettled political process.

In light of the uncertain election results, Iraq was almost certainly heading towards another government of national unity. The majority of parties that did well in the election would likely be rewarded with ministerial positions in the cabinet and would benefit from the resources and jobs that these carried. But the horse-trading could take months to sort out. Maliki's refusal to give up the job of prime minister was hindering progress: his performance in the elections was not decisive enough for him to claim victory but was sufficiently strong to make him difficult to dislodge. The Kurdish Alliance, along with the Sadrists, would have to be given major concessions as a price for backing the next prime minister. These concessions would probably include overt restraints on the prime minister's power, along with recognition of the Kurdish regional government's right to negotiate separate oil-development deals with multinational companies. The office of the president, held since 2006 by veteran Kurdish politician Jalal Talabani, was also thought to be at the top of Kurdish demands. This apparent requirement removed one possible route to a compromise solution, whereby Allawi would be given the presidency in return for Maliki's retaining the premiership. In any case, the government that would eventually emerge was likely to be faction-ridden, weak and indecisive.

The American military withdrawal

The timetable for the US troop withdrawal from Iraq intensified the political uncertainty surrounding the elections. The Status of Forces Agreement (SOFA) negotiated between Baghdad and Washington at the end of the George W. Bush administration mandated the removal of American troops from Iraq's towns and cities by June 2009. Article 24 of the agreement went much further, unambiguously stating that 'all US forces are to withdraw from all Iraqi territory, water and airspace no later than

31 December, 2011'. President Barack Obama increased the momentum of the exit by committing his administration to withdrawing all US combat troops from the country by August 2010. In July 2010, US troop strength stood at 74,000, which meant that a very speedy pullout of American soldiers would be required if the US administration was to meet its own deadline. However, Obama and his senior commander on the ground, General Raymond T. Odierno, publicly committed themselves to this timetable. Privately, Odierno expressed a desire to keep between 3,000 and 5,000 US combat troops in the north of the country to continue their role of separating the Kurdish regional and Iraqi central government's forces, but both Washington and Baghdad vetoed this request.

With such a rigid schedule in place for the complete removal of all US combat troops, the Iraqi government's ability to impose law and order lay in the hands of its own army, police force and intelligence service. Officially, the command and control of the Iraqi security forces was centred at the Iraqi Joint Forces Command, which was subordinate to the National Operations Centre in Baghdad. But Maliki had worked hard to subvert the formal chain of command. He sacked senior intelligence chiefs, army commanders and generals within the Ministry of Interior, and established informal personal alliances with senior army commanders and paramilitary units. In addition, Maliki used a number of operational commands to bring both the army and the police force together under a series of regional organisations and appointed favoured generals to run each of them. To a significant extent, it was this personal control of the Iraqi security services that made many of Iraq's political parties so keen to remove Maliki.

At the start of 2010, the Iraqi security services employed 669,000 people, spread across the Ministries of Interior and Defence and the Iraqi National Counter-Terrorism Force. In spite of an annual budget for 2010 of $4.9 billion, the Iraqi army remained dependent upon the US military for close air support, communications and logistical infrastructure. Beyond the lack of capacity in these areas, three other major challenges hindered the security forces' ability to operate independently of the United States. The first was the influence of pre-regime-change Ba'athist ideology and rules of operation. The speed with which the Iraqi army was reconstituted after 2003 meant that up to 70% of the old officer corps were eventually re-integrated into the new officer corps, producing considerable friction. Corruption has had an even more corrosive and destructive effect. Devastating mass-casualty truck-bomb attacks in Baghdad throughout 2009 and early 2010 revealed how insurgents could penetrate the capital's security cordons by bribing corrupt military officers to let them through. The third weakness hampering the Iraqi security forces was the tendency towards sectarian and religious divisions amongst its rank-and-file and mid-level officers.

On this last score, however, progress had undoubtedly been made. Given that Iraq was mired in civil conflict until at least the end of 2007, it was not surprising that sectarian tensions still existed. But the army and national police were no longer active players in sectarian violence. In addition, the Iraqi army, in partnership with the United States, played a major role in reducing the violence that dominated Baghdad from 2005 to 2007. Also indicating the improved capability of Iraq's security forces were its successes against senior al-Qaeda in Mesopotamia (AQIM) operatives in April 2010. In conjunction with US forces, the Iraqi military killed the two most senior members of AQIM, Abu Omar al-Baghdadi and Abu Ayoub al-Masri. They went on to kill another senior official, Ahmed al-Obeidi. Unfortunately, though, the removal of the top level of AQIM's organisation did not have any noticeable effect on its capacity to deliver mass-casualty attacks in an around Baghdad. After US forces had severely reduced AQIM's operational capability in 2007–08, the organisation rebuilt itself, launching a series of deadly truck-bomb attacks against major government buildings in the centre of Baghdad in the latter part of 2009 and early 2010. In August 2009, AQIM did extensive damage to the Ministries of Finance and Foreign Affairs, killing 95 people. In January 2010, the group successfully targeted three international hotels in central Baghdad used by the foreign press corps.

At its height, US forces detained over 90,000 Iraqis but released all but 2,900 before the handing over control of three major detention facilities – Taji, Camp Buca and Camp Cropper – to the Iraqi government in August 2010. Senior staff in the Iraqi security services in Baghdad linked the rising capacity of AQIM to the mass release of prisoners from US-run jails as part of the SOFA. Even so, the levels of politically motivated violence in Baghdad and across Iraq in 2009 and the first half of 2010 were nowhere near as high as they were at the height of communal conflict in 2007, when 2,700 civilians were murdered in one month. In May 2010, the website Iraq Body Count estimated that 395 people had been killed, compared to 376 the previous month and 311 in March. The main reason for this comparatively low casualty rate was that the Shia militias, specifically Sadr's Jaish al-Mahdi, which played a central role in the civilian murders of 2007, did not retaliate for AQIM's attacks on Iraqi civilians. Unlike in the period 2005–07, the Iraqi security forces were now perceived by the wider population to be able to deliver some semblance of order and could stand between the two sides of another potential civil war, maintaining enough control over security to stop a resumption of the mass killings.

Finding effective compromise

Iraq was sitting at both a political and military crossroads in 2010. Politically, the ruling elite installed by the United States after the invasion of 2003 had yet to find a mechanism that could peacefully allocate power among them without alienating major sections of the electorate. One way could be to choose a compromise candidate for the premiership other than the two front-runners, Maliki and Allawi. Yet the surprising success of Allawi's coalition showed that the previously alienated Sunni section of Iraq's population had responded positively and effectively to the 2010 elections. If they are not meaningfully integrated into political system – in particular, if Iraqiyya is not given major cabinet posts and the resources they bring with them – there may be a real danger that sections of the Sunni community will again turn their backs on the political process and resort once more to widespread political violence. As US combat missions end and American troops are withdrawn, the Iraqi security services will be increasingly compelled to bear the majority responsibility for providing law and order. Neither the political instability caused by the elections nor the uncertainty produced by the transition to Iraqi-provided security need undermine the overall integrity of the post-invasion political settlement. A manageable dispensation, however, requires both Iraq's political and military leaders to exercise their newfound responsibilities with a great deal more skill than they have previously shown.

Saudi Arabia and the Gulf: Concerns over Iran and Economic Challenges

The last year saw the countries of the Gulf Cooperation Council (GCC) wrestling with the impact of the global recession on local economies and with the implications of the continuing stand-off between the West and Iran over Tehran's nuclear programme. The extent and persistence of political opposition within Iran to the results of the Iranian presidential election of June 2009 added a new, unpredictable element to Gulf states' assessments of their vulnerability in the face of an intransigent Tehran. In Yemen, terrorism from a resurgent al-Qaeda group, coupled with conflict in the northern part of the country and increasing dissidence in the south, revived regional fears of outside intervention and of state failure of the one non-GCC state in the Arabian Peninsula. Meanwhile, GCC governments (Bahrain, Kuwait, Oman, Qatar, Saudi Arabia and the United Arab Emirates (UAE)) were disappointed by the lack of progress made by the Obama administration on the Arab–Israeli dispute. However, the recovery in oil prices in early 2010 was an encouraging signal for Gulf economies beset by debt overhangs linked to the property sector and by worries over semi-sovereign debt.

The Gulf and the wider region

The Gulf states were most concerned throughout the year with the threat from and developments in Iran. They shared Western worries about Tehran's nuclear programme and its possible early acquisition of a nuclear-weapon capability, but expressed such worries with a greater sense of urgency, especially in private. They feared they could be subject to retaliatory attacks were Israel or the US to launch strikes on Iran, with Qatar, Bahrain and Kuwait especially vulnerable as hosts to large US military bases. In June 2009, the US Navy confirmed it was expanding its facilities at Mina Salman in Bahrain, base of the US 5th Fleet. In late May 2009 a new French base in Abu Dhabi was formally inaugurated.

In response to the Iran-related threat, Gulf governments looked to the United States in 2008-09 to install or upgrade missile-defence systems and help them build military capability. Kuwait and Saudi Arabia sought to upgrade their *Patriot* anti-missile systems, while the UAE was to spend about $12 billion on acquisitions including *Patriot* and the Terminal High Altitude Area Defence system. These moves drew criticism from Tehran, which claimed it was no threat to its Arab neighbours and that this was an American plot to increase the US military presence. The UAE also expressed interest to Washington in June 2009 in buying the F-35 Joint Strike Fighter, presenting a dilemma for the United States over its long-standing policy of enabling Israel to retain a qualitative technological edge over the Arab states. US defence sales to the Gulf had already doubled in value from $19bn in 2001–04 to $40bn in 2005–08, a measure of American readiness to build up Arab Gulf states' defensive capability, but there remained uncertainty about which weapons systems Washington would sell to them. In 2009 Saudi Arabia took delivery of the first of 72 Eurofighter *Typhoons*, and talked of a S-400 missile shield deal with Russia. In another move illustrating diversification in defence links, Oman conducted its first air-defence exercise with India in October 2009.

The anxieties of Gulf governments over Iran also helped drive their exploration of the potential for acquiring nuclear technology, although their approach was transparent and directed exclusively at civilian applications to meet energy needs.

The Gulf states maintained their traditional concern at the residual threat of Iranian-inspired local unrest or subversion. With the exception of Bahrain's, most local Shia communities were generally quiet, although in Saudi Arabia there was trouble in Medina and the Eastern Province in early 2009. The resumption of the Iranian claim to Bahrain, which the international community had believed resolved in the 1970s, and a new ban by Tehran on aircraft with electronic maps not naming the Gulf as the Persian Gulf from landing in Iran revived old territorial tensions. Since 1971, Iran has occupied the Abu Musa and Tunb islands, which are also claimed by the UAE. In April 2010 the UAE foreign minister compared that occupation to Israel's occupation of Palestinian lands, to Iranian anger. Meanwhile, Oman characteristically took a less anti-Iranian line than most other GCC members; the Omani leader Sultan Qaboos bin Said, accompanied by a senior ministerial delegation, went ahead with a planned but controversially timed visit to Tehran in early August 2009 despite political instability in the Iranian capital.

Consistent with its self-appointed role as regional go-between, Qatar also struck a typically different note with Iran from those of other GCC states with regular exchanges of visits, including one by Crown Prince Tamim bin Hamad bin Khalifa Al Thani to Tehran in February. Meanwhile, Qatar continued to play a mediator role in regional conflicts, for example between the Sudanese government and Darfur rebels.

Having feared an Iran-dominated Iraq, GCC governments were relieved at the political and security progress achieved in Iraq over 2009 and pleased at the success of Ayad Allawi's Iraqiyya alliance in the parliamentary elections of March 2010. They saw him as a secular nationalist who was likely to be more effective, should he become prime minister, than Nuri al-Maliki in standing up to Iranian influence in Iraq and regionally. Relations between Baghdad and Kuwait, however, continued to be awkward. Kuwait considered it had reason to fear the complete withdrawal of US forces from Iraq in 2011. Border issues remained unresolved, and Kuwait was alarmed when Maliki asked in January 2010 for the revision of the maritime border between the two countries. There was still no agreement on repayment of Kuwaiti loans made to Iraq during the Iran–Iraq War, and Kuwait continued to insist on Baghdad paying $24bn in outstanding reparations for the Iraqi occupation of Kuwait in 1990, which currently costs Iraq 5% of its quarterly oil and gas revenue. One positive sign was that Baghdad sent its first ambassador to Kuwait since 1990.

In the absence of major confrontation between Israel and the Palestinians or Hizbullah after January 2009, the Israel–Palestine dispute attracted less direct attention from the Gulf states after mid-2009 than it had in the previous 12 months. Yet after encouraging signals from US President Barack Obama of a new US approach to the Middle East and Islamic world, there was disappointment in Gulf states that Washington failed to force Israeli Prime Minister Benjamin Netanyahu to freeze building of settlements in occupied territory. Israeli intransigence led in April 2010 to unusually public expressions of exasperation by the US administration, which Gulf governments viewed as encouraging. But they saw little prospect of genuine progress with negotiations, especially with the approach of US midterm congressional elections.

Dubai was drawn into the Israel–Palestine issue when an alleged Hamas leader and arms procurer, Mahmoud al-Mabhouh, was killed in his Dubai hotel room on 20 January 2010. This followed the killing of a Chechen leader in Dubai on 28 March 2009, for which an Iranian and a Tajik were jailed by a Dubai court in April 2010. Dubai's police chief, Lieutenant-General Dhahi Khalfan Tamim, drawing on CCTV evidence and other data, unequivocally laid the blame for the killing of Mabhouh on Mossad, the Israeli intelligence service. He noted the use by a large Mossad assassination team of Western passports, some of which ostensibly belonged to UK dual nationals living in Israel. The Israeli government did not acknowledge Mossad's role and international reaction was muted, although the British government required the withdrawal of an Israeli official from the London embassy. The killing was a further blow to Dubai's reputation as a safe international business hub. Abu Dhabi, which in October 2009 had allowed an Israeli delegation at a renewable energy meeting to fly the Israeli flag, did not become involved.

Domestic political developments

In Saudi Arabia, various reformist moves by King Abdullah bin Abdulaziz Al Saud had attracted international attention in early 2009. These included reform of the Council of Senior Ulama (comprised of the kingdom's most senior religious scholars), removal of the head of the religious police, and the unprecedented appointment of a woman to the Council of Ministers. In addition, Interior Minister Prince Nayef bin Abdulaziz was promoted to be second deputy prime minister, next in line to the throne after Crown Prince Sultan bin Abdulaziz Al Saud, who finally returned to Riyadh in December 2009 after a long convalescence overseas. Thereafter there was evidence of continuing tension between the king and the *ulama*, with the former determined modestly to improve the status of women. A new law allowed female lawyers to appear in the mixed environment of the courts, though they could act only for female clients in family cases. The king also supported the mixing of men and women in the newly established research university, the King Abdullah University for Science and Technology near Jeddah, and fired a loyalist scholar for making a mild public criticism in October 2009. In February 2010 an old, respected scholar, 'Abd al-Rahman al-Barrak, said that advocates of mixing men and women were infidels and apostates who should be executed, to which the only official reaction was to take down his website. His fatwa, which was heavily criticised in the media (and by officials in private) for its call for violence against the regime, was supported publicly by 28 other scholars in March. Nevertheless, Saudi women took an increasingly visible part in public life and the grip of the religious police was relaxed. Visa restrictions on the families of expatriates were loosened, and foreign women on business were allowed to visit the country on their own.

The Ministry of Interior continued to make progress in dealing with the threat of terrorism, depleting al-Qaeda-related networks in the kingdom through regular arrests. The announcement in early 2009 of a merger between al-Qaeda elements in Saudi Arabia and Yemen into a group called al-Qaeda in the Arabian Peninsula – with its (Saudi) leadership in Yemen – reflected this success. Saudi Arabia's security situation has been transformed from the dark days of 2003–04. However, the attempted assassination in Jeddah in August 2009 of Vice-Minister of Interior Prince Muhammad bin Nayef by a Saudi al-Qaeda member who was pretending to reconcile with the Saudi regime, was a reminder of the continuing threat, as well as of al-Qaeda's capacity to develop new tactics. The episode highlighted the limitations of the Saudi deradicalisation programme and the danger to Saudi security from Yemen, a long-standing concern. In March 2010 the government announced a major series of arrests of Saudis and Yemenis who were said to be planning to attack key Saudi economic targets.

The al-Houthis' rebellion in the north of Yemen against the Sana'a regime finally drew in the Saudis in November 2009 when the rebels moved into Saudi border areas and stayed there for at least two months. This led to Saudi mobilisation and deployment of the air force, artillery and special forces to expel the al-Houthis with major loss of life, including some Saudi casualties.

In November 2009 Jeddah was hit by heavy floods which killed over 100 people, with many more declared missing. The poorer districts of southern Jeddah were especially badly affected. The scale of the damage was widely blamed on inadequate infrastructure, poor public works and corruption, and gave rise to vociferous criticism of local government in public forums and media, and on the Internet. The king appointed a commission to investigate, and the episode led to the detention of suspect officials and property developers, as well as casting a pall over the real estate market.

In Kuwait, signs emerged of new maturity in the democratic process. In April a parliamentary election was called by the emir to break the long-running deadlock between the government, which is dominated by the ruling Al Sabah family, and the conservative opposition in the assembly. This led to an election campaign dominated by accusations and threats, including the designation by an Islamist politician of one high-profile female candidate as an infidel for not wearing traditional dress. On 16 May she and three other others became the first women to be elected to the national assembly. The Islamists made some apparent gains in an assembly in which political parties are banned but blocs allowed. The emir then reappointed his nephew Sheikh Nasser Al Sabah as prime minister in a move that promised a further stand-off between government and opposition.

> "One female candidate was called an infidel for not wearing traditional dress"

In December, Nasser survived a parliamentary interrogation by deputies of himself and three other senior ministers during an unusually long parliamentary session, and comfortably defeated a vote of no confidence. The conservative opposition had employed the perceived ignominy of parliamentary interrogations to threaten to force pre-emptive resignations of cabinet members or dissolution of the assembly. Nasser's success took the sting out of this threat, which had contributed to the resignation of five cabinets and the holding of three elections in the previous three years.

This breakthrough strengthened the hand of the government in pursuing its development plans. Parliamentary opposition had led to the abandonment of a proposed $17.4bn joint venture with Dow Chemical in 2008 and the shelving of a planned fourth oil refinery in 2009. In February 2010 Kuwait's parliament passed the government's $104bn four-year development plan, the first for decades, which envisaged increasing power and oil production as well as several infrastructure projects. It also approved a long-delayed capital markets law establishing a stock-market regulator along the lines of successful Saudi legislation from 2003. Meanwhile, the government opposed a populist move by deputies in January 2010 to force it to buy all $23.3bn of consumer loans in the country, write off the interest and reschedule the payments. This debt-relief bill was designed to alleviate the distress of Kuwaitis who had borrowed heavily to invest in real estate and the stock market. There were precedents for such a move following the Suq al-Manakh stock market crash in 1982 and the Iraqi occupation in 1991. The government considered that it would fuel moral hazard, but the issue remained outstanding.

In Bahrain, there was less visible political progress. Alternating between paternalism and suppression, the government continued to try to balance political pressure from the Shia majority, who complain of sectarian discrimination over housing and jobs, against the fear of the Sunni minority of Tehran-fomented unrest and subversion of Al Khalifa rule. There had been Shia riots in December 2008 and then controversy in early 2009 over the fairness of the trial of 35 young Shia activists who were charged with overthrowing the government. They were pardoned by the king in April 2009, among 170 people who had been accused of national security offences. In the same month the Ministry of Interior detained two young Sunnis who possessed weapons and sounded the alarm about Internet radicalisation of youth. They were sentenced to five years' imprisonment. On 16 March 2010 a Sunni attacked the British Embassy with a Molotov cocktail in protest at the British ambassador's meeting with the Shia political association al-Wifaq, which local Sunnis condemned as interference in Bahrain's internal affairs. The al-Wifaq parliamentary bloc, with 17 of the 40 seats in the Council of Representatives Assembly, continued campaigning for the cabinet to be chosen by the representatives and not appointed by the king. The next Council of Representatives elections are due in November 2010.

The Gulf and the economic crisis

The shocking announcement on 25 November 2009 by Dubai World, responsible for many of the grandiose property projects in the emirate, that it was suspending repayment of its debts pending debt restructuring was the most high-profile illustration of the extent to which the economic boom in the Gulf in 2007 and 2008 gave way in 2009 to the global forces of recession. In the boom years monetary policy had been loose because local currencies were pegged to the US dollar, creating excessive credit growth and asset bubbles. Fiscal policies, benefiting from high oil prices, were similarly lax. Economies throughout the Gulf became overheated, and the ensuing problems were compounded by poor levels of transparency, financial reporting and data availability. International markets started to focus on these deficiencies and on the links between sovereign governments and state-linked enterprises, as well as the lack of clarity in the relationship between public and private money, and in particular the blurred distinction between state funds and the privy purses of ruling families. Governments, especially those of Saudi Arabia and the UAE, avoided the worst of the downturn through counter-cyclical fiscal expansion but the recession was damaging even for states with large oil and gas reserves. The test in future will be whether governments avoid a repeat by tightening both fiscal and monetary policies during the next boom.

The Dubai World affair exemplified the problems encountered as Gulf states seek to preserve existing modes of business while exploiting access to global financial markets. Although there had been warning signs in Dubai, markets were surprised by Dubai World's announcement. They had believed official assurances that all was well, and had assumed that the emirate would stand behind the company, and Abu Dhabi behind Dubai. After a period of shock and confusion, compounded by poor official communication in both Dubai and Abu Dhabi, the latter made a $10bn loan to enable Dubai World to meet the obligations of Dubai World's Nakheel subsidiary in respect of a $4.1bn Islamic bond (*sukuk*). This grudging, last-minute move raised questions about the health of the relationship between Dubai and Abu Dhabi. It also reflected the desire of Abu Dhabi, as champion of federalisation of the UAE, to exert greater political and commercial leverage over its more freewheeling neighbour, which had always sought to retain a great deal of autonomy. It conveyed a clear signal that Abu Dhabi did not intend to bankroll past or future commitments by Dubai and would look at support purely on a case-by-case basis. However, the delay over Abu Dhabi's reaction, confusion caused by UAE structures, and lack of transparency about ownership of quasi-state entities led to international media criticism and concern in financial markets.

The restructuring process at Dubai World did not deliver a proposal to creditors until March 2010. Even then, it left unresolved questions over terms and its affordability for Dubai, as well as over the status of other Dubai companies and quasi-state entities. Together with some Abu Dhabi equivalents, their creditworthiness suffered as lenders started to insist on explicit state guarantees. The episode highlighted uncertainties about local bankruptcy laws and aspects of *sukuk*, including the compliance of some types of bonds with sharia law.

While Dubai World was the most notorious example of the impact of the global downturn on the Gulf, two Saudi family-owned conglomerates, Saad Group and Ahmad Hamad Algosaibi and Brothers, had also run into problems on $20bn of debts. In Kuwait the emirate's 100 over-leveraged investment houses were severely affected. Buoyed by cheap short-term credit and excessive liquidity, they had created an industry that at its peak commanded assets of more than $50bn but was now in trouble with debt repayments. There were two high-profile defaults on international loans in late 2008 and early 2009, and many houses sought to restructure and reschedule their debts, bonds and other liabilities. Kuwaiti money-market funds were also in deep trouble, having lost much of their value. Local banks became reluctant to extend credit, and some Kuwaitis found it difficult to accept that the government should act simply as a regulator rather than as lender and owner of last resort.

The Gulf avoided a generalised banking crisis since regulation was generally conservative and local banks were mostly well capitalised. However, 2009 was a year for Gulf banks to clean their loan books: lending declined and bank profits dropped by 10%. This and some reduction in government spending led to a credit squeeze which had a particular impact on the real estate and construction sector at the core of local economies. Residential prices in Dubai declined by 60% from the 2008 high, while in Qatar they declined by 30% (with a further drop of 10–15% predicted for 2010) and in Bahrain by 20%. Property over-supply resulted from overambitious plans, the credit squeeze and an overall decline in the expatriate population. A slowdown in construction resulted in some large construction companies being forced into the arms of government or mergers. Dubai's stock market fell by 75% after hitting a 21-month peak in January 2008. Dubai's problems were mainly responsible for a drop in UAE real GDP in 2009 estimated at 0.7% by the International Monetary Fund (IMF), which estimated growth for 2010 of only 1.3%, set against 6.1% in 2007 and 5.1% in 2008. Qatar was also seriously affected but, with oil and gas accounting for half of its GDP and 70% of government revenue, it could be confident of renewed growth in 2010, especially because of a massive expansion in natural gas facilities, from 54m tonnes of LNG export capacity to 77m tonnes. The IMF estimated an 18.5% increase in GDP in 2010, while Saudi GDP was expected to grow by 3.9% in 2010. Meanwhile Oman managed to escape the worst of the downturn by increasing oil production in 2009, and suffered only a small drop in non-oil exports. Its economy grew by 3.7% in 2009. Inflation in the Gulf, which had been running high (in the case of Saudi Arabia at over 11% in July 2008), fell back sharply, with Dubai experiencing some deflation.

Despite investment in economic diversification and the cushion for some of enormous financial reserves, Gulf governments remained at the mercy of oil and gas prices, with GCC stock-market indices other than in Dubai continuing to track oil price movements and oil price volatility remaining a problem for both governments and investors. The price of Saudi heavy crude, however, which had sunk to below $40 per barrel at the start of 2009 and led to a drop in oil production reflecting the record cut agreed by OPEC in December 2008, traded in the range of $63–77 for the rest of 2009 and into 2010. The start of global recovery and the resilience of Asian demand suggested that prices would remain well supported throughout 2010.

The global downturn assisted the cause of those in the Gulf who advocated structural reforms, although traditional attitudes and rivalries persisted at the GCC level. In June 2009 the GCC agreed to establish a Gulf monetary council in 2010 as a prelude to a single currency in the region and a Gulf central bank. However, in early 2010 the UAE withdrew as the council was to be based in Riyadh rather than Abu Dhabi, and Oman stood to one side because it could not yet accept the preconditions. Kuwait called for the council's launch to be delayed.

There were limited moves to reduce protectionism and to encourage foreign investors. In November 2009 Qatar announced it would reduce taxes on foreign companies from 35% to 10% and in January 2010 Oman said it would tax foreign businesses at the same level as domestic ones. In mid-2009, at the instigation of the Economic Development Board chaired by the crown prince, Bahrain abolished the system of sponsorship (*kafala*) for foreign workers, under which they can reside in the country only while still working for the specified employer, who thereby acquires unhealthy leverage. It was the first Gulf state to abandon the system which has long attracted strong criticism from human-rights organisations and prevented expatriates from committing themselves long-term to GCC states. In March 2010 the Saudi Supreme Judicial Council approved the establishment of commercial courts in Riyadh, Jeddah and Dammam.

Broadly viewed, the Gulf's economic experience of the previous two years has cast doubt over the sustainability of the current model of growth. An important aspect of this was industrial and infrastructural overcapacity spread across a patchwork of closely clustered states, a consequence partly of intra-GCC rivalries and partly of distortions created by the rentier system with its dominating governmental role in the economy and enormous revenues derived from hydrocarbons. The risks inherent in duplication and doubts about the power of the Gulf states to continue to attract qualified people to staff grandiose new schemes have placed a question mark over the remarkably similar long-term development plans outlined by governments across the GCC. There was also more explicit recognition within the GCC of the growing imbalance between soaring energy demand (caused by increasing population, adoption of middle-class lifestyles, and resource-intensive infrastructure) and inadequate energy and water resources, stretched by new industries, desalination plants and attempts to diversify economies.

In 2009–10 the Gulf states, with 23% of the world's proven gas reserves, started to appreciate, if not actively to confront, the need for energy conservation, accepting that current usage, with consumption rising 7% a year, was unsustainable. The head of Saudi Aramco warned that, unless energy efficiencies were made, Saudi domestic energy demand would rise from the equivalent of 3.4 million barrels per day (b/d) last year to 8.3m b/d equivalent in 2028, thereby cutting oil available for export by 3m b/d. Only Qatar in the GCC has enough gas to meet the accelerating demand for electricity generation, yet throughout the GCC electricity prices remain subsidised for domestic, industrial and agricultural uses. One potential approach would be to raise electricity prices to control consumption and deliver higher revenues, so as to encourage investments in gas production. However, raising local energy costs would arouse strong local opposition, even if it made renewable power more competitive and cut down the Gulf's contribution to global emissions, which stands at 2.4% from 0.6% of the world's population. Rather than seeking to control demand and consumption, Gulf governments were considering alternative sources of energy.

New interest in nuclear energy was highlighted by the award by the UAE, a net importer of gas, in December 2009 of a contract worth $20.4bn to a South Korean consortium for the construction of four nuclear reactors. Abu Dhabi had assessed that its natural-gas reserves would be able to meet only 50% of electricity demand by 2020. The first reactor is due to supply power to the electricity grid in 2017 and the others in 2020. The UAE was the first GCC state to make a substantive national move towards nuclear power. The others remained tentative about proceeding with national programmes, although Kuwait and France signed a civilian nuclear cooperation agreement in April 2010, and Saudi Arabia announced that it was establishing a new civilian nuclear and renewable energy centre, the King Abdullah City for Nuclear and Renewable Energy to based in Riyadh, to help meet increasing demand for power. The region's caution was due to inadequate infrastructure and also, partly, to diminishing available capital and potential domestic opposition. In 2009 Bahrain formed a national nuclear-energy committee but took no practical steps forward. Both Oman and Qatar decided against national programmes at this stage. Moves towards a GCC-wide programme stalled, although in July 2009, as a useful initial step, the first stage of the GCC power grid was completed, linking Kuwait, Saudi Arabia, Bahrain and Qatar with the UAE and Oman due to be included by 2011.

> " Water also became an issue for GCC governments "

Water also became an issue for GCC governments. Agriculture consumed about 80% of the region's water resources, but contributed less than 2% of regional GDP. The depletion of water resources had previously forced the Saudi government to phase out wheat production. As local production dropped and population grew, food security became an increasing issue for GCC states and a driver for increased overseas agricultural investment.

Overall, the experience of GCC countries in 2009–10 suggested that they would face a tough set of challenges in the coming period, on the economic and financial front and in dealing with energy issues, as well as in being vulnerable to negative developments across the Gulf in Iran.

Yemen: terrorism highlights regime's difficulties

Regional awareness of deterioration in security and governance in Yemen over 2009 was extended to the wider international community when a Nigerian apparently trained in Yemen and directed by al-Qaeda attempted to blow up an aircraft on its approach to Detroit on 25 December 2009. This brought home to the United States and others the risk that Yemen could become a failed state in which al-Qaeda would exploit ungoverned areas to launch terrorist attacks internationally or across the Bab al-Mandab strait. Al-Qaeda, operating since January 2009 as al-Qaeda in the Arabian Peninsula, had already demonstrated its regional ambitions and capability with the failed suicide attack on Saudi Deputy Minister of Interior Prince Muhammad bin Nayef in Jeddah on 27 August, when he received a Saudi al-Qaeda member who had travelled from Yemen and was claiming to seek rehabilitation. The terrorist threat emanating from Yemen left local and regional commentators particularly concerned that further attacks might impel the United States to intervene directly, with potentially destabilising results.

While the threat from al-Qaeda in Yemen seized international attention late in 2009, the government's concern was more focused on the continuing conflict with Zaydi Shia rebels, also known as al-Houthis, in the area around Sa'dah in the north. It also faced growing dissidence in the south of the country, which constituted the People's Democratic Republic of Yemen (PDRY) until unification in 1990. Though widely different in terms of culture and religious affiliation, both regions have suffered from political and economic marginalisation and underinvestment in the last two decades.

In the north the al-Houthis have been in rebellion against the regime of President Ali Abdullah Saleh since 2004. In August 2009 the Yemeni army launched a fresh offensive against them using aerial and artillery bombardment, causing heavy civilian casualties and turning tens of thousands of local inhabitants into refugees. This led to clashes between the al-Houthis and Saudi security forces along the Yemeni–Saudi border after the al-Houthis attacked a Saudi border patrol on 3 November. Saudi Arabia's mobilisation of its army and air force enabled Yemen to recover territory occupied by the rebels, and in late January the leader of the al-Houthis announced their readiness to accept a ceasefire. At mid-2010 this was still holding with prisoner releases taking place. However, there were no apparent concrete moves by the parties to resolve the underlying conflict, which involved a number of tribes from the al-Houthis' Bakil federation ranging themselves against a regime dominated by the rival Hashid federation. Claims of Iranian involvement in the form of material support for the al-Houthis, which the Saudis take seriously and which have led to the trading of accusations between Riyadh and Tehran, remained unsupported by publicly available evidence.

In the south, the rumbling dissident movement, centred around disillusioned former PDRY officials and officers, grew in intensity. Their cause, which emerged in 2006 and was focused initially on pension rights, benefits and the northern bias in job allocation, developed a more secessionist and nationalist flavour in 2009. The year saw a series of isolated attacks by southerners on police posts and government offices, demonstrations and protests, some calling for the restoration of ousted PDRY President Ali Salim al-Bidh. The regime in Sana'a responded with detentions and declarations of local emergency. However, the various groups that make up the so-called Southern Movement, many with leaders lodged in exile overseas, showed no unified purpose or approach, nor did they enjoy the support of any foreign government that might enable them to turn the tables on the regime in Sana'a. It was a telling signal of local desperation and opportunism that Tariq al-Fadhli, an Afghan jihadi ally of Saleh who joined the southern cause in April 2009 with a demand for complete secession, sought to catch the attention of the United States and distance the seccessionist movement from al-Qaeda by raising the Stars and Stripes in his Abyan compound on the south coast in early 2010.

The al-Houthi rebellion and southern disaffection distracted the Yemeni regime from addressing the al-Qaeda threat systematically. It had some successes, achieved with US support and encouragement, such as the claimed killing of then al-Qaeda military chief Qasim al-Raymi in an air strike. Al-Qaeda also failed over the year to launch insurgent-style attacks on Western official targets, as it had done in 2008 when it assaulted the US embassy twice. In April 2010 there was an unsuccessful attack attributed to al-Qaeda on the UK ambassador in Sana'a. Meanwhile, the United States and Yemen were unable to resolve the fate of the hundred or so Yemenis still held at the US detention facility at Guantanamo Bay, Cuba, who represented a potentially serious source of future terrorist threat.

Ominously for the country's longer-term future and prospects for halting the spread of radical ideology, the regime failed to devote much effort to political and economic reform. The last round of parliamentary elections scheduled for early 2009 was delayed until 2011. Reform stalled and politics remained stagnant, dominated by the Sanhan tribe and Saleh's patronage network. Most commentators believe Saleh intends to transfer power in due course to his son Ahmad, who commands the Republican Guard, although this arrangement may be challenged by senior Sanhanis.

Also threatening the regime's stability was the continued deterioration of the economy in 2009. Oil production, which supplies 70% of government revenue and finances the president's patronage network, dropped in volume and price, causing a 75% year-on-year fall in export revenues in the first quarter of 2009. Yemen's oil is due to run out by 2017. Water resources, traditionally depleted by diversion to the growing of the local narcotic khat, are also running out. Meanwhile tourism has continued to be hit by sporadic violence against foreign visitors, including the kidnapping of nine tourists in June 2009. A third of the fast-growing population (currently 23.8m) remain on the breadline.

The failed Detroit aircraft bombing again drew international attention to the terrorist threat. A conference on Yemen on 27 January 2010, called in London by UK Prime Minister Gordon Brown, saw another international attempt to grapple with Yemen's future and renewed pledges of development assistance. This outcome was reinforced by a GCC meeting in Riyadh in late February, but the Yemeni government's inability to manage and deploy aid effectively was a serious obstacle to the international development agenda, and long-standing distrust between foreign governments and Sana'a remained undispelled. The former have long felt manipulated, while the Yemeni regime fears international attempts to fetter its room for manoeuvre. It is a measure of the Saudis' concern for the future that in early 2010 they began to clear inhabitants from border areas and to install a frontier fence along the long and difficult border with Yemen. Meanwhile, in April 2010 the US administration declared it had authority to kill or capture Yemen-based Sheikh Anwar al-Awlaki, a US citizen of Yemeni origin, who was implicated in both the November 2009 massacre by a US Army major at the Fort Hood military base and the attempted Detroit bombing. All the signs are that the Detroit incident did not break the dispiriting pattern of deteriorating internal security and deepening international distrust that has led many commentators to categorise Yemen as a failing state.

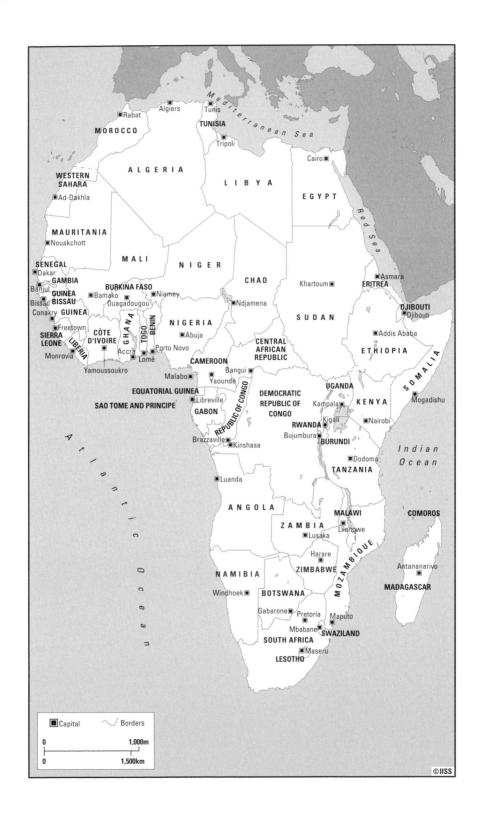

Chapter 7

Africa

As of mid-2010, the prevailing sentiment in Africa was cautious optimism. In early 2009, there had been fears that the global recession would engulf Africa's economies and lead to increased conflict. To be sure, the continent was suffering financial malaise. Africa's economies contracted by 3% in the first half of 2009 as commodity prices fell and investment dipped. The recession hit South Africa especially hard, as the depressed commodity prices and chronic labour disputes dragged down the country's manufacturing sector. In mid-2009, Nigeria's banking sector had to be rescued by a N420 million ($2.8 billion) state bailout akin to the government bailouts of American, British and European banks a few months earlier. But there was no continent-wide collapse of Africa's financial institutions or catastrophic decline in investments, as some had feared. This was in part because Africa's economic growth was propelled by the informal sector, and by public–private partnerships. By mid-2009, and into 2010, most African countries were predicting increased growth and reduced deficits. Africa was also raising its global financial presence by way of the London and Pittsburgh G20 summits in April and September 2009, respectively. This was all good news, but it did not obviate continuing problems of chronic poverty and unequal resource distribution across Africa.

In 2009–10, there were national elections in 12 African countries, and referendums in four. Generally, the election results produced few surprises, with the incumbents returned to power. And although there were plenty of disputes between incumbents and opposition groups about whether the electoral process was genuinely free and fair, Africa's 2009–10 elections did not lead to violence on the scale of previous elections in Kenya (2007) and Zimbabwe (2008). At the same time, debate about whether electoral democracy had really taken root in Africa, or whether African elections represented more form than content, reignited. The issue of establishing 'standards' for monitoring and judging elections, particularly in Sudan and Ethiopia, was still prominent.

Many long-standing conflicts continued, particularly in Somalia and elsewhere in East Africa and the Horn, and the intersection of transnational jihadism and organised crime with local insurgencies remained a major challenge. Multinational task forces could not end piracy in the Red Sea, the Gulf of Aden or the Indian Ocean, as pirates – mainly Somalis – widened their area of operations. But there were a number of positive security-related developments. The African Union (AU) and regional organisations continued to make incremental progress towards realising serviceable African capacities for peace operations and conflict resolution. The African Standby Force (ASF) peace and stabilisation brigades were due to be formally launched by the end of 2010. The AU also flexed its diplomatic muscle against coup leaders in Guinea, Guinea–Bissau, Niger, Madagascar and Mauritania. Unexpected rapprochements between Rwanda and the Democratic Republic of the Congo (DRC) and between Chad and Sudan also improved intra-regional dynamics in the Great Lakes and Horn of Africa regions.

US President Barack Obama visited Ghana in July 2009, stressing in a speech in Accra the importance of the US–Africa partnership and the need to build Africa's institutions. In August, Secretary of State Hillary Clinton visited South Africa, Angola, the DRC, Nigeria, Kenya, Liberia and Cape Verde. These visits attracted a great deal of attention, but arguably a bigger story was the deepening of the continent's economic ties with the Middle East and Asia. Iran, Turkey, India and China, among other countries, launched charm offensives to win military and commercial deals in Africa, while African entrepreneurs also launched overseas business initiatives. On the political side, Turkey hosted a major conference on Somalia in May 2010; Iranian President Mahmoud Ahmadinejad, seeking to bolster Iranian military assistance and infrastructure development ties as well as obtain African support for Iran's nuclear policy, visited Zimbabwe and Uganda in April 2010.

South Africa: Competing Agendas in the ANC

The African National Congress (ANC) comfortably won the April 2009 elections, falling just short of the two-thirds majority needed to unilaterally alter the constitution. Helen Zille's opposition Democratic Alliance (DA) won 17% of the vote, slightly lower than expected, while the newly formed Congress of the People (COPE) won 7%. Jacob Zuma, the former ANC president, was sworn in as South Africa's president on 9 May, and his new cabinet reflected both continuity and change. His political task had already been eased by the resignations of many of former President Thabo Mbeki's ministers following his ouster in October 2008. Many of the post-Mbeki ministers were retained, but Zuma announced some changes, as well as a restructuring of the housing and education ministries. A National Planning Commission was also established, to be chaired by former Finance Minister Trevor Manuel. Zuma stressed that service delivery, jobs and professionalisation of government departments would be priorities.

South Africa's economy was buffeted by the global recession. Commodity prices and manufacturing dipped during the first quarter of 2009, but by the end of the year a rise in commodity prices had rallied the economy. Economic policy became a major issue within the ANC and between the ANC and its Tripartite Alliance partners – the Congress of South African Trade Unions (COSATU) and the South African Communist Party (SACP). Broadly speaking, there were three policy groups in the ANC. Firstly, there was a 'conservative' group within the Finance Ministry and National Treasury whose members argued that a continuation of the pro-business, pragmatic approach of the Mbeki years was essential to retain investor confidence. The second group included recent cabinet appointees from the Tripartite Alliance, such as the SACP's

Rob Davies, appointed to the Department of Trade and Industry; SACP Secretary-General Blade Nzimande, to the Ministry of Higher Education; and Ebrahim Patel of COSATU, named to head the new Ministry of Economic Development. The SACP and COSATU had long advocated greater centralisation, with movement towards a command economy and state-led redistribution. The third group was a loose consortium of business groups favouring a continuation and expansion of the Black Economic Empowerment policy.

Zuma and the ANC appeared to balance these competing economic agendas and groups adroitly, but pressure on the ANC to produce an economic dividend seemed bound to increase. In May 2010, the South African Transport and Allied Workers' Union (SATAWU) and other unions launched crippling strikes. April to May is traditionally the season for wage negotiations and strikes in South Africa, so the action was not unexpected. But the size of the agreed wage increases – 11 to 13% – was. The strikes also cost the economy an estimated R7bn ($1bn) as exports of metal, fruit and wine were temporarily halted. More broadly, the strikes raised fresh questions about the balance of power between the ANC and its union-affiliated allies. Mindful of the job-creation promises made during the run-up to the 2009 elections, the ANC launched a Policy Action Plan (PAP) in February 2010. The PAP pledged to create 2.4m jobs over ten years, and to expand the nation's manufacturing sector. But it remained unclear whether the PAP was adequately resourced, especially since the government has had to borrow R5bn from the World Bank to fund the South African public utility Eskom's revitalisation of South Africa's electricity infrastructure.

Malema and the Youth League

Since becoming president, Zuma has faced numerous political challenges. Julius Malema, leader of the ANC's Youth League (ANCYL) and *enfant terrible* of South African politics, generated continuous publicity for his hardline, anti-white and pro-poor position. Malema's populist rhetoric won him considerable support from South Africa's urban poor. It also allowed the ANC to maintain that it was in touch with the urban and rural underclass and to intimate that Malema was a 'bridge' to the more militant SACP and COSATU groupings within the alliance. But it was clear that Malema was increasingly becoming a liability to the ANC. By early 2010, he was in open conflict with the ANC senior leadership. His rhetoric during a visit to Zimbabwe compromised the ANC's stance as a neutral mediator between the country's two main parties. On 8 April, Malema was involved in a verbal scuffle with BBC reporter Jonah Fisher.

More controversy followed when the ANCYL persisted in singing the song, *Ayesaba amagwala; dubl'ibhunu* ('The cowards are afraid, shoot the Boer'), which was subsequently banned. While Zuma himself had cast the song as symbolic of black South Africans' liberation history, many worried that when Malema sang about shooting the Boers – that is, white South Africans – he meant it. When Eugene Terreblanche, former leader of a white extremist group, was found murdered at his farm on 29 April, Malema's inflammatory rhetoric was seen as an indirect cause. On account of his outspokenness and legal troubles (he was also being investigated for corruption), the ANC compelled him to issue a public apology and attend anger-management and 're-education' classes. For some, this was enough; but the opposition criticised the ANC for retaining Malema as the Youth League leader.

> "Malema was increasingly becoming a liability"

The ANC tightened its focus on youth and security issues. In April 2010, Defence and Military Veterans Minister Lindiwe Sisulu proposed a National Service for unemployed youths, who would be trained by the South African National Defence Force (SANDF). The main objective was to instil discipline in and enhance the skills of South African youth, but opponents feared that the programme would lead to a politicisation of South Africa's military and could produce militias similar to those used by Zimbabwean President Robert Mugabe to brutally suppress political rivals. It remained unclear how the youth would be integrated with the regular military, Meanwhile, the SANDF was undergoing a review to upgrade its capabilities for coping with complex conflicts. The SANDF was also a key contributor to the Southern Africa Development Community (SADC) Brigade of the ASF, the AU's nascent permanent rapid-deployment force for peace operations. *Operation Golfinho* was the SADC Brigade's first major exercise; conducted in the Free State and Northern Cape, it included practice mobilisation, intervention, peacekeeping and demobilisation. After preliminaries involving 5,000 personnel from February to May 2009, the full exercise involving 8,000 military and civilian personnel from 12 SADC states was held in September. There were simultaneous SADC naval manoeuvres off Walvis Bay in Namibia. In May 2010, a review of SADC Brigade in Maputo concluded that the force was ready to become operational in the latter half of 2010.

The World Cup

The quadrennial FIFA World Cup football tournament, which South Africa hosted from 11 June through 11 July 2010, was an enormous and costly undertaking. Although a Saudi national, Azzam al-Qhatani, was arrested in Iraq and claimed to be involved in a plan to attack the Danish and Dutch teams during the World Cup, the key security threat was seen as local and transnational organised crime rather than jihadist terrorism. The government guaranteed the safety of players and visitors to allay safety fears. However, security concerns and high ticket prices did affect visitor numbers. Urban infrastructure was revamped across the ten cities involved. The Cup, the first to be held in Africa, energised the South African Police Service (SAPS). In June 2009, Bheki Cele was appointed as the new national police commissioner. His calls for the SAPS to be allowed to use 'deadly force' against criminals earned him both support and opprobrium, sparking a national debate about the uses and limits of force by the police. Controversy aside, Cele established an intensive training and skills programme within the SAPS. Transnational intelligence links were also upgraded and SANDF–SAPS cooperation was increased.

Although the South African squad failed to progress beyond the group stage, there was no gainsaying the huge surge in national pride and unity which the event created, which looked to favour the ANC in the short term. But the party was likely to come under pressure to provide World Cup 'dividends' by ameliorating poverty, unemployment and corruption. Race relations are another long-standing challenge that the ANC as well as its critics will need to manage carefully.

Kenya and Zimbabwe: Fragile Coalitions

The coalition governments in Kenya and Zimbabwe continued to function, despite predictions of early demise. They had a great deal in common. Both had emerged as the direct result of political crises arising from disputed election results. Both were preceded by surges in political violence that threatened civil war. In both cases the coalition partners were reluctant political bedfellows who had been pressured and coaxed by the regional and international community to agree to a power-sharing deal. There was also a more direct diplomatic link between the two coalitions: the National Accord that had created the February 2008 Kenyan Government of National Unity (GNU) greatly influenced Zimbabwe's Memorandum of Understanding, which led to the creation of its own GNU in February 2009.

Nevertheless, there remained significant differences. On one hand, the gulf in political ideology between the Zimbabwe African National Union-Patriotic Front (ZANU-PF) and the Movement for Democratic Change (MDC), the main stakeholders in Zimbabwe, was much greater than the party-political differences between the Party of National Unity (PNU) and Orange Democratic Movement (ODM), their counterparts in Kenya. Security forces have also played a much greater role in politics in Zimbabwe than in Kenya; at the height of its powers in mid-2008, Zimbabwe's Joint Operations Command effectively usurped the role of the state and virtually turned Zimbabwe into a military cantonment. Kenya's military has been a powerful political stakeholder, but has tended to operate behind the scenes. On the other hand, ethnicity and resource struggles have been a much more acute source of conflict in Kenya than in Zimbabwe. Further, Kenya's PNU and ODM are themselves coalition parties, and this added layer of intra-party politics has made decision-making more difficult.

Kenya

For much of 2009, the energies of the coalition government were focused more on managing PNU–ODM rivalries than with implementing the explicit reform agenda of the National Accord. In January 2009, President Mwai Kibaki's signing of a controversial media law precipitated another freeze in relations between himself and Prime Minister Raila Odinga. The prime minister and much of civil society had criticised the law, saying that it further eroded press freedoms. In March 2009, Constitutional Affairs Minister Martha Karua and Medical Services Assistant Minister Danson Mungatana both resigned. But the coalition endured despite public infighting between Odinga and Kibaki and their respective parties.

There was also increasingly bitter tension between Odinga and his former ally, Minister of Agriculture William Ruto. In the 2007 elections Ruto had 'delivered' the Kalenjin tribe's vote for Odinga, who is a member of the Luo tribe, Kenya's second largest after Kibaki's Kikuyu tribe. In July 2009, Ruto insisted that Odinga had failed to handle Kenya's vexing land question and demanded a vote of no confidence with respect to the prime minister. The vast ecosystem of the Mau Forest is Kenya's largest water-catchment area, with five giant towers providing water to towns in the area. But given the political value of agricultural patronage, its rich soil attracted the attention of the government, which in 1997 settled thousands of landless peasants in the region. The result was increasing environmental degradation; by 2009 there was broad cross-party consensus that the Mau Forest and its water towers needed to be preserved. This would entail the displacement and relocation of the approximately 60,000 settlers in the area. Moreover, the 2008–09 Commission of Inquiry into Illegal Land Grabbing and the 2009 Ndungu Report on land listed various members of Kenya's current and former political elite as living on improperly acquired land, and recommended a number of measures (including eviction), which Mau Forest settlers and some Kalenjin and other members of parliament – including Ruto – resisted. In February 2010, Odinga suspended Ruto and Minister of Education Samuel Ongeri. While the stated reason was their complicity in a national maize corruption scandal, many observers felt that Odinga was seeking revenge against Ruto for the no-confidence vote as well as trying to remove a potential challenger from within his own party ahead of the 2012 presidential elections. Kibaki revoked the sus-

> **Members of Kenya's elite were living on improperly acquired land**

pensions, and in April 2010 reshuffled the cabinet, moving Ruto from agriculture to the less powerful education ministry, reportedly on the advice of Odinga.

Constitutional reform

The government drew increasing criticism from Kenyan civil society and the international community for its reluctance to address political, security-sector and judicial reform. To ease the pressure, the government established a Committee of Experts to prepare a new draft constitution for Kenya. The committee consulted with the political parties as well as the general public as the draft underwent a series of revisions between November 2009 and April 2010. The main sticking point was the allocation of powers between the president and the prime minister. The committee recognised that the lack of convergence between the PNU and ODM on this issue could lead to a renewed political crisis and further violence. The committee's 'final draft' constitution of 23 February 2010 recommended a presidential system without a prime minister. On 1 April, the Kenyan parliament unanimously approved the proposed constitution, which incorporated a presidential system but also greater oversight of the executive branch. It also proposed legalising dual citizenship for Kenyans who were holders of non-Kenyan passports, and offering limited devolution to regions and counties. A referendum was scheduled on the draft constitution in August 2010.

Although the coalition parties joined forces in advocating a 'yes' vote, there was a significant emergence of contrary opinion. Deputy Prime Minister and Finance Minister Uhuru Kenyatta and MPs Isaac Ruto and Peter Muringa complained that it enshrined an 'imperial' presidency. The GNU planned a series of nationwide promotional rallies to press for a 'yes' vote. However, heckling at the first rallies raised doubts about whether the PNU and ODM would continue to hold them jointly. The looming question was whether the constitutional referendum would foster political reform and nation-building, or whether it would lead to renewed factionalism and violence, as occurred in Kenya following the 'no' vote in 2008. The question became acute on 13 June when three explosions ripped through a prayer meeting in Nairobi's Uhuru Park, held jointly by church leaders and activists campaigning against the draft constitution. Five people were killed and more than 70 injured. Subsequently, Assistant Roads Minister Wilfred Machage and MPs Joshua Kutuny and Fred Kapondi were arrested for 'hate speech'.

In June 2009, Kenyatta presented a budget that combined stimulus and austerity. The main focus was on social development, infrastructure and security. There were increased allocations for food security, water conservation, health and youth empowerment activities, in line with the official Kaz Kwa Vijana youth initiative. Funding was also made available for youth involvement in community policing and for the construction of 30,000 houses for the estimated 200,000 internally displaced persons uprooted by the 2007–08 violence. But Kenyatta also announced a drive for efficiency by reducing allocations for departmental overheads such as telephones and vehicles. The budget was generally well received, and a decrease in Kenya's inflation from 13.11% in 2008 to 11.8% in 2009 softened the impact of the reductions. The onset of late rains in early 2010 also lessened fears of widespread food shortages, which had arisen following the 2009 drought.

For the United States, Kenya is an important strategic ally in East Africa and the Horn, particularly in the fight against jihadist terrorism and transnational organised crime. For Kenya, the United States is a key trading partner and major source of donor and tourist revenue. President Obama's Kenyan ancestry had been expected to yield a 'special relationship' between Nairobi and Washington. Instead, relations between the two countries became increasingly fractious. Obama did not include Kenya in his itinerary when he made a brief visit to Africa in February 2009. The main impediment to warmer relations was the Kenyan government's delay in following the agreed reform agenda. American concerns were increased by the publication in July 2009 of a damning UN report detailing largely unpunished police and army abuses. However, Hillary Clinton's visit in August 2009 did demonstrate continued US interest in Kenya, and she emphasised the long-standing ties between the two countries. Bilateral relations were tested again when the US State Department sent letters to some coalition ministers, warning that their visas to enter the United States would be revoked if they continued to resist reform in Kenya. By early 2010, relations had improved again.

Zimbabwe

Zimbabwe's economic recovery continued, buoyed by the continued, albeit often fractious, partnership between ZANU-PF, the opposition MDC-Tsvangirai (MDC-T) led by party founder Morgan Tsvangirai and the much smaller MDC-Mutambara (MDC-M) grouping headed by former student leader Arthur Mutambara. The coalition GNU was established on 11 February 2009, with Robert Mugabe remaining president and Tsvangirai becoming prime minister. When he took office, Tsvangirai stated that the government would promote what he called the 'democratisation agenda' and the rule of law. Stabilising the economy was the other key priority.

ZANU-PF and the MDC-T competed for state and international resources and recognition. ZANU-PF had retained the defence, foreign-affairs and agriculture ministries, while the MDC-T acquired finance, health and education. Although this allowed Mugabe's party to retain its 'hard power' in the coalition, the MDC's control of the Treasury gave it a good deal of 'soft power' and inter-party leverage under new Finance Minister Tendai Biti. In effect, inter-party rivalries yielded parallel governments. Inter-party cooperation on health and education was marred by confrontations on the rule of law and official appointments. On the same day Tsvangirai was inaugurated, his party's Deputy Agriculture Minister-designate Roy Bennett was arrested on charges of conspiring to overthrow Mugabe. In April 2010, Bennett was acquitted of the treason charges, but the state immediately appealed the ruling. It appeared likely that the ZANU-PF–MDC deadlock over his appointment would continue to cloud their relationship.

Other sticking points included the status of pro-ZANU-PF Reserve Bank Governor Gideon Gono, whom the MDC groupings wanted removed; the appointment of provincial governors and Zimbabwe's ambassadors; continued farm invasions by those claiming to be 'war veterans' with ZANU-PF support; and the role of the security sector. On 6 March 2009, Tsvangirai was badly injured in a car crash in which his wife Susan was killed. Zimbabwe has a long tradition of dubious 'car accidents', and circumstantial evidence caused many to doubt that it had been an accident at all, but Tsvangirai, undoubtedly aware that any allegations of a ZANU-PF conspiracy to murder him could destroy the fragile unity government, stated that he considered it as such. Tensions were further heightened by another surge in farm invasions from February to May 2009, when another 120 of the remaining 300 white-owned commercial farms were occupied.

While infighting between the coalition partners garnered most of the headlines, there were some major achievements that stabilised the country. The dollarisation of Zimbabwe's currency brought inflation, which in December 2008 had been the highest in history, down to double digits, and GDP rose by 4%. In March 2009, the government launched the 100-day Short-Term Emergency Recovery Programme. In April 2009, South Africa established a regional SADC Task Force to map out a programme for regional and international economic assistance to Zimbabwe. And in November 2009 the government initiated a Medium-Term Plan, which set an agenda for sustainable development. These developments helped Zimbabwe regain some donor and investor confidence.

During the latter half of 2009, the constitutional review process continued apace with nationwide consultations on a draft. The stated goal was a constitutional referendum in October 2010. In July 2009, Associated Newspapers of Zimbabwe, publishers of the banned *Daily News* and *Daily News on Sunday*, were given a licence to operate. In April 2010, Professor Reg Austin, former head of the Legal Affairs Division in the Commonwealth, was appointed head of the Human Rights Commission, while Judge Simpson Mutambanengwe, a former chief justice, was appointed chair of the Media Commission. The establishment of the commissions, and the appointments of technocrats to run them, was widely seen as a positive step in widening and de-politicising civil society in Zimbabwe. In addition, the infighting between Finance Minister Biti and Reserve Bank Governor Gono was not as disruptive as many had feared, as the Treasury had substantially weakened Gono's institutional power. For the MDC, the bigger obstacle was Johannes Tomana, the partisan attorney general.

Contested leadership

On 18 April, Tsvangirai attended Zimbabwe's independence celebrations (the first time the MDC–T was represented), which led to a mild thaw in his relations with Zimbabwe's military establishment. In July

2009, Tsvangirai met formally with the Joint Operations Command (JOC) – comprising officers from the Zimbabwe National Army, Air Force of Zimbabwe, Zimbabwe Republic Police, Central Intelligence Organisation and the Zimbabwe Prison Service – for the first time at a National Security Council (NSC) meeting. Throughout the decade the JOC had militarised and politicised Zimbabwe's state institutions, and had performed a 'quiet coup' in March 2008 to roll back the MDC's election victory. JOC leaders had also repeatedly stated that they would never accept an MDC-led or MDC-partnered government. Accordingly, the July meeting and subsequent ones between the MDC and the security sector in the NSC carried considerable symbolic significance.

Jacob Zuma succeeded Thabo Mbeki as the regional SADC mediator on Zimbabwe. An SADC Troika comprising South Africa, Mozambique and Botswana was appointed to coordinate SADC policy on the Zimbabwean GNU coalition and ensure that all sides adhered to the terms of the legal agreement, known as the Global Political Agreement (GPA), binding the three parties in the coalition. The involvement of South Africa as chief mediator, and the SADC as guarantor of the GPA, afforded the MDC parties channels for airing allegations of ZANU-PF's 'bad faith' and therefore some external leverage. By late 2009, the GNU had become more fractious than ever, with a resurgence of political violence and squabbles about sanctions threatening to sink the coalition. Zuma visited Harare in August 2009 to encourage discussions, but the deadlock continued. On 28 November 2009, the MDC briefly 'disengaged' from the GNU, putting more pressure on South Africa to engage in firmer mediation. The April 2010 visit to Zimbabwe by Julius Malema, the controversial pro-ZANU-PF ANC Youth League leader, caused further embarrassment to the South Africans, also motivating them to assume a more assertive role.

Tsvangirai, for his part, endured a rough ride. In June 2009, Zimbabweans booed him at a presentation at Southwark Cathedral in London, when he urged those in the UK to return home. Allegations of fraud led to the suspension of the local MDC party executive in Chitungwiza (outside Harare) and in London. In May 2010, an assault on MDC Director-General Toendepi Shonhe led to an internal MDC inquiry and the suspension of five youths from the MDC. Tsvangirai's party was also plagued by factionalism in Midlands South province, which led to the creation in May 2010 of another breakaway party, MDC-99, led by a former MDC-T official, Job Sikhala. With elections looming in 2011 and growing criticism about the failure of MDC ministers to perform, Tsvangirai reshuffled ministers within the GNU on 22 June 2010. Home Affairs Co-Minister Giles Mutsekwa was replaced by the more hardline Theresa Makone; Energy Minister Elias Mudzuri was replaced by Elton Mangoma, formerly minister of economic planning.

Within ZANU-PF, there were long-standing fissures between Minister for Mines Emmerson Munangagwa and Vice-President Joyce Mujuru in the race to succeed Mugabe. Moreover, in February 2010 an internal report by ZANU-PF National Political Commissar Webster Shamu revealed a dearth of grass-roots support and party-infrastructural problems.

While Zimbabwe had begun an economic recovery and the GNU had improbably survived, investment was limited. With elections likely in mid-2011 and rifts growing over the draft constitution, the fear was that absent smoother relations between ZANU-PF and the MDC, 2011 could be a repeat of 2000, when a referendum–election cycle triggered a protracted period of violence and decline.

West Africa's Political Challenges

Nigeria: new leadership, old problems

The year 2009–10 was tumultuous for Nigeria. While it saw concerted state action against financial corruption, and the Niger Delta amnesty brought marginally greater stability to the conflict-ridden area, the failing health and eventual death of President Umaru Yar'Adua, and the succession question within the ruling Nigeria Peoples Party (NPP), dominated events.

Sanusi's tsunami

Despite Yar'Adua's frailty, two key developments occurred under his stewardship during the first half of 2009. Firstly, in May, northerner Lamido Sanusi was appointed governor of Nigeria's Central Bank.

Sanusi, a technocrat, made it clear that he saw his mission as cleaning Nigeria's banking system. That same month, Arunma Oteh, the former vice-president of the African Development Bank, was appointed the new head of Nigeria's Securities and Exchange Commission. The appointments signalled the accession of a new generation of technocrats into Nigeria's top financial echelons.

As the global financial crisis took hold, a July 2009 preliminary audit of Nigeria's key banks illuminated severe financial shortfalls. To prevent the demise of these institutions, Sanusi reluctantly bailed out Afribank, International Bank, Oceanic Bank, Fincor and several others with N420bn ($2.8bn) in state funds. But the banks' chief executives were sacked and Sanusi – in partnership with the Economic and Financial Crimes Commission – authorised a full audit of the banks and a criminal investigation of fraud. Nigerians called the purge 'Sanusi's tsunami'. The interventions, which won widespread support, allowed Sanusi to begin deep-seated banking reforms. In February 2010 he laid out a comprehensive plan for the structural reform of Nigeria's financial institutions. The key, he believed, lay in the quality rather than the quantity of staff and regulations, as well as the stability of the banks.

Niger Delta insurgency

In a May 2009 offensive, 20,000 Nigerian forces killed and captured dozens of economically motivated insurgents across the Niger Delta, but abductions of soldiers and foreign workers in the Delta continued. In July, war-weary negotiators agreed to a 60-day truce and amnesty. Rebels were to surrender their weapons in exchange for cash and official pardons. One of the 'showpiece' insurgent surrenders was that of Ateke Tom, leader of the Niger Delta Vigilante group, in August. Tom, who had been a formidable opponent of the national forces, formally disarmed with approximately 5,000 of his followers at a ceremony at Government House in Abuja. But a number of groups, including the Movement for the Emancipation of the Niger Delta (MEND), refused to surrender. An amnesty programme was established with Yar'Adua as patron, but his increasing debility and the government's limited resources raised questions about the sustainability of peace. In May 2010, the Joint Revolutionary Council, a network of Delta insurgent groups, expressed serious reservations about the lack of funding and jobs under the programme.

The absent president

Eclipsing these developments was the political crisis that followed Yar'Adua's disappearance from public life in late 2009. In November, the president was flown to Saudi Arabia for emergency treatment for chronic liver problems. During his absence, which was not officially announced for some weeks after his departure, Vice-President Goodluck Jonathan, a Christian southerner and former governor of Ekiti state, took over the day-to-day running of the government. However, Jonathan's status as a southerner in a ruling party – the Peoples Democratic Party (PDP) – traditionally dominated by northerners prompted backstage plotting and factionalism. While Jonathan quietly fortified his political alliances, constitutionalists insisted that he could not perform legislative functions until Yar'Adua had formally nominated him to act during his absence. After weeks of silence and speculation, Yar'Adua officially nominated Jonathan to be president during a 13 January 2010 BBC interview in Riyadh. This bizarre handover was recognised by the Supreme Court and the National Assembly, though a number of civil-society groups contested its legality. On 9 February, Jonathan was formally appointed acting president. Keen to assert his authority, he reassigned controversial Justice Minister Michael Aondoakaa to the Special Duties Ministry, and in late March further reshuffled his cabinet, including former Yar'Adua ministers as well as new appointees.

On 5 May 2010, Yar'Adua died. Although he was criticised during his tenure for frequent absences, many had appreciated his insistence on constitutionalism and reform in Nigeria. On 18 May, the National Assembly ratified Jonathan's nomination of former Kaduna state Governor Namadi Sambo as the new vice-president. It appeared likely that any respite from political infighting would be brief. With presidential elections due in 2011, the crucial question was whether Jonathan would stand as the PDP nominee. A standing, tacit agreement to rotate the party leadership between north and south every two terms put pressure on the party to nominate a northerner for the candidacy in 2011. However, Jonathan was building a support base.

Raging insecurity

Sectarian and religious strife remained a key challenge for the new administration. In July 2009, gun battles amongst members of the Boko Haram sect in Bauchi and Maiduguru killed or injured hundreds of civilians. The death of sect leader Mohammed Yusuf in police custody on 30 July also raised questions about the professionalism of the security forces and the integrity of the rule of law.

However, increased Muslim–Christian conflict was the most immediate security challenge. Clashes in Jos, in Plateau state, in November 2008 and January and March 2010 killed hundreds and left a residue of interfaith bitterness. The failed attempt by 'Christmas bomber' Umar Farouk Abdulmutallab, a Nigerian Muslim, to bring down a US airliner with an explosive device also indicated the growing dangers of transnational radicalisation and jihadism that Nigeria faced. Although Abdulmutallab had been radicalised in the UK and Yemen, he had also been exposed to, and influenced by, radical preachers in northern Nigeria. His bombing attempt resulted in Nigeria's inclusion in the US list of 'countries of interest', which meant that Nigerian nationals would face increased US screening and restrictions. Nigeria protested the US policy and relations cooled between the two countries. In April 2010, the United States quietly dropped Nigeria from the list.

There was a general wary optimism regarding the future of the Jonathan government. The fact that the military did not intervene during the Yar'Adua crisis was salutary, and Nigeria's status as the ranking regional power was a source of some stability. Jonathan did, however, face numerous challenges. To consolidate civilian power and advance national reconciliation, he needed to continue Nigeria's economic growth and push the financial reforms initiated by Yar'Adua. Jonathan would also have to deal with Muslim–Christian and intra-faith strife. Most importantly for Nigeria's near future, he would have to establish a workable and equitable template for the 2011 elections.

The Democratic Republic of the Congo: Whither the UN?

Despite a large United Nations presence, the eastern DRC remained a zone of conflict. Questions were increasingly being raised about the role of the United Nations Organisation Mission in DRC (MONUC), which has about 20,000 troops in the country, of whom 15,000 are in the strife-torn eastern provinces.

From November 2006 through December 2007, dissident Tutsi forces of the National Congress for the Defence of the People (CNDP) under the command of Laurent Nkunda had routed demoralised government forces in the area, and besieged the eastern city of Goma, capital of North Kivu province. In 2007–08, the province was wracked by battles between government forces and various militia groups. The failure of the November 2007 Nairobi Agreement between Rwanda and the DRC and of the January 2008 Goma Actes d'Engagement signed by the Congolese government, CNDP and several dozen other armed groups to restore peace to North and South Kivu, to foster reconciliation and promote development resulted in a continuation of armed conflict throughout 2008. A December 2008 report showed Rwandan support for Nkunda's forces, exerting pressure on Rwandan President Paul Kagame and DRC President Joseph Kabila to uphold the 2007 agreement.

A second Nairobi summit in November 2009, however, produced a surprising diplomatic volte-face, as Kabila and Kagame agreed to normalise relations and cooperate against the rebel groups in the DRC. The result was the joint Rwandan–Congolese *Operation Umoja Wetu* against the Forces Democratiques de Libération du Rwanda (FDLR) rebel groups (formerly allies of the DRC army) in North Kivu from 20 January to 25 February 2009. The operation was inconclusive. Although the alliance claimed to have inflicted hundreds of casualties against the FDLR, the rebels divided into smaller units and dispersed into the Kivu forests. From March to December 2009 DRC forces, bolstered by logistical support from MONUC, launched *Operation Kimia II* against the FDLR. The stated goals were the forcible disarmament and demobilisation of the FDLR rebels. There were some notable successes. Key FDLR leader Gregoire Ndahimana was arrested and indicted by the International Criminal Court (ICC) on war-crimes charges. In addition, MONUC reported in November 2009 that it had demobilised nearly 1,500 FDLR combatants that year. Government forces also claimed to have killed or captured more than 700 FDLR personnel by the year's end.

Meanwhile, following Nkunda's arrest by Rwandan forces in January 2009, his deputy Bosco Ntaganda agreed to end the CNDP insurgency and to integrate CNDP forces into the Congolese army. DRC and UN military operations also reduced the insurgency in Equateur province, where the Nzobo Yalobo ('New Groups') insurgency erupted in October 2009 in the town of Dongo. Insurgent leader Odjani Mangbama was reportedly captured by Congolese forces in May 2010. Nearly a quarter of a million civilians fled into neighbouring Rwanda in late 2009, but in mid-2010 some were starting to return.

Problems remain. The 2009 campaigns and the January 2010 offensive against the FDLR did not destroy the rebel group. Its leadership remained intact and, with an estimated 6,000 fighters still active, the FDLR was still a major threat. Hundreds of thousands of civilians had been displaced, and rape, kidnapping, murder and violent conflict continued in Kivu. The Ugandan Lord's Resistance Army (LRA) also continued to terrorise civilians in Orientale province. In December 2008, forces from Uganda, Sudan and the DRC launched an offensive against the LRA in the DRC. The LRA, however, dispersed into smaller groups. LRA massacres of civilians at Niangara in December 2009 and Kpanga in February 2010 demonstrated that the LRA remained the most formidable transnational militant group in the Great Lakes region.

Questions about MONUC

The UN mission, which has 93 bases nationwide and conducts continuous patrols, has played a key role in the demobilisation, disarmament and re-integration of rebels in the DRC, and has also assisted in retraining the national army. MONUC is the key – and often the only – force for protecting civilians in some parts of the DRC.

However, the MONUC–DRC partnership has frayed. The UN has been widely criticised for failing to fulfil its civilian-protection duties in the DRC, particularly during operations in Kivu from 2008 to 2010. Donor nations questioned the cost and duration of the mission, and in September 2009 the Kabila government insisted on its withdrawal by September 2011. MONUC itself was arguing for a gradual drawdown rather than an abrupt pull-out. With elections looming in 2011, and a host of unresolved conflicts in the DRC, it remained unclear whether the DRC military – or the wider region – had the resources, or the will, to provide security for the people of the DRC.

Guinea–Bissau, the Republic of Guinea and Côte d'Ivoire
Guinea–Bissau

Guinea–Bissau's tradition of crisis politics and military intervention continued in 2009–10. On 1 March 2009, General Batista Tagme Na Wai, head of the Joint Chiefs of Staff, was assassinated in a bomb blast. The next day President João Bernardo Vieria was shot dead in his home by a group of soldiers in an apparent revenge killing. Although some initial speculation linked the murders to Guinea–Bissau's drug trade, they were almost certainly a result of the long-standing personal animosity between the two men. Vieria had little support from the military, in part because he was from the minority Papel tribe. He was maintained in power by a small militia and through the support of Lansana Conté, former president of neighbouring Republic of Guinea, who died in December 2008. By contrast, General Tagme was from the majority Tagma tribe, the dominant military caste in Guinea–Bissau. A history of mutual acrimony resulted in Vieria becoming the military's chief suspect in both an attempted assassination of Tagme in January 2009 and the successful attack on 1 March. The next day, a group of Tagme loyalists murdered Vieria; military spokesman Zamora Induta acknowledged that the president's murder was revenge for 'President Vieria's responsibility for the death of General Tagme'.

The tit-for-tat killings did not, however, herald a descent into anarchy or a formal military takeover. Indeed, the military, which faced pressure from ECOWAS, the AU and the international community, took pains to stress that this was not a military coup, and that they would respect a constitutional transition. National Assembly Speaker Raimundo Pereira took over as interim leader, as mandated by the constitution. In July 2009, fresh presidential elections were held; Malam Sanha, who had been defeated by Vieria in the June 2005 presidential run-off, emerged as the new president. Sanha was a veteran of Guinea–Bissau's anti-colonial wars, and a PAIGC insider. After months of relative stability, a fresh crisis erupted in April 2010 when the military arrested Prime Minister Carlos Gomes Jr, Territorial Administration Minister Luis Sanca, and Zamora Induta, the new army chief. Soldiers also seized Bubo Na Tcuto, former head of the navy, from UN offices in the capital Bissau. In a bizarre political twist, it was soon revealed that Induta was in fact one of the ringleaders of the mutiny. After negotiations, the principals were released and Induta later dismissed the event as an 'incident'. The uneasy juxtaposition of fledgling democracy and perennial military intervention looked to continue in Guinea–Bissau. The politics of fear and uncertainty has also proved toxic for the economy; Guinea–Bissau remained one of the world's poorest countries and had also become a major hub in the Latin America–West Africa–Europe drug trade. The military was reputedly heavily involved in the drug trade and this link was expected to continue to stifle development.

Republic of Guinea

The death of Guinea's long-serving head of state, President Lansana Conté, in December 2008 triggered a military takeover, with Captain Moussa Dadis Camara emerging as junta leader. The military intervention evoked little surprise locally or internationally; Conté had survived through military patronage. Guinea has a tradition of mutinies over pay, and each time, Conte had increased military pay and privileges to ensure his survival.

Immediately following Conté's death the junta established a 32-man National Council for Democracy and Development which named Camara as interim president. ECOWAS, the AU and the EU all denounced the takeover and implemented an arms embargo and targeted sanctions against Guinea. The council promised to hold elections in 2010, after a two-year transition, but a combination of internal rifts within the council, and regional and international isolation, made Camara's hold on power increasingly tenuous. In September 2009, pro-democracy activists protesting Camara's decision to contest the presidential elections were attacked by the military. Hundreds of civilians were killed, and there were scores of gang-rapes of women by Camara's forces. This led to a tightening of sanctions, and more isolation for the council. With Camara becoming more and more of a liability, it was clear that his days were numbered. In December 2009, a failed assassination attempt left him with serious head injuries and forced him to relinquish power. His successor was General Sekouba Conate. Conate proved to be more serious about containing military power and instituting a measure of constitutionalism than his predecessors. Some of the more extreme elements in the army and ruling council were quietly purged, and in May 2010 Conate enacted a new constitution which barred members of the council from standing for office. A total of 24 candidates were standing for the presidential elections in June–July 2010, and there were high expectations that the result would deliver a civilian head of state. Conate appointed a military task force to maintain order during the polls and invited ECOWAS to monitor the polls. Former Prime Minister Dalein Diallo won the first round, but failed to get a majority, and was to face veteran opposition leader Alpha Conde in a run-off in mid-July.

Côte d'Ivoire

What has been described as Côte d'Ivoire's 'perpetual transition' continued in 2009–10. Positive developments included the continued disarmament, demobilisation and reintegration of former combatants from the Forces Armées des Forces Nouvelles (FAFN) rebel group. The fragile political and military truce with FAFN continued to hold, as did the political coalition agreement between the two sides, but Côte d'Ivoire's electoral crisis continued to destabilise the country's politics and economy.

The 2007 Ouagadougou Peace Agreements were the blueprint for political reconciliation and peacebuilding in the country; in March of that year, Burkina Faso brokered a power-sharing deal between the government and the Forces Nouvelles (FN), in which FN leader Guillaume Soro became prime minister. The 2007 agreements helped solidify a post-2003 on-again, off-again peace process. They also held the promise of a sustainable political process and elections which could, in turn, revive the economy. But the electoral process proved to be a major problem; presidential and parliamentary polls due to be held in December 2008 were shelved because of security concerns and voter-registration irregularities. Presidential polls scheduled for 29 November 2009 were again postponed. In February 2010 there were violent nation-wide demonstrations as protesters took to the streets to express their anger at what they saw as a corrupt electoral process. President Laurent Gbagbo dissolved the government and the Federal Electoral Commission; this, in turn, sparked more unrest. In March 2010, Soro formed a new coalition government as President Blaise Campaore of Burkina Faso put pressure on Côte d'Ivoire to resolve its political problems swiftly.

2009 was also a year of ups and downs for peacebuilding and economic transformation. In May 2009, former FAFN rebels handed over ten northern districts to civilian administrators as part of the peacebuilding and civilianisation process. In June 2010, 600 FAFN insurgents disarmed and entered the demobilisation process. Since 2008, the UN has provided funding which entitles demobilised insurgents to CFA150,000 ($300) per month (for three months) and skills training. The UN has also been important in facilitating the establishment of an integrated national army. However, the uncertainty regarding the duration of the UN Operation in Cote D'Ivoire (UNOCI) and the associated French *Licorne* force increases the likelihood of violence. The February 2010 riots were at their most violent in the western parts of the country, where there was minimal or no UN presence.

April 2009 brought some good news on the economic front, as the IMF wrote off $3bn of the country's nearly $13bn national debt. But this was tempered in October 2009, when the UN renewed its ban on Côte d'Ivoire diamonds and on weapons sales to the country for another year. The government urged the lifting of sanctions, saying that revenues from diamonds would allow the government to alleviate the crisis in services – there are frequent power cuts and most towns, including the capital Abidjan, do not have reliable supplies of running water. The UN Security Council argued that lifting sanctions would be premature and could further stoke conflict in the country.

Sahel–Sahara: Towards a pan-regional security alliance

Transnational jihadism and terrorism have spurred a common approach to pan-regional security. Over the past several years, al-Qaeda in the Islamic Maghreb (AQIM) has established training camps in the desert regions near the Algerian, Malian and Mauritanian borders, and committed kidnappings, ambushes and suicide bombings across the region. The abduction of foreigners has become the most conspicuous insurgent tactic. In December 2008, two Canadian diplomats were seized. On 22 January 2009, AQIM kidnapped four European tourists in western Niger, near the Malian border, executing one of the hostages, Briton

Edwin Dyer, in the following May. More kidnappings followed. A major battle in August 2009 between Malian forces and AQIM insurgents near Timbuktu produced dozens of casualties.

The region faces additional security challenges. In early 2009, Malian forces launched offensives in Gao and Kidal provinces in northern Mali against Tuareg insurgents. Ethnicity, resource competition and political marginalisation lie at the heart of the Tuareg insurgency, which has become interwoven with insurgencies in Algeria and Niger. On 2 November 2009, a Boeing cargo plane believed to be used for shipping cocaine was found in Mali, leading UN drugs chief Antonio Maria Costa to warn that the Sahara desert was a new centre for drug smuggling across Africa. Evidence also surfaced that the Saharan drug trade was linked to transnational jihadism.

A strong response

In March and April 2010, Algiers hosted the first formal meeting of foreign ministers, intelligence and defence chiefs of Algeria, Libya, Burkina Faso, Mali, Chad and Mauritania for a major Sahel–Sahara security conference. Although there had been previous Sahel–Sahara meetings and agreements, the one in April was notable for the pervasive sense of urgency and the general willingness of participants to mend political fences in the pursuit of a strategy. If the agreements reached in Algiers are implemented, a pan-regional collective security and diplomatic architecture – and greater political unity – could become feasible.

Integrating security approaches was the key theme of the Algiers meetings, which featured separate ministerial, intelligence and defence conferences. The ministerial meeting in March 2010 called for greater attention to pan-regional anti-terrorism and anti-crime strategies. Regional agreement also emerged over cross-border cooperation, non-negotiation with terrorist groups and observation of UN Security Council Resolution 1904, which discourages the 'payment of ransoms to terrorist individuals, groups, foundations or entities'. The hope was that these accords would close an acrimonious chapter in regional affairs, which had begun when Mali released four AQIM militants in exchange for a French hostage in February 2010, to the dismay of Mauritania and Algeria. It was also agreed that long-standing regional terrorist extradition treaties would be implemented. At the intelligence and defence chiefs' meetings in April 2010, it was announced that a regional intelligence partnership would be formalised. In addition, a Joint Operations Centre would be established at Tamanrasset in southern Algeria to coordinate operations and information within the Sahel–Saharan region and build capacity to fight terrorism and organised crime. An initial force of 25,000 soldiers from across the region was proposed for the centre, and enhancing airlift and airborne surveillance capability in the region was an agreed priority.

The prospect of a regional security partnership sits well with the AU's vision of regional security as the linchpin for continental security. It does, however, pose a challenge for American involvement in the region. Washington has established military partnerships at bilateral and regional level through the Trans-Saharan Counterterrorism Partnership and the Pan-Sahel Initiative. These are implemented through the annual *Operation Flintlock* multinational counter-insurgency desert exercises. The May 2010 exercise involved the militaries of Mauritania, Burkina Faso, Senegal, Niger and Chad. But the military relationship with the West is delicate, as issues of sovereignty and hidden agendas can hinder African–Western cooperation. The Algiers summit thus could be read, to some extent, as a statement of intent to the West that North African states would seek greater security autonomy for the region. But while the establishment of a regional security initiative was a major development, it looked unlikely that a purely military solution would end jihadist insurgency. For this to happen, the region's states would also have to address long-standing socio-economic and political grievances.

The Horn of Africa: Making Up and Breaking Up

The Horn of Africa is the continent's most volatile region. As a new decade began, many of the Horn's traditional fault lines remained. Important elections in Sudan, Ethiopia and Somaliland in 2009–10 held the potential for greater stability, but also for increased civil discord. In a region of porous borders, close economic linkages and shared vulnerabilities, security continued to be the paramount concern.

Sudan: back to the future

The six-year interim period under the Sudanese Comprehensive Peace Agreement (CPA) – aimed at restoring unity between the north and south of the country – was set to expire in June 2011, but much of the accord had resisted implementation. President Omar al-Bashir continued to defy his January 2009 ICC indictment for crimes against humanity, and human-rights abuses by government forces, rebels and criminal actors, particularly in Darfur, continued. International groups also cited the government's invocation of a 2001 anti-terrorism law against human-rights campaigners and suspected rebels as cause for alarm.

In Darfur, the 2006 peace agreement has proved weak, and violence and humanitarian strife have continued. The expulsion of 13 international aid agencies from the region in March 2009, together with an increase in kidnapping, led to serious concerns that the food, health-care and clean-water needs of at least a million people would not be met. But although more than half of Darfur's 8m inhabitants remained aid-dependent, in 2010 the UN noted that the 'Sudanisation' of humanitarian work had not led to the expected catastrophe. Conflict in Darfur broke out intermittently over the year, with heavy aerial bombardment claiming civilian lives. After seven years of war, a framework peace agreement signed in February 2010 between the Khartoum government and one rebel group, the Justice and Equality Movement (JEM), in Doha was hailed as a major step forward. Still, the ceasefire was shaky and a stalemate in discussions meant that the March 2010 deadline for agreeing on a final deal was not met. JEM withdrew from negotiations, and skirmishes between government forces and rebel fighters resumed.

Elsewhere the LRA's depredations in the southern borderlands persisted. Sudan and Chad, however, enjoyed a rapprochement, as a January 2010 accord normalised relations and the border reopened in early April 2010. Nevertheless, ongoing violence in Darfur meant that tensions between the neighbours could not be completely eradicated. In the south, cattle-raiding escalated into serious inter-communal fighting in 2009, particularly in Jonglei state. An upsurge in violence between the Lou, Dinka and Nuer tribes was a symptom of enduring insecurity in the south, compounded by ineffective disarmament, poor civilian protection and a weakly mandated UN peacekeeping force. Evidence also suggested that in 2009 Khartoum revived the proxy warfare it had waged through organised militia attacks prior to the signing of the CPA.

An electoral milestone

2009 was dominated by preparations for Sudan's 2010 national elections. The latest census, conducted in 2008, contributed to soured relations between the main and primarily Muslim National Congress Party (NCP) and the largely Christian southern Sudanese People's Liberation Movement (SPLM) into mid-2009. The census results had assigned just 21% of the population to the south, reducing the number of allocated seats in the National Assembly as well as the south's proportion of national revenue. In February 2010, two months before planned elections, 40 additional seats were allocated to the south. Yet in the first week of April, a number of opposition parties declared an electoral boycott because of ongoing violence and insecurity in Darfur, failure to implement reform on the controversial national-security law, and concerns about voter registration and basic electoral fairness. Although the ballot papers had already been printed, some opposition candidates, including presidential contenders from both southern and northern parties, withdrew.

The general election on 11–15 April returned Bashir as national president and Salva Kiir to the southern presidency. Nationally, the votes confirmed expected patterns, with the NCP holding sway in the north and the SPLM in the south. Local and international observers reported widespread logistical failures and technical irregularities, including late or incomplete voting materials, faulty ballots, incorrect voter lists and inconsistent identification methods. Civil-society organisations reported abuses such as the detention of local observers and activists, intervention by security forces in polling states, intimidation and manipulation of voter preferences. Additional problems encountered during counting and tabulation included alleged vote rigging and ballot stuffing. There was limited voting in Darfur because of the security situation and the boycott. The National Elections Commission announced in May that voting in 33 constituencies would need to be repeated. The upshot was that Sudan's first multiparty elections in 24 years failed to be nationally inclusive.

While the international community was aware of the risks of post-ponement to the CPA and therefore had generally encouraged the elections, observers from the Carter Center and European Union ultimately gave the elections a cautious assessment – including a notable pronouncement by the former that the elections fell below 'international standards'. The Arab League, AU and China, on the other hand, were more tolerant of irregularities in consideration of the historical obstacles that had been surmounted. US Special Envoy Scott Gration noted that millions of people voted, dozens of parties contested the elections across the country and Sudan experienced a renewed sense of civic engagement and political invigoration.

Two Sudans?

In May 2010, an international consultative meeting in Addis Ababa affirmed the diplomatic partnership between the NCP and SPLM, and stressed the need to determine a political settlement for Darfur before the January 2011 referendum on self-determination for southern Sudan. As Sudan looked ahead to 2011, both the NCP and the SPLM were focusing on internal dynamics and trying to consolidate power in their respective domains. It was also incumbent on them, however, to undertake coordinated and organised dialogue on border demarcation, citizenship and oil revenue. In mid-2010, partition was looking increasingly likely. That eventuality could augur civil conflict if, as some believe, Khartoum refused to accept it, and in any case could alter the balance of power in the region.

Ethiopia: Zenawi's hold on power

Ethiopia is widely regarded as the Horn of Africa's powerhouse. Although more than two-thirds of its population are engaged in agriculture and the country has low purchasing-power parity, it has experienced year-on-year growth over the last four years, and the fifth largest inflation-adjusted GDP increase in the world. Ethiopia received over \$2bn in US aid in 2009, as well as significant help from the United Kingdom, EU and World Bank. This foreign assistance has been ploughed primarily into poverty alleviation and infrastructure projects. But widespread reforms that could improve the lot of ordinary Ethiopians have not been forthcoming. In 2009 Ethiopia had the lowest human-development index rating in the region except for Somalia, based on low life expectancy, exceptionally low adult literacy rates and lack of access to potable water.

Ethiopia's government was burdened by ongoing counter-insurgency campaigns against separatist movements in the Ogaden and Oromo regions, which chafed under the rule of Prime Minister Meles Zenawi, a member of the Tigray ethnic group (the Ogadeni and Oromia peoples' traditional rival). Enhanced cooperation between Sudan and Ethiopia on intelligence-sharing and border control sought to reduce cross-border infractions, but was unable to significantly reduce the insurgency threat. In addition, Ethiopia's ongoing border dispute with Eritrea continued to simmer despite the August 2009 Claims Commission ruling awarding both countries compensation. Ethiopia expected 25,000 more Somali refugees in 2010, in addition to an existing refugee population estimated by the World Food Programme to exceed 100,000 people.

Politics

On 23 May 2010, Ethiopia went to the polls. The ruling Ethiopian People's Revolutionary Democratic Front (EPRDF), in power for nearly two decades, won over 90% of parliamentary seats, and Zenawi retained power. The 2005 elections, in which the opposition made unprecedented gains, had ended in a bloody crackdown. Since then, the EPRDF coalition had consolidated power through intimidation and the imprisonment of senior opposition members, also winning over 90% of council seats in April 2008 local elections. A Human Rights Watch report in March 2010 highlighted fears that laws restricting charitable work, media freedom and, on the pretext of national security, individual rights (in particular, an oppressive anti-terrorism bill) had weakened democracy in the months leading up to the elections. The ruling party denied these charges, pointing instead to the joint code of conduct signed by four leading political parties in October 2009 that purported to provide a method of redress for any violations. In any case, the overwhelming EPRDF win in 2010 sidelined the issues raised by Ethiopia's opposition, such as enhanced regional autonomy to counteract the centralising tendencies of the governing party, land reform and privatisation, and opposition to Article 39 of the constitution, which permits self-determination for every people, group and nation in Ethiopia.

Somalia: a 'stable crisis'?

In 2010 Somalia celebrated the 50th anniversary of its independence, but the country perennially labelled the quintessential failed state continued to struggle. Half the population, an estimated 3.75m people, required food assistance, though the difficulty of operating without a functioning state infrastructure continued to hinder aid providers. The internal displacement of Somalis worsened, with thousands fleeing the capital as armed conflict between Islamist forces and those of the largely secular, internationally recognised Transitional Federal Government (TFG) escalated. Human-rights abuses by both government and Islamist forces were also widespread, and fighting often produced civilian casualties.

The writ of the five-year-old TFG remained restricted to a few streets of the capital Mogadishu, with little authority and almost no institutional presence elsewhere. Handicapped by a dearth of resources and authority, the administration made only marginal progress in establishing a sustainable, civil regime capable of providing security and administering justice. Unable to forge a rapprochement with the Islamist groups of south-central Somalia, the TFG had to resort to tenuous agreements with clan and militia leaders, and was dependent on the 5,600-strong African Union Mission in Somalia (AMISOM) force, composed substantially of Ugandan and Burundian soldiers, for its survival. AMISOM has been deployed mainly around Mogadishu's Presidential Palace, seaport and airport. Although AMISOM has secured strategic zones, it has mainly been on the defensive. This is in considerable part because its rules of engagement are reactive rather than pre-emptive; limited resources and funding are also a factor, although in 2009 both AFRICOM and the UN signalled their intention to increase logistical assistance.

In May 2010, an informal alliance among the TFG, AMISOM and Ahlu Sunna Wal Jama'a (ASWJ) – a moderate armed Sufi Muslim group formed in 2009 to oppose militant jihadism – fought running battles against the al-Qaeda-linked al-Shabaab, the extreme Islamist militia, and the slightly tamer and more nationalistic Hizbul Islam, for control of Mogadishu. Sheikh Ali Mohammed Hussein, the al-Shabaab 'governor' of Mogadishu, urged his forces to take the Presidential Palace, but AMISOM artillery repelled repeated assaults. Political turbulence within the TFG – particularly continued infighting between President Sheikh Sharif Ahmed and Prime Minister Omar Sharmarke – also crippled its internal coherence and political capacity.

Al-Shabaab and Islamist insurgency

The increase in foreign nationals trained in Afghanistan or Pakistan and members of the Somali diaspora in al-Shabaab's ranks heightened international fears that Somalia could become a haven for – or branch of – al-Qaeda in the Horn. Four alleged al-Shabaab members attempted a suicide attack on Holsworthy army base, near Sydney, Australia, in August 2009. In November, eight Somali-American men were charged in the United States with attending camps in Somalia and training with al-Shabaab. Having claimed its affiliation with al-Qaeda since 2007, al-Shabaab formally declared its allegiance to the group on 2 February 2010. Al-Shabaab's material support continued to come from the Middle East and from the Somali diaspora via *hawala* informal remittance systems. Yemen is host to both al-Qaeda in the Arabian Peninsula (AQAP), which was largely ousted from Saudi Arabia and absorbed al-Qaeda's Yemeni wing, and Somali refugees. Yemen is a probable source of and transit route for arms, money and personnel into Somalia, though as of mid-2010 there remained little evidence of collaboration between al-Shabaab and AQAP. Overall, however, it appeared likely that al-Shabaab and core al-Qaeda would grow closer, ideologically if not operationally.

Al-Shabaab's marriage of convenience with Hizbul Islam, the Islamist faction led by Sheikh Hassan Dahir Aweys (former head of the Islamic Courts Union, which controlled most of southern Somalia from June 2006 until the US-backed Ethiopian invasion and occupation in December 2006) suffered in 2009 when al-Shabaab expelled Hizbul Islam from the southern port of Kismayu in September after fierce fighting. Although the alliance was subsequently resuscitated, local opposition to al-Shabaab was becoming more substantial and organised. In 2009, ASWJ expelled al-Shabaab from Galguduud, in central Somalia, after the former had dominated the town for months. In March 2010, ASWJ reached a tentative agreement with the government to combine military efforts to defeat al-Shabaab. Thus, while al-Shabaab remained the main threat to stability into 2010, the shifting allegiances and deal-making typical in Somalia began to work to its disadvantage in 2010.

Accordingly, the threats of Somali jihadists to international security appeared to be tenuously contained. While the United States in particular will continue to watch Somalia carefully and to take direct counter-terrorist action on an opportunistic basis, it is likely to do so very selectively. The United States, UN, EU, regional multilateral organisations and regional powers are likely to continue to diplomatically support the TFG, as Hillary Clinton pledged during her August 2009 meeting with Sheikh Sharif in Kenya, and especially to endorse and support any of its efforts to defeat or co-opt al-Shabaab.

Persistent piracy

From mid-2009 to mid-2010, US Combined Task Force 151, EU *Operation Atalanta*, NATO's *Operation Ocean Shield*, and the operations of other navies as well as enhanced private security arrangements comprised a well-coordinated international effort to interdict piracy and capture and prosecute pirates in the Gulf of Aden and the Indian Ocean, using high-tech surveillance – in particular, US unmanned aerial vehicles, or drones – to gather intelligence. But even modern blue-water navies and sophisticated technology cannot identify and target all of the small pirate vessels operating in vast expanses of water. While the total number of ships seized fell for a while, the pirates became savvier and increased the number of attacks during late 2009. Hostage-taking continued throughout 2009 and into 2010, with millions of dollars paid out in ransom, though hostages were often kept for months at a time. In March 2010 alone, over 150 hostages were believed to be held captive.

Pirates continued to operate almost exclusively out of Puntland, the semi-autonomous region in the northeast and one of the poorest areas of Somalia. While the international anti-piracy mobilisation resulted in more effective enforcement, the financial rewards of piracy continued to outweigh its costs. On the ground, a weak legal regime, complicit local authorities and continuing ransom payments created a permissive environment. A promised crackdown by Puntland President Abdurrahman Mohammed Farole in April 2009 resulted in some arrests, but this had little deterrent effect on an enterprise that supports thousands of people on the mainland. The trial of pirates in Kenya and the United States generated media attention abroad, but had had little deterrent impact. In early 2010, Kenya announced that it would no longer prosecute pirates, citing lack of multinational support.

Persistent piracy on the Somali coast has led to fears of linkage between Islamist insurgents and pirates. Such an alliance could imperil the relative stability of Puntland and, potentially, Somaliland, the comparatively peaceful breakaway autonomous region in the northwest part of the Horn. In May 2010, Hizbul Islam captured Haradheere, one of the main pirate towns in Puntland, but it was unclear whether this indicated any meaningful coalescence of pirates and jihadists. In any event, Puntland's claim to being the model of the 'building block' approach to political reconciliation in Somalia was increasingly undercut by the entrenchment of the shadow pirate economy, and the prevalence of powerful clan-based interests that sidelined the formal institutions of the quasi-state.

Somaliland's frustration

Somaliland has long been touted as an exemplar of peace and stability for Somalia. Over the last two years, however, a stalled electoral process and subsequent political crisis threatened to throw it off course. Elections were rescheduled five times. Constitutional manipulation and systematic fraud marred electoral preparation efforts since April 2008, driving a wedge between the government and the opposition as well as dividing parties. Elections planned for March 2009 were pushed back to September, but political tensions escalated to dangerous levels, with mass street protests occurring during the summer. In August, opposition members disrupted parliament on several occasions, and civil war seemed to loom. A memorandum of understanding and electoral code, signed by Somaliland's political parties, averted a crisis on 25 September 2009. Presidential elections were held on 26 June 2010, but whether they would overcome political dysfunction remained uncertain. Opposition candidate Ahmed Mahmoud Silanyo defeated incumbent President Dahir Ruyale Kahin.

A number of armed groups – particularly the Northern Somali Unionist Movement (NSUM) – advocate a Greater Somaliland that would include parts of southern Somalia and western Ethiopia. In May 2010, Ethiopian forces skirmished with NSUM militias at Buhodle village on the Somaliland–Ethiopia border. While Ethiopia, which has strong trade links with Somaliland, has at times shown signs of recognising its sovereignty, Addis Ababa is wary of inferences that it seeks regional hegemony and of jeopardising a strong relationship with the TFG. The broader consensus is that politically recognising Somaliland and other self-declared Somali entities like Puntland could set a troublesome international precedent. A unitary state would square with the preferences of the UN, the United States and Europe, as well as the 'one Somalia' policy of neighbouring countries like Djibouti and Kenya, which regard a unified Somalia as the natural geopolitical balancer against Ethiopia and as less susceptible to destabilising mischief by Eritrea.

The African Union: Seeking to Match Ambitions

In February 2009, Libya's Muammar Gadhafi became chairman of the African Union in accordance with its rules for the regional rotation of the annual chairmanship. Gadhafi's populist rhetoric did not prove to be as divisive as some had feared, but the majority of AU leaders opposed his continued advocacy of a 'United States of Africa', and saw increased regional integration as the key to Africa's development. When Gadhafi attempted to extend his tenure as AU chair for another year at the January 2010 AU summit in Addis Ababa, delegates rebuffed him in favour of Malawian President Bingu wa Mutharika. But the AU's struggle to match its capabilities and authoritativeness with its high ambitions continued.

International law

The AU's relationship with the ICC has grown tense over the court's requests that Sudanese President Bashir be handed over for trial. At the February 2009 AU summit in Addis Ababa, Ethiopia expressed 'serious concern' about ICC Chief Prosecutor Luis Moreno-Ocampo's request for an arrest warrant. The AU Commission was tasked with convening a meeting of African ICC states to 'exchange views on the work of the ICC in relation to Africa' in Addis Ababa the following June. That meeting seemed to support the ICC, yielding recommendations on combating the non enforcement of international law and on the renewal of the AU's commitment to the ICC. In July 2009, however, the AU summit in Sirte, Libya, produced an apparent reversal of AU support for the ICC. Citing the failure of the UN Security Council to act upon an AU request to defer the ICC's case against the Sudanese president, the AU called for member states not to cooperate with the ICC with respect to the arrest of Bashir.

The Sirte decision was not unanimous, and the ICC debate has widened rifts between African civil-society groups and African governments. On 24 May 2010, 124 civil-society groups from 28 African countries released a declaration calling for African governments to improve accountability and to reduce impunity. The AU's two-week ICC Review Conference in Kampala in May–June 2010, which was marked by heated debate, resulted in an agreement on the definition of the crime of aggression. Delegates passed a resolution which criminalised 'the use of armed force by one state against another and carried out in contravention to the UN Charter. On this basis, individuals responsible for unlawful acts of war may be subject to prosecution before the [ICC].' There was also an agreement that the definition of war crimes should encompass acts committed in intra- as well as inter-state armed conflicts. In broad terms, the Kampala conference was a breakthrough for cross-cutting consensus on jurisdiction between the ICC, the AU and African civil society.

Increasing peacekeeping capacity

The AU has had to adapt its resources to the challenges of peace and stabilisation operations. Since 2002, the AU has deployed forces in Burundi (2003), Darfur (2007–) and Somalia (2007–). The AMISOM deployment in Somalia has proved to be a particularly protracted and costly urban-warfare effort. Joint AU–UN forces also remained deployed in Darfur, reflecting the broadening of the AU's transnational security partnerships. The AU–EU–UN African Peace Facility, for which €300m ($440m) was pledged for 2008–09, has been an important support organisation, particularly for the AMISOM operation. In October 2009, the Joint

Experts Group meeting in Addis Ababa agreed on a roadmap for security cooperation.

Through the ASF, the AU is fielding permanent regional rapid-deployment brigades with civilian as well as military capabilities to bolster AU capacity in peace and stabilisation operations. These include ECOWAS Brigade (West Africa), North African Brigade, Central African Brigade, Eastern African Brigade, and SADC Brigade (Southern Africa). Each regional brigade held exercises in 2009 in anticipation of their formal launch as Africa Standby Brigades, scheduled for late 2010. In addition, the Continental Early Warning System, also slated for a formal launch in 2010, was designed to facilitate preventive security efforts. In supporting international sanctions on Guinea and Eritrea, the AU also demonstrated a willingness to use economic coercion and an appreciation that it could be an effective and relatively economical governance and security tool.

Maritime security

The AU has tightened its focus on maritime security. The Sirte summit committed the organisation to formalising a continental agenda and roadmap for AU and regional-led maritime security in the naval and commercial domains. At the subsequent summit in Addis Ababa, AU heads of state endorsed the AU Maritime Transport Charter, the Maritime Transport Plan of Action and the Durban Resolution on Maritime Safety, Maritime Security and Protection of the Environment, the latter two of which were agreed at a ministerial conference in Durban in October 2009. US Africa Command (AFRICOM) – the United States' new regional combatant command, established in 2007 – has also endeavoured to bolster African maritime safety and security capabilities through its Africa Partnership Station. AFRICOM was due to host a maritime safety and security conference keyed to developing AU operational and institutional capacity at its headquarters in Stuttgart, Germany, in autumn 2010.

Chapter 8

South and Central Asia

The contrasts to be found in the region became more marked during the year to mid-2010. While India's economic powerhouse marched on, violence deepened in Pakistan and little progress seemed to be made against the insurgency in Afghanistan. Western leaders were increasingly looking for political solutions that would enable them to call time on the foreign combat presence in Afghanistan.

Pakistan: Facing Up to Insurgency

Pakistan saw continuing high levels of violence over the past year, but the country's troubled political system showed signs of returning to a more even keel.

Underlining the persistent threat from extremist insurgents, a record number of suicide bombings were carried out: there were 87 in 2009, compared with two in 2002. In a new effort to counter the home-grown insurgency, the Pakistani army launched operations on an unprecedented scale against insurgents in the Swat region and in South Waziristan, and recorded military successes. The United States extended its campaign of strikes from unmanned aircraft in Pakistan's Federally Administered Tribal Areas (FATA), but this served to heighten popular

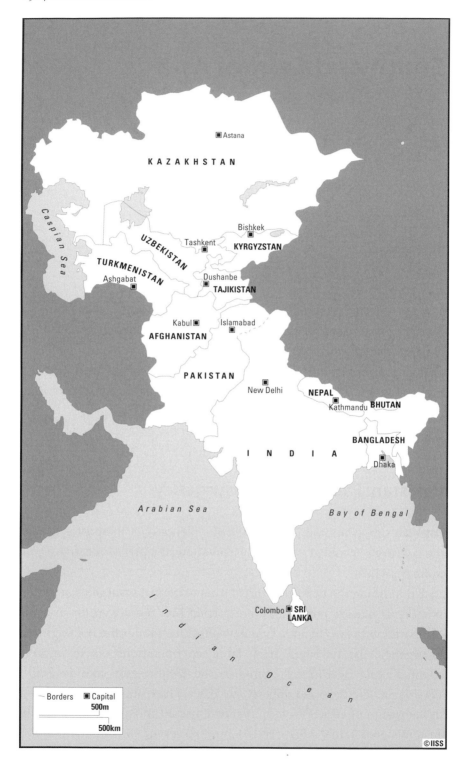

opposition. According to opinion polls, the level of distrust towards the United States exceeded that towards India and al-Qaeda, even though Washington's new level of attention towards Pakistan was accompanied by the promise of a significant package of civilian aid. Meanwhile, domestic political tension surrounding the unpopular President Asif Ali Zardari, husband of the late Benazir Bhutto, eased as wide-ranging presidential powers introduced by his predecessor, General Pervez Musharraf, were rescinded.

The government's approach to domestic insurgency saw the most significant developments. In recent years, faced with growing opposition and violence in the tribal regions in western Pakistan, the army and other authorities had entered into formal agreements with insurgent leaders under which the army would halt military operations, allow local leaders some freedom of action and restore confiscated weaponry, all in return for a pledge to keep the peace. These agreements all collapsed, most of them quite quickly, because the counterpart signatories had no intention of keeping their side of the bargain. The presence of the army, in which Punjabis predominate, was resented by the local Pashtun inhabitants. In such circumstances, surrounded by opposition, military operations were doomed to failure, as several humiliating incidents had proved all too clearly. The home-grown insurgent groups, known collectively as the Pakistani Taliban, which included sizeable criminal elements, capitalised on this situation. In directly threatening the state, they ultimately provoked a military clampdown.

Army acts against militants

The tide seemed to turn in July 2009. In February the government had capitulated to the local Pakistani Taliban leader in the Swat region and agreed, in the form of the Sharia Nizam-i-Adl Regulation, that sharia law should apply within the Malakand division, which comprises about one-third of North-West Frontier Province (in what is known as the 'settled area', as distinct from FATA). But the agreement collapsed spectacularly in April 2009. The Tehrik-e-Nifaz-e-Shariat-e-Mohammadi (TNSM), under the leadership of the veteran Sufi Mohammed and the operational command of his son-in-law Maulana Fazlullah, reverted to violence. Interpreting sharia in a manner quite at odds with local traditions, insurgents bombed girls' schools, closed markets and extended their operations further south to Buner, just 110km from the capital Islamabad. This behaviour, and especially a video recording of the beating of a teenage girl, appalled the hitherto sympathetic local people, who turned to the army for help. Estimates of the size of the ensuing military deployment varied between 30,000 and 54,000 troops, but by July, with the help of a week of air-strikes, the army had prevailed, killing or capturing some 7,000 opponents. About 2 million inhabitants were displaced during the fighting. Although most returned to their homes relatively swiftly, employment opportunities generated by craft industries and through tourism and pilgrimages to the formerly idyllic Swat Valley had evaporated.

The army then turned its attention to South Waziristan, the homeland of the Tehrik-e-Taliban Pakistan (TTP), whose leader Baitullah Mehsud was reportedly responsible for directing most of the suicide bombings which had proliferated since 2005. Baitullah was killed in August 2009, apparently in a US drone attack, and the army instituted a blockade supplemented by artillery and air-strikes against Taliban bases. Major military operations were launched in October against, the army claimed, some 10,000 Taliban and 1,500 foreign fighters led by Baitullah's successor, Hakimullah Mehsud. The Taliban, choosing not to engage in pitched battle, mostly melted away into other tribal regions. This may have been the army's intention in delaying their main offensive, thereby reducing the number of casualties and grounds for revenge. In November the UN High Commissioner for Refugees had registered some 275,000 refugees from South Waziristan in two neighbouring districts alone, but a great many more had fled the area without registering, seeking traditional Pashtun hospitality from relatives and others.

These operations were backed by parliament and Pakistan's political leadership. The Pakistani Taliban espoused Salafist objectives, sought the return of the Caliphate, challenged the writ of the constitution, and therefore presented a direct threat to the state itself. In this regard they were different from the Afghan Taliban, led by Mullah Mohammad Omar, who claimed to have no designs on Pakistan. In practice, however, conduct of the campaigns, organisation of assistance for refugees, and reconstruction (such as it was) were left to the army. No official civilian agency was capable of administering relief operations of such magnitude, as had been demonstrated after the earthquake in Kashmir in 2005, nor were mechanisms for civil–military coordination adequate to allow for civilian oversight and control. One of the consequences was to reinforce the power and prestige of Chief of Army Staff General Afshaq Parvez Kayani, whose cool and discreet effectiveness contrasted with the extrovert ebullience of his predecessor Musharraf.

If the inhabitants of Swat had welcomed the army's role in quelling the violence, however, their support for central government and its institutions was by no means unqualified. Displacement and material losses may have reinforced pre-existing distrust and resentment. Similarly, the army and federal institutions have never been welcome in the fiercely independent FATA. While the military operations in Swat and the South Waziristan tribal agency in FATA may have had a measure of success, the militants infiltrated into other FATA agencies, which required the army to engage more widely there also. By mid-2010 the army were engaged in four major operations: in Swat, Bajaur–Mohmand, Khyber–Kurram–Orakzai and South Waziristan. It was also increasingly engaged in North Waziristan, which became a haven for fleeing militants, and had therefore been drawn into all seven of FATA's agencies.

> "Inhabitants of Swat had welcomed the army's role in quelling the violence"

Pakistani official figures show that civilian and military deaths in 2009 resulting directly from insurgency amounted to at least 3,000, almost 50% more than in the previous year. However, according to other reputable monitors, if deaths from operational clashes are included, the number of fatalities rises to 10–12,000.

In retaliation against the army operations, militants stepped up attacks against soft targets inside Pakistan, including mosques and markets, as well as against facilities of the army and the Inter-Services Intelligence directorate (ISI), Pakistan's security agency, in Peshawar and Rawalpindi. In April 2010, the US consulate in Peshawar was attacked.

In addition, with the objective of forcing US-led coalition troops out of the region, indigenous Pakistani insurgent groups such as the TTP and TNSM forged deeper operational links with al-Qaeda, as well as with terrorist organisations such as Lashkar-e-Tayiba (LeT), Hizb-e-Islami led by Gulbuddin Hekmatyar, elements of the Afghan Taliban, and the Haqqani network, which is responsible for many attacks on US troops in southern and eastern Afghanistan. The insurgency also permeated other parts of Pakistan, especially southern Punjab, where the LeT and its parent organisation Jamaat-ud-Dawa were increasingly worrisome, and the violent and heavily populated southern city of Karachi. Whatever the distinctions of ideology among the various groups, the increased connections between them reduced grounds for hope that some could be peeled away from violence by accommodating grievances or offering financial inducements.

This situation led to serious tension in Pakistan's internal security policy. On the one hand, the declared official position was that the government made no distinction between groups that espouse violence within Pakistan and would vigorously deal with all of them; it was just a matter of sequencing, with the more directly threatening TTP and TNSM to be brought under control first. On the other hand, however, senior army officers emphasised privately that, notwithstanding recent arrests of some of its senior members, there could be no question of alienating the Afghan Taliban and that the American leadership was deluding itself if it thought otherwise. Kayani said in February 2010 that 'a peaceful and friendly Afghanistan can provide Pakistan a strategic depth'. He asked the United States and NATO to enunciate a clear strategy on Afghanistan. Implicit in his request was what other senior Pakistanis explain more explicitly privately: that Pakistan must wait and see precisely how the United States will execute the strategy towards Afghanistan and Pakistan that President Barack Obama announced in December 2009. Pakistan cannot afford to tie itself too closely to a US operation which might prove short lived.

Against that background, the arrest of Mullah Abdul Ghani Beradar Akhund, the Afghan Taliban's second-in-command, and others in February 2010 in a joint operation in Karachi by US and Pakistan intelligence personnel did not necessarily demonstrate that the Pakistanis were now prepared to eliminate the Afghan Taliban within Pakistan. But at least they now acknowledged, having repeatedly denied it in the past, the presence in Pakistan of the 'Quetta Shura' – that is, the top leadership of the Afghan Taliban. There was also reason to suspect that, by detaining Beradar, a member of the shura who was reportedly willing to explore Afghan President Hamid Karzai's overtures about reconciliation, the Pakistani army aimed to limit the scope for independent action between Karzai and the Taliban and reinsert itself in any negotiation for ending the Afghan war.

Violence in Pakistan was, however, by no means limited to Afghanistan-related issues or reactions to externally driven factors. The turmoil in the tribal regions allowed violent sectarian organisations such as the Sunni Lashkar-e-Jhangvi to establish operating bases there. Sectarian violence, also involving the Shia group Tehrik-e-Jafria, reached a high level by comparison with the previous year. Nor did violence abate in the south-western province of Baluchistan, where the army pitted itself against the Baluch Liberation Army and others amidst Pakistani accusations that the Afghan authorities were harbouring militant refugees.

Management of the country's counter-insurgency efforts was hampered throughout this period by inadequate coordination and consultation between military and civilian authorities. The chief of army staff stepped up his briefings to the parliament and the civilian leadership. But the Defence Committee of the Cabinet and the National Security Council (NSC), both of which in theory were intended to bring military and political issues together, were in practice almost totally neglected. The NSC, weakened by the sacking in January 2010 of National Security Adviser Mahmud Ali Durrani, was effectively wound up. Steps were taken to create a National Counter Terrorism Authority to coordinate the activities of the Intelligence Bureau (IB), the Federal Investigation Agency (FIA) and the ISI. But by mid-2010 this appeared to be little more than an extra administrative tier, which some regarded as best suited to administration and analysis rather than operational coordination.

Self-regarding politics

While the army and its intelligence subsidiary, the ISI, took the lead in dealing with internal security and policy towards Afghanistan, the country's political leaders continued to be caught up in their own disputes. The arena was dominated by controversy about Zardari. Dogged by concerns over corruption and other aspects of his murky past, and

further weakened by a series of political gaffes, he was deeply unpopular with the army, the general population and within his own Pakistan
People's Party (PPP). Rumours were rife throughout 2009 that Zardari
would imminently be ousted. But it was hard to see how this could come
about, short of something close to a coup with military backing, since
his election to the presidency had been generally regarded as fair and
regular; and the military were reluctant to be seen to intervene in politics yet again, following humiliations in the latter stages of Musharraf's
regime.

In November 2009, Zardari stepped down as chairman of the National
Command Authority and passed authority for Pakistan's nuclear arsenal
to Prime Minister Yousaf Raza Gilani. But such conciliatory moves were
insufficient to stem the tide against him. In December the Supreme Court
overturned the 2007 National Reconciliation Ordinance, which had provided immunity for Zardari and others against corruption charges. And
efforts to rescind Zardari's immunity arising from his position as president continued. In April 2010, Zardari finally agreed to implement his
earlier pledge that the 17th constitutional amendment, introduced by
Musharraf to give him extraordinary powers, should itself be amended.
After endorsement by both houses of parliament, the 18th amendment
passed into law on 21 April, transferring important powers from the
presidency to the prime minister and parliament. These included the
power to dissolve parliament and appoint military chiefs, judges or the
chief election commissioner. Zardari's position as president thus became
largely titular and the political crisis surrounding his role seemed largely
defused, although he retained importance in his capacity as leader of
the PPP.

In contrast to the unpopularity of Zardari and his immediate coterie,
former Prime Minister Nawaz Sharif, leader of the other main national
party, the Pakistan Muslim League-Nawaz (PML-N), retained a high
popularity rating in opinion polls. Punjab province, which contains
over 60% of Pakistan's population and where Nawaz's brother Shahbaz
is chief minister, is Nawaz's political heartland. Speculation continued
that Nawaz might force an early general election and, since constitutional changes now allowed him to have a third term, bid for the prime
ministership. But in view of the many challenges facing the country, he

may not have been in a hurry to assume such responsibility, at least until there was a greater prospect of stability.

IMF support

The political turmoil in 2007 and 2008 was accompanied by neglect of economic management. This and profligate expenditure had brought the economy close to collapse. A former Citibank executive, Shaukat Tarin, was appointed finance minister in 2008 and reinstated much-needed discipline, which underpinned a stabilisation effort supported by the International Monetary Fund (IMF). In July 2009 the IMF agreed to increase its original $7.6 billion loan to $11.3bn.The economy was further boosted by $8.8bn of remittances from Pakistani workers abroad, which eclipsed much-publicised pledges of $1.6bn made by foreign donors in Tokyo in April 2009, of which only $750m had been disbursed by year's end. Aid from Pakistan's traditional major donors, Saudi Arabia and China, was apparently held back by concerns about Zardari's leadership. GDP rose by only 2% in the 2008/09 financial year and was projected to rise by 2.5–3.5% in 2009/10, well below the levels needed as the country's 170m population grows by 2.7% a year. Chronic power outages, which affected industries and households alike, were constant reminders of the deficiencies of central planning and administration.

In December 2009 the National Finance Commission introduced a much-needed change to the distribution of the state's revenues to the provinces. Each province's share, which had formerly been allocated in proportion to its population, now took account also of poverty and inverse population density. As a result, Baluchistan's share increased while those of the others, especially the populous and relatively prosperous Punjab, decreased. Possible protest was assuaged by increasing the share of total national revenue allocated to the provinces at the expense of the federal government. These steps, together with a financial package for Baluchistan announced in November 2009, may also help ease the widespread resentment in that sparsely populated and deprived province.

Tarin, who had been a vocal critic of corruption, resigned suddenly in February 2010, apparently frustrated by a number of appointments which smacked of cronyism. He was replaced by Abdul Hafeez Shaikh, a former World Bank official who had been a minister under Musharraf.

Difficult relations with Washington

In 2009 it became clear that the United States was set to become a major donor of civil aid, having largely limited its financial contributions since 2001 to military-related contributions averaging about $1bn a year. This had done little for Pakistan's social development or for generating employment; and funds available for such needs had been further eroded by Pakistan's purchase from the United States of big-ticket military hardware which had little relevance to counter-insurgency or operations in the western sector. The Kerry–Lugar–Berman bill, which passed into law in October 2009 as the Enhanced Partnership with Pakistan Act, provided for $7.5bn in aid for civil development over a five-year period. In January 2010 the US State Department released an Afghanistan and Pakistan Regional Stabilization Strategy which provided broad details of how this might be spent. But in Pakistan the act provoked considerable opposition. Perceived as an attempt to 'control' Pakistan, the conditionalities attached to it revived the prospect of sanctions. It was seen as a continuation of the US tendency towards a transactional approach which took little account of the wishes and wider interests of the Pakistani people: Pakistanis would be paid to do US bidding and penalised if they did not come up to the mark. The army leadership portrayed it as an insult to the country's honour. While the funding was vitally needed, how Pakistan's weak institutions would be able to absorb it, and how they could provide the sort of transparency and accountability which the US Congress was likely to demand, was unclear.

The aid controversy underlined the problematic nature of relations with Washington. In August 2009 a poll conducted by Pew Research Center suggested that 64% of Pakistanis regarded the United States as an enemy while only 9% saw it as a partner. Obama's announcement on 1 December 2009 of a revised strategy towards Afghanistan and Pakistan closely associated the two countries. Although he pledged that the United States would 'remain a strong supporter of Pakistan's security and prosperity', many Pakistanis considered that, on the contrary, the United States had proved to be a fickle friend who had, both before and after 2001, damaged rather than supported both its security and its prosperity. And, despite Obama's pledge that 'our resolve is unwavering', his undertaking in the same speech to begin the transfer of US forces out of Afghanistan in July 2011 seemed to confirm the popular view that Pakistan would be left to pick up the pieces after an American withdrawal.

In this context, Pakistani attitudes towards the Afghan Taliban assumed particular significance. Obama was highly critical of Taliban leaders in view of their linkages with al-Qaeda. Pakistan, by contrast, had a strong interest in both maintaining contact and not alienating them. Uncertainty about the prospect of US withdrawal and concern that Afghanistan would become a battleground for proxy wars convinced the Pakistanis that they should wait and see, and not be drawn precipitously into American-led policies which might soon be changed. Meanwhile, the arrest or elimination – to a great extent by US drone attacks – of some of the Afghan Taliban leadership seemed sufficient to maintain the appearance of a willingness to crack down on the sources of violence, while blurring the distinction made between the various groupings. Multiple visits to Pakistan by top US military leaders engendered a deeper understanding of Pakistan's constraints and complexities. The view developed among the US leadership that nothing was to be gained from the previous tendency towards bitter public recrimination. Progress had to be made as a result of patient dialogue and cooperation, with any complaints to be uttered in private. Kayani played a leading role throughout the process of dialogue, and in March 2010 a US–Pakistan Strategic Dialogue in Washington between Foreign Minister Mahmoud Qureshi and US Secretary of State Hillary Clinton was accompanied by pledges to strengthen strategic ties, to establish a multi-year security-assistance package and to resolve differences over the Pakistani insistence that it was owed $2bn in compensation for military support for Afghanistan-related activity. As part of the continuing military cooperation, Pakistan acquired significant new counter-insurgency capabilities, including helicopters and night-vision equipment. Pakistani military commanders privately acknowledged the effectiveness of the US drone attacks in killing al-Qaeda and other terrorist leaders, despite what they termed the strategic disadvantage of public resentment of violations of Pakistani sovereignty.

There remained, nevertheless, a significant and very public imbalance in US–Pakistan cooperation. While US military assistance was gathering momentum and proving increasingly productive at the tactical level, it was doing nothing to reduce the public's animosity against the United States or a possible 'Talibanisation' of parts of the population. Civilian developmental assistance, however, which could help offset such toxic tendencies by boosting employment, remained frozen by the difficulties of devising, administering and assessing development programmes and, above all, by the absence of results visible to a sceptical population. These obstacles were real enough in relatively peaceful parts of Pakistan, and all the more formidable in those areas where visible progress was most needed, in the turbulent tribal regions of the north and west.

For its part, US willingness to persist in its efforts to allocate, disburse and replenish its assistance to Pakistan might also have been coloured by US perceptions of Pakistan's real intentions and the adequacy of its actions. The arrest in May 2010 of Faisal Shahzad, a Pakistani-born US citizen who sought to detonate a car bomb in New York City, renewed American concern about the global nature of the threats emanating from Pakistan. Shahzad had lived in the United States for some ten years, but had reportedly visited Pakistan frequently. Later, it was reported that a Pakistani Army major had been arrested over suspected links with Shahzad, who was also alleged to have links with the Pakistani Taliban. Shahzad pleaded guilty to all charges.

India: Economic Progress, Regional Tensions

The first year of the second Manmohan Singh government saw a rapid recovery of economic momentum, the first steps towards renewed engagement with Pakistan, heightened conflict with domestic Maoist insurgents, and efforts to manage new tensions with China.

Politically, the ruling coalition's 'inclusive development' agenda took the form of a draft food-security programme that would give heavily subsidised food grain to the 37% of the population officially deemed to be poor. A new law on the right to education made schooling free and compulsory for all children up to the age of 14 (the literacy rate is currently 65%). Then, in May, the government attempted to introduce caste-based counting in the 2011 census, for the first time since the census of 1931. This was set to introduce a new dynamic to the arithmetic of caste-based politics, since many educational posts and government jobs are reserved for the underprivileged castes, whose relative numbers had been little more than guesswork for many years. The coalition was unable to reach consensus on the issue, and it was referred to a Group of Ministers in June.

On the economic front, surveys showed that business confidence in summer 2010 was at a new peak, reflecting a sharp upswing in economic activity in the early months of the calendar year. The stock market was up 40% in the year to May 2010, buoyed by a surge in corporate profits (up 40% in the March quarter on a year earlier), export growth of over 36% in April, and industrial output growth in the January–March quarter of 15% on a year earlier. GDP growth for the financial year that ended in March 2010 was 7.4%, and was projected to be 8.5% for 2010/11, encouraging the finance minister to propose a budget with a lower fiscal deficit and lower taxes on personal incomes. Inflation remained a worry, with consumer (and especially food) prices 16% higher than a year earlier.

In parliament, the government was frustrated in its bid to get legislative approval for a new law limiting liability in the event of civil nuclear disasters, seen as a requirement for attracting private foreign investment in nuclear power generating stations, one of the anticipated benefits of the 2008 civil nuclear agreement with the United States. The bill was introduced on the last day of the budget session in May, amidst an opposition walkout in protest, and was to be referred to committee. Another important bill, reserving for women a third of seats in the Lok Sabha (the lower house of parliament), made it through the upper house but was not presented in the lower house for want of majority support, and remained in limbo.

The general view at the end of the first year of the second United Progressive Alliance (UPA) government was that it should and could have done more to fight inflation, to open up the economy to foreign investment (in retail trade, insurance and media), to allow free pricing of petroleum products (cutting the large government subsidy), and to undertake financial reform. The government seemed at times to lack cohesiveness, as ministers spoke out of turn, while coalition partners frequently ploughed their own furrow. A junior minister had to resign following his involvement in some questionable cricket dealings, and there was speculation that the communications minister might be moved over the arbitrary manner in which he gave out telecoms licences. Even more seriously, questions were beginning to be asked about whether the government's strategy to tackle Maoist insurgents was working.

Maoist violence

The Maoist insurgency in central-eastern India took centre stage as the principal internal security problem over the last year. The high point came when government forces drove the Maoists out of Lalgarh, an area in West Bengal's West Midnapore district, which the insurgents had controlled for eight months. In all, the Maoist insurgency claimed some 800 lives across the country in 2009.

Singh has called the insurgency the country's 'gravest internal security threat', and it has been so for some time. During the first Singh government (2004–09), an ineffective home minister allowed the Maoists to spread from fewer than 40 to 76 of India's 626 districts; by mid-2010 there was at least some Maoist presence in nearly 200 districts. Maoists from different states came together under a common umbrella in 2004. They have gained purchase in the poorest districts, populated mostly by tribal people whom development has bypassed. The areas are typically forested, with hilly terrain, and therefore difficult to access. It has not helped that state police forces are usually poorly trained and not very motivated. The dilemma for the government has been to tackle the Maoists without alienating the broader population from which they draw their recruits, and to bring education, health care and jobs to remote areas to cut the ground from under the insurgents.

Besides Lalgarh, the biggest flashpoint was the Dantewada region of Chhattisgarh state, where 76 men of the Central Reserve Police Force (CRPF) were gunned down in a forest in a dawn attack by Maoists in April. This was the biggest ever toll on Indian security forces in a single attack, and sent the country into a state of shock. Home Minister P. Chidambaram offered his resignation, but was asked to continue in office. But in May the Maoists blew up a bus carrying civilians and policemen heading for Dantewada, killing at least 30, and a splinter group blew up a railway track in West Bengal, causing a train crash that killed at least 100. By early June, the problem had assumed dimensions which prompted the government to reconsider bringing in the armed forces to supplement central and state police forces. Chidambaram had acted with purpose after moving from the finance ministry in the wake of the 2008 attack on Mumbai. He focused on improving intelligence coordination (seen as having failed in the run-up to the Mumbai attack), better cooperation between state and national governments and between states, and building capacity to deal with the insurgents. He was, however, criticised for treating the Maoist issue as a pure security problem, saying repeatedly that development could take place only after government control had been re-established in Maoist-dominated areas. Others, including Singh, put things differently. The prime minister emphasised the importance of winning hearts and minds, recognising that the Maoist ranks were filled by marginalised people who had enjoyed none of the benefits of rapid economic growth. Facing criticism in and outside parliament, Chidambaram himself appeared to shift emphasis after the Dantewada fiasco, which had been, according to an inquiry report, the consequence of a botched operation by the CRPF (among other things, a radio set had fallen into the hands of the Maoists, who used it to track what the CRPF unit was doing so as to lay an ambush).

> "The Maoist ranks were filled by people who had enjoyed none of the benefits of growth"

Chidambaram's task was made difficult by the fact that mainstream political parties were not above doing deals with the Maoists, especially at election time. The Congress Party in Andhra Pradesh was widely seen to have been soft on Maoists after coming to power in the state in 2004, only to get tough later and force most of the insurgents to flee to neighbouring states such as Chhattisgarh. More recently, the Trinamool Congress in West Bengal was accused of being soft on the Maoists, who had taken on the state's ruling Left Front, which Trinamool hoped to unseat in state elections due in 2011. A similar suspicion was aired about Shibu Soren, chief minister of Jharkhand state, who made some soft statements about the Maoists immediately after taking office in December 2009. While all these allegations were denied, they were freely bandied about by rival political parties.

Talks with Pakistan

Relations between India and Pakistan remained clouded throughout 2009 by reactions to the terrorist attacks in Mumbai in November 2008. By February 2010 they had stabilised sufficiently to allow a meeting between the two foreign secretaries (top officials of the respective foreign ministries). This published no conclusions and fell short of a resumption of the stalled Composite Dialogue which, when established in 2004, envisaged discussion of all outstanding issues including Kashmir. But in late April the two prime ministers met in the course of a wider regional meeting and agreed that the dialogue should be resumed and that the foreign secretaries should meet again.

Singh, however, told Indian officials that the diplomatic stand-off that set in after the Mumbai attack was not sustainable. He believed Pakistan was in trouble and needed India's help, but the general political mood in India favoured a tougher line with Islamabad. Singh had gone out on a political limb to clinch the Indo-US civilian nuclear agreement of 2008, and seemed willing to do so again on Pakistan. Pakistani leaders seemed to recognise this, but were unable or unwilling to deliver the minimum that India expected on the terrorism issue to create the right environment for serious talks. For all that, the movement was in the direction of more talks and, before too long, some real engagement.

Following the 2008 Mumbai assault there were no fresh jihadi attacks (despite recurring warnings), other than a relatively minor strike at a bakery in Pune frequented by foreigners. Ajmal Amir Kasab, the Pakistani terrorist captured during in the Mumbai attack, was found guilty in May 2010 on five counts, including murder and waging war against the state, and was sentenced to death, although he had the right to appeal.

The Kashmir valley remained relatively quiet, though there were occasional militant strikes, street protests over excesses by security forces, and an attack by militants on the popular new railway line intended eventually to connect Jammu and Kashmir's summer capital of Srinagar to the winter capital Jammu and to the national rail network.

The ceasefire along the Line of Control (LoC) between Indian- and Pakistan-administered Kashmir, which took effect in November 2003, continued to hold, though there were occasional reports that Pakistan was organising increased infiltration of militants into the Indian side, and some isolated incidents of firing across the LoC. In late 2009, the Indian army responded to the easier security situation and withdrew about 35,000 troops from the state, but stopped further withdrawals after seeing increased infiltration across the LoC. The lower Indian army profile helped Pakistan focus its own forces near its western border with Afghanistan, to deal with the challenge from militant Islamist groups.

There was significant improvement in bilateral ties between India and Bangladesh, especially after a visit to New Delhi by Bangladeshi Prime Minister Sheikh Hasina, in January. Indian officials said the visit marked the start of a new chapter. Several agreements were signed, including one on extradition and another on transit rights for Bangladesh to Nepal across Indian territory. The main gain for India was on the security front. In December, Bangladesh sent Arabinda Rajkhowa, chairman of the outlawed United Liberation Front of Assam, the outfit's deputy commander-in-chief Raju Baruah and his senior aides back to India, where they were taken into custody. In early May, Dhaka also handed over Ranjan Daimary, chief of the National Democratic Front of Bodoland, who had been hiding for years in Bangladesh. Through these actions, Dhaka made it clear that it would not provide safe harbour for Indian militants. The next major issue on the India–Bangladesh agenda looked to be the use of Bangladeshi ports for goods to transit to India's landlocked northeastern states.

Tensions over water

The new hot-button issue between India and Pakistan was not Kashmir but water. Pakistan accused India of violating the Indus Basin Water Treaty as a result of upstream activity which, Islamabad claimed, reduced the flow into Pakistan-administered Kashmir. The 1960 treaty, brokered by the World Bank, divided the waters of the Indus and its five tributaries that flow from India into Pakistan by allocating the three western rivers (Indus, Chenab and Jhelum) to Pakistan and the relatively minor share from the eastern rivers (Ravi, Beas and Sutlej) to India. The treaty has worked well for half a century, although work on several navigation and hydroelectric projects has been held up for years or decades by formal disputes under the treaty's resolution and arbitration mechanisms. The Pakistani media regularly accuse India of using water that belongs to Pakistan, and the issue is politically sensitive in Pakistan's agricultural regions in Punjab.

Pakistanis charge that India's upstream storage and discharge decisions disrupt the downstream flow. Indian officials argue that the country's record is clean, pointing out that India has not even used the water from the three eastern rivers, which continue to flow unimpeded into Pakistan. The real problem, they have said, is profligate use of water by Pakistan. This was acknowledged in April 2010 by Pakistani Foreign Minister Mahmoud Qureshi, who said that one-third of the water that flows into Pakistan goes to waste. The issue has concentrated minds in Pakistan over fears of a long-term decline in water flow, at least in part due to deforestation upstream, something not provided for in the Indus treaty. There have been calls on the Pakistani side for abrogating the treaty on such grounds, but as it gives Pakistan the bulk of the Indus waters, this could actually lead to a greater reduction in available water. On the other hand, under the right political circumstances, upstream reforestation could be an effective arena for cooperative action.

Water has also in the past dominated relations between India and Bangladesh (which, like Pakistan, lies downstream), as well as between India and upstream Nepal. More recently, it has become a source of tension between India and China, after India raised the issue of dams in Tibet on the Tsangpo river, which becomes the Brahmaputra in India and the Jamuma in Bangladesh. Beijing initially denied any dams were to be built, but admitted in April 2010 that a dam then under construction was the first of a planned five. Although all five were to be run-of-the-river (that is, they were not planned to involve diversion or seasonal storage of water and thus would not reduce downstream flow), India feared that an attempt might eventually be made to divert Tsangpo water to irrigate China's parched northwest, which would negatively affect the river's hydroelectric potential in India's Arunachal Pradesh, an area disputed with China. There is no bilateral water agreement between the two countries; although it did inform India about its plans, China asserted it was not obliged to do so.

Nepalese dissatisfaction over past river cooperation projects with India has hampered joint exploitation of common Himalayan rivers such as the Sharda, Saptakosi and Sun Kosi – all tributaries of the Ganges – for hydropower and flood control. In contrast, India and Bhutan have worked well together to develop hydroelectric projects at Tala and Chukha in Bhutan. The power generated has been bought mostly by India (about 1,400MW), and provides an important source of revenue for Bhutan. Another four projects were agreed over the last year, bringing the power pacts between the two countries to 5,000MW.

Wariness towards China

India's relations with China continued to be marked by wariness with regard to Chinese plans and intentions in South Asia as well as issues related to their disputed border. In 2009, China protested strongly over Singh's visit to Arunachal Pradesh to campaign in state elections, and over the visit by the Dalai Lama to his birthplace in Tawang in the disputed state. China also signalled that it may supply two nuclear power reactors to Pakistan, which many saw as a violation of the letter or spirit of Nuclear Suppliers Group (NSG) rules. China argued the reactors were allowed under grandfather provisions when they joined the NSG in 2004. Observers interpreted this as an indication of Beijing's unhappiness over the Indo-US civilian nuclear agreement, which, however, China had not blocked in the NSG. (Russian Prime Minister Vladimir Putin signed a deal with India for 16 nuclear plants when he visited New Delhi in March 2010, but this was within the rules, as the NSG had put India on a different footing in 2008.)

India, for its part, moved to block imports of Chinese manufactured goods, especially telecoms equipment, for fear that such equipment could help China tap into India's phone networks, as it had previously targetted sensitive government computer networks. A large order placed with a Chinese firm by the state-owned Bharat Sanchar Nigam was cancelled, and private telecoms operators were told that the government would have to vet their equipment-purchase decisions. There was also pressure to limit the Chinese role in India's power programme after Chinese companies began to win the bulk of new orders for thermal power equipment, shutting out domestic suppliers. Chinese companies had been using business visas (in lieu of employment visas) to bring in thousands of Chinese workers to work build plants; these rules were also tightened.

China did not complain officially about these moves, but Chinese companies signalled that they would try to get around import restrictions by setting up production facilities in India. But regulations were being tightened in this area; foreign investment applications now required specific security clearances, especially in sectors deemed sensitive.

An application by India to the Asian Development Bank (ADB) in 2009 for a $2.9bn development loan to part-finance projects that included $60m for flood management, irrigation control and sanitation in Arunachal Pradesh provoked a diplomatic row with Beijing. China, which holds one of the 12 seats on the ADB board, objected that the bank should not fund projects in disputed territory. The loan was eventually approved, without the Arunachal Pradesh component, and India's 2010 ADB loan application did not include finance for any projects in the territory.

India and China also showed, however, that they can work together, particularly at the climate summit in Copenhagen in December 2009. The two prime ministers have established a pattern of meeting every year, and they have also met at periodic summits of the BRIC (Brazil, Russia, India, China) countries, held in Russia in June 2009 and Brazil in April 2010, with the next scheduled for Beijing in 2011. In 2008/09 China surpassed the United States as India's largest trading partner and enjoys a large trade surplus with its neighbour.

Worries over US moves

The regional security situation was influenced heavily by the US-led war in Afghanistan and its overflow into Pakistan's tribal areas. India watched the Obama administration's moves to deal with what the United States sees as 'moderate Taliban' elements with growing concern. It was also worried by Washington's moves in 2010 to embrace Islamabad for the first time as a strategic dialogue partner, increase economic and military aid to Pakistan, and put pressure on India to lower its profile in Afghanistan. Pakistan asked in early 2010 for its own equivalent of the US–India civil nuclear agreement; the Americans refused because of Pakistan's poor record on nuclear non-proliferation, but some comments from Washington seemed not to rule out such an agreement in future.

New Delhi saw risks to its own interests in these moves. It also saw America's embrace of Pakistan as demonstrating a lack of US commitment to pressure Pakistan to dismantle its jihadi networks focusing on India, despite Hillary Clinton's tough comments after the failed bomb attack in New York in May 2010.

India was also incensed by a sentence in the statement issued after Obama's visit to Beijing in late 2009, which gave China a role in monitoring events in South Asia. Both the United States and China subsequently discounted the statement as non-significant, but India remained wary. There was a noticeable lowering of expectations in New Delhi regarding India–US ties, after the warmth of the later Clinton years and during the George W. Bush administration, driven by a sense that India did not figure on Obama's list of priority countries. Nevertheless, Singh was hosted at Obama's first state banquet in November 2009, and Obama was expected to visit India in November 2010 – an occasion that was expected to give a fillip to bilateral ties, perhaps in non-security-related areas such as education and agricultural research.

Amidst persistent regional tensions, India's arms-procurement programme remained active. With competitive bids from global defence manufacturers subject to procedural bottlenecks that typically delay purchase decisions for years or decades, however, many of the new orders were government-to-government deals, including the purchase of 145 howitzers from the United States in early 2010. The protracted dispute over the price of an aircraft carrier being refitted by the Russians, for delivery in 2012, was finally settled in March 2010 at $2.35bn. In April, the navy commissioned its first stealth frigate, to be built by Mazagon Dock Ltd, while the army was getting ready to place orders for indigenously built tanks. The most significant development, however, was the launch in July 2009 of an Indian-built 6,000-tonne nuclear-powered submarine, which will be commissioned after trials that could last three or four years. In spite of these moves, defence spending in relation to GDP remained modest at 2.1%, of which less than half was for buying hardware.

Central Asia: Turmoil in Kyrgyzstan

The key event in Central Asia in the year to mid-2010 was the ousting of Kyrgyzstan's President Kurmanbek Bakiyev, five years after he had seized power in the so-called Tulip Revolution. His regime's pervasive corruption and authoritarianism were the main factors behind the April 2010 unrest in Bishkek, in which 85 people were killed in clashes with the armed forces. Bakiyev fled the country and was replaced pending new elections by Roza Otunbayeva, one of the leaders of the 2005 revolution.

Bakiyev's removal served as a reminder of the absence of real democracy in the Central Asian states (Kazakhstan, Kyrgyzstan, Tajikistan, Turkmenistan and Uzbekistan), the majority of which are ruled by presidents who have concentrated power in their hands and are unwilling to leave their posts in the foreseeable future. The Kazakh and Uzbek leaders have ruled since the Soviet period and the Tajik president came to power in 1994. Increasing authoritarianism in Central Asia has been largely overlooked in the West due to the region's geo-strategic location – a factor that reasserted itself over the past year as the United States initiated the Northern Distribution Network (NDN) to transport supplies to Afghanistan via ground and air routes through the North Caucasus and Central Asia. An early act of the provisional government in Kyrgyzstan was to extend the American lease on the Manas air base. Bakiyev had announced in February 2009 that this would be terminated following the promise of large investments by Russia, but later agreed to allow the US to stay in return for tripled annual rent of $60m.

Bakiyev had come to power as a result of mass demonstrations that caused his highly unpopular predecessor, Askar Akaiev, to flee the country. His arrival raised hopes in Kyrgyzstan that he would combat the corruption and political nepotism that had marred the Akaiev regime. He quickly showed a desire, however, to centralise political control, and allowed corruption to flourish. His regime was characterised by the pervasive involvement of military officials in political affairs – a shift from the Soviet era in which the military was strong yet submissive to political control. Bakiyev's brother Zhanysh, as head of the National Security Service, began to assert greater independence. The increasing involvement of the military was reflected in the decision to use force against protesters in the April unrest.

Otunbayeva, a strong strategic thinker who had once been described by Akaiev as a 'locomotive' of the opposition movement, again played an important role, first in mobilising crowds to protest against Bakiyev and then in forming a provisional government. Once again, hopes were raised in Kyrgyzstan about greater democracy: the three major political parties represented in the provisional government – Social Democratic Party, Ata-Meken and Ata-Jurt –reached a consensus on building a democracy in which the power of any one leader would be limited. A new draft constitution was being developed with the participation of international experts. Parliamentary elections were due to take place in October 2010, with the number of parliamentary seats likely to be increased and election rules to be changed to minimise vote rigging.

> **The fighting spread beyond Osh to other parts of the south**

In mid-June, ethnic tensions between Kyrgyz and Uzbeks erupted into violence and looting in the southern city of Osh. The interim government, which had struggled to establish control in Bakiyev's power base in the south, blamed forces loyal to the former president, drug traffickers and Islamist militants from Uzbekistan for fomenting the violence. The fighting appeared to have been initially sparked by a fight between two youth gangs, but quickly spread and intensified. There were reports that rogue security forces participated in or permitted attacks on Uzbeks. The fighting spread beyond Osh to other parts of the south, including Bakiyev's home town of Jalalabad; after two weeks it had left at least 200, and perhaps as many as 2,000, dead, nearly 2,000 buildings destroyed and some 400,000 people displaced, many across the border to Uzbekistan. Otunbayeva called first on Russia and then on the Russia-chaired Collective Security Treaty Organisation (CSTO) to send peacekeeping troops or police. When these requests were declined, she appealed to the Organisation for Security and Cooperation in Europe (OSCE) to provide a police-training mission; this was still under consideration as of the end of June.

Kyrgyzstan was the first example of cooperation between the big powers in Central Asia, rather than the geopolitical competition which had previously been the norm. Russia played a key role; it was the first to recognise the new interim government and offered $20m in urgent economic assistance. A general decision to support the ouster of the Bakiyev regime was taken in Washington on the fringes of the nuclear security summit, with the involvement of Presidents Dmitry Medvedev and Barack Obama, as well as Kazakhstan's President Nursultan Nazarbayev. Russia and China also coordinated their responses bilaterally and through the framework of the Shanghai Cooperation Organisation (SCO). Both the European Union and the United Nations sent special representatives, who helped stabilise the situation by providing economic aid and assisting in the development of a more stable political system. This cooperation helped to contain the regional and international implications of the Kyrgyzstan crisis.

Kazakhstan, as the chair of the OSCE for 2010, was closely involved in persuading Bakiyev to leave Kyrgyzstan in order to prevent further clashes between the provisional government and his supporters. Kazakhstan provided a military aircraft to transport Bakiyev from Jalalabad to Kazakhstan (he later found refuge in Belarus). Nazarbayev had long sought the OSCE chair in order to enhance Kazakhstan's international image, and in 2010 it became the first post-Soviet state to chair the organisation. Human-rights activists, however, criticised the decision to offer Kazakhstan the chair, given its poor record on democracy and human rights. Supporters within the OSCE hoped that the chairmanship would compel Kazakhstan to improve its domestic situation to avoid embarrassment while in the international spotlight. Kazakh NGOs, however, continued to warn of a worsening human-rights situation, including government moves to draft a law on religious practices, regulate Internet-based mass-media outlets, and restrict freedom of assembly.

Tajikistan's President Emomali Rakhmon, who had altered the constitution by referendum in 2005 so that he could remain in power until 2020, continued to seek to bolster public support though construction of the planned 3,600MW Rogun Dam – at 350m tall, it would be the highest in the world, surpassing China's Three Gorges Dam. Rakhmon presented it as a potential breakthrough in national development. However, the project's future remained unclear due to the government's ineffective and corrupt management, the poor economy and the projected $2bn cost. International investors, including development organisations, proved reluctant to provide finance. The government therefore sought domestic finance, asking each adult to buy at least $690 worth of specially issued stock – an amount greater than most citizens' annual income.

Central Asian states have focused on strengthening military capacity to protect incumbent regimes, often at the expense of regional cooperation. Inter-state trust thus remained low, especially between Uzbekistan, Kyrgyzstan and Tajikistan. However, military cooperation has increased under the umbrellas of the China-dominated SCO and the Russia-led CSTO. Both bodies have become important channels for maintaining national and regional security.

Afghanistan: Flawed Election, New Strategy, Doubtful Prospects

The year to mid-2010 saw major new political and military developments in Afghanistan and a strategic re-think on the part of the United States. The appointment in June 2009 of US Army General Stanley McChrystal as commander of the NATO-led International Security Assistance Force (ISAF) heralded a new military approach, with a greater emphasis on counter-insurgency techniques intended to minimise the loss of civilian lives. Politically, it was hoped that presidential elections in August would invigorate Afghanistan's democracy by offering the people a clear choice and the option of change. But blatant manipulation of the election, protests about which did not prevent Hamid Karzai's inauguration for a second term in November, cast serious doubts over the legitimacy of his presidency and government.

Following McChrystal's appointment, divisions emerged among Obama's advisers over how best to pursue US interests in Afghanistan. McChrystal requested the dispatch of 40,000 additional troops in order to execute his new strategy. After an intensive review, Obama made a major new policy announcement in December. He declared that, though not lost, Afghanistan had for several years moved backwards and that the status quo was not sustainable. A further 30,000 US troops would be sent to the country. He also announced, however, that after 18 months 'our troops will begin to come home'. He reiterated that the main US target remained al-Qaeda in Afghanistan and Pakistan and affirmed that success in Afghanistan was 'inextricably linked to our partnership with Pakistan'.

This policy speech influenced much of the activity that followed. At a conference in London in January 2010, many coalition partners, whose support for the Afghanistan campaign was palpably waning, advocated a process of reconciliation and reintegration with the Taliban and other insurgents and pledged funds for this purpose. Later that month US Secretary of State Hillary Clinton launched an Afghanistan and Pakistan Regional Stabilization Strategy which described plans to support civilian reconstruction and development efforts. A 'Peace Jirga' in Afghanistan, held at the end of May, was intended to promote the reintegration of former insurgents and strengthen governmental legitimacy. Future hopes were then pinned on the prospect of parliamentary elections, due to be held in September 2010.

Military operations were consonant with this approach. A major NATO offensive, *Operation Moshtarak* in the Marjah district in Helmand province, was launched in February with the intention of driving out insurgents and filling the vacuum with Afghan political leadership. This was intended to be followed by a much more ambitious politico-military operation in the city of Kandahar, which had long been identified as the Taliban centre of gravity.

Each of these elements of activity experienced setbacks. Then Obama's attempts to promote a visible 'unity of effort' were severely damaged in June 2010 by revelations in *Rolling Stone* magazine of animosity among McChrystal's coterie and to some extent on the part of McChrystal himself towards some of Obama's advisers, including Vice President Joe Biden and Special Representative Richard Holbrooke. McChrystal was speedily relieved of command and replaced by his boss, General David Petraeus, who previously had been commander in Iraq.

Few if any of the developments over the year offered much material for governments of coalition countries to counter growing popular opposition to the deployment of troops in Afghanistan. Perceptions by mid-2010 tended to discount any notion of 'victory' but focused more on a political solution that would permit the drawdown of combat troops while avoiding the appearance of defeat.

Political setbacks

The presidential elections, dogged by allegations of fraud and vote rigging, raised doubts in the West about the validity of an international effort in support of an incumbent associated with electoral malpractice. Preliminary results gave Karzai 54.6% of the vote. Claims of fraud were endorsed by the UN-backed Electoral Complaints Commission (ECC). A certified result, accepted by the Afghan Independent Election Commission (IEC), invalidated nearly one-third of the votes and gave Karzai just short of the 50% needed to avoid a run-off with the next-placed challenger, Abdullah Abdullah. After pressure from Washington, Karzai agreed to a run-off, but the vote scheduled for 7 November was cancelled when Abdullah Abdullah pulled out, arguing that a fair election was impossible. Karzai was inaugurated for a second five-year term on 16 November.

With parliamentary elections due in September 2010, the issue of electoral reform became a high priority and a condition for further international assistance. The ECC prohibited 6,000 election workers from working in future elections for failing to follow correct procedures. Karzai introduced initiatives to improve voting procedures and measures to tackle corruption, including the establishment of an independent High Office of Oversight and an independent Monitoring and Evaluation Mission. But his contentious proposal to appoint all five ECC commissioners was partially resolved when he agreed that the UN Special Representative in Afghanistan would select two international experts to sit on the ECC for the parliamentary elections.

The most conspicuous outcome of the London Conference on 6 January was international support for the persuasion of Taliban leaders to distance themselves from al-Qaeda. Efforts would be made to reconcile senior Taliban commanders who were willing to negotiate and, as a separate process, to reintegrate local insurgent commanders and their followers into society. A Peace and Reintegration Trust Fund was established at the conference for this purpose. At Karzai's request eight former

Taliban government ministers were removed from the list of the United Nations al-Qaeda and Taliban Sanctions Committee, meaning they were no longer subject to sanctions such as a freeze on their assets.

The plan did not proceed smoothly. Karzai envisaged that King Abdullah of Saudi Arabia would act as an interlocutor to guide and legitimise any peace settlement, but Riyadh stated that the Taliban must first deny sanctuary to al-Qaeda. Claiming that he had reservations about its agenda, Karzai cancelled a meeting with the Organisation of the Islamic Conference (OIC). International human-rights groups condemned a new law granting immunity to those accused of human-rights abuses prior to the removal of the Taliban in 2001. The Quetta Shura, the Afghan Taliban leadership based in Pakistan, explicitly rejected Karzai's reconciliation proposals.

Contacts with Taliban leaders did, however, take place. UN Special Representative Kai Eide met Taliban representatives, among them the son of Gulbuddin Hekmatyar, leader of the Hizb-e-Islami Gulbuddin (HiG) insurgent group, in the Maldives in parallel with discussions between the Taliban and Afghan representatives. Eide stated that several rounds of talks had occurred from January 2010 onwards between the UN and the Taliban, though the latter denied any such contact. On 22 March a HiG delegation held talks with the Afghan government and demanded as a precondition for peace that all foreign forces withdraw within six months of July 2010. Two days later the new UN Special Representative, Staffan de Mistura, who had replaced Eide, met a HiG delegation for talks in Kabul.

Karzai had planned that a 'Peace Jirga' should take place at the end of April to develop a consensus on the inclusion of former insurgent groups in the Afghan political process. After postponement to 29 May, the three-day event involved some 1,600 participants from all parts of Afghan society. The Taliban, however, refused to attend and launched a series of attacks in Kabul in an attempt to disrupt it.

While the international community hoped that the jirga would enhance Karzai's political authority, it was criticised by parliamentarians and leaders from northern groups for being biased towards the needs of the Pashtun tribes of the southern provinces. Opposition leader Abdullah Abdullah boycotted the event, saying it was no more than a public-relations exercise. The jirga nonetheless ultimately agreed upon the need for negotiation with the Taliban.

Worsening security situation

Meanwhile, security in Afghanistan continued to deteriorate. There was a significant increase in the tempo and spread of insurgent activity in the run-up to the presidential elections in August. In the third quarter of 2009 there were a monthly average of 1,244 violent insurgency-related incidents, a 65% increase over the previous year. The use of improvised explosive devices (IEDs) and suicide attacks increased, with insurgents operating with greater boldness across the country.

McChrystal assumed command in June 2009 after US Defense Secretary Robert Gates relieved US Army General David McKiernan of his command. McChrystal, whose background was in special-forces operations, sought to apply counter-insurgency expertise to the worsening situation. Recognising the importance of support from the Afghan people, he centred his approach on 'protecting the population' and the reduction of civilian casualties. He tightened rules of engagement and sought to reduce the number of NATO air-strikes. Nevertheless, in September, a NATO air-strike killed up to 150 people, most of whom were civilians clustered around two hijacked petrol tankers. The strike was called in by a German officer and the incident provoked a political furore in Germany, resulting in several resignations (see Germany, pp. 143–4).

McChrystal's creation of a new three-star Intermediate Joint Command (IJC), headed by US Army Lieutenant-General David Rodriguez, enabled better command and control over Regional Commands, which had been mostly operating independently of each other. With Rodriguez running day-to-day operations, McChrystal was better able to coordinate political-military aspects of the campaign. He devoted more time to the relationship between ISAF and the Afghan government, including Karzai, and this enabled better mutual understanding. Nevertheless, tensions remained over NATO tactics.

In August McChrystal submitted a confidential report to Gates which was subsequently leaked to the *Washington Post*. Expressing serious concerns about the way the campaign was being waged, McChrystal sought

40,000 more troops. This proposal gave rise to disagreements within the US administration, with Vice President Biden and the US Ambassador to Kabul, Karl Eikenberry, taking a contrary view. These tensions and the controversy surrounding the Afghan presidential election led to delays in decision-making. In an apparent attempt to accelerate the process, McChrystal set out his view in a public speech at the International Institute for Strategic Studies in London on 1 October. He referred dismissively to a CIA report that had suggested a scenario whereby international forces might withdraw from Afghanistan and that combat operations might then be managed remotely, from outside the country – a plan he called 'Chaosistan'. Adding support to the CIA scenario, Biden proposed that the United States could pursue its strategic goals in the region by simply using air power to attack al-Qaeda in Afghanistan and Pakistan.

Obama's speech on 1 December at the West Point Military Academy finally sought to present a comprehensive new strategy. It endorsed a counter-insurgency approach and allocated additional extra resources and 30,000 more troops. However, his additional announcement that a drawdown of troops would begin in July 2011 sent several messages: to Karzai, that US support to Afghanistan was not open-ended; to other countries in the region who may have been concerned that the United States intended to maintain a long-term presence; and to the US elector- ate who were tiring of the campaign. The risk, however, was that Taliban leaders would receive an additional message, that they simply needed to outlast a time-limited American military presence.

The change of command and the policy review did not, however, halt the military campaign. Launched in July 2009, *Operation Khanjar* was the first major US offensive following an increase in US ground forces in January and involved 4,000 US Marines and 650 Afghan National Army (ANA) soldiers in the Now Zad Valley district of Helmand province, with the objective of taking and holding ground in Taliban-controlled areas. At the same time, a British-led operation, *Panther's Claw*, in Nad Ali enabled 27 polling stations to be established, although only a small proportion of the 88,000 residents voted. Both operations demonstrated the change in tactical tempo demanded by McChrystal, whilst empha- sising tighter rules of engagement and holding population centres to facilitate reconstruction.

The largest operation of the campaign so far, *Operation Moshtarak*, was launched in February 2010 to drive insurgents out of the town of Marjah in central Helmand and extend the influence of the Afghan government. ISAF/ANA troop deployments were publicised in advance to minimise civilian casualties. Many families fled to the provincial capital of Lashkar Gah, and about 1,800 refugees took shelter in neighbouring Nimroz province. Initial clearance operations in Marjah met little resistance. However, success was dependent on the establishment of effective governance within Marjah district after military operations ceased. McChrystal referred to this as 'government in a box'. The operation was to be a model for his strategy of securing population centres, but it failed to install sustainable governance and the Taliban began to re-infiltrate the area. Senior officers attributed this outcome to unreformed and corrupt police, whom McChrystal accused of creating a 'bleeding ulcer'. *Operation Moshtarak* was a foretaste of a larger, sustained and more complex operation to secure Kandahar, the birthplace of the Taliban, which was expected to last through summer 2010 and which was seen as the key to future progress.

> " McChrystal called it 'government in a box' "

The volatile security situation and heightened counter-insurgency efforts led to an increase in casualty rates among coalition forces. By mid-2010, 228 had been killed that year, of whom 143 were American and 45 were British. This compared with 520 for the whole of 2009, the highest number since the intervention began in 2001. About three times as many troops were seriously injured. Half the deaths were caused by IEDs. In the less-volatile north of Afghanistan, Germany suffered a total of seven casualties in 2009 and lost the same number in the first half of 2010. Afghan National Security Forces (ANSF) losses in 2009 were 465 army and 794 police. Civilian casualties numbered 2,412 in 2009, with 67% attributed to insurgent action, according to the US Congressional Research Service. UN figures put civilian casualties caused by Afghan government and international forces at 25% lower than in 2008.

The total number of foreign troops in Afghanistan increased to approximately 135,000 by mid-2010, with the United States contributing

94,000 (including some 15,000 troops outside ISAF), due to rise to 98,000 by the end of the year. The United Kingdom was the next largest contributor, with 10,000. The Netherlands was contributing 1,800 troops, of whom 1,400 were based in Uruzgan province, but in February 2010 the Dutch government collapsed, having lost a vote to extend the deployment of its troops beyond August. Australia, which shared responsibility for Uruzgan, announced that it would not assume a lead role there and would not increase its troop numbers. The Dutch pull-out reinforced pressure in Canada to withdraw Canadian forces from Kandahar province, scheduled to leave in the second half of 2011. In Germany, support for military deployment remained precarious, but Berlin approved the dispatch of an additional 850 troops, to a total of 5,350, the third-largest contribution.

The increased tempo of operations and numbers of troops required greater logistic support. With the southern supply lines from Pakistan through the Chaman and Tor Kham crossing points under threat from insurgents, a Northern Distribution Network (NDN) was established. Russia and the Central Asian states agreed to the transit of logistics supplies, and a second trans-Caspian route brought supplies via the South Caucasus.

Afghan forces: slow development

Obama's December speech emphasised the need to increase the capacity of the ANSF as a prerequisite for the drawdown of US forces due to begin in July 2011. Much of the US troop build-up was devoted to training the ANSF. One trainer was assigned to every 29 recruits, compared to one to 466 in some areas in 2009.

Recruitment to the ANA increased to approximately 7,000 per month. While there were many Pashtuns in the ANA, only 2–3% were from the south, where Pashtuns are dominant and insurgent activity is greatest. High drop-out and absentee rates added to concerns that manpower targets would not be met. According to NATO figures, 92% of operations were carried out jointly with the ANA, of which 61% were Afghan-led. By mid-2010 there was cautious optimism that the increased training effort for the ANA was making progress and that target strengths would be met. Troop numbers were expected to rise to 134,000 by October 2010, from a mid-2010 figure of 125,694; the target of 171,600 would be reached in October 2011. But the slow growth in numbers of trained non-commissioned officers, and to a lesser extent officers, risked jeopardising the ANA's capability to take over operations from NATO. At 25%, the annual drop-out rate in the Afghan National Police (ANP) was especially worrying: it was as high as 60–70% in its elite paramilitary unit. The target strength for the ANP in 2010 was 109,000.

US forces also engaged in 'community defence initiatives'. Although the creation of local militias remained controversial, ISAF command circles cautiously accepted that they could be beneficial in the short term. In Wardak province, for example, the Afghan Public Protection Force numbered approximately 1,200, recruited by local elders and financed by the Ministry of the Interior. Units received some US training and were required to arm themselves. In addition, the role of private security contractors operating in Afghanistan increased substantially. According to the Afghanistan Conflict Monitor, numbers rose to 71,000, well above the 10,700 revealed in a September 2009 US congressional study. This was largely in support of the US 'surge'. Most personnel were Afghan nationals employed by international companies or Afghan private security firms. Several incidents gave rise to accusations of lawlessness on the part of some firms.

Economy and narcotics

The economy continued to grow, albeit from a low base, as agriculture recovered from the previous year's drought. Higher spending by the Afghan government and international forces supported other sectors of the economy. In the 2009/10 fiscal year, revenue collection was expected to surpass $1bn for the first time. Despite this, opinion polls suggested that Afghans' perception of the economy had worsened. Food prices had risen, but lack of electricity was the greatest source of complaint: more than half of the population were without electricity in their homes, and only one in 20 homes had power all day. A third of Afghanistan's electricity supply was imported from neighbouring countries.

Corruption was also of continuing concern. The UN Office on Drugs and Crime (UNODC) reported in January 2010 that, in the past 12 months, one out of two Afghans had had to bribe public officials and that an estimated $2.5bn – 23% of Afghanistan's GDP – was paid in bribes. A majority of those interviewed by the UNODC described 'public dishonesty' as a greater source of worry than insecurity or unemployment. On his inauguration in November, Karzai – under considerable international pressure – said that 'ending the culture of impunity and strengthening integrity' was a key priority for his administration.

More positively, the Afghanistan Investment Support Agency (AISA) reported a 150% increase in domestic and foreign investment since 2008. As of December 2009, approximately 3,000 Afghan workers and 70 Chinese engineers were on site at the Aynak copper mine in Logar province, to which China Metallurgical Group had been awarded development rights in 2008. But private-sector development was hindered by weak governance, inadequate access to power, land-tenure issues and lack of access to credit.

The economy seemed nonetheless likely to be dependent on aid for many years. At the London Conference, amidst increased concerns about the effectiveness of disbursement, donors pledged to direct 50% of development aid through the Afghan government within two years. Of some $36bn disbursed since 2001, 77% was spent on donor-designed and -implemented projects with no government input. Of the remaining $8.7bn assistance delivered directly through the Afghan treasury, only some $770m was placed fully at the discretion of the government. In January a report by eight international NGOs criticised the channelling of aid donations through military-dominated institutions and the delivery of aid projects by the military. In particular, US Provincial Reconstruction Teams (PRTs) were criticised for co-opting aid funds for the purpose of counter-insurgency, and for hindering sustainable development because of the lack of civilian engagement.

In line with this criticism, it was increasingly recognised that greater civilian involvement was needed alongside military efforts. As part of a 'civilian surge' called for in Obama's December speech, the number of American civilian experts in Afghanistan was to be increased to 1,000. As of October 2009, 603 US civilians had been deployed, including lawyers, agronomists and development specialists from the State Department and other departments. However, the UN Assistance Mission in Afghanistan (UNAMA), with 1,500 staff at 18 offices, was struggling to attract international staff due to security concerns. An October attack on a guest house in Kabul, which killed five UN international staff members, heightened these concerns.

The economy continued to be heavily distorted by narcotics. The UNODC reported that, although production and cultivation of Afghan poppy decreased in 2009 and the number of poppy-free provinces had increased from 18 to 20, four provinces (Uruzgan, Faryab, Baghlan and Sari Pul) showed an increase. Helmand and Kandahar provinces were expected to maintain a high level of cultivation and production in 2010. Another UNODC survey in April 2010 showed that Afghanistan was the world's leading producer of hashish as well as of opium products. Cannabis was fetching $3,900 per hectare compared to $3,600 per hectare for opium. Over two-thirds of cannabis farmers reported paying *ushr*, an informal tax of approximately 10%, to groups who control territory in rural Afghanistan. The UNODC estimated that 30–50% of *ushr* levies went to the Taliban, yielding an annual income of $125m. The Taliban sought to disrupt the Afghan National Drug Control Strategy (NDCS). In March a suicide bomber in Helmand targeted farmers receiving fertiliser and seed handouts as part of NATO's Food Zones project.

In June 2009, Holbrooke announced a new US approach to assisting the Afghan government's counter-narcotics strategy, having described the previous approach as 'the most wasteful and ineffective programme I have seen in 40 years in and out of government'. US efforts were intended to re-focus away from eradication towards the creation of alternative livelihoods for farmers. Interdiction efforts were henceforward to be conducted by special forces rather than as part of conventional counter-insurgency operations.

Growing concern

In the ninth year of the international campaign in Afghanistan there were some signs of positive change in a number of areas. The economy offered hope for a better future, with more inward investment. However, Karzai and his government were still unable to exercise authority across the country and some foreign countries were wearying of the task of supporting a weak government. Systemic corruption that continued to affect all parts of society had not been dealt with. Unless this was addressed, there was a feeling that the sustained governance that was essential for the handover of responsibility for security to Afghan control would not be achievable. *Operation Moshtarak* demonstrated the military challenges involved in delivering setbacks to the Taliban, and the fact that governance in Afghanistan required more than a 'government in a box'. Accordingly, there was general recognition in the international community that resolution of the Afghan situation would require some form of conciliation, and that this would have to embrace at least some elements of the Taliban. The key question was how such rapprochements should be negotiated. In absence of political progress, it was likely that Western backing for the military mission in Afghanistan would steadily dwindle. In any case, major contributors of troops appeared to be on a path towards reducing their combat presence.

Chapter 9

Asia-Pacific

China: Balancing Competing Interests

As the world continued to suffer the effects of the worst economic downturn since the Great Depression, China emerged from the rubble more quickly and successfully than most other countries. The world's third-largest economic power made impressive economic gains and continued to be the leading financier of America's fast-growing debt. The rapid rise in Chinese influence over the past year had two somewhat conflicting effects on China and its international profile. On the one hand, while market economies struggled to regain their footing, a rebounding China gained confidence in its development model and its policies at home and abroad, resulting in greater Chinese confidence and increased assertiveness on the global stage in defence of its national interests in economic prosperity, social stability and national unity. China's behaviour at times aroused concern in some countries about whether Beijing would continue to adhere to its pledge to rise peacefully and not pose a threat to other nations as it re-emerges as a great power. On the other hand, the rise in Chinese influence led to increased demands and expectations in other countries, which increasingly looked to China to play an active and constructive role in advancing shared international interests, such as rebalancing the global economy, combating climate change and preventing proliferation of nuclear weapons.

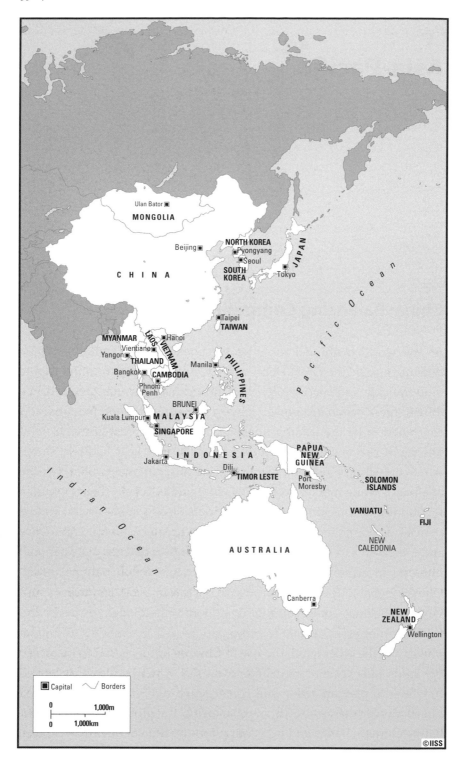

Yet Beijing remained reluctant to contribute substantially to the resolution of such global problems. Time and again over the past year, China grappled with striking an appropriate balance between defending its national interests and being a full participant in efforts to solve international problems.

China at Copenhagen

In 2009, China passed the United States to become the world's leading carbon-dioxide emitter, placing it at the centre of the United Nations Climate Change Conference in December. The major question ahead of the meeting was whether the developed world could strike a deal with the developing world, symbolically 'led' by China, to reduce international carbon emissions and minimise climate change. China had announced a plan to reduce its carbon intensity – emissions per unit of GDP – by 40–45% by 2020, compared to 2005 levels. The decision provoked criticism because of its focus on carbon intensity rather than carbon emissions: under the Chinese plan, if China's GDP continued to grow at current rates, per capita and overall emissions would continue to increase (albeit at a lower rate) and thus would have little effect on efforts to reduce emissions globally.

> " China showed willingness to butt heads with developed nations "

At Copenhagen, China repeatedly demonstrated willingness to butt heads with developed nations, primarily over the issues of financing and oversight. The crux of the confrontation between the PRC and the developed world was the clash between China's interest in sustaining high levels of economic growth and mounting Western demands that China behave as a 'responsible' power. Beijing argued that developed nations should be primarily responsible for reducing global emissions and for financing reductions made by developing nations, including China, while the developed nations maintained that China, as the world's third-largest economy and top polluter, should play a larger, more constructive role in combating global warming by cutting emissions more significantly, by self-financing these cuts, and by agreeing to independent compliance verification.

The discussions among national leaders were blunt, even confrontational. When German Chancellor Angela Merkel presented Europe's proposal for 50% reductions in global greenhouse-gas emissions by 2050, China's negotiator interrupted: 'Thank you for all your proposals. We've already said we cannot accept the long-term goal of 50%.' To this, French President Nicolas Sarkozy countered that the West had already committed itself to an 80% reduction by 2050. 'And China, who will soon be the biggest economy in the world, now tells the world "these engagements are for you, not for us." This is unacceptable. One has to react to this hypocrisy.'

On the final day of the conference, world leaders met in hopes of reaching an agreement, but Chinese Premier Wen Jiabao did not attend, remaining in his hotel room and sending a lower-level official in his stead. Tempers quickly flared as Chinese and Indian negotiators refused to accept binding emissions targets, preferring instead to make voluntary cuts. There was considerable frustration that the Chinese negotiator repeatedly delayed talks to ask the premier for instructions. At one point, a portion of the Indian and Chinese delegations left the conference and headed for the airport; both, however, returned for a final meeting with the leaders of South Africa and Brazil. To their surprise, the discussion was interrupted by US President Barack Obama, who arrived early for a scheduled meeting with Wen. A non-binding framework for emissions reductions – the Copenhagen Accord – was agreed after the United States removed draft language that called for 'examination and assessment' – language that Beijing saw as overly intrusive. Although the American and Chinese leaders both proclaimed satisfaction with the accord, many European leaders favoured a legally binding agreement and blamed the two powers, particularly China, for the failure of the conference.

China subsequently submitted its proposed mitigation actions to the UN Framework Convention on Climate Change (UNFCCC) on 28 January and officially associated itself with the Copenhagen Accord in a letter to the body in early March. In the letter, China reaffirmed earlier announcements that it would reduce its carbon intensity by 40–45% by 2020 from 2005 levels; increase the share of non-fossil energy in its primary energy consumption to around 15% by 2020; and increase forest coverage by 40 million hectares and forest stock volume by 1.3 billion cubic meters by 2020 from 2005 levels.

Sino-US Relations

In contrast to the past pattern, in which US–China relations experienced troubles in the first year of a new American presidency and improved in subsequent years, the relationship developed relatively smoothly throughout Obama's first year in office before entering a rocky period at the start of his second year. An important change over the past year was the centrality of global issues compared to a previous focus on bilateral and regional issues. Rebalancing the global economy, combating climate change and countering proliferation challenges increasingly occupied centre stage in the relationship.

Although there were some important achievements, the overall record was decidedly mixed, falling short of US hopes a well as international expectations. In some cases, greater progress was hampered by diverging interests. A deficit of mutual strategic trust and persisting suspicions of each other's long-term intentions also inhibited greater cooperation. China remained wary that the United States sought to prevent its re-emergence as a great power, while Washington harboured uncertainty about how Beijing would use its ever-growing national power in the future.

The second half of 2009 saw a series of cooperative and congenial bilateral meetings. In July 2009, the United States hosted the first round of the newly created Strategic and Economic Dialogue (SED), a mechanism that Obama and Chinese President Hu Jintao agreed to establish when they met for the first time on the margins of the London G20 meeting in April. The dialogue consisted of two tracks: a strategic track co-chaired by US Secretary of State Hillary Clinton and Chinese State Councillor Dai Bingguo, and an economic track, co-chaired by US Treasury Secretary Timothy Geithner and Chinese Vice Premier Wang Qishan. Obama stressed crucial areas of common interest for the two nations, including economic recovery and rebalancing, clean energy advancement, nuclear non-proliferation and transnational threats. He told the delegations that 'the relationship between the United States and China will shape the twenty-first century, which makes it as important as any bilateral relationship in the world'.

In the strategic channel, discussion touched on North Korea, Iran, counter-terrorism, Afghanistan and Pakistan, and the two sides pledged to strengthen future cooperation on non-proliferation and arms control. In the economic talks, the dialogue focused on measures to promote recovery from the global financial crisis and on charting a course towards sustainable and balanced growth. Geithner pledged US efforts to increase private savings rates and called on China to increase the share of domestic consumption in its GDP, while both sides reaffirmed the need for financial regulatory reform. A memorandum of understanding established 'regular ministerial consultations to deepen mutual understanding and promote and guide bilateral cooperation on climate change, clean and efficient energy and environmental protection'.

Visiting China on November, Obama held six hours of discussions with Hu, during which he reportedly told the Chinese president that the United States would continue to abide by the Taiwan Relations Act – which meant it would sell arms to Taiwan – and that he would soon meet with the Tibetan spiritual leader, the Dalai Lama. According to administration officials, the two leaders spoke frankly on issues such as human rights, Tibet and Taiwan. They then released a joint statement – the first time the nations had done so since 1997 – reflecting the growing depth and breadth of the relationship. The document included a Chinese statement welcoming the US role in maintaining the peace and security of the Asia-Pacific region and a joint pledge to increase military-to-military contacts. Of greatest importance to the Chinese side, however, was a sentence that read: 'Respecting each other's core interests is extremely important to ensure steady progress in US–China relations'. From China's perspective, the term 'core interests' refers to issues related to Chinese sovereignty and territorial integrity: Taiwan, Tibet, Xinjiang and even the South China Sea. Agreement on this language, combined with the overall positive tenor of relations and the importance that Obama attached to cooperation with Beijing, led to expectations among many Chinese that the United States would forgo any action antithetical to China's perceived core interests, such as arms sales to Taiwan. According to American officials, however, the paragraph that included the reference to core interests was understood by both Chinese and US negotiators to relate solely to Tibet and Xinjiang, not to Taiwan.

The Obama administration soon showed that the joint statement did not represent a significant departure from previous American policy when, on 29 January, it notified the US Congress of its intent to sell $6.4bn worth of arms to Taiwan. The package consisted almost entirely of items approved by the Bush administration in October 2001, including PAC-3 missiles, *Black Hawk* helicopters, *Harpoon* anti-ship missiles, mine-hunting ships and fighter jet communications systems. Notably, the arms-sale notification did not include funding for a submarine feasibility study, long desired by Taipei and previously approved by the Bush administration, or for advanced F-16 fighter jets to upgrade Taiwan's aging air force.

A formal démarche was promptly issued by Beijing to US Ambassador Jon Huntsman, and the Chinese government subsequently announced three forms of punishment. Firstly, consistent with its response to previous such sales, China said that it would suspend military exchanges and postpone vice-ministerial-level consultations on international security, arms control and non-proliferation issues. Secondly, it warned that bilateral cooperation on major international and regional issues

> **China's reaction turned out to be more bark than bite**

would be adversely affected. Finally, and most dramatically compared to previous Chinese reactions, Beijing threatened to impose sanctions on American companies involved in the sale of weapons to Taiwan. In the end, the United States did not back down from its decision, and China's reaction turned out to be more bark than bite; cooperation with Washington on international and regional issues was not significantly affected and no action was taken to sanction US companies. The one threat Beijing carried out was the suspension of military-to-military exchanges, which by the end of June 2010 had not yet resumed.

As the Chinese government and media fumed over the arms sale, three other issues cropped up simultaneously that further strained bilateral relations. Firstly, in January 2010, Google, the US Internet company, alleged that Chinese hackers had used a software glitch to infiltrate the company's servers and enter the e-mail accounts of leading Chinese dissidents. As a result, the company announced that it was ceasing its practice of censoring the results of its Chinese search engine and threatened to end its China operations. This spat led to a back-and-forth exchange between Washington and Beijing over Internet censorship policies, with Clinton calling on China to allow full freedom of access and China's Foreign Ministry accusing the United States of interfering in its domestic affairs. In March, Google relocated its Chinese search engine from the mainland to Hong Kong but retained much of its operation in mainland China, including research and development and its local sales force. As of the end of May, the Chinese government had not taken steps to censor search results from Google's Hong Kong website.

Secondly, on 18 February Obama held a long-anticipated meeting with the Dalai Lama. The Tibetan spiritual leader had requested a meeting with the president in autumn 2009 but the administration demurred, not wanting to offend China on the eve of Obama's visit to Beijing. This marked the first time since 1991 that the Dalai Lama had travelled to Washington without meeting with the American president. The protocol for the February 2010 meeting was in line with past practice: the two met in the White House Map Room instead of the more formal and politically charged Oval Office, and no media were permitted. Nevertheless, the Chinese Foreign Ministry condemned the meeting, accusing the United States of 'conniving and supporting anti-China separatist forces'.

Finally, Sino-US economic frictions reached a zenith in early 2010. Throughout the economic downturn, the countries had clashed on numerous occasions within the World Trade Organisation over duties imposed by each in retaliation for perceived protectionism. But the most contentious and conspicuous economic spat was over Chinese currency policy. The issue gained prominence when reports surfaced that the US Treasury Department was considering labelling China a 'currency manipulator' in its semi-annual report to Congress. American politicians, ranging from Obama to prominent senators Charles Schumer and Lindsey Graham, seized the opportunity to criticise China's exchange-rate policy, which, they charged, deliberately keeps the renminbi undervalued to boost exports, hampering American competitiveness. Wen used a press conference in Beijing at the end of the annual meeting of the National People's Congress to accuse Washington of practising protectionism by artificially undervaluing the dollar. This set off a firestorm on Capitol Hill, with 130 congressmen and senators signing a letter to Geithner and Commerce

Secretary Gary Locke demanding the administration take action against China for its currency policies.

Almost as quickly as tensions rose they were greatly eased, after intense negotiations between senior US and Chinese officials. Reconciliation was guided by a shared recognition that, despite persisting differences, the bilateral relationship was critically important to both American and Chinese interests. Deputy Secretary of State James Steinberg reaffirmed the US commitment to the 'one China' policy and its position that Tibet is part of the People's Republic. The following day, Obama personally received the credentials of incoming Chinese Ambassador Zhang Yesui. After the meeting, the White House released a statement saying the president had reaffirmed the American commitment to the 'one China' policy and stressed the importance of cooperative Sino-US relations. Two days later, Obama and Hu held an hour-long telephone conversation to discuss the overlapping interests of the two nations and a path forward for cooperation.

> " Obama reaffirmed America's commitment to the 'one China' policy "

In the days that followed these carefully choreographed events, additional results of the behind-the-scenes diplomacy came to light. Firstly, the Chinese Foreign Ministry announced that Hu would attend the mid-April Nuclear Security Summit in Washington, a major gathering of world leaders. Secondly, US State Department officials announced that China had entered into negotiations at the UN Security Council on sanctions against Iran. Finally, the US Treasury announced that it was delaying the release of its report on international currency policies. After two months of public and heated disagreements and accusations, the relationship had returned to an even keel in all realms except for ties between the US and Chinese militaries.

This easing of tensions paved the way for a successful second round of the SED, held on 24–25 May in Beijing. The two tracks were chaired again by Dai, Wang, Geithner and Clinton. With over 200 American officials travelling to Beijing for the talks, the second SED was the largest bilateral dialogue ever held between the two nations. Although the talks were at times contentious, especially over the issues of an appropriate international response to the sinking of a South Korean naval vessel, the

Cheonan, and the scope of sanctions against Iran, the dialogue ultimately resulted in 26 'outcomes', including seven new memoranda of understanding between the two nations on topics ranging from gas-shale development to infectious-disease cooperation and declarations to continue expanding cooperation on clean-energy issues.

Of particular importance to the US business community, China pledged to gradually adjust its currency valuation, followed on 19 June (on the eve of the opening of the G20 meeting in Toronto) by an announcement by the People's Bank of China that Beijing would allow more exchange-rate flexibility. At the SED, China also committed to submit a revised offer to join the WTO Agreement on Government Procurement, which would require the Chinese government to accept foreign company bids for government purchasing. While many American commentators focused on what the two sides did not agree to at the SED, those in China largely welcomed the dialogue's progress and their nation's expanded negotiating power on the world stage.

Nevertheless, the Chinese–US military-to-military relationship remained essentially frozen. The differences between the two sides were on full display at the International Institute for Strategic Studies' Asia-Pacific Security Summit (the Shangri-La Dialogue) in June 2010. In the run-up to the conference, China rejected a proposed visit by US Defense Secretary Robert Gates, with Beijing saying that the timing was inconvenient. At the dialogue in Singapore, Gates and Deputy Chief of Staff of the PLA General Ma Xiaotian openly clashed over arms sales to Taiwan. In his speech, Gates told the audience that 'only in the military-to-military arena has progress on critical mutual security issues been held hostage over something that is, quite frankly, old news'. The US defence secretary also expressed regret that the military-to-military relationship was 'affected by every change in the political weather'. Ma, speaking after Gates, insisted that US arms sales to Taiwan could not be regarded as 'normal'. He cited US weapons sales to Taiwan, US reconnaissance activities in China's Exclusive Economic Zone, and restrictions on US–Chinese military cooperation in the 2000 National Defense Authorization Act as obstacles to the resumption of normal US–Chinese military interactions.

It remained unclear whether the Chinese would continue to insist on US actions to address at least some of their concerns before agreeing to resume bilateral military exchanges or whether the passing of a longer period of time after the January arms sale to Taiwan would be all that was necessary to restore military-to-military ties. Even if the US–China military relationship returned to the status quo ante, however, it was likely to develop slowly and would remain superficial, contentious and vulnerable to repeated suspensions irrespective of progress in other areas of the bilateral relationship.

China and nuclear proliferation

The continuing nuclear dilemmas in the Democratic People's Republic of Korea (DPRK) and Iran posed challenges for Chinese foreign policy. North Korea's continued survival and stability were essential for Chinese economic and security interests, while a regular flow of oil from Iran – provider of 11% of Chinese crude – was needed for China's energy security. As both nations' nuclear programmes advanced, however, the international community increasingly called upon Beijing to play a larger role in responding to the challenges posed to the international non-proliferation regime. Thus China has been forced to walk a tightrope when dealing with these two nations, attempting to balance its national interests with its international responsibilities.

In May 2009, Pyongyang's second underground nuclear detonation led to international demands for another round of UN sanctions, which tested Beijing's ability to balance its interests in preserving North Korean stability with China's international image as a responsible stakeholder. After intense negotiations in which China played a central role, UN Security Council Resolution 1874 was approved, putting in place a set of strong but targeted sanctions intended to limit Pyongyang's ability to finance its nuclear programme. In the months following the passage of the resolution, China worked with the United States and others in the region to implement the sanctions, and Beijing played a pivotal role in the July 2009 reversal of the North Korean vessel *Kang Nam I*, which the United States believed was carrying sanctioned cargo to Myanmar.

China did not allow the sanctions and its role in their enforcement to sour its friendly relationship with Pyongyang, however. On the contrary, Beijing increased its economic investment in the North and stepped up Sino-DPRK exchanges. In the latter half of 2009, three high-level Chinese delegations travelled to Pyongyang in consecutive months – Hu in August, Dai in September and Wen in October. Wen met Kim Jong-il, the North Korean leader, who promised to return to multilateral dialogue on denuclearisation upon improvement in US–DPRK relations. For its part, China reportedly agreed to provide additional aid and grants to the North totalling $20m.

In May 2010, Kim travelled to China, his first international trip since visiting the PRC in 2006. Although dubbed an unofficial visit at Pyongyang's request, Kim was hosted by Hu at a banquet in the Great Hall of the People in Beijing and met every member of China's Politburo Standing Committee. Kim pledged to create 'favourable conditions' for the resumption of denuclearisation talks and, according to the North Korean news agency, told his Chinese hosts that the North would 'implement the [September 2005] joint statement adopted at the Six-Party Talks and pursue a peaceful solution through dialogue'.

The sinking of the *Cheonan*, a South Korean corvette, on 26 March 2010 also posed a significant challenge to Beijing's balancing act. Beijing called the incident 'unfortunate' and refused to be drawn into the condemnations of North Korea and its leader. While other national leaders offered condolences to Seoul within hours of the incident, which took the lives of 46 South Korean sailors, Hu did not offer condolences until 1 May, an exhibition of Beijing's reluctance to appear to be taking sides on the sensitive issue. On 19 May, investigators announced they had found conclusive evidence that North Korea was responsible for the sinking; Beijing urged all sides to remain calm and not risk an escalation of tensions. South Korea and the United States turned to the UN Security Council to respond to what they saw as an act of aggression. Other global developments compelled discussion of the *Cheonan* incident to be deferred for several months, but China, as a permanent member of the council, faced the eventual necessity of choosing between supporting its traditional ally and bolstering its international reputation as a responsible player.

Following the unmasking in September 2009 of a secret Iranian nuclear facility near the city of Qom, all eyes were on China to see how it would react. Again, Beijing worked to balance its national interests in energy security and non-interference in the affairs of other nations with its international responsibilities. In November, it supported an International Atomic Energy Agency (IAEA) resolution demanding that Tehran halt uranium enrichment. While numerous parties attempted to strike a deal with Iran over enriched uranium, Beijing continually called for diplomacy and dialogue and tirelessly restated its opposition to sanctions. For example, Foreign Minister Yang Jiechi reiterated in March 2010 that 'sanctions do not provide a fundamental solution to the Iranian nuclear issue, ultimately this issue has to be resolved through peaceful negotiations'.

Beijing then, however, reached a turning point. As part of the complicated diplomatic deal with Washington to ameliorate tensions caused by US arms sales to Taiwan and Obama's meeting with the Dalai Lama, China agreed to join discussions at the UN on a resolution that would impose new sanctions on Iran. On 1 April, while Iran's top nuclear negotiator was in Beijing, US State Department spokesman Philip Crowley told reporters that 'China has indicated a willingness to be a full participant' in negotiations on sanctions against Tehran. As the parties negotiated, steps were taken to alleviate Chinese concerns about energy security: the United States and other members of the Security Council coordinated to ensure that China's energy needs would be met in the event that Iran reduced oil supplies to China in retaliation for its support for sanctions. On 18 May, Hillary Clinton announced that the five permanent members of the Security Council had reached an agreement on sanctions. On 9 June, a fourth round of UN sanctions against Iran, targeting the nation's Revolutionary Guard, its ballistic-missile programme and its nuclear sector, were approved, with China voting in favour of the resolution.

Cross-Strait relations

During Ma Ying-jeou's first year as president of Taiwan, cross-Strait relations witnessed a dramatic improvement, with stepped up people-to-people exchanges and the signing of numerous bilateral agreements. By mid-2009, however, many of the least controversial issues, from tourism exchanges to mail delivery, had been tackled, while thornier matters began to come to the top of the agenda. In addition, domestic politics in Taiwan slowed progress as the Ma administration was dogged by criticism over its slow and ineffective responses to the global recession and to Typhoon Morakot in August 2009, and faced persistent accusations from the Democrat Progressive Party (DPP) that cosiness with Beijing would negatively affect Taiwanese sovereignty.

Cooperation continued, but negotiations became increasingly difficult and drawn out. Memoranda of understanding regarding regulation of finance and banking were signed in November, about five months later than expected. In December 2009, the mainland's Association for Relations Across the Taiwan Strait (ARATS) and Taiwan's Straits Exchange Foundation (SEF) held their fourth round of talks in Taichung, Taiwan. Although deals were reached on fishing, agriculture and industrial inspections, an agreement on the most important agenda item, double taxation, was delayed.

In 2010, the Economic Cooperation Framework Agreement (ECFA) emerged as the major issue facing Taiwan and mainland leaders. The Ma administration maintained that by signing ECFA, which would reduce tariffs and other trade barriers between the island and the mainland, Taiwan would avoid being excluded from the regional economic integration process. The DPP argued, however, that ECFA would hurt many Taiwanese industries and would make the island uncomfortably dependent on mainland China. The DPP also criticised Ma's government for lack of transparency throughout the negotiating process. Formal negotiations on ECFA were launched in January 2010 by ARATS and SEF, and while Beijing was cautious to avoid committing to a deadline for the conclusion of negotiations, Taiwan leaders repeatedly expressed hope that an agreement could be reached by June.

After three rounds of intense negotiations, the ECFA was completed and signed on 29 June. The final and most controversial aspect – the 'early harvest' list of products immediately eligible for tariff benefits after ratification of the ECFA – was resolved in the final round of negotiations in early June. The agreement was weighted in Taiwan's favour, with 539 Taiwan products eligible for tariff exemptions or reductions amounting to $13.84bn per year, nearly five times the value of the 268 Chinese products that will enjoy similar preferential tariff treatment. Facing a tough political environment for municipal and mayoral elections in December, conclusion of the ECFA was of particular importance to Ma and his

Kuomintang (KMT) party. Recognising the forces of Taiwan's domestic politics, both Hu and Wen publicly stated that a bilateral economic agreement would be mutually beneficial, with Wen even noting the need to sacrifice some of Beijing's interests for Taiwan's benefit. Beijing also offered assurances that the ECFA would contain no political dimensions and would protect the island's agriculture sector.

Another sticking point in cross-Strait relations was the path forward on discussion of political and security issues. Following Hu's speech on cross-Strait relations at the end of 2008, in which he attempted to promote closer ties, Beijing pressed Taipei to launch informal discussions on military confidence-building measures and political topics, such as the definition of 'one China'. Due to the controversial nature of the ECFA and the lack of domestic consensus in Taiwan on political and security issues, however, the Ma administration was reluctant to tackle these issues and did not look likely to alter this position in the remaining two years of Ma's presidential term. The risks of entering into dialogue on political and security issues prematurely were highlighted in November 2009 when a delegation composed of retired military officers, former ambassadors and senior scholars from the PRC travelled to Taiwan to discuss 60 years of cross-Strait relations. Sharp differences of opinion between the two sides (and amongst the Taiwanese participants) underscored the need to progress slowly in accordance with Ma's guideline to proceed from easy matters to more difficult ones; and to tackle economic issues before taking on more sensitive political and military issues.

> " China continued to increase missile deployments opposite Taiwan "

China also continued to increase its missile deployments opposite Taiwan, despite repeated calls from Ma to remove them. The US arms sale announced in January 2010 was intended in part to shore up Taiwan's confidence in dealing with its much more powerful neighbour. Although the failure to make progress towards a resolution of political and military differences did not appear to have negatively affected cross-Strait relations, such issues must eventually be addressed if the objectives of ending cross-Strait hostility and signing a peace accord, which leaders on both sides have endorsed, are to be realised.

Domestic situation

Over the past year, the Chinese economy almost fully recovered from its slowdown; most indicators pointed to the stimulus package launched in November 2008 as the turning point. Economists had debated whether the credit-driven stimulus would be able to ensure continued high-level growth, but the plan ultimately had the positive impact Beijing had anticipated. The end result was a GDP increase of approximately 8.7% in 2009.

But this stellar performance did not prevent questions about whether the Chinese government and its state-owned banks were simply fuelling another credit bubble. In April 2010 alone, property prices rose 12.8%, the largest monthly gain since 2005. Inflation continued to be a concern for Chinese leaders during the early stages of global recovery, as producer prices surged 6.8% and consumer prices rose 2.4% in April. Expectations were growing that the central government would soon be compelled to increase interest rates and appreciate the renminbi; in other words, the spigot of easy money that the central government had opened to stimulate the economy during the recession might need to be closed to prevent out-of-control inflation.

Though the Chinese economy recovered quickly, the government was forced to limit the growth of spending in many sectors. While the number that drew the most attention internationally was the 7.5% growth in military spending, the smallest increase in over two decades and the first time since 1989 that China's defence spending had grown by less than 10%, other sectors saw more significant reductions in year-on-year growth. Some of the most dramatic declines were in housing (which increased by 1.4% after 202.7% growth in 2009), health care (up by 8.8% after 49.5% growth in 2009), public security (increased by 8% after 47.5% growth in 2009) and transport (decreased by 2.7% after 38.6% growth in 2009).

Despite unpredictable economic conditions and a number of sensitive anniversaries, including the twentieth anniversary of the 4 June 1989 Tiananmen incident, the tenth anniversary of the Falun Gong protests in Beijing, and the sixtieth anniversary of the founding of the People's Republic, the Chinese leadership was largely able to ensure social stability. A major exception, however, was the Xinjiang rioting of July 2009, the spark for which was a 25 June dispute at a Guangdong toy factory between Uighur and Han workers that resulted in the deaths of at least two Uighur employees.

On 5 July, thousands of Uighur citizens in Urumqi, the capital of Xinjiang, held a protest to demand a full investigation into the toy-factory incident. Although the demonstrations started peacefully, they quickly led to violent clashes between the city's Uighur and Han populations – the culmination of long-bubbling tensions in the autonomous region. These clashes soon spread from the capital to other parts of Xinjiang. Beijing quickly deployed the People's Armed Police (PAP) and limited communications networks while blaming Uighur activist Rebiya Kadeer and her 'separatist forces' in the United States for taking advantage of the toy-factory incident to promote ethnic unrest. After days of violence, order was restored, but only after at least 197 citizens were killed (most of them Han) and 1,721 were injured, according to official Chinese reports. Thousands of others, both Uighur and Han, were arrested, and at least nine people were executed for their roles in the violence. In January 2010, the central government announced that it was increasing Xinjiang's public-security budget by 90%. Then, in April, Wang Lequan, the hard-line party secretary in Xinjiang, was replaced after 15 years on the job, a move largely interpreted as a vote of no confidence in his handling of the unrest. Ten months after the rioting, full Internet service was finally restored in Xinjiang, marking the longest and most widespread blockage in China since the Internet became readily available a decade ago.

The other major domestic development of the year to mid-2010 was the ritual meeting of China's top leadership, the fourth plenum of the Chinese Communist Party's 17th Central Committee, held in September 2009. The meeting was most notable for what did not occur: the expected appointment of Hu's presumptive successor as party sec-retary, Xi Jinping, to be vice-chair of the Central Military Commission (CMC). Although such leadership changes are far from institutionalised in China, observers anticipated that Xi would be placed in a top position on the leading military body based on the pattern of Hu's own career. Failure to become a CMC member deprived Xi of the opportunity to acquire the military-leadership credentials that many see as essential for assuming the position of China's top leader. The fourth plenum demon-strated the continued unpredictability of Chinese leadership politics.

China in the world

China's rising influence in the past year was accompanied by both the growing visibility of its military and by the nation's augmented role in international institutions. In particular, the People's Liberation Army Navy (PLAN) continued to modernise and expand its international operations, a development that had both negative and positive impacts on regional and global security. As China's navy operates more frequently beyond its territorial waters, its presence and behaviour is alarming other nations and revitalising discussion about whether the opaque and substantial growth of the Chinese military poses a threat. In the South China Sea, through which pass most of the shipments needed to satisfy China's insatiable appetite for oil and natural gas, the navy continued to flex its muscles by increasing deployments of nuclear-armed submarines. Other countries in the region, including Vietnam, Indonesia and the Philippines, expressed concern that China was more aggressively defending its territorial claims in the South China Sea in violation of the 2002 Code of Conduct. In December 2009, for example, Vietnamese Deputy Defence Minister Nguyen Chi Vinh told reporters that 'the situation with regard to disputes over sovereignty in the East Sea [South China Sea] causes certain concerns for Vietnam's national defence and creates new challenges'. The United States voiced its concerns about Chinese behaviour in the South China Sea in June 2010 when Gates, in his speech at the Shangri-La Dialogue, condemned 'any effort to intimidate US corporations or those of any nation engaged in legitimate economic activity'.

In the East China Sea, the PLAN made headlines in April 2010 when a flotilla comprising two submarines and eight destroyers passed narrowly between two Japanese islands without prior notification to Tokyo, en route to an exercise in waters off the disputed Okinotori Islands. Though the ships were operating in international waters, Japanese media and officials expressed concern when a Chinese helicopter reportedly flew within 100m of Japanese Maritime Self-Defense Force vessels.

China's navy also made positive contributions to the supply of public goods. A fifth flotilla was dispatched to the Gulf of Aden in March 2010 to participate in anti-piracy operations; while China was not officially integrated into the 30-nation combined task force in the Gulf, its role in the mission was welcomed. For example, US Rear Admiral Scott Sanders, then commander of the task force, said in November 2009: 'Piracy is an international problem that requires an international answer ... It is clear that China is a reliable partner and that our efforts are mutually beneficial.' In March 2010, two Chinese warships docked in Abu Dhabi, marking the first PLAN port call in the Middle East.

China's role in international institutions expanded as well. In response to the economic crisis, the world's largest economies all but abandoned the G8, whose meetings China had attended as an observer, and paid growing attention to the G20, of which China is a member. China played a constructive central role in G20 summits held to discuss the financial and economic crisis. At the UN, China agreed to boost its financial support in 2010 from 2.7% of the total operating budget to 3.2%, and became the seventh-largest funder of UN peacekeeping activities. Finally, in April 2010 China's voting power in the International Monetary Fund rose to 4.42% from 2.77%, ranking it third behind the United States and Japan.

A more active approach

Since China's reform and opening up began three decades ago, Chinese national interests have focused overwhelmingly inward on economic growth and domestic stability. In many ways, the People's Republic became accustomed to adjusting to changes in the international environment (since it was too weak do otherwise) and focused its efforts on ensuring that the periphery would remain stable enough to allow for continued prosperity at home. The onset of numerous regional and especially global challenges in the past few years, including the proliferation threats posed by North Korea and Iran, climate change and, most importantly, the collapse of the global financial system in 2008, thrust China onto the world stage almost overnight. Calls mounted from inside and outside China for policies to actively shape its environment and to play a central role in protecting core national interests and shared international interests. In many ways, China's own views of its interests have been slow to catch up to the world's expectations, and a nation so long focused inward is only now discovering that its diplomacy must contribute to the provision of public goods as well as secure resources, markets and technology for the continued augmentation of Chinese national power. Over the past year, China walked a tightrope, balancing its national interests with what it still saw largely as excessive international burdens that should be avoided lest they divert Beijing from its central task of development. In the future, however, this approach may become less viable. As an emerging global power, China's interests and the world's increasingly intersect, and to truly secure its domestic interests, Beijing may find that it has to take a leadership role in seeking to resolve international problems.

Korean Peninsula: Heightened Tensions

North Korea's sinking of a South Korean warship on 26 March 2010 raised tensions on the Korean Peninsula sharply, preventing any prospect of diplomatic progress in the foreseeable future. This was the most dramatic incident in a year during which North Korea endured self-imposed economic turbulence amid uncertainty about the health of its leader Kim Jong-il, while South Korea balanced a more ambitious global role with its continuing reliance on the United States.

Nuclear diplomacy stagnates

Efforts to denuclearise the Korean Peninsula had appeared to have entered reverse gear during 2009. In April the DPRK quit the Six-Party Talks and conducted ballistic-missile tests, which were followed by a successful second nuclear test in May. In June the UN Security Council responded with Resolution 1874, which included an extension of the arms embargo against North Korea, banning all weapons imports apart from small arms and all exports without exception. Successful enforcement of the resolution was made more likely after South Korea joined the Proliferation Security Initiative (PSI) in May. Unbowed, the DPRK announced that South Korea's participation in the PSI – under which countries interdict cargo suspected of carrying materials related to nuclear, biological or chemical weapons – rendered void the armistice agreement between the two countries, and in June announced that it would 'weaponise' its remaining plutonium stockpiles. It also repeated a claim it had first made in April that it would begin enriching uranium, notionally to fuel a future light-water reactor. In the same month, the DPRK sentenced two American journalists, detained in March 2009 for apparently crossing the border with China, to 12 years in a labour camp. As in 2006, Pyongyang went on to test-fire cruise and ballistic missiles to coincide with the American 4 July public holiday.

The DPRK later claimed to have reprocessed 8,000 additional spent fuel rods by the end of August, enough to produce around 8kg of plutonium or at least one nuclear weapon. This would be in addition to its existing plutonium stockpile, estimated to be equivalent to 4–8 weapons. To add further to its stockpile, North Korea would have to reverse previous disablement measures and restart the 5 MWt Yongbyon reactor. This would take approximately six months and, once operational, the reactor would be able to produce about 6kg of plutonium a year, roughly sufficient for one nuclear weapon. However, as of June 2010, there had been no indications of any rebuilding having taken place at the reactor site.

Enriching uranium would be the alternative way for Pyongyang to produce fissile material. While it was likely that the DPRK has pursued some level of enrichment for many years (indeed, American suspicions about a clandestine programme precipitated the collapse of the Agreed Framework in 2002), the US intelligence community has expressed less certainty about the progress that Pyongyang has made in this area. The technical significance of the declaration in a September 2009 letter from Pyongyang's delegation at the UN to the head of the Security Council that its 'experimental uranium enrichment has successfully been conducted to enter into completion phase' was unclear. It would be significantly easier for it to add to its nuclear arsenal by producing plutonium. It was probable that the DPRK hoped to use enrichment as a means to bolster its desired image as a nuclear-weapon state and to provide it with further leverage in international negotiations. In the same announcement Pyongyang made clear it was ready for 'dialogue', even while it said it was prepared to respond to sanctions with a strengthened nuclear deterrent.

This was typical of the way in which North Korea's confrontational diplomacy was leavened with occasional conciliatory gestures towards the United States and South Korea throughout the year. Following its belligerent activities and statements, the DPRK allowed former US President Bill Clinton to travel to Pyongyang in August to secure the release of the two journalists. Pyongyang also released an imprisoned South Korean worker (formerly employed north of the border at the Kaesong Industrial Zone) and a captured South Korean fishing crew, eased restrictions on travel to Kaesong, and allowed a new round of reunions between family members separated by the Korean War. These reunions were one-time events and, like the rest of the gestures, were not indicative of a real change in relations. Hopes were raised by North Korea's decision to send a delegation to the 18 August funeral of former South Korean President Kim Dae-jung, the architect of the 'sunshine' policy repudiated by President Lee Myung-bak. The delegation met Lee and conveyed a personal message from Kim Jong-il that called for improved relations. Optimistic that the funeral may have prompted a rapprochement, a presidential aide remarked to the press that 'simply put, we can say there has been a paradigm shift'.

These hopes were swiftly dashed. Pyongyang boasted of its enrichment advances less than two weeks later, and two days afterwards North Korea released water from at least one of its dams, drowning six South Koreans camping downriver. Pyongyang rejected a public offer from Lee Myung-bak of a 'grand bargain' in which the DPRK would receive economic assistance and security guarantees in return for denuclearisation.

By autumn 2009 North Korea was hinting that a resumption of the Six-Party Talks could be possible, despite having declared the talks to be 'dead' in April and 'gone forever' in July. These suggestions were most likely designed to satisfy China's demands for progress while delaying any actual return to multilateral negotiations on the nuclear programme, as well as in hope of extracting further concessions. In October Kim Jong-il reportedly told Wen (during the first visit of a Chinese premier to Pyongyang in 18 years) that the DPRK would rejoin the talks if the United States was willing to engage in bilateral negotiations first. Washington was prepared to reach out to the DPRK, as long as such discussions served as the precursor to renewed multilateral negotiations. The visit of Stephen Bosworth, US special representative for North Korea policy, to Pyongyang in December 2009 was the first high-level contact between the Obama administration and the Kim regime. But in a diplomatic snub, Bosworth was met upon his arrival by a mid-ranking official and later told that a peace treaty between the United States and the DPRK, excluding South Korea, would be a precondition for North Korea to rejoin the Six-Party Talks. The North Korean Foreign Ministry released a communiqué in January 2010 reiterating the need for such a treaty, and proposed that it be signed within the year. North Korea also demanded that sanctions be lifted before it returned to the Six-Party Talks.

Although Bosworth announced after his visit to Pyongyang in December 2009 that there was a 'common understanding' between the United States and North Korea on the need to implement the September 2005 Joint Statement on denuclearisation and to resume the Six-Party Talks, Washington responded with caution to North Korean overtures such as the release in February of Robert Park, a Korean-American journalist seized illegally entering North Korea on Christmas Day 2009, and an offer to reopen talks on finding US soldiers missing in action. North Korea, as the United States knew, was repeating a long-standing pattern of combining threats with inducements. This mixture had previously secured economic and political concessions in return for promised progress on denuclearisation that, in the end, either never materialised or was reversed. Pyongyang had repeatedly engineered crises so that it could extort assistance as payment for a return to the status quo. While the United States was prepared to engage in dialogue on other issues if North Korea were to demonstrate its willingness to move ahead with denuclearisation, Gates had made clear at the IISS Shangri-La Dialogue in May 2009 that it was 'tired of buying the same horse twice'.

> "Gates made it clear that America was 'tired of buying the same horse twice'"

It was reasonable to interpret North Korea's insistence on a peace treaty being concluded with the United States before the Six-Party Talks resumed – only months after it had insisted that it was indifferent to the prospect of normalising relations – as evidence that it was not serious about reviving the diplomatic process, and would never be persuaded to trade its nuclear capabilities for improved relations and economic aid.

The demand suggested that Pyongyang's ultimate goal was in fact to be acknowledged as a nuclear state and to use its nuclear capabilities as a means to extract concessions through coercion. On this view, North Korean references to the possibility of future multilateral negotiations were cynical gestures intended to buy the regime further concessions and time to manage its dynastic succession. The DPRK declared in a letter to the UN Security Council in October that it would be 'unthinkable even in a dream' for it to give up its nuclear weapons, and that these could never be relinquished until the United States completely disarmed. Washington emphasised that it would not consider lifting sanctions or signing a peace treaty until Pyongyang returned to the Six-Party Talks, and that it would in no way recognise North Korea as a nuclear-weapons state.

Rather than respond to North Korean provocations, the Obama administration attempted to follow a policy of 'strategic patience'. Its immediate focus therefore shifted to enforcing the sanctions mandated by UN Security Council Resolution 1874 and containing North Korea's proliferation potential, in particular by inspecting suspicious shipping. Although the resolution did not authorise the use of force if the vessel's flag-state withheld authorisation for an inspection, it did appear to enjoy some success in constraining North Korean action. An early victory was the statement by Myanmar's foreign minister, made public by US Secretary of State Hillary Clinton in July 2009, that his country would comply with UN sanctions against North Korea. That month, the North Korean ship *Kang Nam I*, believed to have been destined for Myanmar, had aborted its voyage and returned with its unknown cargo to the DPRK without requiring a forced interdiction by the US Navy. In August 2009, citing UNSCR 1874, India intercepted a North Korean vessel off its coast, although no illicit materials were discovered. In the same month the United Arab Emirates intercepted a ship sailing under a Bahamian flag that was transporting North Korean munitions and explosives apparently intended for Iran. In December 2009 the Thai authorities seized a Georgian aircraft containing 35 tonnes of weapons from North Korea, including man-portable air-defence systems. The Kazakh crew were eventually released and deported to their homeland. A leaked report by Thailand to the UN Security Council suggested that the consignment had been destined for Iran. In May 2010 the Israeli foreign minister claimed that the weapons had been ultimately intended for Hamas and Hizbullah, while the Israeli president stated that North Korea acted as a 'duty-free shop' for Iran and its proxies.

Further clampdowns on North Korean activity in December included the imprisonment of two Russian-based North Korean diplomats in Sweden for smuggling cigarettes, and the EU's imposition of a travel ban on 12 senior DPRK officials, including Jang Song-thaek, Kim Jong-il's brother-in-law and a possible future regent if Kim's young son Kim Jong-un eventually succeeds his father. These actions, as well as other interceptions of suspicious North Korean vessels, demonstrated that at least part of the international community was willing to enforce the measures contained within UNSCR 1874, although in May 2010 a senior US official warned that Myanmar might be intending to ignore the resolution and attempt to purchase weapons from Pyongyang. Moreover, China's decision in October 2009 to cease issuing detailed data on its trade with the DPRK suggested that its enforcement of UNSCR 1874 was inconsistent at best, and it remained North Korea's largest trading partner. In November South Africa stopped a ship destined for the Republic of the Congo with North Korean parts for tanks onboard. The components for T-54/55 main battle tanks had been loaded onto the ship at a Chinese port. The Panel of Experts on North Korea concluded in two reports to the UN Security Council that 111 states had failed to submit reports on their implementation of UNSCR 1874 and UNSCR 1718 (passed in 2006 after the first North Korean nuclear test), and that various assessments indicated continuing North Korean involvement in nuclear and missile-related activities in countries such as Syria, Iran and Myanmar.

Inter-Korean tension

Relations between the South and North, while interspersed with occasional moments of concord such as Seoul's dispatch of medical supplies to help the North to tackle an outbreak of swine flu, were generally characterised by confrontation and sometimes overt hostilities. After taking office in 2008, Lee had ended the unconditional 'sunshine' policy pursued by his two predecessors of sending substantial material assistance to North Korea, pursuing engagement and avoiding criticism of its regime. Lee spoke of a 'lost decade' in which the North had pocketed concessions while developing a nuclear arsenal and testing an atomic device and ballistic missiles. Seoul would now condition aid to the DPRK on reciprocal North Korean efforts towards denuclearisation. The North's refusal to take such measures and its rejection of Lee's offers for a 'grand bargain', combined with the lack of appetite within South Korea for decisive confrontation, meant that Seoul would be forced to calibrate a careful response to Pyongyang's periodic provocations.

On 12 October, around a week after Wen's visit to Pyongyang, North Korea fired short-range missiles into the Sea of Japan and announced a navigation ban off its eastern and western coasts. On 10 November the most serious naval skirmish for seven years occurred when a North Korean vessel crossed the disputed Northern Limit Line (NLL) and sustained heavy damage in an exchange of fire. South Korea prompted furious responses from Pyongyang when it co-sponsored a UN resolution on human rights in North Korea in November and when its defence minister stated in January that it could launch a pre-emptive strike if a North Korean nuclear attack appeared likely. Naval tensions continued in January when North Korea fired artillery rounds into the sea on its side of the NLL; Seoul responded in kind.

At the same time, however, North Korea appeared eager to restart or sustain the revenue flows generated by South Korean commercial investment and tourism. In January and February the two Koreas held talks on conditions in the Kaesong Industrial Zone, which employed approximately 40,000 North Koreans earning around $30m a year in salaries and lend-lease fees. February also saw talks on restarting tourism to Kaesong and Mount Kumgang; tourism to both sites had been suspended since 2008 after the shooting of a South Korean visitor and the distribution of anti-regime propaganda. North Korea unsuccessfully tried to brush aside Seoul's concerns about the safety of South Korean citizens in order to restart the tourism projects. On 25 March Pyongyang threatened to take 'extraordinary measures' if Seoul refused to lift its ban on tourism to Mount Kumgang. The following day, in response to South Korean press reports that experts from South Korea, China and the United States would examine contingency plans to react to scenarios of future chaos in the DPRK, the North Korean military declared that 'those who seek to bring down the system ... will fall victim to the unprecedented nuclear strikes of the invincible army'.

That night the *Cheonan*, a 1,200-tonne South Korean navy corvette, sank near the NLL after an explosion that split it in two. Forty-six of its 104-strong crew were killed. Lee's government, aware of the potential for catastrophic escalation if it were clear that North Korea had been responsible, initially reacted cautiously, amidst a national outpouring of grief and some criticism of the defence establishment's slow response to the crisis. Seoul established a Joint Civilian–Military Investigation Group composed of experts from South Korea, the United States, Britain, Australia, Canada and Sweden.

On 20 May the results of the investigation were made public: the *Cheonan* had been sunk by a torpedo fired from a North Korean submarine. Supported by strong forensic evidence, South Korea argued that there was 'no other plausible explanation'. North Korea responded that the evidence was fabricated and threatened to respond to any new sanctions with all-out war. It countered South Korean suggestions of renewed psychological warfare against the Kim regime with threats to close the border and trap South Koreans within Kaesong and to destroy South Korean loudspeakers broadcasting propaganda across the frontier, and even a 'merciless strike' that could turn Seoul into a 'sea of flame'. Pyongyang also announced that it would cut all ties and contact with South Korea for the rest of Lee's time in office, including military-assurance agreements designed to prevent accidental conflict. South Korea stated that nearly all inter-Korean trade was to cease (with the exception of Kaesong, although firms operating there were requested by the Ministry of Unification to delay payments to North Korea), and that North Korean merchant ships would be barred from using South Korean sea lanes.

> " The *Cheonan* had been sunk by a North Korean submarine "

The United States pledged its support for South Korea and planned joint anti-submarine exercises. While under pressure to respond to North Korea's behaviour, neither Washington nor Seoul was keen for the situation to escalate into open conflict. Yet their desire for a firm UN Security Council response was complicated by China's ambivalence. Despite its frustration with Pyongyang's obstinacy in recent years, China's continuing diplomatic and economic engagement with North Korea reflected its determination to revive the Six-Party Talks and its priority of preventing regime collapse in North Korea. Despite a request to Hu by Lee that a planned trip to China by Kim Jong-il be delayed, the visit proceeded in May – Kim's first trip to China in four years and his first time abroad since his stroke in 2008. Although Chinese press reports said Kim had reaffirmed to Hu the DPRK's commitment to denuclearisation and readiness to rejoin the Six-Party Talks, no tangible steps to restore confidence in the diplomatic process were announced. China waited a month after the *Cheonan* sinking to send condolences to South Korea, describing the event as 'unfortunate'. After the release of the investigation results, it urged restraint, apparently reluctant to accept the conclusion that North Korea was culpable.

Nor were these the only manifestations of peninsular tensions. In April, while the investigation of the warship incident was under way, an assassination plot against the prominent North Korean defector Hwang Jang-yop was uncovered, the DPRK froze South Korean assets at Mount Kumgang, and 24 South Korean employees were expelled from the resort in May.

During Kim's visit to China, Lee had convened a meeting of top military commanders and vowed 'clear and resolute measures' against whoever was responsible for the sinking. By June, Lee was seeking a clear admission of responsibility from Pyongyang. In a speech to the IISS Shangri-La Dialogue in Singapore, he said that North Korea should 'admit its wrongdoing; it must pledge to never again engage in such reprehensible action'. He urged Pyongyang to abandon its nuclear ambitions and accept the terms of his proposed grand bargain, and emphasised that 'we do not seek confrontation and conflict'. But in response to a question, he made clear that 'we must not let the enemy look down upon us' and that Seoul needed to strengthen its deterrence against North Korea.

On the same day as Lee's address, South Korea referred the *Cheonan* sinking to the UN Security Council. After presenting its evidence, South Korea said it hoped that the Security Council would take 'timely and appropriate measures'. North Korea threatened that any condemnation by the Security Council could lead to war. While the United States emphasised the importance of the world sending a 'strong message' to North Korea over the sinking, as of June neither Russia or China had either refuted or endorsed the results of the international investigation, and their support for any UN condemnation of North Korea appeared uncertain.

North Korea: self-inflicted economic troubles

Kim Jong-il appeared to have recovered since suffering a stroke in 2008, yet his health remained the topic of much speculation throughout the year. South Korean press reports in July 2009 suggested that he was fighting pancreatic cancer, while the head of a South Korean state-run research institute suggested in March that Kim also suffered from diabetes and kidney problems that required dialysis. In January a report by another government-affiliated research institute estimated that Kim would live for no more than another two years, while it was reported in March that a senior US official had said during a private meeting with the US ambassador to South Korea, a South Korean politician and activists that Kim was unlikely to live past 2013.

Nevertheless, Kim was able to make an increased number of public appearances from spring 2009 onwards, including his meeting with Bill Clinton in August 2009 and his trip to Beijing in May 2010. Although there were widespread press reports in mid-2009 that Kim had ordered officials, the military and diplomatic missions abroad to recognise his youngest son Kim Jong-un as his successor, it appeared that efforts to establish his son's legitimacy slowed somewhat after this point. Although his status had not been made official, Kim Jong-un remained the most likely contender to succeed his father. Kim's desire to cement the legitimacy and status of his son, despite his youth and lack of military experience, may have contributed significantly to the confrontational policies pursued by the DPRK since late 2008. An amendment of the constitution in April 2009 to denote the notion of *songun* ('military-first') as equal to the national principle of *juche* ('self-reliance'), and an expansion of the National Defence Commission (NDC), seemed to suggest that Kim was eager to secure his power base within the military in advance of any leadership transition. In June 2010 Jang Song-thaek, Kim's brother-in-law and probable future regent, was promoted to vice-chairman of the

NDC. The previous month a long-standing rival of Jang had died, apparently in a car accident, and an elderly member of the NDC had been dismissed. Another senior official had died of a heart attack in April. Whether or not these deaths were suspicious, they symbolised efforts by Kim to install a new generation within the leadership that would support his son's succession.

The lack of reliable statistics pertaining to North Korea's dysfunctional economy (exacerbated by China's decision in October 2009 to stop issuing data on its trade with the DPRK) made assessments highly dependent on anecdotal evidence and conjecture. It was clear, however, that the DPRK's economy suffered problems from the imposition of sanctions through UNSCR 1874, particularly due to interdictions against its shipments of conventional weapons. It was not helped by the drying up of the revenue stream from South Korean tourism to Mount Kumgang and Kaesong since 2008, and the gap left by what had been an unconditional annual aid supply from South Korea of 500,000 tonnes of rice and 300,000 tonnes of fertiliser. These shipments, which had covered 50% of the DPRK's yearly shortfall, ended once Lee's presidency began in 2008. In addition, from March 2009 onwards North Korea refused American food aid. In September the UN World Food Programme assessed that a third of North Korean women and young children were malnourished, while in February the South Korean Ministry of Unification reported that the North's 2009 grain harvest had been poor, some 5% lower than the previous year.

On 30 November 2009 the regime suddenly implemented currency reform. New currency was issued, with old notes transferable for new ones at the ratio of 100:1. Since only a limited amount of the old currency could be converted, this move had the effect of eliminating most savings. The redenomination, which was accompanied by an ineffective ban on foreign currency, was presumably intended to curb inflation and to strengthen the regime's control over the economy, particularly by targeting the 'merchant class' involved in black-market activity. The regime probably calculated that targeting the small traders and corrupt junior officials who would be most affected by the reform would be a popular policy, especially since many state salaries continued to be paid at the same nominal rate, effectively increasing wages of state employees a hundred-fold. However, mass confusion and uncertainty encouraged hoarding of commodities, while the boosted state salaries increased demand for goods that could not be adequately supplied. Both of these factors, along with the collapse of local markets, produced rampant inflation. Moreover, since the collapse of the Public Distribution System during the famines of the 1990s, local markets had become essential for food distribution. Reports emerged of serious food shortages, and a South Korean NGO claimed that Korean War veterans had mounted a protest in a town where deaths from starvation had been reported.

While it was impossible to verify press reports that spoke of widespread unrest throughout North Korea, it was clear that the situation was serious enough to merit some displays of regret by the regime. Pak Nam-gi, head of financing and planning for the Korean Workers' Party, was used as a scapegoat: he was dismissed, and, according to unconfirmed reports, was executed by firing squad in March 2010. The DPRK's premier, Kim Yong-il, reportedly apologised to government officials and local leaders for having enacted the reforms 'without sufficient preparation, causing pain among the people'. Even Kim Jong-il himself made an oblique apology by referring in the Korean Workers' Party *Rodong Sinmun* newspaper to a pledge made by his father Kim Il-sung that North Koreans would not have to rely on corn: 'I am most heartbroken by the fact that our people are still living on corn … What I must do now is feed them generous amounts of white rice, bread and noodles.' In February the bans on foreign currency and markets were lifted, and prices appeared to have stabilised somewhat: 1kg of rice that ostensibly cost some 20 won just after the re-evaluation had risen to 1,000 won in mid-March, before retreating to 500–600 won by April. Yet unconfirmed reports by South Korean NGOs suggested that food shortages remained severe, and that by late May the North Korean government had removed the last remaining restrictions on the operation of private markets, a tacit acknowledgement that it was unable to manage food distribution via a planned economy.

> " Even Kim Jong-il made an oblique apology "

South Korea: focus on US relations

Under Lee South Korea has pursued a more prominent global role. It was to chair a G20 summit in November 2010 and host the next Nuclear Security Summit in 2012 – no doubt partly to highlight Pyongyang's isolation during what will be the centenary year of late 'Great Leader' Kim Il-sung, Kim Jong-il's father, and the date set by North Korea to become a 'strong and prosperous nation'. Seoul contributed more than 200 peacekeepers to UN efforts in Haiti, and on 25 February 2010 the National Assembly agreed to deploy 350 troops to Afghanistan, three years after Korean forces had left the country following the kidnapping of South Korean missionaries. A South Korean rear-admiral took command of the multinational task force combating Somali piracy, and Seoul has plans to create a blue-water navy.

Bilateral relations with the United States improved after the elections of Presidents Lee and Obama, who exchanged visits in 2009. In an opinion poll, 49.9% of South Korean respondents believed that the alliance with the United States was 'strong', compared to only 19.3% in 2007. In general, military cooperation with the United States improved after Lee succeeded Roh Moo-hyun as president. In November 2009 it was announced that both countries had finally completed OPLAN 5029, a document that laid out plans for emergency scenarios in North Korea, including regime collapse. Roh had been reluctant to plan for such eventualities out of concern that it could provoke the North – and indeed, a North Korean journal announced that the completion of OPLAN 5029 was a 'declaration of war', and the document itself was stolen by computer hackers based either in China or North Korea. In addition to joint exercises with the United States, South Korean forces participated for the first time in the six-nation *Cobra Gold* exercises held in Thailand in February 2010.

Other legacies of the Roh's administration's military policies raised more serious problems. Plans to move US forces away from the de-militarised zone (DMZ) and relocate them south of Seoul sparked disagreements over transfer costs and suffered severe delays. For example, the move of the United States Forces Korea (USFK) headquarters from Yongsan in central Seoul to Pyeongtaek, south of the capital, was originally scheduled for 2008, then moved back to 2012, and further delays looked possible, with some even suggesting 2019 as a more feasible date for completion. Relocation of US forces, as well as their planned smaller footprint within the country, would assuage some of the fierce opposition from the left towards the US military presence, although many Korean conservatives were anxious that America's retrenchment was proceeding too swiftly.

In 2007 the US had agreed with the Roh government to transfer wartime operational control (OPCON) to Seoul, with the handover due to be completed by 17 April 2012. However, some in South Korea feared that this was too hasty and could jeopardise the country's security. In February 2010 Chung Mong-joon, chairman of Lee's Grand National Party (GNP), described the transfer as 'an irresponsible decision made by the Roh government without an objective assessment of security conditions'. In January Defense Minister Kim Tae-young argued that given the symbolic importance of 2012 for the North Korean regime, the date set for OPCON completion had made for 'bad timing'. In March another senior GNP lawmaker called for the United States and South Korea to establish a Joint Study Group to review the transfer, while in May Lee Sang-woo, head of the newly established Commission for National Security Review, recommended a delay in the transfer due to Seoul's inability to deal with growing threats from North Korea on its own. In a statement to the US Congress the USFK commander confirmed that the transfer was on schedule to be completed by April 2012 and that the process would not lead to a reduction in US forces on the peninsula. However, other US officials indicated some willingness to discuss a delay in the transfer. While there were concerns that any delay could be interpreted as 'pusillanimity' in the face of North Korean aggression, at the end of June Lee and Obama agreed to postpone the transfer until 2015 due to the *Cheonan* incident.

Lee's government was to receive assurances that America remained committed to the defence of South Korea, including through its extended nuclear deterrence. In June 2009, a month after the second North Korean nuclear test, Lee met Obama in Washington and secured a written joint statement that confirmed the importance of the US nuclear umbrella. Concerns that the new Nuclear Posture Review (NPR) would weaken America's commitment to nuclear deterrence were not realised.

The free-trade agreement signed with the US in 2007 remained dormant. The GNP pledged to ratify the agreement once it moved forward in the US Congress, but the Obama administration did not send the bill to Capitol Hill. The White House hesitated to submit the agreement for ratification due to concerns over bilateral trade imbalances, as well as being occupied by more pressing domestic priorities. In May 2010 Senators John Kerry and Richard Lugar sent an open letter to Obama, noting that China had replaced the United States as South Korea's largest trading partner in 2004, and urged him to submit the bill for ratification as soon as possible, preferably before Seoul hosted the G20 in November.

Nuclear ambitions

South Korea's nuclear ambitions bring with them the potential for future tensions with the United States. Twenty nuclear power reactors currently meet around 40% of South Korea's domestic electricity needs, and by 2020 its nuclear-power capacity is due to expand by 56%. In addition, South Korea has ambitions to become a major nuclear-power exporter. In December 2009 Seoul secured a landmark deal with the United Arab Emirates (UAE) for a Korean consortium led by the Korea Electric Power Corporation (KEPCO), in which the Korean government owns a 51% controlling stake, to be paid $20.4bn to construct, commission and provide the initial fuel loads for four 1,400MW APR-1400 third-generation pressurised-water reactors. The first reactor is due to become operational in 2017. It is likely that KEPCO will be awarded another $20bn contract to operate the reactors over the next 60 years. KEPCO reportedly substantially underbid its French and American/Japanese rivals and attached other favourable conditions to the contract in the hope of securing this landmark first export deal for the Korean nuclear industry and thus obtain a showcase for future contracts. The government stated that Seoul hoped to sell 80 reactors worth $400bn by 2030, making it the third-largest nuclear-power exporter.

Given the planned expansion of both its domestic and export nuclear-power sectors, South Korea was lobbying for a relaxation of constraints on its fuel-cycle activities. The Korean nuclear industry hopes to become completely independent by 2012, and the Korean Atomic Energy

Commission envisages a national development plan involving fast breeders and fuel recycling. Reprocessing would reduce the problem of spent nuclear fuel storage (current storage sites will reportedly be full by 2016) and Seoul's dependence on foreign fuel suppliers, but poses proliferation risks. Both the 1974 nuclear cooperation agreement with the US and the 1992 Joint Declaration on Denuclearization of the Korean Peninsula prevent South Korea from reprocessing spent fuel. Since 1997 South Korea has been developing a technique known as pyroprocessing. Unlike the more common PUREX reprocessing method, pyroprocessing does not separate plutonium from other elements in spent fuel, and has therefore been portrayed by South Korea as proliferation-resistant – although further chemical separation would be relatively simple to perform. The current US nuclear cooperation agreement will expire in 2014, and in July 2009 the South Korean government announced plans to negotiate an amendment to any new deal that would permit it to perform pyroprocessing. In a speech at a nuclear-power conference in March 2010, Prime Minister Chung Un-chan repeated his government's desire for pyroprocessing to form a key part of Korea's future fuel cycle. It was reported in June that the priority of responding to the *Cheonan* incident meant that negotiations between Washington and Seoul to revise the nuclear cooperation agreement would be postponed until later in 2010.

The United States has sought to limit the spread of fuel-cycle technology since the 1970s. The one major exception in its policy has been Japan, the only non-nuclear weapon state with significant reprocessing capabilities. This disparity has angered many in the Korean nuclear establishment, who question why Seoul must forgo its 'sovereign rights' if Tokyo need not do so and believe that concerns over the legality of South Korean reprocessing are misplaced, given North Korea's blatant violation of the 1992 Joint Declaration. In January the United States and South Korea agreed to launch a technical and economic feasibility study on pyroprocessing before negotiations begin. Previous assessments by the US Department of Energy had concluded that pyroprocessing only boasted minimal increased protection against proliferation compared to PUREX. There were no indications that the US saw South Korea's demand for pyroprocessing rights as motivated by a desire for a nuclear-weapons capability, although a March 2010 report by the US Joint Forces

Command assessed that both South Korea and Japan were 'highly advanced technological states and could quickly build nuclear devices if they chose to do so'. The United States is aware that granting Seoul the right to reprocess spent fuel could complicate long-term hopes of denuclearising the peninsula, antagonise China, and set an unfortunate precedent in negotiations with other countries about their own fuel-cycle activities, regardless of how proliferation-resistant pyroprocessing may actually be.

Ratings recover with economy

South Korea did not escape the effects of the global recession, suffering an economic contraction of 5.1% in the final quarter of 2008. Yet it had begun a solid recovery by the second quarter of 2009 (indeed, the fastest economic recovery of any OECD country, bar Australia), leaving it with an overall growth rate of 0.2% for 2009 and a projected GDP growth rate of 4.5% for 2010. The economic resurgence contributed to Lee's improved approval ratings, which had plunged to 30% by June 2009 but increased to around 50% by December. The Korean Confederation of Trade Unions (KCTU) had failed to mobilise mass demonstrations effectively during the same month, and Lee's increased political capital helped him to take legislative measures against them in 2010.

Despite mounting opposition fury against Lee in mid-2009, when former President Roh's supporters blamed Lee for his suicide in May 2009 over allegations of corruption and blockaded the National Assembly building, the Democratic Party failed to gain ground in opinion polls. However, Lee faced opposition from a faction within the GNP support-ing Park Geun-hye, his rival from 2007 and a likely candidate to succeed him as president in 2013. Park's opposition complicated Lee's efforts to modify the planned relocation of government agencies to Sejong City and his $18bn initiative to clean and beautify South Korea's four largest rivers. Both policies, along with Lee's handling of the *Cheonan* incident, were key issues in the 2 June local elections. Belying pre-election polls, the GNP performed poorly, winning only six mayoral and gubernato-rial seats compared to the Democratic Party's seven. Although Lee's firm policy towards the North following the *Cheonan* disaster had won him praise from abroad, many South Koreans suspected that the ship had in fact been sunk by the United States and feared that his determination to hold North Korea to account could provoke wider conflict. Although the elections did not directly affect the composition of the National Assembly and hence the GNP's overall majority, the GNP chairman resigned over the party's poor showing, and its leader in the National Assembly warned that the GNP would no longer give unconditional support to the administration, further complicating Lee's reform plans.

South Korea's growing trade and technological prowess looked to continue to give substance to Lee's theme of 'global Korea'. However, it looked likely that the North would continue to find ways to drag Seoul back to the preoccupations of peninsular security.

Southeast Asia: Political Conflict and Stresses

Southeast Asia's political complexity was apparent in the upheaval, unease and democratic consolidation that variously characterised parts of the region. Thailand's political conflict worsened to the extent that clashes between protesters and security forces in April and May 2010 raised the prospect of widespread civil conflict as a result of the gulf between the aspirations of the populist 'red shirt' movement aligned with exiled former prime minister Thaksin Shinawatra and the country's 'yellow shirt' political establishment. In Myanmar, the regime's plans for elections during 2010 did not seem to offer a way of resolving the long-running stand-off between the military government on one hand and the democracy movement and ethnic-minority rebels on the other.

The political outlook elsewhere in Southeast Asia was more positive. Elections in Indonesia in July 2009 resulted in Susilo Bambang Yudhoyono winning a second term as president, though politically inspired corruption allegations against key figures in the new administration undermined its credibility and reformist drive. Elections in the Philippines in May 2010 raised fears that the country's development would continue to be constricted by the political dominance of a self-perpetuating, economically powerful elite. However, the election of Benigno 'Noynoy' Aquino III as president raised hopes of a tougher line against the country's crippling corruption. In Malaysia, Prime Minister Najib Tun Razak's assumption of national leadership strengthened the position of the ruling Barisan Nasional coalition, though political and religious tensions continued to characterise the national scene.

Internal-security concerns remained prominent in several Southeast Asian countries. On the positive side, there were renewed hopes for a settlement between the Philippine government and the Moro Islamic Liberation Front (MILF), while the Indonesian security forces registered major counter-terrorist successes. However, the Abu Sayyaf Group in the southern Philippines persisted as a threat, as did Malay-Muslim insurgents in southern Thailand. Meanwhile, Southeast Asian governments remained as concerned as ever about the implications of the shifting regional distribution of power – and particularly China's growing power – for their countries' security, but were keen to defend the existing structure of regional institutions based on the Association of Southeast Asian Nations (ASEAN) in the face of suggestions for a new regional security architecture.

Thailand's protracted agony

The lethal clashes between 'red-shirt' protesters and government security forces in Bangkok during April and May 2010 were the culmination of the country's drawn-out political crisis since 2005. The conflict was not simply between the populist Thaksin's poor, rural supporters and an urban middle class backing the Bangkok political establishment and the monarchy. Indeed, Thai army estimates suggested that 70% of red-shirt protesters involved in the 2010 demonstrations came from Bangkok or nearby provinces. Moreover, the red-shirts displayed diverse political positions: while many supported Thaksin (who lives in exile in Dubai and Montenegro) and demanded his return, others were critical of him, arguing that as premier he had failed to deliver on his promises and that he was no longer essential to their cause. Voting in the 2007 general election suggested that around 40% of Thais sympathised with the red-shirt cause, while a similar proportion supported the yellow-shirts; around 20% of Thais appeared to be undecided, or unwilling to take sides.

The urban violence in early 2010, and indeed the country's overall political instability, took place in the context of deep uneasiness in

Thailand regarding the prospective succession to the widely revered but ailing 82-year-old King Bhumibol Andulyadej. Throughout Thailand's often tumultuous history since 1945, the king has provided a sense of continuity and has frequently legitimised significant political developments, most recently in 1992 by intervening to halt street protests against a military-led government. The royal palace engages in politics extensively, if indirectly, through a loose alliance of pro-royalist forces emanating outwards from the Privy Council and including the judiciary, armed forces, parts of the bureaucracy, universities and even non-governmental organisations. What particularly alarms royalist and conservative political forces is the prospect of Thaksin being in power when Crown Prince Maha Vajiralongkorn, who is somewhat unpopular and is widely expected to be a weak monarch, ascends to the throne. Their fear is that the new king would allow Thaksin too much leeway to govern Thailand in his own style and for the benefit of his own business interests.

An army-led clampdown in Bangkok in April 2009 temporarily ended violent protests by the United Front for Democracy against Dictatorship (UDD) group, which backed Thaksin, against Prime Minister Abhisit Vejjajiva's coalition government. The red-shirts deemed Abhisit's administration illegitimate because of the way it was installed in a 'silent coup' following the November 2008 Constitutional Court judgement that dissolved Thaksin's proxy People's Power Party and two other parties and toppled the pro-Thaksin government that had been in office for less than a year. Opposition to Abhisit's government remained widespread and substantial, and in February 2010 the government strengthened its domestic security apparatus, establishing 38 'security centres' in the country's north and northeast, and deploying 5,000 troops to prevent protesters from entering Bangkok, where a large-scale UDD protest was expected following the Supreme Court's announcement on 26 February of its verdict on whether to seize Thaksin's assets. Although the court found that Thaksin had used his position as premier to benefit his Shin Corp telecommunications company while he was prime minister from 2001 to 2006 and confiscated $1.4bn from a total of $2.2bn in frozen assets, the anticipated protests did not materialise. Nevertheless, the UDD announced that it would organise a demonstration involving a million protesters in Bangkok on 14 March to call for elections. Although in the event the demonstrators numbered only around 150,000, many of them from the heartland of Thaksin's support in north and northeast Thailand, over the following two months a hard core of activists and supporters provoked mayhem in Bangkok, including the most violent clashes between demonstrators and security forces since 1976.

Following a series of peaceful UDD marches in Bangkok in late March, the government in early April declared a state of emergency in the city when protests expanded to the Ratchaprasong intersection in the city centre. Because many police personnel sympathised with the UDD (Thaksin himself was a former senior police officer), the army had necessarily to take the lead in countering the protests. However, even the army's efforts to control the disturbances were slow and, according to some foreign observers, less than competent because of lack of relevant training and effective leadership. On 10 April, violent clashes between the army and protesters at Phan Fah bridge resulted in 24 deaths (including those of five soldiers and a Japanese journalist), and more than 800 people were injured. The army subsequently admitted that troops had fired live rounds directly at protesters, who used rocks, petrol bombs and (the army claimed) firearms and grenades. The army was unable to seize the protest site and retreated, leaving behind substantial quantities of arms and other equipment, including assault rifles, heavy machine guns, armoured personnel carriers, ammunition, riot shields and body armour. Despite the carnage on 10 April, neither side was willing to step back from confrontation and on 14 April UDD leaders – whom Deputy Prime Minister Suthep Thaugsuban called 'terrorists' – announced that they would regroup in the up-market Rajaprasong shopping area for a final showdown with the security forces. On 22 April, the army command moved 10,000 troops into central Bangkok and warned that it was willing to use live ammunition again if necessary. Negotiations between Abhisit's government and the UDD, following the latter's offer to end the protests in return for a dissolution of parliament within a month and elections days later, failed to produce agreement on an election date, with Abhisit claiming that the dissolution of parliament needed to benefit 'the whole country' and to occur 'at the right time'. After more violent clashes, the UDD tentatively accepted a political 'roadmap' involving parliamentary dissolution in September and a mid-November election that the admin-istration offered on 3 May, but then demanded additional concessions – including Abhisit's arrest for the deaths on 10 April – which caused the government to withdraw its offer on 13 May. Speculation suggested that the UDD rejected the roadmap because it made no reference to an amnesty for Thaksin; however, it was also clear that government's offer had divided the red-shirt movement.

On 14 May, the army and police surrounded the main red-shirt camp and its several thousand remaining protesters, but met heavy resist-ance. A sniper (presumably from the security forces) fatally wounded Major-General Khattiya Sawasdipol, who had defected from the army to become the red-shirts' unofficial security chief. Central Bangkok effectively became a war zone, with mounting casualties on both sides and among bystanders. After several days of skirmishing, and Khattiya's eventual death, on 19 May the army launched a long-delayed final assault on the pro-testers' encampment using armoured personnel

> " The offer had divided the red-shirt movement "

carriers. UDD leaders surrendered in order to avoid further casualties, but a hardline core of red-shirts continued to resist and set fire to the Bangkok stock exchange, shopping malls, banks and a TV station. There were also disturbances in provincial centres in the north and northeast, with several town halls burnt down. By 22 May, violent protest had sub-sided, leaving a total casualty toll since April of 88 dead (most of whom were protesters) and almost 1,400 injured.

Speaking to the nation three weeks after the final assault on the red-shirts in Bangkok, Abhisit presented a 'letter to the Thai people' which introduced a five-point roadmap towards national reconciliation intended to address the socioeconomic disparities that underlie Thailand's politi-cal schism, to control the media (which the government claims to have stoked the disturbances), to discuss constitutional reform, to uphold 'the honour of the monarchy', and to investigate the recent violence. However, despite Abhisit's insistence that announcing the roadmap was just the start of a lengthy process, critics pointed to his statement's brevity and lack of detail. These features made it ideal for propagation through the medium of the Twitter social-networking site, following the example of the UDD which had used the electronic medium extensively during the protests, but at the same time it perplexed many Thais who had expected a fuller statement of intent from the prime minister.

With the rift between Thailand's two main political camps deeper than ever, continuing fears concerning the royal succession, no consensus on when to hold new elections, and 40% of the electorate unlikely to accept the legitimacy of whatever government is elected, the prospect in mid-2010 was for continuing political conflict and possibly further violence. The economic impact of Thailand's acute political stability was already severe: in late May, Finance Minister Korn Chatikavanij estimated that economic growth for 2010 was likely to be at least two percentage points lower than the 7% that had been expected earlier in the year. The tourism sector was particularly badly affected. According to Korn, growth for the rest of the year would depend on 'how quickly we can put our house in order'.

Myanmar: grounds for hope?

Thailand's neighbour, Myanmar, moved towards its first elections for 20 years in a state of great uncertainty. It became increasingly clear that the elections, a key milestone in the seven-stage 'roadmap to democracy' that the State Peace and Development Council (SPDC) junta announced in 2008, were unlikely to satisfy domestic opponents and external critics of the military government.

In March 2010, the SPDC announced long-awaited electoral legislation, the Political Parties Registration Law, which decreed that parties intending to participate in the elections must register within 60 days. However, it also prohibited anyone serving a prison sentence from being a member of a registered political party: parties with disqualified members were required to expel them or face dissolution. This law effectively excluded Nobel laureate Aung San Suu Kyi, leader of the National League for Democracy (NLD) and victor in the 1990 elections (following which the military did not allow her and the NLD to form a government), from participating in the forthcoming elections, given the failure two weeks earlier of her appeal against conviction for breaching the terms of her house arrest. At the end of March, the NLD said it would not take part in the elections because of the 'unjust' election laws. This was unsurprising in light of the NLD's Shwegondaing Declaration of April 2009, in which its participation in the elections was made conditional on, among other things, the release of Aung San Suu Kyi and other political prisoners. However, the effect of the boycott was that the NLD would cease to exist as a political party, though its social development work would continue. Moreover, the significant proportion (perhaps a majority) of the electorate that would have voted for the NLD would have to decide whether to vote for other parties or to abstain. Though the NLD leadership's decision was supposedly unanimous, dissenting pragmatists within the party argued for participation in the elections and subsequently announced they were forming a new party which would apply to register itself for the elections. Other NLD dissenters might stand as independent candidates.

By late May 2010, 39 parties had applied to register, and all applications had been approved. Of these, around 15 were national parties, the others smaller and regionally based. The national parties included the new Union Solidarity and Development Party (USDP), a political spin-off from the regime's social organisation, the Union Solidarity and Development Association. The USDP's candidates included current government ministers, who resigned from the Tatmadaw (armed forces) in order to qualify as civilian candidates. Such candidates prospectively increase the military's influence substantially beyond the 25% of total seats allocated to it under the constitution. Another pro-regime party to register was the National Unity Party, the successor to the late General Ne Win's Burma Socialist Programme Party.

Whether the election can be conducted smoothly and without disruption will depend in large measure on the SPDC's relations with the numerous non-Burman ethnic minority groups that populate Myanmar's periphery, constitute around one-third of the population, and have supported some of the world's longest-running insurgencies (which in turn have provided a major justification for military rule over the country as a whole). Since the 1990s, the Yangon regime has agreed ceasefires with 18 ethnic minority rebel groups, including the substantial armies of the Kachin, the Wa and some Shan militias. The 2008 roadmap envisaged that these 'ceasefire' militias would be transformed into border guards under Tatmadaw command. By mid-2010, 17 armed ethnic-minority groups had acquiesced in such arrangements: various Kachin, Karenni and Kokang groups were transformed into Border Guard Force (BGF) battalions, while others were allowed to form semi-autonomous local militias.

In late 2009, the refusal of the Kokang minority to join the BGF led to conflict with the Tatmadaw close to the Chinese border, causing ethnic Chinese citizens of Myanmar as well as illegal Chinese immigrants to flee into China. Ultimately, the Kokang suffered defeat and agreed to join the BGF. However, more powerful ethnic-minority groups such as Kachin Independence Organisation (KIO), the New Mon State Party, the United Wa State Army, the Shan State Army–North and the Karen Peace Council all rejected the regime's proposals and rearmed. The government warned ethnic-minority groups that if they continued to resist government offers after a deadline on 28 April 2010, it would revoke their ceasefire status and declare them illegal. If this happened, it seemed likely that the regime would declare a state of emergency in non-ceasefire regions and bar residents there from voting: the election laws stipulate that elections can only be held in the absence of conflict. The likely resultant inadequacy of ethnic-minority representation threatened to undermine the legitimacy of the elections still further.

Despite the severe constraints that the regime was imposing, some observers were optimistic that the elections would be another step in a gradual process of liberalisation that had been apparent in Myanmar since Cyclone Nargis in 2008 provided an opportunity for international organisations and charities to establish a presence in the country. Such observers pointed to a limited but noticeable amount of public debate, and a growing minority view in Myanmar that even a flawed liberalisation process was better than none at all. The more prevalent opinion in the country, though, seemed to be one of deepening cynicism regarding the intent of the military, whose primary interest was evidently to retain effective long-term control of Myanmar's political, economic and social systems rather than to initiate a process that would lead in the foreseeable future to real liberalisation of the country's political system.

During 2008–09, unconfirmed reports that the SPDC regime was developing nuclear weapons increased sharply, following the appearance in Thailand of defectors from Myanmar who claimed to have directly knowledge of a secret nuclear-weapons programme. At the ASEAN Regional Forum meeting in Phuket in July 2009, Hillary Clinton said that the US government was concerned over military cooperation between North Korea and Myanmar. International reactions were generally muted, however, with concerned governments and international organisations erring on the side of caution because of a lack of sufficient information on which to make a well-founded judgement.

Maritime Southeast Asia: a mixed picture

Compared with Thailand and Myanmar, the three main states of maritime Southeast Asia manifested greater stability and provided international observers with relatively little cause for concern. Nevertheless, their political scenes were far from untroubled. Indonesia continued its democratic consolidation. Following legislative elections in April 2009 which revealed continuing strong support for Indonesia as a secular state despite it being the world's most populous Muslim country, in July Susilo Bambang Yudhoyono (widely known as 'SBY') received a resounding mandate for a second term as president, this time with a former Bank of Indonesia governor, Boediono, as his vice-president. This winning ticket received 61% of the vote, compared with 27% for Megawati Sukarnoputri and Prabowo Subianto, and 12% for Jusuf Kalla and Wiranto.

Following his inauguration on 20 October 2009, however, it was not long before SBY's new administration faced major problems, with opposition parliamentarians levelling corruption allegations at Boediono and Finance Minister Sri Mulyani Indrawati – the two leading economists in the government, both of them technocrats rather than party-political figures. These charges related not to any personal corruption but rather to the decision by Boediono (then central bank governor) and Sri Mulyani (who had also been finance minister in the initial SBY administration) to bail out a relatively small Indonesian bank, Bank Century, after it defaulted on major loans at the height of the global financial crisis in late 2008. While the bailout helped Indonesia ride out the financial crisis by preventing depositors from panicking, the measures cost more than anticipated, and some key depositors may have benefited more than the bank itself. Leading the attack on Boediono and Sri Mulyani was Aburizal Bakrie, a wealthy businessman and former coordinating minister for the economy, who in 2009 had become chair of the Golkar party, which was formally part of SBY's ruling coalition.

Sri Mulyani, widely-respected domestically and internationally as a tough-minded reformer credited with increasing foreign investment and guiding Indonesia's economy through the financial crisis, resigned her ministerial post in May 2010 to become a managing director at the World Bank. This may have a move calculated by SBY to ensure the survival of the coalition with Aburizal Bakrie and Golkar. As of mid-2010, Boediono remained vice-president, amid speculation that he might ultimately also opt to resign rather than face a protracted impeachment-style procedure with the attendant damage that this would do to the administration. Against this backdrop, sympathetic observers expressed concern that the second SBY government seemed to be drifting without a clear agenda.

In Malaysia, the Barisan Nasional (National Front) coalition government, led by the United Malays National Organisation (UNMO), faced an uphill struggle to reassert its political primacy under Prime Minister Najib Tun Razak, who succeeded Tun Abdullah Ahmad Badawi in April 2009. Abdullah's national leadership was widely seen as lacklustre, and the Pakatan Rakyat opposition coalition led by Wan Azizah Wan Ismail, wife of and proxy for former Deputy Prime Minister Anwar Ibrahim (who was still disbarred from direct involvement in politics as a result of a criminal conviction) made significant gains in the March 2008 elections, taking control of five state governments and denying the Barisan Nasional the two-thirds majority that it held in the federal parliament since independence in 1957. Anwar soon returned to parliament to lead the opposition and, for several months, claimed that he could persuade sufficient Barisan Nasional legislators to defect to bring down the government. In the event, the federal government faced down this threat, and in February 2009 managed to re-assume control of the Perak state government by securing the defection of Pakatan Rakyat assembly-men. The opposition, however, continued to pose an extremely serious challenge.

Once he took office, Najib – whose father and uncle were both prime ministers in their time – avoided rhetoric emphasising the interests and rights of the majority Malay community, instead stressing his government's intent to tackle matters of concern to all ethnic groups, notably poverty, and the need for a higher-quality and more accessible education system. Najib's cabinet included a minister of unity and performance, reflecting his concern to reduce tensions between ethnic and religious groups, and to implement the Government Transformation Programme aimed at making the public service sector more effective, efficient and transparent. In May 2009, Najib announced the New Economic Model, intended to accelerate Malaysia's transition to developed-country status and emphasising the development of knowledge-based industries and the need to attract increased foreign investment. The government will allow foreign investors majority stakes in businesses apart from 'strategic industries' such as banking, telecommunications and energy. The economic initiative also reduced the Malaysian government's traditional emphasis on boosting the economic stake of the Bumiputra (Malay and other indigenous Malaysian) community, whose minimum ownership stake in publicly listed companies it cut from 30% to 12.5%. In June 2010, Najib announced the 10th Malaysia Plan, the government's economic development programme for the next half-decade, which targeted real annual GDP growth of 6%.

> " There was widespread disdain for what many saw as empty rhetoric "

There were few signs, however, that these initiatives were swaying public opinion in favour of the government, particularly among the ethnic minorities. Indeed, there was widespread disdain for what many saw as the government's empty rhetoric, while popular concern focused on police ineffectiveness in the face of rising crime, the continuing prevalence of high-level corruption, the federal government's inefficiency, and major economic disparities between regions.

Meanwhile, though, while the opposition retained substantial and possibly growing support (winning 8 out of 11 federal by-elections between 2008 and mid-2010), Anwar Ibrahim's leadership of the Pakatan Rakyat seemed ineffectual, and his own party, Parti Keadilan Rakyat, appeared to be the opposition coalition's weakest component. Anwar lost considerable credibility when his pledge to take power at national level by September 2008 came to nought. Moreover, since June 2008 he had faced new criminal charges – which he claimed were part of a conspiracy to force him out of politics again – relating to sodomy. His trial began in February 2010, and was supposed to resume in mid-July. If convicted, Anwar would face up to 20 years in prison. In an apparent attempt to reassert his role as opposition leader in March 2010 (and subsequently) Anwar resorted to populist anti-semitism (a common theme in Malaysia's modern political discourse, despite the country's lack of a significant Jewish community), pointing to a supposed conspiracy between Najib's administration, the United States and APCO, an American public-relations firm retained by the government to develop the '1Malaysia' campaign intended to enhance national solidarity in the face of the country's ethnic divisions, and claiming that APCO was controlled by Jews who were manipulating Malaysia on behalf of the United States. These claims suggested a degree of desperation on Anwar's part to re-take the initiative in the national political debate and, more specifically, to attract greater support from within the Malay community.

More worrying from the perspective of the country's stability was the emergence of ultra-nationalist pressure-groups which stood firmly against what they claimed to be the erosion of Malay rights implicit in new government policies. Maverick member of parliament Ibrahim Ali founded Perkasa ('Strength') after the 2008 elections, and by early 2010 it had become a vehicle for conservative elements in UNMO who feared that new government policies seemed to pay too much attention to the interests of ethnic and religious minorities. In January 2010, the group made a strong stand in response to the *Malaysia v. The Herald* case, in which the High Court decided that government regulations prohibiting non-Muslim publications from using the term 'Allah' were unconstitutional. Immediately after this ruling, Gertak (an acronym standing for People's Awareness Movement, which also translates as 'intimidate') was formed, with the supposed aim of uniting the Malay community. Many Malaysians blamed a subsequent rash of fire-bomb attacks on churches near Kuala Lumpur and elsewhere in early January, apparently in response to the High Court judgment, on such extremist groups.

In the Philippines, the run-up to the May 2010 general election (involving presidential, legislative and local components) was marred by violence, notably the mass-murder motivated by clan rivalry of 57 unarmed civilians, mainly women and journalists, in Maguindanao province, part of the semi-autonomous Muslim region of Mindanao in the country's south. The women had been intending to register the candidacy of a male relative for the provincial governorship. The gunmen who carried out the massacre were allegedly working for the Ampatuan clan, which tightly controls the province, in part through its state-condoned private militia which had supported government counter-insurgency efforts against Muslim separatists. Subsequently, Andal Ampatuan Sr, the clan's patriarch, and provincial governor at the time of the massacre, was charged with murder alongside his son, who allegedly led the murderers.

Although Esmael Mangudadatu, the Ampatuans' opponent, won the Maguindanao gubernatorial election, for many observers the massacre was symptomatic of a political system which despite its democratic facade including regular elections, vibrant mass media and a supposedly independent judiciary, was actually dominated by privilege, money politics and violence. These shortcomings help to explain the Philippines' relative economic regression and extreme social inequality. Corruption is estimated to consume 30% of the national budget.

In May 2010, many of the candidates for the presidency, vice-presidency and Congress were scions of prominent political families. These candidates included the clear victor in the presidential election, Benigno 'Noynoy' Aquino, son of former president Cory Aquino and assassinated opposition leader Benigno ('Ninoy') Aquino Jr. As an opposition senator, 'Noynoy' Aquino was a strong critic of graft and electoral fraud, and was party to several efforts to impeach President Gloria Macapagal Arroyo (who took office in 2001). His election-campaign focus on the need to eradicate corruption undoubtedly contributed significantly to his success. However, Philippine political observers pointed out that once Aquino took over as president on 30 June 2010, in attempting to tackle corruption he would confront the challenge posed by an entrenched and politically powerful elite. Nevertheless, when he was proclaimed president-elect in early June 2010, Aquino renewed his anti-corruption promises and identified tackling 'smugglers' in the Bureau of Customs as an initial priority.

The second major challenge for Aquino as president looked to be providing tangible improvements in the Philippines' economic plight, particularly in terms of reducing the budget deficit and managing inflation. After corruption, the high cost of basic goods was the most important election theme and a large part of the electorate wants 'pro-poor' policies. At the same time, Aquino and his administration will need to deal more effectively than the previous government with the Philippines' broad spectrum of internal security threats, including the continuing Maoist insurgency of the New People's Army across much of the country, the complex troubles in Mindanao and other parts of the Muslim south, and a human-rights environment that deteriorated seriously under Arroyo's presidency.

Internal security concerns persist

After the intense resurgence of fighting between the MILF and the Armed Forces of the Philippines (AFP) that followed the breakdown of peace negotiations during 2008, a ceasefire ordered by the government in July 2009 precipitated the MILF's return to talks. At the end of the month, negotiations resumed under Malaysian auspices in Kuala Lumpur. In mid-September, under the so-called Ramadan Accord, the two sides signed a framework agreement establishing an International Contact Group (ICG) to support the peace process. By the end of 2009, the ICG comprised Japan, Turkey and the United Kingdom, as well as several NGOs. The new negotiations survived the Maguindanao massacre in November (which some in the AFP and the media sought to blame on the MILF), continued fighting between the AFP and the Abu Sayyaf Group in which MILF personnel were sometimes implicated, a dispute between the two sides over the fate of MILF commanders whom the government accused of 'atrocities', and an apparently still wide gulf between the positions of the Philippine government and the MILF on the appropriate status for the Moro entity that should result from the negotiations. During February and March, the international sponsors of the peace process – led by Malaysia – began reconstituting the International Monitoring Team, which had supervised the 1997 ceasefire agreement before it broke down in 2008. The new team was expected to include military observers or civilian experts from the European Union, Indonesia,

Norway and Qatar as well as from original contributors Brunei, Japan, Libya and Malaysia. During early 2010, however, it became clear that the government and MILF were unlikely to achieve final agreement under Arroyo's administration and that some sort of interim agreement was the best that could be achieved before Aquino took office on 30 June. On 4 June, the two sides' peace panels signed a 'Declaration of Continuity for Peace Negotiations' to ensure that the peace process continued despite the change in government in Manila.

Meanwhile, the Philippines' security forces seemed to make little progress in countering the activities of Abu Sayyaf, whose area of operations in the south of the country overlapped with that of the MILF, despite continuing support from 600 US troops deployed in the southern Philippines as part of *Operation Enduring Freedom*. In the face of intensified operations led by the Philippine Marines in early 2010, Abu Sayyaf continued to kidnap and murder civilians, and in mid-April mounted five simultaneous gun and bomb attacks in Isabela City, the provincial capital of Basilan island, leaving 14 civilians, police officers and troops dead. The AFP subsequently attacked Abu Sayyaf bases and training camps, and in late May a senior military officer claimed rashly that the 'AFP has effectively curtailed the terror campaign of the Abu Sayyaf'. Two days later, a group of 30 Abu Sayyaf gunmen kidnapped three government employees whom they subsequently murdered, prompting what the AFP claimed was a 'full blast' offensive against the terrorist group in early June.

For security and intelligence agencies in the region and further afield, one worrying aspect of Abu Sayyaf's resilience was the persistent evidence that operatives from the pan-Southeast Asian terrorist group, Jemaah Islamiah (JI), had not only sought refuge with it, but had also provided bomb-making expertise for joint operations. AFP raids on Abu Sayyaf bases in March and April 2010 discovered evidence of the presence of JI personnel, who may have participated in the Isabela City attacks. Evidence also emerged in early 2010 that the southern Philippines provided a sanctuary which had contributed to the emergence of a significant new terrorist group in Indonesia. Reports suggested that, from 2003, leading JI bomb-maker Dulmatin – reputedly a mastermind of the 2002 Bali bombings – found refuge with Abu Sayyaf, provided them with technical training and participated in operations. Probably in late 2007, after evading capture by Philippine security forces, Dulmatin moved to Aceh in Indonesia, where he assembled a new terrorist group that included former contacts from JI and other violent Indonesian extremist groups including KOMPAK and Darul Islam, as well as new recruits from Aceh. This *lintas tanzim* or 'cross-organisational project' apparently repudiated JI's ideological shift away from violent jihad towards religious outreach and Islamic community-building. At the same time, though, it sought to assert a longer-term strategy than the JI splinter group led by Noordin Top, responsible for the 2003 Marriott hotel and 2004 Australian Embassy bombings in Jakarta, the 2005 Bali attacks and, finally, the twin attacks on the Marriott and Ritz-Carlton hotels in Jakarta in July 2009. The July 2009 attacks caused nine deaths, including those of two suicide bombers. Responding to these first major terrorist bombings in Indonesia for almost four years, Jakarta's security forces stepped up their hunt for Noordin, who was eventually killed in mid-September alongside three other terrorist suspects during a police raid near Solo in Central Java. Noordin's death effectively concluded an important chapter in Southeast Asian Islamist terrorism.

Unlike either the mainstream JI or Noordin Top's group, the ideology of Dulmatin's *lintas tanzim* stressed the waging of jihad as a means of establishing Islamic law, in the first instance from a secure zone which could be the nucleus of an Islamic state as well as an operational base. The aim was to do this without causing Muslim casualties. However, while the group established a primary base in Aceh, it was not to last long. In late February 2010, a chance encounter between a local police intelligence officer in Aceh and members of Dulmatin's group based there provoked a series of police raids in Aceh and Java over the following two months that led to the arrests of 48 jihadis, and the deaths of eight others, including Dulmatin. Perhaps 15 other individuals from the coalition remained at large and posed a continuing security threat. The discovery of Dulmatin's group highlighted the possibility of new terrorist threats evolving out of other groups that had been broken up, and from newly radicalised individuals. Nevertheless, the disruption of the Noordin Top and Dulmatin groups amounted to important victories in Indonesia's counter-terrorism campaign.

There were no signs of success, however, in the Thai authorities' efforts to manage the Malay insurgency in their country's three southernmost provinces. Indeed, the Abhisit government's primary focus on countering the red-shirt challenge continued to distract it from dealing more effectively with the southern insurgency. Despite measures including the expanded use of civilian militias to support security-force operations, and new economic stimulus measures for the region, insurgent activity continued at a high tempo with an average of almost 20 rebel attacks occurring weekly during the first four months of 2010.

Concerns over the emerging regional order

Southeast Asian governments have become increasingly concerned over the nature of the emerging regional security order. These concerns derive largely from pervasive evidence that the regional distribution of power is in long-term flux, particularly as a result of China's growing wealth and strategic extroversion on the one hand, and the apparently growing challenges to the long-term capacity of the United States to maintain its regional security role on the other. Individual Southeast Asian states and their regional grouping, ASEAN, have adopted a policy of hedging towards their relations with the United States and China. This reflects their vital interest in preventing Chinese regional hegemony while at the same time avoiding entering wholeheartedly into any balancing strategy against China. Equable relations with China are important for economic as well as security reasons: it is an increasingly crucial, even if sometimes resented, trading partner and investment source for Southeast Asia.

However, China's behaviour has hardened attitudes in some Southeast Asian capitals, particularly in the context of their conflicting territorial claims with Beijing in the South China Sea. During 2009, China's navy reportedly detained 17 Vietnamese fishing vessels and more than 200 Vietnamese fishermen in disputed areas, and at the end of the year Hanoi requested the return of boats that the Chinese still held. At the very end of the year, China's announcement of plans to develop tourism in the Paracel Islands (which it seized from South Vietnam in 1974) further increased tensions with Hanoi. Vietnamese efforts to internationalise the South China Sea issue became more evident in November 2009, when Hanoi convened a regional conference of maritime experts.

Vietnam also continued efforts to upgrade its naval capabilities, in large part as a deterrent to any future Chinese attempt to seize disputed features in the Spratly Islands, and in December its prime minister signed an arms-sale agreement in Moscow that included the purchase of six *Kilo*-class submarines. In early 2010, one short-term response by Beijing to this development was apparently to direct Chinese think tanks and academics to highlight repeatedly the issue of 'provocative' Southeast Asian military programmes. Vietnam was not alone in resisting Chinese pressure in the South China Sea: according to Beijing, during May 2010 Malaysian naval vessels 'harassed' Chinese fishing vessels (which may have been naval intelligence-gathering auxiliaries) in the Spratlys. Meanwhile, the United States' latest Quadrennial Defense Review in February 2010 mentioned Washington's interest in not only developing existing alliance relations with the Philippines and Thailand and its strategic partnership with Singapore, but also in developing new strategic partnerships with Indonesia, Malaysia and Vietnam. These countries' governments were all, to a greater or lesser extent, keen that the United States should remain involved in regional security, but doubts persisted in Southeast Asian capitals over America's will and capacity to do so in the longer term. The third postponement of US President Barack Obama's much-heralded visit to Indonesia dented repeated US statements concerning Southeast Asia's importance, while Southeast Asian governments were not oblivious to America's severe economic problems and the impact these could have in the future on its ability to project power in Asia if China's wealth and military strength continued to grow.

There was also a degree of anxiety in Southeast Asia over the future institutional structure for regional political and security cooperation. Since the late 1960s, ASEAN and more recently its pan-regional extensions in the form of the ASEAN Regional Forum (ARF), ASEAN+3 and the East Asia Summit (EAS) have provided the so-called 'regional security architecture' for not only Southeast Asia but also the wider East Asian and Asia-Pacific regions. However, the shortcomings of these institutions in the politico-security sphere were evident, for example, in the failure of ASEAN to deal more effectively with the problems generated by one of its member states, Myanmar; in the apparent inability of the ARF to advance its 'preventive diplomacy' agenda; and in frustrations in Northeast Asia and Australasia over ASEAN's determination to remain in the driving seat of regional institutions. These stimulated new thinking in the wider region about the appropriate institutional framework for managing regional security.

The most controversial proposal, and one which provoked some strong reactions within Southeast Asia, was then Australian Prime Minister Kevin Rudd's suggestion for an all-encompassing Asia-Pacific Community (APC), first enunciated in June 2008 and subsequently refined in later speeches during 2008–09. Southeast Asian responses – notably at the June 2009 IISS Shangri-La Dialogue and a December 2009 conference that the Australian government sponsored in Sydney – focused on concerns that the proposal failed to recognise ASEAN's achievements in constructing a regional order, and on the danger that a new institution based on the APC proposal might lack the inclusiveness of ASEAN and might exclude smaller ASEAN members. To the extent that a consensus emerged at the Sydney conference, it favoured building on existing ASEAN-led institutions such as the EAS (particularly through membership expansion to include the United States) rather than creating any grand new regional body. After the Sydney meeting, less was heard of the APC proposal, which effectively expired with Kevin Rudd's ouster as Australian Labor Party leader and prime minister in June 2010.

> "The proposal effectively expired with Kevin Rudd's ouster as prime minister"

However, other suggestions emerged, including Japanese Prime Minister Yukio Hatoyama's September 2009 proposal for an East Asian Community (EAC) along the lines of the European Union, and the notion of a 'KIA' (Korea–Indonesia–Australia) axis to promote the interests of these three medium powers amidst the flux that seemed almost certain to characterise the distribution of power in the Asia-Pacific for the indefinite future. While Southeast Asian governments asserted the continuing utility of ASEAN-centred institutions, it seemed likely that challenges to their primacy would re-surface unless they demonstrated newfound competence in the political and security sphere.

Australia, New Zealand and the Southwest Pacific

Australia: Juggling Global and Regional Priorities

The rise of Chinese power and the prospect of strategic conflict between China and the United States, Australia's traditional major-power ally alongside the United Kingdom, have become Australia's central strategic concerns. This situation is new and unsettling for Australia. Its post-1945 trade expansion came primarily with Asian partners aligned with the United States for their defence: Japan, South Korea, Taiwan and the original core group of the Association of Southeast Asian Nations (ASEAN). Since 2007, however, China has supplanted Japan as Australia's biggest bilateral trading partner. In early 2010, it became the biggest export market too, as China's rapid rebound from the global economic crisis led to frenetic demand for iron ore and other raw materials. Thus, the Australian government found itself pulled between strong strategic alignment with the United States and a broader, more hedged brand of regional engagement fuelled by economic as well as prudential security considerations.

Seeking a balanced China policy

In its May 2009 Defence White Paper, Canberra's first new strategic review since 2000, the Australian Labor Party government of then Prime Minister Kevin Rudd, elected in November 2007, raised the possibility of a contested Western Pacific, with American dominance no longer assured. But the document was equivocal in its judgement, and Canberra sought to dispel notions that it feared receding American power and interest. In February 2010, Foreign Minister Stephen Smith said that 'the United States, which has underwritten stability in the Asia-Pacific for the last half-century, will continue to be the single most powerful and important strategic actor in the region for the foreseeable future'. Smith added that, while China's rise was a defining element in Asia's growing influence, as power shifted from the Atlantic, it was 'not the only story or the whole story', citing the rising strength of India, the ASEAN economies, the individual potential of Indonesia and the enduring strengths of Japan and South Korea.

Canberra's ostensible policy was to engage China as a 'responsible stake-holder' in global affairs, in line with the approach advocated by the George W. Bush administration in 2004. Indeed, aside from a wobble at the start of John Howard's premiership in 1996, Australian policy has been directed towards that goal since the 1970s. Yet to some, the White Paper continued to suggest worries in Canberra that an amicable partnership between Beijing and Washington might not develop. Although the document reasserted the primacy of the 'Defence of Australia' and an Asian focus for the alliance with the United States, as opposed to a more expeditionary and global flavour, it also supported force components that would enable Australia to augment US military efforts far from Australian shores. At the same time, there were doubts about Australia's ability to meet cost, technology and manpower challenges. For example, the Royal Australian Navy has experienced continuing operating and personnel problems with its six domestically built *Collins*-class submarines, and has proposed replacing them with 12 larger submarines to be built in Adelaide to a unique design that ministers have admitted will be at 'the margins of Australia's scientific and technological capacity'.

The prevailing view in Canberra foreign-policy circles accordingly favoured a policy of continued engagement and persuasion vis-à-vis China, including containment of the Taiwan and North Korea problems. There remained a strand of conservative thought which argued that Beijing's good behaviour as a 'responsible stake-holder' meant only that it was biding its time for a later strategic contest for influence, and that explicitly regarding China as a strategic competitor would produce a better outcome. To some Australian analysts, the contest had already started, with the assertive patrols by PLA Navy flotillas around the Japanese archipelago and harassment of ostensibly routine US ocean surveillance operations in international waters off China. These activities, not the PLA Navy's occasional blue-water forays, seemed to have the most strategic significance insofar as they directly challenge the US sea-based alliance system and the corresponding regional order. Australian forces already reinforce the American strategic presence in East Asian seas. A small number of EP-3C maritime surveillance aircraft carry out patrols into the South China Sea from the Butterworth air base in Malaysia, and Australian warships regularly exercise with the US and Japanese fleets. Projected upgrades in terms of submarines, *Aegis* destroyers, cruise missiles and strike aircraft will sustain Australia's ability to contribute to US military activity in the region.

China's often enigmatic economic moves posed a subtler and less momentous challenge. In July 2009, only weeks after the White Paper stirred indignation in Beijing, China's Ministry of State Security arrested four Shanghai-based staff of the Anglo-Australian mining company Rio Tinto – one Chinese-born Australian citizen and three Chinese nationals – on suspicion of bribery and obtaining state secrets. The arrests deepened Australian suspicions of Chinese government retaliation for Australia's allegedly discriminatory foreign investment standards. Earlier in 2009, the Australian government, wary of Chinese control of Australian national resources, had held up an attempt by a large state-owned Chinese metals corporation, Chinalco, to double its 10% stake in Rio Tinto, which was struggling with high debt after the September 2008 financial crisis. It emerged that the Chinese Commerce Ministry's primary motivation was simply to support large state-owned steel makers against private Chinese steel entrepreneurs for control of iron-ore imports. In the event, pragmatism prevailed on both sides. The case was transferred to the Chinese police, the charges reduced, and the four Rio Tinto employees sentenced to jail terms in March 2010. Rio Tinto disowned them, and announced plans for a joint-venture iron mine with Chinalco in Guinea, West Africa. Chinese investments in metals ventures in Australia's west and north and in coal strip-mines along the eastern coast gained clearance.

Diplomatic friction was harder to finesse. China objected strongly to the attendance of exiled Uighur leader Rebiya Kadeer at the Melbourne Film Festival, where a movie about her life was shown. In January 2010, while showcasing the new Cyber Security Operations Centre in Canberra run by the Defence Signals Directorate (DSD) – counterpart of the United Kingdom's Government Communications Headquarters and the United States' National Security Agency – Defence Minister John Faulkner disclosed that the DSD had been fending off more than 200 cyber attacks on defence information systems a month, and a smaller number of attacks on non-defence systems. Although Faulkner was careful not to name China, it has been a prime suspect in sophisticated cyber attacks, and Beijing probably regarded Faulkner's pointed mention of the frequency of such attacks as a veiled accusation. Even so, the two governments have sought to ensure diplomatic cordiality. Vice-Premier Li Keqiang, expected to become premier in the 2012 generational change of Chinese leadership, went forward with an official visit to Australia in October 2009, followed in June by Vice-President Xi Jinping, who is likely to succeed Hu Jintao as party chief and president.

Accommodating America

Kindred thinking between Rudd and US President Barack Obama on multilateralism, climate change, social welfare and financial regulation kept US–Australia relations warm. The Australian government also welcomed Obama's interest in Indonesia, his childhood home for several years, as a valuable source of American attention to a nation of great potential weight in regional security and the world Islamic community. But Canberra resolutely refused to be drawn into further military involvement in Afghanistan. This issue became acute after the collapse of the Dutch government in February 2010 over its deployment of 1,950 troops in Uruzgan province, where they provided force protection for an Australian deployment of 1,500 soldiers tasked largely with reconstruction. The Dutch contingent was expected to be withdrawn in August 2010. Faulkner argued that forces had to be retained at home to cope with regional emergencies and declined to add to the Australian contingent. Almost simultaneously, however, he announced that Australian forces in Timor Leste would be cut from 650 to 400 by February 2010 because of an improving security situation. Military analysts had thus concluded that Australia could at least marginally increase its forces in Afghanistan without compromising its regional posture.

Canberra's reluctance to do this stemmed less from operational incapacity than from strategic doubt, largely unvoiced, that the United States' aggressive programme of counter-insurgency and state-building in Afghanistan would achieve lasting positive results. As of mid-2010, Canberra intended to split the difference with Washington by maintaining a localised approach in Uruzgan, training up Afghan Army units, police and civil administration ahead of an expected exit in mid-2011. There remained some anxiety that if, as seemed likely, US forces replaced the Dutch, more aggressive tactics could heat up conflict in the province.

Active in Asia

Australia's relations with traditional friends in Asia continued to be stable, though Canberra analysts watched with some concern the rising political tensions in Thailand and Malaysia. Relations with Indonesia were unusually steady, with President Susilo Bambang Yudhoyono's address to the Australian parliament on a March 2010 bringing an effusion of goodwill.

The formation, for the first time, of a government by the Democratic Party of Japan (DPJ) after elections in August 2009 raised questions in Canberra about a potential loosening of US–Japan strategic ties, and a shift of Tokyo's attention to East Asian neighbours. During US President George W. Bush's two terms, Howard's tenure and successive conservative Japanese administrations, a 'trilateral' strategic relationship between the US, Japan and Australia had been at least tacitly consolidated. Despite then Japanese Prime Minister Yukio Hatoyama's somewhat iconoclastic inclinations, a visit to Australia by Japanese Foreign Minister Katsuya Okada revealed little change in Tokyo's broadly favourable position on this arrangement. Neither did Hatoyama show much movement on the vexed issue of Japan's 'scientific' whaling expeditions in the Southern Ocean, opposed by both the Australian and New Zealand governments and harassed by environmentalists operating from Australasian ports.

Asian governments were generally lukewarm about Rudd's June 2008 proposal for a new Asia-Pacific Community to provide a framework for security and economic cooperation. In particular, Hatoyama's East Asian Community proposal diluted Japanese interest, while Southeast Asian nations were concerned that such a forum would marginalise ASEAN. At the same time, Indonesia, ASEAN's most powerful member, was frustrated at the body's inability to effectively tackle regional issues like Myanmar's governance and human-rights problems. In March 2010, Indonesian Foreign Minister Marty Natalegawa suggested that adding the United States and Russia to the existing East Asia Summit list (which includes the ten ASEAN nations plus Japan, China, South Korea, India, Australia and New Zealand) would achieve a close semblance of the grouping envisaged by Rudd. When Rudd was deposed by his deputy prime minister, Julia Gillard, in June 2010 in an internal Labor Party convulsion over his faltering support in opinion polls, the proposal looked to drop back in Canberra's priorities.

Two factors inhibited Rudd's declared goal of forging a closer relationship with India. First, his party's position barring uranium exports to non-signatories of the Nuclear Non-Proliferation Treaty (NPT) led to a reversal of Howard's earlier clearance of uranium sales if they were merely subject to safeguards against diversion to weapons use, which had been in line with US policy. The May 2009 NPT Review Conference brought no inkling of any shift in Canberra's position. Foreign Minister Smith told the conference that Australia was committed to a universal NPT, and called on non-signatory states to accede 'as non-nuclear weapon states and without preconditions'. While India sought no immediate uranium supplies from Australia, the policy irked New Delhi in light of its strong record on non-proliferation in contrast to that of China, which nonetheless enjoys access to Australian uranium.

The other factor was a string of attacks against Indian students in Melbourne and Sydney, leapt upon by India's many television news channels and other popular media as evidence of Australian racism. The violence stemmed from a massive influx of young Indians taking advantage of a 2004 change in migration policy allowing graduates of vocational courses to obtain permanent residency, with Indian students seeking homes and part-time jobs in disadvantaged suburbs. After some initial reluctance on the part of state police forces, the issue was addressed as a specific crime problem and steps were taken on both sides to delink education and migration.

Despite these hindrances, in November 2009, Rudd and Indian Prime Minister Manmohan Singh announced a formal 'strategic partnership' with enhanced security cooperation and the possibility of a free-trade agreement. With Indian steel production expected to quadruple by 2020, and the first sale of Australian liquefied natural gas from the offshore Chevron-operated Gorgon Project to India agreed in August 2009, Australia's trade with India appeared poised to grow considerably, as it had with China. At the same time, Canberra has pursued an enhanced if still modest level of support for Pakistan, doubling the number of training positions in Australia for Pakistani defence personnel to 140 and raising development assistance.

Effective pragmatism

The Rudd government showed a willingness and ability to use foreign policy with agility and instrumental purpose in the region, and Gillard was expected to try to do the same. For instance, in early 2010, an increased influx of Sri Lankan boat people, displaced in the wake of the May 2009 military defeat of the Tamil Tigers, to Australia's outlying Christmas Island moved Rudd's conservative opponents to accuse him of 'losing control' of Australia's borders. The government then stepped up Australia's efforts to help the Sri Lankan government 'win the peace' by ameliorating treatment of the Tamil population and thus lessening pressure on Tamils to seek asylum in Australia. Although, according to a poll released in May 2010 by the Lowy Institute, domestic approval of the Rudd government's foreign policy was tepid, the main complaints concerned immigration policies that were considered lax and the government's perceived stand-down on climate change in delaying the implementation of a carbon-emissions trading scheme until 2013. Poll participants still gave the Rudd government high marks (seven on a scale of ten) for maintaining a strong alliance with the United States, while registering ambivalence about China's rise that was generally reflected in national policy. Overall, the Australian government's constructive pragmatism in international affairs appeared well-suited to enabling Australia to navigate the fluid strategic environment in the Asia-Pacific region and, in particular, to calibrate its key relationships with the United States, China and India effectively.

New Zealand's Modest Extroversion

The steady thaw in Wellington's strategic relationship with Washington accelerated during Obama's presidency. New Zealand had been virtually cut out of the trilateral Australia–New Zealand–United States (ANZUS) alliance with the United States and Australia after Labour Party governments in the 1980s banned the entry of nuclear-armed and -powered ships to its ports. By the end of the George W. Bush era, with tactical nuclear weapons long withdrawn from US warships, New Zealand regained standing as a steadfast ally, maintaining a continuous army presence in Afghanistan from 2001 (though quietly declining to join the US-led invasion and occupation of Iraq) and contributing to numerous regional security operations.

Prime Minister John Key's centre-right government, replacing Helen Clark's Labour administration in November 2008, stepped up New Zealand's Afghanistan deployment in August 2009, ordering a return of Special Air Service units after a four-year break and assigning more armoured vehicles to aid the army reconstruction unit in Bamiyan province. His government meanwhile began a comprehensive review of the defence forces in mid-2009, aimed at squeezing more front-line capability from the NZ$2.1 billion defence budget. The review was expected to result in a new Defence White Paper in September 2010.

Having become the first developed nation to sign a free-trade agreement with China in 2008, New Zealand was notably active in the pursuit of greater regional economic integration, and looked possible to reach a similar deal with India after negotiations slated for 2010. The New Zealand government, maintaining a foreign-policy focus on developing nations and emerging Pacific economies, also sought to bolster regional stability, particularly through efforts, alongside Australia, to advance governmental reform in Fiji through the Pacific Islands Forum.

Southwest Pacific: Political Dysfunction, Economic Fragility

Issues of poor governance and poverty continued to be the main preoccupations in the Southwest Pacific. Fiji remained the most glaring sore spot, with the military's suspension of parliamentary democracy into its fourth year. The military commander and regime prime minister, Commodore Frank Bainimarama, held out against a May 2009 deadline from the Pacific Islands Forum, a 16-member regional body, to call elections before the end of the year, and Fiji was suspended from the forum. The government went on to announce tighter controls on the media, including a ban on 'negative reporting' and a prohibition against foreign ownership of greater than 10% that threatened to force the *Fiji Times*, one of the island's two major daily newspapers, to cease operating.

Bainimarama promised elections for 2014, under a controversial new electoral system that sweeps away a racially based system that had assured ethnic Fijians of political dominance since independence from the United Kingdom in 1967. Ethnic Fijian institutions, including traditional chiefs and the Methodist Church, bitterly opposed the reforms. Meanwhile, the Fijian economy suffered from sanctions, with the poverty level rising to about 45%, and a steady exodus of more skilled ethnic Indians. About half of the island's 840,000 people now live in Suva and surrounding squatter settlements, which has produced high potential for civil unrest. After tit-for-tat expulsions of diplomatic envoys in 2009, Australia and New Zealand agreed to new dialogues at the ministerial level, but these produced little perceptible change in Bainimarama's policies.

Tonga continued its transition from monarchy to parliamentary rule, with a new electoral system announced in April 2010 that would provide for 17 elected members in a 26-member parliament, replacing the existing 30-member parliament which had only nine elected members. But the government's decision to abolish the independent commission that appointed judges and make direct appointments itself led to the resignation of the attorney-general, an Australian lawyer, and threats by New Zealand to halt its financial aid, which had substantially financed the judiciary.

The region's largest country, Papua New Guinea, has had uninterrupted elected parliamentary rule since independence in 1975 and in recent years has enjoyed a return to macro-economic stability. Yet it was rated at 154 out of 180 countries on Transparency International's index of corruption, and was widely seen as getting worse. Several members of Sir Michael Somare's government were cited for serious abuses by the main government watchdog, the Ombudsman Commission. The response was an assassination attempt against the chief ombudsman in late 2009, and moves by Somare to weaken the commission's powers. His government ignored the recommendations of an official inquiry that 57 highly-placed persons face criminal prosecution over alleged conspiracies to siphon large sums in false compensation claims against the government.

The ability of traditional aid donors, notably Australia, to wield influence over Port Moresby and demand accountability has waned. In mid-2010, Papua New Guinea was poised to sign final agreements on two huge liquefied-natural-gas projects, which would bring in some $20bn in investment and double GNP from 2014. Additional revenue to the government would top $1bn a year, more than three times Australia's aid, increasing the government's effective autonomy. It remained to be seen whether a run-down, demoralised administration would be willing or able to use this economic bounty for the benefit of the Papua New Guinea's broader population, comprising 6.6m people, of whom 40% were living in poverty.

Increasing Chinese influence and capital in the Southwest Pacific has had mixed results. Chinese diplomacy has been generally responsible and cooperative. Assistance to the military in Papua New Guinea and Fiji has been limited to provision of uniforms and routine equipment, rather than weaponry. Civil aid has concentrated on infrastructure and some showpiece items such as football stadiums and government office blocks. Since the election of Taiwan's President Ma Ying-jeou in March 2008, there has been a truce in the competitive vying for diplomatic recognition through largesse.

Chinese capitalism has been more disruptive. The $800m Ramu nickel project undertaken by a Chinese state metal corporation near Madang, Papua New Guinea, has been marked by disregard for established rules on the importation of Chinese labour, compensation to local landowners, and working conditions. Local environmentalists obtained a court injunction over the proposed outfall of mine tailings into the sea, which held potential for further friction. Across Papua New Guinea and other island nations, individual Chinese entrepreneurs, mostly from Fujian province, have been arriving and setting up 'trade stores', supplanting other retailers with their alternative goods from China. In Papua New Guinea, the storekeepers have become noted for running entirely cash businesses and disregarding value-added tax obligations. Resentment has burgeoned, producing riots against Chinese stores in Lae, Popondetta and Port Moresby. Similar anti-Chinese sentiment has fuelled riots in the Solomon Islands and Tonga over the past decade.

Japan: New Party Meets Old Difficulties

Japan experienced a long anticipated regime transformation in 2009–10. The Liberal Democratic Party (LDP), after nearly 54 consecutive years in office, finally lost its grip on power in September 2009 after a landslide defeat at the hands of the Democratic Party of Japan (DPJ). New

DPJ Prime Minister Yukio Hatoyama took office pledging fundamental change in both Japan's domestic politics and foreign policy. Japan under the DPJ would seek to break free from the previous pattern of bureaucratic-led and interest-group-centred politics and economy, and instead emphasise stronger and more open political leadership and broader social-welfare programmes. The party also sought to revitalise Japan's foreign policy by shifting away from perceived over-dependence on the United States and rebalancing its international relations through strengthening ties with East Asian neighbours and fostering more effective frameworks for region-wide cooperation. At just over eight months into its term, the signs were that the implementation of the DPJ administration's new domestic and international strategies would be fraught. As of mid-2010, the DPJ had failed to follow through on many of its planned domestic reforms, and had not found a new equilibrium for Japan's international relations. In particular, the US–Japan alliance has become less stable, with Hatoyama forced to resign in early June over his botched handling of the issue of Okinawan bases.

LDP downfall, DPJ triumph

The LDP administration of Prime Minister Taro Aso was unable to gain a handle on the domestic political agenda, with approval ratings for Aso's cabinet falling below 20% in mid-2009. The prime minister staked the survival of his administration on combating the effects of the global financial crisis on Japan's ailing economy, and by reverting to pork-barrel-style interest-group politics, passing in May 2009 a third successive stimulus package worth ¥15 trillion ($155bn), or 3% of GDP. But these measures made little dent in the opinion polls, compelling Aso to call an election in August, a month before he was constitutionally mandated to do so.

Aso fought the election on a platform contrasting the LDP's experience and competency to the untested DPJ, and on his party's ability to defend Japan's national security in the face of recent threats from North Korea. The Japanese electorate was unmoved. The DPJ inflicted the worst-ever defeat on a governing party in modern Japanese history, gaining 195 seats for a total of 308 – an absolute majority in the 480-member house. The LDP, having itself won an absolute majority in

2005 under Prime Minister Junichiro Koizumi, lost 177 seats and was reduced to a rump of 119. Hatoyama was installed as prime minister on 16 September. Although he had pledged to break the ossified pattern of Japanese politics, he was the fourth successive prime minister who was the son or grandson of a past premier.

The DPJ victory, though stunning, was not total. Exit polls suggested that many voters viewed the election as an opportunity to punish the LDP rather than to embrace the DPJ's policies. The Japanese electorate's growing impatience and consequent propensity to swing strongly between the two main parties, as evidenced in the 2009 and 2005 elections, suggests that the DPJ cannot take for granted its future hold on power. The DPJ's freedom of action has been further constrained by its need to seek a coalition with two much smaller parties – the Social Democratic Party of Japan (SDPJ) and People's National Party (PNP), with a combined total of only 20 seats in the National Diet – to gain the extra nine seats necessary for a working majority in the Upper House. The SDPJ left the coalition in early June 2010 in protest at the DPJ's failure to relocate US military facilities out of Okinawa.

Hatoyama has also had to contend with potential divisions within his own party, which is a fusion of former socialists, social progressives and moderate and right-leaning conservatives. The potential for intra-party discord is exacerbated by the intimidating figure of Ichiro Ozawa, party leader until May 2009 (when irregularities discovered in the reporting of political donations between 2004 and 2007 forced his resignation) and DPJ secretary-general from September 2009 to June 2010. Ozawa, once an LDP heavyweight, masterminded the DPJ's electoral triumph. As a result, Ozawa gathered around him a loyal grouping of around 120 or more DPJ National Diet members, perhaps the largest factional grouping in Japanese political history, and formed an alternative pole of power to the prime minister. Ozawa's rising influence invited tensions with other leading faction leaders in the DPJ, and he was rocked by recurring accusations from the LDP and media over the suspect political donations. Ozawa escaped criminal indictment in early 2009, with former aides taking the fall, but the possibility of fresh investigations and indictments surfaced in late April 2010, and contributed to Ozawa's resignation as DPJ secretary-general in June. Hatoyama, too, was tainted by revelations that his political support organisations had falsified reports on the source of ¥1.25bn ($13m) in donations between 2002 and 2009, later found to be gifts from the prime minister's mother, heiress to the Bridgestone Corporation fortune.

Hatoyama was eventually cleared, in April 2010, of direct involvement, but these scandals cast doubt on his claims that the DPJ would break from the past pattern of 'money and politics' in Japan and, alongside his need to maintain his fragile coalition, called into question his ability to control his party and cabinet. Minister of Finance Hirohisa Fujii resigned in January 2010, ostensibly for health reasons, but also possibly because of his inability to formulate a budget in the absence of strong prime ministerial support, and in the end it was left to Ozawa to intervene and forge an intra-party compromise. The tougher figure of Naoto Kan, who also served as deputy prime minister, succeeded Fujii. Hatoyama consistently defended Ozawa's position, knowing that he was key to maintaining a large portion of DPJ Diet strength and ties with the SDPJ and PNP, and was willing to accommodate the policy preferences of the junior coalition partners out of proportion to the actual level of national support these parties commanded. Hence, PNP leader Shizuka Kamei, appointed as minister of state for financial services and postal reform, was allowed to pursue his pet project of largely halting the privatisation of the Japan Post Office, and SDPJ leader Mizuho Fukushima and the PNP were indulged over the fractious issue of relocating the United States Marine Corps (USMC) base in Futenma on the island of Okinawa. Hatoyama's intent was to hold the DPJ and coalition together in the run-up to Upper House elections in July 2010 in the hope of securing a single-party majority and enhancing the government's freedom of action. But the decline in approval ratings from 70% to 20% indicated the riskiness of this strategy. In the event, with half the seats up for election, the DPJ and PNP both lost seats, bringing the coalition below a majority in the Upper House.

Notwithstanding these difficulties, the DPJ looked to have the wherewithal to stay in power for some time. Under Ozawa, the DPJ developed a formidable electoral machine far superior to that of the more loosely organised LDP even in its heyday, and the electoral system lends itself increasingly to a two-major-party system, in which smaller parties can survive only if led by figures with strong personal support bases. Thus, DPJ electoral fortunes have been increasingly tied to centralised support from the party, which reduces the incentives to split and the possibility of the DPJ's displacement by a new multi-party coalition. Furthermore, the DPJ was unlikely to allow internal party dissension to squander its ten-year quest for power, especially given the LDP's political maladroitness. Sadakazu Tanigaki, elected as the LDP's new leader in September, had as of June 2010 proved incapable of re-forging the party into an effective opposition. The LDP was divided between nationalistic elder statesmen complacent with their electoral fiefdoms and reform-minded younger members keen on redefining the party by transitioning to a more neo-liberal economic ideology. Dissatisfaction with Tanigaki's failure to establish a new agenda for the party led to a number of high-profile departures, including former Finance Minister Kaoru Yosano, who founded the Sunrise Party of Japan, and former Health and Welfare Minister Yoichi Masuzoe, perhaps the LDP's most popular figure, who formed the New Reform Party. The LDP lost 13 Diet members between the election and June 2010, and its approval rating in mid-2010 was only in the high teens.

> " Tanigaki's failure led to a number of high-profile departures "

Against this political background, the DPJ made mixed progress on its domestic agenda. Hatoyama, in line with his pledge to overturn political–bureaucratic collusion in decision-making and to elevate the role of the cabinet, created the National Policy Unit in the Prime Minister's Office (modelled on the UK's 10 Downing Street Policy Unit) to take the lead in formulating and directing overall national policy and budgets. Hatoyama also abolished the practice of weekly meetings of administrative vice-ministers, where in the past policy was decided by senior bureaucrats and then presented to politicians as a virtual fait accompli. In addition, the DPJ did away with its own internal policy council, with an eye to avoiding the LDP's penchant for catering to special-interest groups by formulating policy in parallel with the cabinet.

The DPJ's economic programme was to try to move Japan away from the previous model of export-led growth and domestic spending on construction projects in favour of stimulating domestic demand and countering rising demographic problems through enhanced state welfare. The DPJ passed a record ¥92tr ($1.03tr) budget in March 2010, with a 10% increase in welfare spending. The budget included a ¥26,000 monthly child allowance, a tuition waiver for all high-school students, and long-term incentives for larger families. However, the DPJ remained constrained in its spending plans by parlous public finances, with the government deficit running at 200% of GDP. The DPJ, through its new Government Revitalization Unit, for the first time in 2009 publicly vetted ministerial budget requests and managed to find savings of ¥690bn, but this fell far short of its election pledge of ¥9.1tr in savings. The public-works budget was slashed to its lowest level in 30 years, but still the DPJ could only finance its plans by backpedalling on a pledge to cut petroleum taxes and by issuing an extra ¥44tr in government bonds. In the long term, the DPJ only looked likely to be able to fund its plans and address the government deficit by breaking an election promise and raising the consumption tax above the current 5%.

US–Japan alliance: crisis brewing

Aso's government, in its latter stages, attempted to maintain close alliance cooperation with the United States, but signs of cracks in the relationship emerged. Japanese policymakers, at first frustrated by the US agreement with China to respond to North Korea's April 2009 missile test by agreeing only to a UN Security Council president's condemnatory statement, were more encouraged by Washington's tough stance following the North's 25 May 2009 underground nuclear test. Japanese Defense Minister Yasukazu Hamada and US Secretary of Defense Robert Gates met with South Korean Defense Minister Lee Sang-hee at the 2009 IISS Shangri-La Dialogue on 30 May (the first-ever trilateral meeting of these officials) and pledged a unified stance against North Korean provocations. Japan, as a non-permanent member of the Security Council, then worked closely with the United States to pass Resolution 1874, which imposed further economic and commercial sanctions on North Korea and encouraged UN member states to search North Korean cargo.

The Japanese government welcomed the Obama administration's initiatives for a 'nuclear free world' as broadly consistent with Tokyo's non-nuclear stance. At the same time, LDP politicians and Ministry of Foreign Affairs (MOFA) officials expressed quiet concerns regarding the impact of US policy on extended deterrence (Japanese confidence in the US nuclear umbrella having already been shaken by Washington's inability to prevent North Korean nuclearisation) and were reported to have requested that the United States maintain tactical nuclear weapon deployments in the Asia-Pacific region. Japanese policymakers were further disappointed with the Obama administration's decision to discontinue production of the F-22 Raptor fighter aircraft and not to consider an export version. Japan had sought the F-22 as the Air Self Defence Force (ASDF)'s next-generation fighter. The LDP in mid-2009 also failed to push ahead with the plans it had negotiated with the United States for the relocation of the USMC Futenma facility.

On taking power, the DPJ found the stewardship of the US–Japan alliance its greatest foreign-policy challenge, and one that significantly affected the stability of Hatoyama's premiership. The party campaigned on a platform of enhancing Japanese autonomy in foreign policy, whilst maintaining and strengthening the US–Japan alliance as the foundation of Japan's security. The DPJ accused the LDP of pursuing a blind devotion to the alliance at the risk of entangling Japan in military adventurism in Iraq and the Middle East, to the detriment of emerging opportunities for East Asian regional cooperation. The DPJ argued that the US–Japan connection should become a more 'equal alliance' with a greater concentration on military commitments within the scope of the security treaty in East Asia and 'multi-layered' cooperation beyond security in areas such as international finance and climate change. For their part, US officials, whilst welcoming the successful democratic transition of regime in Japan, viewed the ascendance of the DPJ with some trepidation. The DPJ's pledge to review Japan's commitment to the US-led international coalition in Afghanistan, revise bilateral agreements on US base facilities in Japan, and revisit past US nuclear strategy vis-à-vis Japan have produced tension in the alliance.

Since 2006, the DPJ had opposed the Maritime Self Defense Force (MSDF) refuelling mission in the Indian Ocean in support of *Operation Enduring Freedom* as illegitimate because it transgressed Japan's constraints on the exercise of collective self-defence. During the election campaign, the DPJ demonstrated more flexibility over the MSDF mission, omitting from its manifesto any explicit mention of redeploying the force. After the DPJ took power, Toshimi Kitazawa, the new minister of defence, raised the possibility that the MSDF might shift its refuelling mission to support the anti-piracy coalition in the Indian Ocean and thus share the coalition's maritime burden by freeing up other states' naval assets to be devoted to Afghanistan. Hatoyama, though, announced in mid-October 2009 that the Replenishment Support Special Measures Law authorising the MSDF deployment would be allowed to expire in January 2010. The MSDF duly terminated its nine-year mission at the end of 2009.

DPJ policymakers, aware that the MSDF mission had been Japan's most high-profile contribution to international efforts in Afghanistan, sought to substitute an expanded civilian contribution. Three days before Obama's first visit to Japan in November 2009, Hatoyama announced an assistance package to Afghanistan of $5bn over five years, focused on capacity-building for the Afghan police, the employment of former combatants, and the development of energy infrastructure and agriculture. The deteriorating security situation meant that any operational military deployment that also complied with Japan's constitutional prohibitions would be largely ineffectual, as its symbolic contributions in Iraq had been. The Obama administration, although not pleased about the MSDF withdrawal, had already prepared for the mission's termination, and welcomed Japan's alternative contribution as positive for US–Japan alliance cooperation.

While the new DPJ administration and the United States were able to reach a compromise on Afghanistan, they found themselves at loggerheads over Futenma (see map, p. XV). In 2006, as part of the US–Japan Defence Policy Review Initiative (DPRI), the LDP negotiated a resolution to the long-running issue of the USMC Air Station Futenma in Ginowan City in the southern part of Okinawa. The facility's 2,800-metre runway occupies about one-quarter of Ginowan's land space, and USMC aircraft afflict residential districts with noise pollution and safety hazards. Japan and the US have agreed since 1996 that the facility should be relocated, provided Japan finds another site which offers comparable military operability and the capacity to dispatch a higher number of aircraft in the event of a regional contingency. The LDP's two previous relocation plans foundered due to Okinawan opposition to the impact of the relocation on other local communities and the natural environment, and questions of military feasibility and cost. The 2006 DPRI agreement aimed to relocate Futenma to USMC Camp Schwab in Nago City in the north of Okinawa, and entailed the construction through landfill of two V-shaped, 1,600-metre runways on adjacent Cape Henoko. The plan was sold as part of a larger package of USMC relocations designed to relieve Okinawa's burden, including the movement of 8,000 troops of the III Marine Expeditionary Force (MEF) and their dependents to Guam. Japan agreed to provide $6bn, or two-thirds of the total required, for the Guam relocations, signing an agreement with the United States to this effect in February 2009, and to construct and pay for the new facility at Camp Schwab for an as yet undisclosed cost.

Since 2005, the DPJ has argued that the Futenma facility should be relocated outside Okinawa or even outside Japan altogether. It has objected that the LDP's 2006 plan does not sufficiently relieve the disproportionate burden on Okinawa, cements the long-term presence of the USMC at Camp Schwab, will damage the currently pristine marine environment around Cape Henoko, and fails to support cost estimates for the transfer to Guam and the construction of the additional facilities at Camp Schwab. The military utility of the USMC for the defence of Japan and the surrounding region is questionable. After taking power, the DPJ also signed a coalition agreement with the SDPJ and PNP pledging to re-examine the realignment programme and to relieve the base burden on Okinawa. Hatoyama's government from late September to early October 2009 intimated that it would move ahead with a review of the 2006 plan and began to publicly air possible alternatives.

US Defense Secretary Gates visited Japan in mid-October and stated that the US preferred, and saw no feasible alternative to, the existing Futenma plan, and that if the agreement were not implemented then there would be no additional relocations of Marines to Guam and no return of other facilities in Okinawa to Japan. Thereafter, DPJ ministers scrambled to try to find a relocation formula that would fulfil election promises, satisfy the US, placate coalition partners and mollify local Okinawans. Okada investigated relocating Futenma to the nearby US Air

Force base at Kadena, but operational inadequacy, local opposition and possibly inter-service rivalry scuppered this option. Kitazawa argued that the existing agreement would meet election pledges by facilitating the move of Marines to Guam and relieving the burden on Okinawa.

Japanese and US officials attempted to contain the emerging crisis by establishing in early November 2009 a high-level bilateral working group to discuss Futenma. Obama's visit later that month proceeded smoothly without overt controversy over Futenma. But in a major speech in Tokyo, the American president did comment that he hoped the existing plan would be implemented expeditiously, whereas Hatoyama in media remarks after the Asia-Pacific Economic Cooperation (APEC) summit the same month commented that he saw no point in the bilateral working group if the US aim was simply to pursue the existing agreement. The growing divergence in Japanese and US positions barred any progress, and the working group was suspended in December. Hatoyama then announced that no decision would be made until the end of May 2010.

The Futenma issue, however, rumbled on into early 2010. US Secretary of State Hillary Clinton reportedly summoned Japanese Ambassador Ichiro Fujisaki to her office and left him waiting outside in the snow before calling for quick implementation of the existing agreement. US officials have since adopted indirect pressure tactics, avoiding engagement with their Japanese counterparts: Ozawa cancelled a trip to Washington in April because he was not granted an audience with the president. The United States has also placed the onus on Japan to provide a feasible alternative supported fully by local consensus. The SDPJ and PNP pro-duced their own plans in March. The SDPJ prioritised relocation outside Japan to Guam, Saipan or Tinian, or if inside Japan to shared JSDF facil-ities on the mainland. The PNP proposed constructing a new 1,500m runway inland at Camp Schwab, but this drew opposition from the neighbouring wards of Nago City, and it appeared impractical to the US, which needed a longer runway to operate MV-22 *Ospreys*. The DPJ has accepted the indispensability of the USMC deterrence role in East Asia, and, after examining a number of other alternatives, agreed that the new Futenma site should still principally be located in Okinawa. In late April, the DPJ finally made formal proposals to Washington whereby Futenma was to be relocated to Camp Schwab and a new 1,800m runway would be constructed off Cape Henoko on piles rather than landfill to protect the marine environment; half of the USMC helicopter or *Osprey* force would be stationed in Tokunoshima for training to relieve the burden on Okinawa, but the new Camp Schwab facility would be large enough for contingency deployments.

The US State Department welcomed the new flexibility of the Japanese government in seeking to implement large portions of the 1996 plan, but the USMC was reportedly against splitting its helicopter force and operationally requires its helicopters to be within 120km of its ground troops, ruling out Tokunoshima. US officials also were sceptical that Hatoyama had the necessary political muscle to implement the agreement domestically. Key SDPJ and PNP figures opposed relocation within Okinawa. In the prefecture itself, the ground shifted under the DPJ. In January, Nago City elected a mayor who had declared total opposition to accepting the Futenma relocation. Okinawa Governor Nakaima likewise adopted a position of total opposition to maintaining the facility in Okinawa, and joined an anti-base rally involving 90,000 local citizens in April 2010. Similarly, all three mayors in Tokunoshima opposed accepting USMC helicopters, and in the same month approximately 60% of the island's population joined a protest rally. Domestic disapproval of the DPJ's handling of the issue was a major cause of the party's decline in popularity.

> " Hatoyama apologised and then resigned "

In the end, Hatoyama's government, stuck between continued strong US pressure to implement the existing agreement and local domestic opposition against it, essentially folded and plumped for pleasing its US ally. The Japanese and US governments agreed at the end of May that the existing agreement would be largely implemented, although as a sop to the Japanese position Washington agreed to investigate moving some training exercises to Tokunoshima. Hatoyama subsequently apologised to Obama for his failure to handle the issue effectively and to the Okinawan people for asking them to continue the burden of hosting the new Futenma facility and then resigned to take responsibility for his failed policies.

During the flap over Futenma, there was concern that the anti-base contagion could spread across Okinawa to affect other US facilities. In line with the DPJ manifesto, Hatoyama pledged in October 2009 to conduct a review of the US–Japan Status of Forces Agreement (SOFA), as well as Host Nation Support (HNS) funding for US facilities. The DPJ has thus far trod carefully on these issues and has expended most of its energy on Futenma. The party's Status of Forces Agreement (SOFA) demands aimed to bring Japan in line with other countries hosting US bases by allowing Japanese police to hold US military personnel suspected of a crime before their indictment and to tighten up environmental standards inside US bases, and these looked to be negotiable with the US. What looked more problematic, though, were potential DPJ moves to significantly cut HNS from Japan's current commitment of 75% of US in-country base costs.

The DPJ's interest in investigating past and current US nuclear policy vis-à-vis Japan, while running the risk of increased bilateral tensions, actually created some new bases for cooperation. The DPJ took power pledging to investigate revelations in mid-2009 by former MOFA officials that during the Cold War the ministry had maintained a range of 'secret pacts' with the US to freely allow the entry of tactical nuclear weapons into Japan. Such pacts could have been in breach of arrangements under the security treaty for prior bilateral consultations regarding any major change in deployments of US military forces in Japan, and also could have contravened Japan's Three Non-Nuclear Principles (not to produce, maintain, or introduce nuclear weapons). Although the United States had acknowledged since the 1970s that Japan had accepted the US stance that 'transit' of nuclear weapons on US Navy vessels should not be defined as their 'introduction', US officials were concerned that the DPJ might insist that Washington abandon its 'neither confirm nor deny' policy for the deployment of nuclear weapons with respect to Japan, complicating US nuclear strategy. Foreign Minister Okada commissioned an internal MOFA panel and external panel of historians to study the secret pacts, and they reported their findings in early March. The MOFA panel denied the existence of the pacts, but the expert panel concluded there were at least tacit understandings between the ministry and the United States to allow nuclear weapons on Japanese territory. The DPJ showed little interest in using this finding to challenge US nuclear-weapons practices, probably to avoid straining bilateral ties further.

The DPJ did seek to press the United States and other nuclear states through the Nuclear Non-proliferation Treaty (NPT) review process to accept a 'no first use' policy, at least vis-à-vis non-nuclear states, with the hope of reducing the military salience of nuclear weapons and dissuading states such as North Korea from seeking or bolstering their own nuclear deterrents. But this proposal in fact chimed well with the Obama administration's Nuclear Posture Review. Moreover, the DPJ appeared more constructive than the LDP on assisting US nuclear-arms reduction policy, with Okada writing to Secretary of State Clinton in December stressing that Japan had no intention of trying to influence specific deployments of US nuclear capabilities in the Asia-Pacific, and thus, in effect, no objection to the planned withdrawal of Tomahawk sea-launched land-attack cruise missiles.

Japan's new activism under the DPJ on nuclear issues hinted that more 'multi-layered' alliance cooperation was possible, but moving into the latter part of 2010 relations remained uneasy between the two new administrations. 2010 was the 50th anniversary of the revision of the US–Japan security treaty, but instead of triumphant celebrations Hatoyama and Obama were obliged to issue in January separate and rather bland statements reaffirming the importance of the bilateral alliance.

Japan and East Asia: steady state

Japan's relations with North Korea under both the LDP and DPJ remained tense in the wake of the 2009 missile and nuclear tests. The LDP strengthened sanctions by reducing the level of undeclared cash transfers that could made from Japan to North Korea, and then sought to pass a new law to enable the Japan Coast Guard and MSDF to inspect ships for nuclear, biological and chemical weapons in international waters, although time to pass the legislation ran out due to the impending elections. North Korea appeared to have expected the DPJ to take a softer line given that its coalition partner, the SDPJ, had traditionally maintained friendly ties with Pyongyang, and rumours surfaced of a possible summit mission by Hatoyama to Pyongyang to try to restart negotiations on the issue of North Korea's abductions of Japanese in the late 1970s and early 1980s. Instead, Hatoyama increased the number of personnel in the Headquarters on Abductions, and Hiroshi Nakai, the minister of state for the abductions issue, attempted in April 2010 to exclude North Korean schools in Japan from a planned high-school tuition-fee waiver. The DPJ extended sanctions on the North, and resubmitted and passed legislation in the National Diet for the interdiction of North Korean shipping.

Japan–South Korea relations proceeded smoothly and pragmatically. President Lee Myung-bak and Prime Minister Aso established an effective working relationship in responding to North Korea's provocations, and agreed to consider restarting negotiations for a bilateral free-trade agreement. Nevertheless, bilateral ties were hampered by the familiar issues of history and territory: South Korea objected to Japan's approval in April of a history textbook seen as justifying the colonial rule of the Korean Peninsula, and took a dim view of the Japan Defence White Paper in 2009 referring to the disputed Takeshima islands as inalienable Japanese territory. Hatoyama and Lee established a similar relationship, but it looked to be less fraught due to Hatoyama's declaration that he would not visit the controversial Yasukuni Shrine for Japanese war dead.

Japan–China relations also experienced a relatively quiet 12 months, although many old problems continued to simmer. Aso visited Beijing for meetings with Chinese Premier Wen Jiabao, and generally sought coordination with China over North Korea's missile and nuclear tests. The Japanese government, however, was frustrated with China's failure to move forward with a June 2008 agreement on the joint development of gas resources in the East China Sea, and protested to Beijing over its apparent activity in preparing to resume operations on drilling platforms near the Shirakaba/Chunxiao field.

The DPJ came to power pledging to redouble efforts to improve relations with China after the deterioration of Sino-Japanese ties under Koizumi, and China strongly welcomed the new government. Hatoyama's assertion that he would follow the 1995 Murayama statement acknowledging the damage of the colonial past and not visit the Yasukuni Shrine was expected to help downplay issues of history on the bilateral agenda. He met with Chinese President Hu Jintao at the UN General Assembly in September 2009, and then at the Japan–China–South Korea Trilateral Summit in Beijing in October, pledging deeper bilateral cooperation and proposing an East Asia Community (EAC). Ozawa then visited Beijing as DPJ secretary-general in December and met with Hu, accompanied on his trip by 143 DPJ Diet members and 496 other participants, the largest-ever Japanese delegation. Ozawa was also believed to be instrumental in prevailing on the Imperial Household Agency to grant, on short notice and outside normal diplomatic proto-col, an audience with the Emperor of Japan to Vice-President Xi Jinping during his visit to Tokyo in December.

All this activity suggested a DPJ gravitating towards China in its foreign policy. Reality checks, however, soon arose. In December, Foreign Minister Okada felt compelled to press his counterpart Yan Jiechi hard on oil development in the East China Sea, stating that if China did not move ahead with bilateral agreements Japan would have to 'take certain actions' of its own, intimating that Tokyo might begin to develop the fields by itself. In a meeting in Tokyo with Wen at the start of June, Hatoyama extracted a pledge that China would negotiate a treaty with Japan to implement the bilateral agreements on joint development. During his visit to Beijing, Ozawa admonished China on the need for greater transparency with respect to its military build-up to preclude a Japanese counter-reaction. In April 2010, Japanese officials watched closely the passage of a People's Liberation Army Navy 'armada' con-sisting of ten warships in international waters around Japan, including movements close to the tiny islet of Okinotorishima, Japan's most south-ernmost territory. China disputes Japan's right to claim an Exclusive Economic Zone (EEZ) around Okinotorishima on the grounds that it is a reef which cannot support human habitation. The DPJ responded to increased Chinese naval activity near Japan's territorial waters by submitting a bill to the Diet in February 2010 that would require the government to preserve Okinotorishima's status as an island through additional construction so as to consolidate Japan's EEZ claim. At mid-2010 Minister of Defense Kitazawa was considering new budget requests to enable the stationing of GSDF units on the southernmost islands of the Okinawa chain, with a clear design to ward off Chinese depredations.

The DPJ's remaining energy for new foreign-policy initiatives was devoted to promoting the establishment of an EAC. Hatoyama's government saw the promotion of regionalism as an important means of reducing Japan's dependence on the United States and enhancing cooperation with China, South Korea and the Association of South East Asian Nations (ASEAN) countries. Hatoyama initially predicated the EAC on the vague concept of *yuai* (fraternity), but in November 2009 articulated a concept of functional regionalism, concentrating on cooperation in energy and maritime security, natural disasters, finance and the environment. The United States expressed concerns that it appeared to be excluded from Japan's EAC plans, and that Japan could become complicit in creating an exclusive East Asian bloc anchored by China. Some considered these concerns excessive, given that Hatoyama advocated a format of open regionalism linked with other regional frameworks such as APEC and global institutions, and that the EAC was designed to enmesh and constrain China rather than cede regional leadership to it. In any case, China did not appear overly enthusiastic about Japan's proposals, preferring the ASEAN+3 framework. EAC developments appeared to be an important gauge of Japanese autonomy in foreign policy.

Defence policy developments

In the final stages of its era in power, the LDP had increasingly sought to shift Japan onto a more radical, outward-looking and active track in defence doctrine and capabilities. Aso's government tried to further this agenda but ultimately ran short of political capital and time. The Prime Minister's Council on Security and Defence Capabilities released a report in August 2009 designed to inform the Ministry of Defence's ongoing review of the National Defence Programme Guidelines (NDPG) scheduled for the end of that year. The report most notably recommended that Japan consider the use of its ballistic-missile defence (BMD) system to respond to North Korean missile launches against the United States, the acquisition of the necessary capabilities to strike against enemy missile bases in conjunction with the United States, and a relaxation of the ban on arms export for joint development of weapons systems with other advanced industrial states as exercises of Japan's legitimate right of collective defence.

After some internal debate, the DPJ chose not to accept these recommendations and to conduct its own review of defence policy. It convened a new council to report in mid-2010, and rolled over the new NDPG to the end of 2010. The council's membership indicated that its recommendations might shift the DPJ in a direction less focused on the US–Japan alliance and more towards increased multilateral cooperation in East Asia and with the UN, and might steer clear of controversial issues such as collective self-defence and the arms-export ban. However, the DPJ was unlikely to diverge radically from LDP policy. The new government accepted the need to upgrade Japan's information satellites and in the 2010 defence budget approved the procurement of 20,000-tonne DDH-22 light helicopter carriers, a third bigger than the existing DDH-16 *Hyuga*-class carriers. The DPJ government also looked likely to maintain the *Aegis*-based BMD programme. It was hesitant to remove restrictions on JSDF participation in UN peacekeeping operations, and maintained the LDP-initiated MSDF anti-piracy missions in the Gulf of Aden.

Uncertain outlook, again

The DPJ's prospects for establishing a more stable government and creating more dynamism in foreign policy had looked promising in September 2009. But the new government quickly become bogged down in the Futenma controversy, and, partly on that account, was beset by declining domestic support. The mini-crisis in US–Japan relations claimed the premiership of Hatoyama, and led to the SDPJ leaving the coalition. Despite hopes for a more stable Japanese government under the new regime, in the end Hatoyama only lasted eight months in office, far shorter than his three LDP predecessors.

Finance Minister Kan then assumed the premiership in early June. The DPJ received a major bounce in the polls, with Kan's cabinet receiving support rates of around 60%, freed from the image of Hatoyama's indecisiveness and Ozawa's financial scandals. The DPJ also was now free of the SDPJ, and the vocal Kamei stepped down from his ministerial post when Kan indicated that he would not accede to all of his plans to halt postal privatisation. The DPJ did win the greatest share of seats in the July 2010 Upper House elections, but failed to gain an absolute majority.

The DPJ looked likely to remain in power for a full first term, if not longer, but how Kan's administration would fare over the next year remained unclear. Kan, a self-made politician, is more of a pragmatist and personally a more resilient figure than the patrician Hatoyama. He was also expected to benefit from the Futenma issue remaining dormant for a few months, giving his administration some breathing space to concentrate on bread-and-butter domestic issues. But Futenma remained unresolved, especially given enhanced Okinawan resistance to the plan. Moreover, the growing tensions with North Korea after the *Cheonan* incident held the potential to further drive Japan back into the arms of the United States. It thus looked unlikely that Kan would find much leeway for any major innovations in Japan's foreign policy.

Chapter 10
Prospectives

The post-2008 economic crisis at first inspired the near-universal appreciation of a global challenge and the need for a response shaped by intergovernmental coordination. By mid-2010, however, Asians were referring to the recession as a 'transatlantic' financial failing and the G20 had to accept that each country would judge for itself whether it would continue with fiscal stimulus or embark on dramatic austerity budgeting. This geo-economic international trend also had its geostrategic parallel. International cooperation on large strategic projects began to stutter and a number of countries began to take more national approaches to regional and global security challenges. The international operation in Afghanistan was subject to wide-ranging domestic debate on its sustainability, while diplomacy with Iran fractured as Turkey and Brazil developed approaches which were ultimately ignored by the UN P5. While the immediate risk of protectionism in the economic realm has so far been averted, strategic protectionism appears on the rise as more countries define their national interests more precisely and act accordingly. This tendency is pronounced in Asia, but also evident elsewhere, and rising and super-middle powers are asserting their independent interests more strongly.

The rise of strategic self-confidence in India and China continues, though their diffidence about shaping the international strategic agenda – as opposed to just defending their core interests – slows that rise. Each, however, is more conscious of the strategic ambitions and reach of the other. They are sometimes brought into uncomfortable strategic contact along their own border, in neighbouring countries including Pakistan, Sri Lanka and Myanmar, and over competitive activities, whether in cyberspace or in Africa. Many Asian countries pressed for India's involvement in the East Asia Summit precisely to ensure a more multipolar Asia, with India serving at least psychologically as some sort of 'balance' for China. The two nevertheless offer comfort to each other on the climate-change agenda and on the need for differentiated international approaches to developing economies. The political and security architecture of Asia will be much shaped by how these two powers act in the region, but also by how a group of Asian middle powers defend their interests. Many perceive a subtle need to hedge against China, either by engaging other powers more obviously or by meeting more directly Chinese capacities.

A growing awareness of the relentless growth of Chinese economic and military power and a feeling that China asserts itself more in the region have provided important reasons for key states, notably Australia and Vietnam, to increase their defence spending and invest in submarines and other military equipment that could help deter future Chinese adventurism. While some states in Asia appear from time to time to bend to presumed Chinese strategic wishes even before they are expressed, others are combating that tendency more overtly. More countries want to avoid being subject to untoward Chinese pressure and are happy to accommodate US efforts to intensify defence cooperation through exercises, exchanges and deployments. Indeed, the US Quadrennial Defense Review recognises that there seem to be realistic prospects for closer bilateral defence cooperation with states identified as potential strategic partners, namely Indonesia, Malaysia and Vietnam, as well as traditional allies and established partners.

More generally, Australia, Indonesia and South Korea appear to be interested in forms of middle-power consultation, to ensure that their interest in a multipolar Asia is preserved. These three countries may in time become a diplomatic force to be reckoned with inside Asian councils and as a protector of a dynamic Asian polity, combining from time to time with Japan and India. Australia, which like all countries in Asia wants the best possible relations with China, conducts its diplomacy in the 'proximate region' mindful that it cannot rely only on the US connection to protect its interests and defend its values. Indonesia, boosted by its G20 status and its domestic successes, while faithful to the rigours and protocols of ASEAN diplomacy, does not want to be uniquely constrained by that structure in developing its wider bilateral relations.

South Korea, in particular, seems to be developing a brand of middle-power activism that extends beyond its own region and mirrors the more individualistic and distinctive approach of middle powers elsewhere. Indeed the successful conclusion of a nuclear-power project with the United Arab Emirates (UAE), where South Korea defeated competition from the French nuclear industry, in essence makes South Korea a strategic actor in the Middle East. While the UAE's choice was expressly taken on commercial grounds, the diversification of political economic links with key Asian countries is manifestly part of its security policy. Hosting a G20 meeting in 2010 and in 2012 the Nuclear Summit, following on from the inaugural one in Washington DC, South Korea clearly wants to give meaning to its Global Korea country brand.

Within the Middle East, and particularly the Gulf, the UAE seems to be doing more than others to diversify its security links and take an individual approach to foreign policy. It is active in strengthening links with Asia and Europe, and at the forefront of the regional debate on Iran. Its ambassador to the United States was willing publicly to contemplate the possibility of military options in the event that nothing else was able to prevent a confirmed acquisition by Iran of a nuclear-weapons capability and lamented the drift towards containment and deterrence options, which he believed were insufficient. The UAE has chosen, with Oman, to stay out of any prospective Gulf Cooperation Council (GCC) monetary union and is willing, as increasingly are other GCC states, to take independent foreign-policy stances.

In Europe, it is Turkey's diplomatic activism and individualism that has most caught the eye. Ankara has worked hard to improve its relations with all of its neighbours. It has also taken a more independent line in pursuing its interests in the Middle East. It is regarded by many, especially in the Gulf, as an important strategic partner. Relations with Europe and the United States have sometimes been strained as a consequence of the occasionally strident attitude that Turkey has taken towards

Middle East issues and its souring relations with Israel. That has not much worried Ankara, whose leadership perceives larger advantages in being seen as a sovereign actor than as constrained diplomatically by alliance obligations. Indeed, while Turkey remains very committed to its long-term ambition of EU accession, its almost Gaullist approach to foreign policy might not be quite so easy to blend in to a common European foreign policy, were it ever in a position to try.

More nineteenth-century English individualism, with a dash of William Pitt the Younger, provided the intellectual fuel for the UK's new stance. The first major speech of William Hague as foreign secretary of the United Kingdom in July 2010 set out the goal of 'a distinctive foreign policy that extends our global reach and influence', noting that 'today, influence increasingly lies with networks of states with fluid and dynamic patterns of allegiance, alliance and connections', and arguing that the UK should 'lead through the power of our ideas' and affirming that 'no country or groups of countries will increase the level of support or protection they offer to us and no-one else will champion the economic opportunity of the British citizen if we do not'. In essence, the speech argued for self-reliance and the renewed expression and defence of national interest. Hague's remarks underscored the need for an active diplomacy with many states and many regions to guarantee this. While emphasising that the United States would remain the UK's biggest single partner to achieve international goals, it was the variety of bilateral relationships that needed to be cultivated that shone through his argument. Over 20 different countries were mentioned. In referring to the European Union (EU), the emphasis was on ensuring that a proper quota of British bureaucrats was seconded to the European Commission, presumably to guarantee that a British perspective more seamlessly entered the thinking of the Brussels technocratic establishment. It is a mistake to over-interpret one speech, especially as this was the first of a series, but the tenor reflected the broader international tendency, doubtless to be reinforced over the next period, to define, protect and advance national interests more forthrightly.

A previous Western conceit that national interests and the global public good were nearly one and the same has dissipated with the economic introspection that the financial crisis has engendered and the sense of flux in international affairs that has been its prime geopolitical consequence. With so many pieces of the international strategic puzzle moving simultaneously, countries small, medium and large are all banking more on their own strategic initiative than on formal alliance or institutional relationships to defend their interests and advance their goals. No one is even pretending to make a bet only on regional or global institutions to do this for them. In Europe, the strange poker game played between various eurozone states, and most of all France and Germany, on the Greek bailout was illuminating. That during the debates, the French president reportedly threatened that France might withdraw from the euro and the German tabloid press loudly recommended that Germany could and should leave, clearly demonstrated the fragility of even the European institutional cause in these troubled times.

The financial crisis has certainly energised national reflexes. With economies and nerves frayed, and the nationalisation of foreign policy all the rage, the appetite for very ambitious collective long-term political-military goals is limited in the West. Liberal interventionism is hardly much trumpeted, but more significantly, security operations generally are going to undergo a much stricter test of necessity if they are to be pursued and if public support for them is to be garnered and sustained.

It is therefore to be expected that the mission in Afghanistan will undergo more public scrutiny and re-examination. The counter-insurgency (COIN) strategy approved by US President Barack Obama was in sum a grand strategy for Afghanistan. The goal was very little short of a secure and stable Afghanistan. As the campaign passes the ten-year mark, public tolerance for the generation-length commitment that political and military leaders in the West have sometimes spoken about is waning. The original strategic goal was to disrupt, dismantle and defeat al-Qaeda in Afghanistan and prevent its return. War aims traditionally expand, but in Afghanistan they ballooned into a comprehensive strategy to develop and modernise the country and its government. Defeat of the Taliban insurgency was seen as virtually synonymous with the defeat of al-Qaeda, even though much of its organised capacities had been displaced to Pakistan. Many worry that the large presence of foreign troops is what sustains and fuels the Taliban fighters. Reconciling the insurgents to a distant government in Kabul whose legitimacy is questioned and authority weak will be hard. Finding a constitutional dispensation that recognises the very loosely federal reality of Afghan regional fealty and governance structures would require an enormous political effort that included not just all local actors but all regional states. That, in time, might be necessary. In the interim, and as the military surge reaches its peak and begins to wind down, it may become necessary and is probably advisable for outside powers to move to a containment and deterrence policy to deal with the international terrorist threat from the Afghan–Pakistan border regions.

British Prime Minister David Cameron said on 14 June in a statement to the House of Commons: 'I am advised that the threat from al-Qaeda from Afghanistan and Pakistan has reduced, but I am also advised that if it were not for the current presence of UK and international coalition forces, al-Qaeda would return to Afghanistan and the threat to the UK would rise.' The first part of this statement is clearly a fact, as the specific international threat from Afghanistan itself is insignificant while that from Pakistan is being dealt with partly by the Pakistani military and partly by the decapitating drone strikes against elements of the al-Qaeda leadership and other 'high value targets' in Pakistan that are being carried out by international forces. The second part of this statement is more of a judgement. It is not clear why it should be axiomatically obvious that an Afghanistan freed of an international military presence would be an automatic magnet for al-Qaeda's concentrated reconstruction. Al-Qaeda's leadership, such as it is, may be quite content to stay where it is, while Taliban leaders who remained in Afghanistan might think twice of the advantages to them of inviting al-Qaeda back, given the experience of the last decade, or at least they could be made to think twice. The problem with judging that al-Qaeda would just return or that the Taliban would turn itself into an international or global threat following a major withdrawal of coalition forces is that this presumes no other policies would be implemented to contain the terrorist threat from the Afghan–Pakistan border areas, or to deter it.

The outlines of a containment and deterrence strategy need now to be more firmly drawn. This is a strategy that at some point will need to be implemented. It will be needed as combat forces withdraw, and is one towards which the international community could move quickly if it was judged that there was sufficient local and regional support for a containment and deterrence approach. Containing the international threat from the Afghan–Pakistan border and deterring the reconstitution of al-Qaeda in Afghanistan would, like all such strategies, have political, diplomatic, economic and military elements. It would require political deals in Afghanistan and among key regional powers including India, Pakistan, Iran and the Central Asian states. It would entail promises of economic and development support to its supporters as well as the threat of military strike against any re-concentration of international terrorist forces. It, too, would be a grand strategy of sorts, but unlike the COIN grand strategy, would not be so dependent on orchestrating near-ideal internal political and developmental outcomes in Afghanistan. Nor would it necessarily require the degradation of Taliban capacities to the point of near surrender, a prospect that is by no means immediate. A containment and deterrence approach would be a strategy limited to dealing with the threat as originally defined by the coalition forces that intervened in Afghanistan. Outlining such an approach earlier rather than later would demonstrate that the long-term strategy need not depend on winning an ever-lengthening succession of tactical local battles against an enemy incentivised by the presence of foreign forces. It would replace the impression that an eventual drawdown of combat forces from Afghanistan would constitute victory for the enemy, with the reality of a strategy that could be maintained for a longer period while meeting the principal security goal.

There is a risk of strategic fatigue in the United States. The antidote to that fatigue is to welcome and to shape the regional activism of newly energised middle powers and to tailor expeditionary military capacity to specific and sustainable purposes. The United Kingdom, as a kind of super-middle power, has argued that a global foreign policy and the development of strong bilateral ties with countries around the world is within its means and is an important way to maintain an individual influence that other countries, even one's closest friends, will not always exercise on one's behalf. France has always felt this way. Powers in other regions are seeking to match global visions for themselves with specific regional goals. In a world of more competitive national foreign policies, neighbourhood politics are inevitably more fraught. Turkey and Iran are key players in determining the eventual government that will emerge in Iraq following the elections this year. South Korea and the UAE will share perspectives on North Korea and Iran, given the proliferation links between the two and the role each thus plays in Asian and Middle East power balances. India and China will judge their economic investments in other Asian countries in geostrategic terms. African, Latin American and European politics are subject to the same bilateral and mini-lateral competition. Balancing diplomatic initiative against weakening economic strength, or bolstering newly acquired financial power with more, if hesitant, foreign-policy impulses, joins rising powers and those hanging on to their rank in complex competition. That competition will not easily be regulated by regional or global institutions. No single telephone number will be enough to conduct diplomacy in any part of the world. In a G20-plus world, many numbers and frequent calling will be necessary. Contact-group diplomacy will be an ever-evolving need. With economic, financial and diplomatic activity moving at such a pace and with such varied outcomes, military operations have to be all the more carefully considered. Precision and adaptability will be essential watchwords. For heavy, large, military deployment, the *longue durée* will be seen as an attitude for other times, other centuries.

Index